Media and Education in the Digital Age

Matteo Stocchetti (ed.)

Media and Education in the Digital Age

Concepts, Assessments, Subversions

PL ACADEMIC RESEARCH

Bibliographic Information published by the Deutsche Nationalbibliothek

The Deutsche Nationalbibliothek lists this publication in the Deutsche Nationalbibliografie; detailed bibliographic data is available in the internet at http://dnb.d-nb.de.

Library of Congress Cataloging-in-Publication Data

Media and education in the digital age : concepts, assessments, subversions / Stocchetti Matteo, ed.
pages cm.
ISBN 978-3-631-65154-4 -- ISBN (invalid) 978-3-653-04437-9 1. Internet in education. 2. Digital media. 3. Education--Effect of technological innovations on. I. Stocchetti, Matteo.
LB1044.87.M43 2014
371.33'44678--dc23
2014006469

ISBN 978-3-631-65154-4 (Print)
E-ISBN 978-3-653-04437-9 (E-Book)
DOI 10.3726/ 978-3-653-04437-9

PL Academic Research is an Imprint of Peter Lang GmbH.

Peter Lang – Frankfurt am Main · Bern · Bruxelles · New York · Oxford · Warszawa · Wien

This publication has been peer reviewed.

www.peterlang.com

Preface

This volume is the first book length publication of the research programme Media and Education in the Digital Age – MEDA.

MEDA is an interdisciplinary research programme whose main goal is to support the circulation of critical knowledge about the educational role of digital technology. It should be clear that MEDA does not promote the use or the rejection of digital technology. Rather it promotes a critical attitude towards the values, goals and ultimately pedagogical projects that inspire its usages in education. In this endeavour, MEDA shares many of the assumptions, interests, intellectual goals and conceptual tools of the critical traditions that pays attention to the changes affecting education as part of a larger reflection on the nature and direction of social change.

The notion of 'critical' that inspires the work and ambitions of MEDA includes at least three features: first an explicit attention to the relations of power implied, reproduced, challenged or otherwise associated with the uses of digital technologies in education. Second, sensitivity towards the idea that the study of social phenomena is not detached from but very much part of and actually influential upon the phenomena investigated. Finally, the normative commitment to the idea that improvement in education should be defined in relation to a notion of the 'individual' as a value in herself and independently from other configurations instrumentally associated with this notion in the economic, political or religious domains.

A number of friends and colleagues have supported this project in several ways. In particular I here gladly acknowledge a debt of gratitude toward, Ana Bermejillo Ibanez and Emiliano Blasco Doñamayor, Universidad San Pablo, Madrid (Spain), Belinha De Abreu, Fairfield University, Connecticut (USA), Jarkko Häutamäki, University of Helsinki (Finland), Alexandra Juhasz, Pitzer College in Claremont, California (USA), Reijo Kupiainen, University of Tampere (Finland), Guy Merchant, Sheffield Hallam University (UK), Nigel Kimberly and Jan-Anders Ray, Arcada University of Applied Sciences in Helsinki (Finland).

Notes on the Contributors

Cristina Aliagas Marín is a Postdoctoral Researcher in the Department of Educational Studies at The University of Sheffield, United Kingdom. Her research interest focuses on the role of literacy in the everyday life of Catalan/Spanish teenagers, particularly those that resist education. Within this broad area, her research covers a variety of topics: ethnography and literacy, digital literacies, literacy/literary identities and the complex interface between vernacular literacies and the curriculum. In 2012, her PhD. Thesis, *El desinterès lector adolescent* (The adolescent lack of interest in reading, 2012) was finalist of the *Joventut* award of the Catalan Government.

Alberto Bitonti has a PhD in Political Theory and Public Affairs (University of Roma Tre, 2011). He is Adjunct Professor of Political Science at IES Abroad Rome (Italy) and Fellow of the School of Public Affairs at American University (Washington DC). His research interests include the theory of power and the political process (especially lobbying and pressure groups), civic and media education and philosophy of science. Recently, he published a book on Italian ruling class.

Scott Bulfin is lecturer in the Faculty of Education at Monash University where he studies 'new literacies' for young people and adults across various educational contexts. He is a member of the Learning/New Media Research Group at Monash University and is currently engaged in a three-year Australian Government (ARC) funded ethnography of digital technologies in secondary schools. He can be reached at scott.bulfin@monash.edu.

Josep M. Castellà Lidón is a Senior Lecturer in Catalan Philology and Discourse Analysis in the Department of Humanities at the Universitat Pompeu Fabra. His interests in research encompasses Discourse Analysis and Social Linguistics. Currently, he collaborates with the research group GR@EL /Critical Literacy. He usually collaborates in conferences and journals of applied linguistics He is the author of the book *Oralitat i escriptura: dues cares de la complexitat en el llenguatge* (2004), and coauthor of *Entendre('s) a classe. Les estratègies comunicatives dels docents ben valorats* (2007) (Educational Research Award Foundation Catalan Encyclopedia 1999).

Verolien Cauberghe is Assistant Professor in Communication Management at the Ghent University. She teaches the courses Marketing Communication, Corporate Communication and Social Marketing. Her research interest lays on advertising effectiveness and social marketing. In the past she did research related to advertising knowledge among minors, the persuasive impact of communication strategies (e.g., two-sided messages) and crisis communication. Among her recent publications: De Vocht, M., Cauberghe, V., Uyttendaele, M., & Sas, B. (2014). 'Affective and cognitive reactions towards emerging food safety risks in Europe', *Journal Of Risk Research* and Claeys, A.-S., & Cauberghe, V. (2013). 'What makes crisis response strategies work? The impact of crisis involvement and message framing'. *Journal Of Business Research.* She can be reached at Veroline.Cauberghe@UGent.be.

Daniel Chazan is Professor in the Department of Teaching and Learning, Policy and Leadership at The University of Maryland College Park, Director of the Center for Mathematics Education, and co-Director of Terrapin Teachers. Chazan studies the teaching of mathematics in compulsory high school settings as a practice, embedded inside societal institutions, within a society with particular kinds of structure, that is carried out by individuals with their own identities and knowledge. Such a view of the teaching of mathematics challenges him to integrate theoretical perspectives and orientations, for example, toward mathematics as a discipline, school as an institution, and students and teachers as members of communities with particular positions in our society. Chazan has studied mathematics from the inside by teaching (*Beyond formulas in mathematics and teaching: Dynamics of the High School Algebra Classroom*, 2000, Teachers College Press) and, more recently, through observational studies (Teachers College Record 115(2)) and experiments into the practical rationality of teaching (Cognition and Instruction, 30(1), 1–38). He has also worked collaboratively with teachers on teaching education and the improvement of teaching (*Embracing Reason: Egalitarian Ideals and High School Mathematics Teaching*, 2007, Taylor Francis).

Vincenzo De Masi (vdemas@gmail.com) is currently a PhD candidate at University of Zurich and Lugano with a dissertation on Chinese animation and he is also assistant in the same Institute and filmmaker. Recent publications include: De Masi V. (2013), *Miss Puff, a new way of communication in China*, KOME Hungarian Communication Studies Association, (ISSN 2063-7330). Benecchi E., De Masi V. (2013), *Media Management in Disaster Events: A Case Study of Japanese Earthquake* in 'Business Strategies and Approaches for Effective Engineering Management', IGI Global, (ISBN-13: 9781466636583, LCC:T56). www.vincenzodemasi.com.

Patrick De Pelsmacker is Professor of Marketing at the University of Antwerp, Belgium, where he teaches courses in Marketing communications, marketing and communication management, marketing research, and research methods. He is the former dean of the Universiteit Antwerpen Management School (now Antwerp Management School). His research interests include consumer behavior, marketing communications and new advertising formats. Among his recent publications: Verhellen Y., Dens N., de Pelsmacker P.,'Consumer responses to brands placed in Youtube movies: the effect of prominence and celebrity endorser expertise' in *Journal of electronic commerce research* – ISSN 1526-6133 - 14:4(2013), p. 287–303 and Charry K., de Pelsmacker P., Pecheux C.- 'How does perceived effectiveness affect adults' ethical acceptance of anti-obesity threat appeals to children? When the going gets tough, the audience gets going' in *Journal of business ethics* – ISSN 0167-4544 - (2013), p. 1–16. He can be reached at Patrick.Depelsmacker@au.ac.be.

David Elliott is a PhD candidate in the Faculty of Education at Monash University. His research interests include video games and new media learning, online cultures as sites of informal literacy activity, and the radicalising of pedagogy and curriculum through emergent technologies. He is currently the online learning developer for the Australian Council for Educational Research (ACER), focusing on the design and implementation of new media learning systems. He can be reached at david.elliott@acer.edu.au.

Judith Faifman is Director of the Digital Media and Learning Program at Centro Argentino de Investigación y Acción Educativa, Buenos Aires, she served as Co-Director of the Media Lab and Digital Cultures Research & Design Program at the Talpiot School in Buenos Aires from 2004–8; was Secretary for Education and Culture at Friends of UNESCO, Buenos Aires; directed the National Youth Film Festival; and has worked on formative digital media education projects in Argentina from the early 1990s.

Julie Faulkner is Senior Lecturer at Monash University, Melbourne. She writes and teaches on matters of literacy, popular culture, identity and digital reading/writing practices. Her publications include the role of new media in curriculum innovation, the development and use of a virtual school in preservice teacher education and the role of pedagogies of discomfort in learning. She has edited *Disrupting Pedagogies in the Knowledge Society: Countering Conservative Norms with Creative Approaches* (IGI Global), and has jointly edited *Learning to Teach: New Time, New Practices* (Oxford University Press), currently in second edition.

Karen Ferreira-Meyers is Senior Lecturer and Coordinator Linguistics and Modern Languages at the Institute of Distance Education, University of Swaziland, in Swaziland (Southern Africa). Her research interests include distance and e-learning with a special focus on the attitudes of stakeholders (students, lecturers, tutors) in online learning environments, learning management systems, blended e-learning, MOOCs, etc. Additional research fields comprise contemporary literature (African literature, autofiction and crime fiction mainly), language teaching and learning, interpreting and translation. Among her recent publications on distance/e-learning Ferreira-Meyers, K. and Nkosi, J. 'How to incorporate academic and digital literacy development in information and communication technology (ICT)-enhanced teaching and learning: the case of Swaziland', in *Talking about learning. The South East European University Language Centre Journal of Teaching and Learning*, Vol. 3, 6 p. http://www.seeu.edu.mk/files/broshurat/LCC-boshura2.pdf.

Megan E. Fromm, PhD, is Assistant Professor of communication at Boise State University in Boise, Idaho and an Adjunct Professor at Johns Hopkins University. She has taught at the Salzburg Academy on Media & Global Change, the University of Maryland, Towson University, and the Newseum in Washington, D.C. She is a former professional journalist and was recently elected to the board of directors for the Journalism Education Association for a three-year term as Professional Support Director. Fromm received her PhD from the University of Maryland in 2010, and her dissertation focused on how newspapers have covered scholastic First Amendment cases. An avid supporter of student free press rights, she received the Colorado Friend of the First Amendment Award in 2005 and the Society of Professional Journalists Sunshine Award in 2004.

Brian Goldfarb is Associate Professor of Communication at UCSD. His research and production focuses on visual/digital culture, disability and education. His book, *Visual Pedagogy*, considers media technologies used in the 20th century to advance models of pedagogy in the US and globally. Goldfarb's current projects include Global Tourette, a documentary and media exchange project engaging cultural and professional responses to Tourette Syndrome internationally; and, *Carescapes*, a "born digital" book exploring patient communities in the digital age.

Gloria Gómez-Diago is PhD candidate at the Department of Sciences of Communication (II) at the Rey Juan Carlos University (Madrid). She has worked as journalist and as researcher in international projects related to the use of new technologies and its applications. In the course 2011–2012, she worked as interim professor at the University of Vigo, where she taught Print Advertising Production and Advertising and Cultural Industries. Her research interests comprise research methodologies in communication science, virtual communication and new uses and applications of online platforms such as Virtual Worlds. She is reviewer for *Empedocles: European Journal for the Philosophy of Communication* andfor *Journal of Virtual Worlds Research.* Since 2008, she maintains the blog 'from-communication' http://fromcommunication.blogspot.com.es/. Among her latest publications is the entry 'Cyberspace and Cyberculture'. in Kosut, M. & Golson, J. Geoffrey (Eds.) *Encyclopedia of Gender in Media*. Sage, 2012.

Yan Han is currently a PhD candidate in Animation and Digital Arts Academy at Communication University of China. Her research interest is in Chinese original animation. She has developed great passion in animation and also made animated short film.

Melissa Harness is currently Ph.D. candidate in Cultural Studies and Education at the University of Tennessee, where she is presently teaching International Education. Her research interests include: the lack of teacher 'professionalization,' public policy, bureaucratization of the educational systems in the U.S. and around the world, globalization of education, women's and racial identity issues, and neoliberal ideologies that play into both world politics and education. She is the author of the book, *Pretending Teaching is a Profession: Why Public School Teaching Will Never Be Considered a 'True' Profession*, published by Lambert Academic Publishing.

Filip Lab is Professor of Photojournalism at the Faculty of Social Science, Charles University, Prague. He is an investigator of the Czech part of Worlds of Journalism Study project, a member of Journalism Studies section of ECREA and project leader of Czech website of European Journalism Observatory (EJO). He is interested in visual communication and transformation of photojournalism practice. He is active as journalist and photographer collaborates with several cultural as well as commercial magazines. For his publications please visit: http://cuni.academia.edu/FilipLab.

Pilar Lacasa is Professor of Developmental Communication and Education at the University of Alcalá. She leads the research group Grupo Imágenes Palabras e Ideas (GIPI) (Images, Words and Ideas Group; http://www2.uah.es/gipi/). The group has developed innovative methodological approaches in a number of areas, and has led the debate about the development of teacher training programmes and educational policy in Spain. Dr Lacasa has been a visiting scholar at the Universities of Utah and British Columbia, and at MIT.

Marlène Loicq is currently a post-doctorate researcher in national project on Transliteracy (ANR TRANSLIT) attached to Rouen University. She has a double PhD in public communication (Laval University, Quebec) and information and communication sciences (Sorbonne Nouvelle University, Paris). Her research interests include media studies, youth mediatic culture and interculturality. She is specialised on media education (policy and theoretical frameworks) and information literacy. She co-edited a book on information pluralism and media diversity and wrote several articles on different national contexts of media education (France, Quebec, Autralia). She promotes an intercultural media education field.

Rut Martínez-Borda is Professor of Developmental Communication and Education and Research Fellow at the University of Alcalá. She is a member of the research group Grupo Imágenes Palabras e Ideas (GIPI) (Images, Words and Ideas Group; http://www2.uah.es/gipi/). She works on videogames, new technologies and new literacies. Her current research on the topic of Computer Games and Narratives is supported by the Ministery of Culture and Education. She has been a visiting scholar at the Insitute of Education at the University of London; University of Westminster of London; University of Delaware of Philadelphia and collaborates with other research groups at the Universidad Autónoma de Madrid, Universidad Nacional de Educación a Distancia (UNED) and Universidad de Córdoba, Spain.

Paul Mihailidis is Assistant Professor in the school of communication at Emerson College in Boston, MA, where he teaches media literacy and interactive media. His research focuses on the nexus of media, education, and civic voices. His forthcoming books, *Media Literacy and the Emerging Citizen* (2014, Peter Lang) and *Media Literacy Education in Action* (2014, Routledge), outline effective practices for participatory citizenship and engagement in digital culture. Mihailidis, who directs the Salzburg Academy on Media and Global Change, and sits on the board of directors for the National Association of Media Literacy Education, was recently named associate director of the newly formed Engagement Labs at Emerson College.

Tobias Olsson is Professor of Media and Communication Studies at Lund University, Sweden. He has extensive research experience within the areas of media and citizenship, internet culture and mediated participation. Between 2009 and 2013 he coordinated the research project "Organized Producers of Young Net Cultures" (funded by the Swedish Knowledge Foundation) and he is currently starting a research project on user generated content within newspaper companies (Hamrin foundation, 2012–2017). His most recent publications include articles in *Javnost – The Public* and *Continuum: Journal of Media and Cultural Studies*. He is also editor of the volume *Producing the Internet: Critical Perspectives of Social Media* (2013).

Ron Owston is Dean of the Faculty of Education and former Director of the Institute for Research in Learning Technologies (IRLT) at York University, Toronto, Canada. His research interests include the evaluation of e-learning programs in schools, higher education, and continuing professional education with an emphasis on blending learning. Recently he has published in *Internet & Higher Education* and *Educational Researcher*.

Katarina Panic is a Researcher and Teaching assistant in the Department of Communication Sciences at Ghent University, where she has been a faculty member since 2009. She is currently working on a Ph.D. on the effect of new media in social marketing. Among her recent publications: Panic, K., Cauberghe, V. & De Pelsmacker, P. (2014). Promoting dental hygiene to children: comparing traditional and interactive media following threat appeals. *Journal of Health Communication*, available online at http://www.tandfonline.com/doi/abs/10.1080/10810730.2013.821551#.Uw2yDPldWSo, and Panic, K., Cauberghe, V., & De Pelsmacker, P. (2013). 'Comparing TV ads and advergames targeting children: The impact of persuasion knowledge on behavioral response'. *Journal of Advertising: special issue on Advergames, In-Game Advertising, and Social Media Games*, 42(2–3), 264–273. She can be reached at Katarina.Panic@UGent.be.

Sara Pereira is Associate Professor at the Communication Sciences Department and researcher at the Communication and Society Research Centre at the University of Minho, Portugal. Currently she is Director of the Communication Sciences Department. She also directs the Master Degree on 'Communication, Citizenship and Education' and she teaches several Curricular Units on Media Education/Literacy in graduate and postgraduate courses. She has been coordinating several research projects on media literacy and on young people and media. Her main research interests are the relationship between children, youth and the media; ICT and media at school; media education and media literacy; media audiences and participation. Among her recent publications: Pereira, S., Pereira, L. (2013), 'Digital Media in Primary Schools: Literacy or Technology? Analysing Government and Media Discourses'. *Educational Policy*, Sage Publications (Published online before print June 20, 2013, Doi: 10.1177/0895904813492378).

Magda Pischetola is Professor in Digital Media in Education at the Pontifícia Universidade Católica do Rio de Janeiro. She has a Ph.D. in Education at the Università Cattolica of Milan, Italy (2006–2010), and has completed a Post-doctorate fellowship at the Universidade Federal de Santa Catarina, Brazil (2012). Her Ph.D./Post-doctorate research was held in Italy, Ethiopia and Brazil on the One Laptop Per Child program. Her current research interests focus on the digital divide from the point of view of Education; the impact of technology on learning practices; the role of social media in political activism; the relationship of ICTs to social development. Among her recent publications are: 'Da crítica à criatividade: olhares sobre os projetos de mídia educação no Brasil' in *Atos de Pesquisa em Educação*, vol. 8 no. 1, 2013, pp. 386–401; 'Il digitale nella didattica: un graduale cambiamento di cultura' in *Media Dialogues – Journal for research of the media and society*, vol. 6, no. 15, 2013, pp. 31–45, and 'Formação de professores para a promoção de projetos de inclusão digital sustentáveis', in *Linhas*, vol. 13, no. 2, 2012, pp. 89–98.

Ulli Samuelsson is Senior Faculty Administrator and lecturer in Education at School of Communication and Education, Jönköping University. Her research interest lies in digital inequality among young people. She has recently published her doctoral thesis, *Digital (in)equality? ICT use in school and pupils' technological capital,* but also articles in *Learning, Media & Technology* and *Nordic Journal of Digital Literacy*.

Sultana A. Shabazz is currently a Ph.D. candidate in Cultural Studies and Sociology at the University of Tennessee, where she teaches a course on the globalization of education. Her dissertation, entitled *Power, Privilege, & Perception: Film as a Discursive Practice in the [de]Construction of Otherness*, uses critical discourse analysis to examine how American constructions of power and marginalization are reproduced in international dialogues. Research interests include: subaltern discourses and social movements, critical film theory, adult education and generational knowledge, critical pedagogy, and discovering how social groups interface with institutions to construct identity. Her article exploring the intersection of race and politics, 'The National Black Republican Association: Toward Post-Racial Politics?', will be published by the Griot Institute at Bucknell University.

Andrej Školkay is the Director of the School of Communication and Media, Bratislava, Slovakia. He has lectured at journalism and media schools across Slovakia and overseas and he has published widely on various aspects of the media, focusing in particular on the relationship between media and politics. He is the author of *Media and Globalisation* (2009) and a book on Media Law in Slovakia (Kluwer Law International, The Netherlands 2012). His research interests include media policy, media literacy, media and politics, media and international relations, new media, among other topics.

Matteo Stocchetti is Adjunct Professor of Political Communication at Åbo Academy University in Vasa and Senior Lecturer at Arcada University of Applied Science in Helsinki, Finland, where he teaches critical media analysis. The primary focus of his research work is the role of communication in the construction and legitimization of relations of power. Within the media field, his main research interest is the role of digital technology in education. Recent publications include 'The Great Transformation Three Centuries Later: double movement, 'market-speak' and sacrifice', in *COLLeGIUM. Studies Across Disciplines in the Humanities and Social Sciences*, 14. Helsinki: Helsinki Collegium for Advanced Studies, 2013, pages 210–226 and 'Critical Thinking and Cultural Recycling: Research notes for the educational use of bad movies'. *Trash Culture Journal*, 2013, Vol. 1 No. 1. Pages 42–65.

Barbara Szafrazjen is Lecturer in Information and Communication Sciences at the Alps Centre of the University of Aix-Marseille, in Digne-les-Bains, France. Main research interests include the construction of meaning through various topics: ICT and organisation, distance education, face-to-face and distance learning tools, virtual distance learners communities, organisational communication, collective intelligence, methods and methodology in Information and Communication Sciences, multidisciplinary perspectives on Information and Communication Sciences and Economics and Management Sciences. Among her recent publications, Szafrajzen B. and Moutouh J. (2013), 'Prise en compte de la construction du sens dans les systèmes d'aide à la décision'. *R2IE: Revue Internationale d'Intelligence Economique, Systèmes d'aide à la décision et Big Data: comprendre la stratégie aujourd'hui*, n. 5, Lavoisier, pp. 167–177.

Alice Nemcova Tejkalova is Assistant Professor of Journalism at the Faculty of Social Science, Charles University, Prague. She is a principal investigator of the Czech part of Worlds of Journalism Study project, a member of Journalism Studies section of ECREA. She is interested in media stereotyping and framing of minor topics, such as Paralympic sport and journalism education. She has been working also as a freelance TV journalist. For her publications please visit: http://cuni.academia.edu/AliceNemcovaTejkalova.

Michal Yerushalmy is a Professor in the Department of Mathematics Education at the University of Haifa, Israel. Yerushalmy is the Director of the Institute of Research and Development of Alternatives in Education, a member of the Learning in Networked Society (LINKS) National Research Center and Vice President for Research of the University of Haifa. Yerushalmy studies mathematical learning and teaching, focus on design and implementation of reformed curricula and on cognitive processes involved in learning with multiple external representations, bodily interactions and modeling. Yerushalmy authored and designed numerous software packages and interactive textbooks (International Journal for Computers in Mathematical Learning, 4 (2–3)). She co- authored the Geometric Supposer (Educational Studies in Mathematics, 57), the VisuaMath algebra curriculum (Technology, Knowledge and Learning 16 (3), Educational Designer, 2(6)), and studies learning of calculus in dynamic and multi-representation environments (Educational Studies in Mathematics, 80 (3)) and designed ways to make technology available for mathematical inquiry learning everywhere using mobile phones (The Math4Mobile project.).

Dennis York is a Distance Learning Specialist at the University of Guelph and a Postdoctoral Research Associate at York University in Toronto, Canada. He holds an MSc and PhD in Education, specializing in e-learning and educational technologies, from the University of West Alabama and York University respectively. He is a past recipient of an Edmund S. Muskie fellowship (USA). He is currently working on the development and evaluation of online and blended learning programs in higher education. His research interests include multimedia instructional design, web-based technologies, engagement strategies and community building in online learning, the role of social media in facilitating teaching and learning in postsecondary education.

Table of Contents

The Politics of Educational Reform in the Digital Age: Concepts, Assessment and Subversions

Matteo Stocchetti

Abstract

Education is a political process in which a variety of actors compete for the control over the future of society. In this process, the role of technology is construed along ideological lines, and the professional role of educators is a reflection of their political role. This introductory chapter offers a preliminary description of a conceptual framework designed to foster critical and hopefully emancipative participation in the debate on the role of digital technology in the politics of educational reform. The main point is that some of the most important themes in this debate can be addressed in terms of concepts, assessment and subversions. The chapters in this collection are contributions to the development of a conceptual framework that enables emancipative participation in the politics of education.

Introduction

The essays collected in this volume discuss the role of digital technology in education from diverse perspectives and in relation to a variety of issues, but share, coherently with the research programme that has inspired them, the intent of promoting informed and active participation in the reform of education in late capitalist societies. In this volume we have deliberately tried to avoid forcing the reader into the discussion of intra-disciplinary theoretical or conceptual development. Those issues are surely relevant and effectively discussed in other fora. In this introductory chapter, however, it seemed a good idea to briefly describe the conceptual co-ordinates of this collection – its starting points, its goals, and the analytical strategy that links them. Informed participation is possible when the participants are in some measure familiar with the relevant debates, issues and positions that constitute the communicative environment of the reform process. Active participation, furthermore, requires the participant to have opinions about desirable or undesirable outcomes of the reform process and about the way to bring about the former and oppose the latter. This goal is important because education is about the future of society and, as I shall argue to a greater length in a moment, this future is always, in one form or a another, a stake in the competition between ideologies inspired by and grounded in competing hierarchies of values.

The politics of education, technology and participation

This collection invites the reader to engage with one particular aspect of this process, i.e. the role of digital technology in education. This is only one, but in my opinion, especially important dimension of the debate about educational reform.

The analyses and the arguments presented in this collection contribute to a conceptual framework that interprets some of the most relevant aspects of the current debate in terms of meanings or 'concepts', the evaluation of the role of digital technology in education or 'assessments', and the opening of intellectual and educational spaces to resist oppressive interpretation of this role, or 'subversions'. To make my case about the analytical value of this framework, I will now present for the attention of the reader three main tenets. First, education is not a technical but a (very!) political process with ideological roots that cannot be ignored. Second, the role of technology is not politically neutral but rather politically indeterminate – subordinated to interpretations that reflect the ideological roots of the political competition. Third, educators must become aware of the key political relevance of their role even and especially when the relevance of this role is challenged by the influence of technocentric culture in educational discourse.

The politics of education

The idea that education is a fundamentally political process construes education as a process in which a number of participants compete for a variety of goals, depending on the nature of the issues at stake. A classical tradition in political science defines the core aspect of this process as a competition for control over the distribution of values in society. In this perspective, the study of politics is, in practice, the study of 'who, gets what, when and how' (Lasswell, 1950 (1936)). Seen as a political process, the study of education is the study of who gets what, when and how in the competition for control over the future of society. This includes the study of the main cleavages, or the fault lines defined by relevant issues at the core of the competition between the main actors, the strategies, or the moves through which main actors try to gain political influence and the nature of the stake. While shared in political studies and also in critical contributions to the analysis of education (Youdell, 2011) this position seems nevertheless far from mainstream in much of the current discussion on media and education. For too many, education is a technical problem: one which has to do primarily with the effective management of available resources, with the identification and implementation of cost-efficient educational models, curricula and technologies, with the co-ordination between the training of teachers and the education of students with the needs of the productive system, or the national economy, or the global markets, and so on.

This technical approach seeks 'optimal solutions' for the role of digital technology in education based on a notion of society interpreted through the organicistic metaphor as the place of order and harmony and on a notion of education as the activity to assure the integration of the individual in a social order endorsed with transcendental traits (e.g. Hobbesian 'Leviathan' or Hegelian 'Spirit') and immutable. Education therefore consists of the transmission of knowledge and values or, more precisely, the knowledge and the values that are necessary to preserve not only the material basis of this society but also the ideas and beliefs supporting its representation in terms of a harmonious whole. In the critical tradition, society is not a place of harmony but rather a place of incessant struggle between the forces that seek to influence the nature of the social order. This order, and the inequalities associated with it, is a more or less contingent outcome of this struggle. In this tradition, education is a crucial battlefield because it is through the control of education – the control of the nature of knowledge and values informing the upbringing of younger generations – that it is possible to control the future of any existing social order: the future distribution of power and the structure of inequalities in society.

One can argue that the stake of the politics of education is fundamentally pedagogical to the extent that the forming of a person, as a citizen, a producer/consumer or as an individual, is the ultimate stake of the competition for the control over the knowledge and the beliefs that formal education is supposed to preserve through generations. This competition, however, does not happen in a vacuum but in a social environment rich in ideas, beliefs, hierarchies of values, understandings of the past, and visions of the future organized in more or less coherent interpretative systems usually referred to as ideologies.

In this part of the century, the main ideological protagonists of this competition are global capitalism, with its political corollary usually referred to as neoliberalism, and democracy. These two ideologies have much in common. Inheritors of some of the great intellectual traditions of the 19th and 20th Centuries, they both contain utopian elements and seek the support of technology to enforce them. The core differences between these two ideologies, however, can be described in relation to the problem of social change or, more precisely, in relation to the problem of change and continuity in the fundamental traits of the social order, and the problem of freedom. In the democratic tradition, egalitarianism is necessary for the participation of the majority of the population in the political competition on the assumption that the legitimacy of decisions is in direct proportion to the extent of the participation. If and when people have equal entitlements and, at least in principle, equal opportunities to effectively participate in the political competition, responsibilities are shared, political violence less attractive, and the possibility of social change less threatening for all. In this ideology, thus, the twin problems of social change and freedom are addressed by prioritizing egalitarianism and collective freedom – the control of the democratic community over its future – over individual freedom.

At the origins of the free-market utopia, in its early formulation, is the idea that societies could be spared the troubles and the violence associated with political competition by establishing the 'free market' as a self-regulating mechanism for the distribution of values in society. The history of this idea, its evolution and its profound consequences on capitalist societies of the 19th and 20th Centuries has been famously described and discussed by economic historian Karl Polanyi in his classic The Great Transformation (Polanyi, 2001 (1944)) (Dale, 2010) (Gammon, 2008). Polanyi argues that the free-market utopia annihilates the 'human and natural substance of society' (Polanyi, 2001 (1944): 3–5) and establishes economic freedom as the fundamental freedom for the sake of which other freedoms have to be sacrificed (Polanyi, 2001 (1944): 265). The effort to establish a non-political order, however, creates inequalities that trigger the reaction of society against the free-market utopia and interpretation of freedom associated with it in the form of communist and fascist dictatorships.

For our purposes, and the understanding of the role of digital technology in education as a dimension of the competition for control over the future of society, the single most important difference, in my opinion, is in the nature of the pedagogical ambitions associated with the utopian elements of these ideologies. By endorsing the utilitarianism of the free-market utopia and seeking to establish a political order based on (in our age, corporate) economic freedom, Neoliberalism needs a dual pedagogy: one for the elites or 'leaders' and one for the masses; one for those in charge of the administration and ideological reproduction of the political order and another one for those who, as producers and consumers, will assure the material reproduction of the same order. Conversely, by endorsing egalitarianism and seeking to establish a political order based on universal participation and consensus, democratic utopia needs a single pedagogy for individuals expected to participate with equal entitlements in the reproduction of a political order based on and legitimated by the endless possibilities of emancipative social change.

The different pedagogical needs of these ideologies and the utopias that inspire them encourage different visions of what education is all about. In the democratic tradition, education is construed as a fundamental resource to pursue the egalitarian ideals through the broadening of participation. Education is therefore a public good, not out of charitable morality but because educated individuals are necessary for the establishment and preservation of an egalitarian society and the participatory management of social change.

In the capitalist tradition, the pedagogical dualism necessary to support a social order that places economic freedom over social justice implies the problem of convincing many that their subjugation to the leadership of the privileged few is both legitimate *and* immutable. An ideology aiming at the establishment and the preservation of a political order based on inequalities needs a dualistic concept of education. Whereas education for participation in the political process is restricted to the 'leaders', education for the masses takes the connotation of 'professional training': the transmission of skills and beliefs relevant for the functional but ultimately passive participation of the vast majority of the individuals in the process of production and consumption.

As Bertrand Russell noted 'in all education, propaganda has a part' and 'the question for the educator is not whether there shall be propaganda but how much, how organized, and of what sort' (Russell, 1932: 213–214). For both these ideologies, education is not only about knowledge and skill but also about beliefs transmitted in the form of propaganda. The important difference here is that democratic propaganda fosters emancipation and the possibility of more egalitarian social order through education, whereas neoliberal propaganda fosters education to facilitate the control of the many by the few in the effort to avoid the subversion of a social order based on inequality.

In democratic propaganda, education is about the transmission of beliefs about the moral quality of egalitarianism, and the importance of participation as the organizing principles of societal order and in the legitimization of political authority. The fundamental skills here are not primarily those that allow the individual to become a capable leader or an efficient worker, but rather those that enable one to actively participate in all the processes through which a democratic society gains and keeps control of its future.

In the educational propaganda of global capitalism, human relations are all contained within the relations of production. People are construed as 'human resources', as producers and consumers; students are seen as 'consumers' (Newson, 2004) of educational services and educated in accordance with the 'need of the labour-market'. The explicit objective of educational reform in neoliberal propaganda is to increase the productivity of the educational process: meaning forming more efficient workers in a more efficient way. The implicit assumption in this discourse is that the problem facing global and national economies is one of productivity or efficiency instead of one of distribution or equity: too much injustice in the distribution of whatever is produced.

This emphasis on production rather than distribution and on economic freedom rather than social justice is a fundamental difference between the hierarchies of values fostered by neoliberal and democratic propaganda, and one with profound pedagogical implications. The neoliberal belief that 'society does not exist'[1] has the pedagogical implication that individuals need not be educated as parts of a community of equals. And they should not since, as the new psychology of leadership suggests, effective leadership depends on the formation of 'collective identities' around the leader constructed as 'entrepreneur of identity', an in-group 'prototype' and 'champion' (Haslam, Reicher, & Platow, 2011: xxii–xxiii). While in democracy people are educated to take pride in the achievements of the community they participate as equals, in neoliberal propaganda people are effectively educated to identify with their 'leaders' and be happy when their leaders are happy.

The sense of urgency that inspires the debate and the call for reform in the educational domain, as well elsewhere, may have to do with the fact that capitalism and democracy are increasingly perceived as incompatible ideologies and, perhaps, with the growing discontent about global capitalism among a large variety of political actors worldwide. To describe this increasing awareness in terms of a 'politicization' of the process of educational reform seems to me a bit naïve and uncritical – as if the reform of education could ever be non-political – but it nevertheless gives us a reason not to ignore the current debate on the reform of education. It shows that what is at stake are not only curricula but very different futures based on different notions of the individual, of freedom, justice and ultimately different ideas about what the future of humanity should look like.

With its emphasis on 'leadership', management and productivity, neoliberal education seeks to enforce the kind of administrative control that, as Herbert Marcuse and others noticed about half a century ago, aims at 'closing the universe of discourse' (Marcuse, 2002 (1964)) and removing the possibility of structural social change at his roots: in the discursive construction of the problem of change itself in terms of production instead of freedom and in terms of the preservation rather than elimination of inequalities. Global capitalism is therefore a threat to democracy because the material opulence of administrative control is exchanged with individual freedom and, most importantly, with the practical possibility of bringing about a more egalitarian social order. Conversely, with its emphasis on egalitarianism principles and participatory skills, democratic education can be a serious obstacle to the spreading of neoliberal ideology in society and, consequently, to the consolidation of global capitalism and the interests of the elites with which it is associated. It should come as no surprise, therefore, that these elites

---

1 This is a sentence attributed to Margaret Thatcher but quickly endorsed among supporters of neoliberalism.

will do whatever is in their capacity to promote the ideology and the education that best serve their interests and oppose the alternative that threatens them.

The sense of urgency, however, may also reflect the impression that, in the current conditions, while the economic crisis inspires both intellectual opposition and social discontent about neoliberalism and the workings of global capitalism, the competition between capitalism and democracy has entered a crucial phase: one in which both the control of education *and* of the role of technology in education are stakes of strategic importance. The crisis of capitalism and the 'free-market' utopia is nothing new. What in the present situation seems unprecedented, however, is the fact that both the current crisis and its response – in support or against global capitalism – are global in scope. In this situation the globalization of the 'free-market' utopia and the globalization of dissent, are twin processes depending on ambivalent communicative affordances associated with digital technology that education can disambiguate in support of or against global capitalism.

Questioning technology

Democracy needs technology to fulfil the egalitarian and participatory ambitions of its utopia through the free circulation of information and knowledge. In democratic discourse, digital technology is the material interface for bringing about universal education and the communicative conditions for the legitimization of political power. Global capitalism needs technology to unite humanity under the rule of the 'free market' and to control the conditions of its stability. In neoliberal discourse, digital technology is the material interface to support its dualist pedagogy and the legitimization of the structures of inequality with which it is associated.

If education is seen as a political process, to discuss the role of digital technology in this process means to look at the impact of this technology on the competition for the control of society. Thus, the second tenet of the conceptual framework I propose here is that this role is not politically neutral[2], or irrelevant for this competition, but rather politically indeterminate: capable in principle of serving the ambitions and hierarchies of values and the strategies of both global capitalism and democracy – and presumably of other ideologies as well. The main reason for this indeterminacy is that the 'power' of technology is not in technology itself but in its usage as a material interface for practices, purposes, goals, and objectives, etc. that are established and justified in relation to ideological ambitions, values

2 Discussing the relationship between technological development and society, the historian of technology, Melving Kranzberg, formulated the 'Kranzberg's First Law…' which '…reads as follows: Technology is neither good nor bad, nor is it neutral' (Kranzberg, 1985: 50).

and visions. This is not to deny the role of corporate and managerial forces which, as many have suggested, support much of the current hype about the digitalization of education. Quite the contrary, the questioning of the ideological roots of technological development aims at shedding a critical light on this process and establishing common grounds for the critical engagement with both the politics of education and the politics of technological development as these processes intersect in much of the current debate.

If one endorses the prescriptions and the ambitions of democratic ideology, the engagement with the role of digital technology cannot be confined to unconditional approval or rejection but it has to be critical: capable of assessing and identifying forms of usage that support the values, practices and purposes associated with democratic ideology.

Uncritical approval is dangerous because it misconstrues the social meaning of the information age and ignores the ideological implications of technocentric discourse. As early observers noted, the emancipative potential of the 'information revolution' is just a potential, at its best, or an illusion at its worst: a 'rhetorical gambit' that promotes a profound misunderstanding of the role of technology (Winston, 1986, 363), ultimately hiding the fact that the 'dominant ideology of the information age' has deep roots in the free-market utopia (Slack, 1987: 11) and 'it is not so much the consumers as the producers who decide what the market "requires"' (MacBride, 1986, vii). Technocentric culture in education represents digital technology as politically neutral, and has a remarkable inclination to overestimate the capacity of this technology to address the problems of education (Selwyn, 2011: 10–21). This culture, however, is not a politically or ideologically innocent one. It assumes that the purposes of education are themselves uncontested, hiding the struggle among competing forces for the control over the nature of these purposes, naturalizing hegemonic visions, values and standards of what technology and education are all about (Ferneding, 2003: 80–84). The representation of technology as a natural and, in a technocentric perspective, essentially benign force hides the 'social' behind the 'technical'; the competition for the control of society behind the organized consensus over optimal solutions; the possibility of social change and the uncertainty about the future of the social order behind an illusion of stability designed to inhibit the possibility of social change. In this perspective, the risks of authoritarian involution are not embedded in technology per se but in the symbolic power of the technocentric discourse. The naturalization of technology as a 'neutral' force is therefore a discursive move in the politics of technological development (the competition for the control over the uses and development of technology), in the politics of education and in the process where these two partially overlap: the debate about the role of digital technology in education.

Rejection is tempting but, politically speaking, is not an option. It is tempting because if the relation between digital technology and the ideology of global capitalism is construed in terms of an end to a means, one may believe that in rejecting the 'means' one can reject the 'end'. But it is not an option for at least two related reasons. First, because it underestimates the transformative power of technology itself and the effects of technological change on the social construction of reality. Second, because this rejection, if motivated on ideological grounds, construes democratic ideals, values and practices dangerously independently from the social relations to which they should be applied.

Even if the digital 'revolution' is construed as a transformative process dictated by the ideological needs of preserving the appeal of the free-market utopia as the fundamental principle of social order in the 21st century, the effective rejection of this ideology, and the order inspired by it, should not be confused with the rejection or denial of the effects of this transformation. From the normative grounds of the democratic ideology, the effective rejection of the capitalist order requires a preliminary appreciation of change: the intellectual understanding of the nature of this transformation and its implications for the effective actualization of democratic ideals.

The notion of technological indeterminacy I suggest here is based on at least two assumptions. The first is that the social role of technology is a 'sticky' one: it can be controlled but not effaced, we can try to understand it and find an effective way to bend it to our purposes, but we cannot ignore it or try to return society to the situation as it was before the new influential technology spread. The second assumption is that the social changes produced by the use of digital technology in education offer opportunities for political antagonism independently from the influence of the actors and the ideology supporting the spread of the same technology. For all practical purposes, this means that emancipative as well as oppressive opportunities are neither intrinsic to nor excluded by the process of technological development.[3]

If one acknowledges the indeterminate nature of technology, the challenge for the political actors inspired by the democratic ideology is to identify the conditions in which the role of digital technology in education can serve egalitarianism and participation rather than the dualist pedagogy of the 'free market'. To pick up this challenge one has to avoid both the rejection of this technology and its uncritical

3 Peter Dahlgren, for example, over two decades ago observed that 'the information revolution now unfolding will no doubt offer still newer methods for subverting democratic participation. Yet it should also hold out possibilities for evolving new strategies to enhance people's political control over their own lives' (Dahlgren, 1987: 24).

embrace along technocentric lines. These positions are based on and reproductive of what, for the lack of a better term, I would argues as the 'moralization of technology': the false idea that digital technology – or technology in general – can be 'good' or 'bad' and therefore endorsed or rejected. This idea hides, rather than exposes, the role of technology in the social construction of reality, and ultimately hinders the effective participation in the debate about the role of technology in the politics of education.

Emancipative opportunities therefore are not intrinsic to digital technology – nor to technology more broadly. Rather, they have to be invented or created. This process requires a number of important steps: the de-familiarization of the technological utopia, first and foremost, and the de-naturalization of its conceptual influence in society: the influence of the way we think, talk and write about technology, taking too many of its benefits for granted.

A more useful approach, and one that in my view is compatible with the idea that the role of digital technology in education is ideologically indeterminate, is described by Karen Ferneding when she suggests that the determinism and the 'language of inevitability' of the dominant discursive framework is opposed by the 'language of possibility' of the emergent discursive framework (Ferneding, 2003: 81–82).

> The language of inevitability assumes an apolitical, artifactual/tool function of technology… this simplistic perspective rationalizes rapid top-down infusion, a conduit or transmission view of knowledge and learning, and an expression of a teacher's role as a mere "delivery system". In contrast, the realm of possibility problematizes technology. Perceiving its functions as both tool and social structures, technology is understood to be intimately connected with culture and politics. (Ferneding, 2003: 83)

Table below summarizes the main differences between the 'discursive frameworks' of competing visions of society participating in the debate over the reform of education. These differences are worth attention also for our discussion, because they offer a clear illustration of how the role of technology in education can be construed along very different concepts, reflecting different ideological roots.

Table 1: The Dialectic of Educational Reform Policy (Ferneding 2003: 81–82)

Dominant Framework	Emergent Framework
Technocentric discourse (fait accompli/ closure)	Discourse of possibility (deliberative/ pluralism)
Technological fix/technological determinism	Questions technology/media infusion
Technology as artefact/tool (apolitical)	Technology as a socio-political process
Information as commodity	"mythinformation" and *techne* as *politea*

Dominant Framework	Emergent Framework
Discourse of progress	Technological pessimism
Functionalist/vocationalist	Politics of meaning/social justice
Techno-utopian social vision	Emancipatory social vision
Efficiency/*technique*	Questions *technique*
Enterprise culture	Questions technical rationalism
Libertarian/technocentric	"cultural wars"/multiculturalism
Privatization/commodification	The public good/social democratic process
Crisis exists and related to the rise of Information Age and global market economy	Crisis exists and related to systemic socioeconomic problems and postmodern crisis in meaning
Educators without agency/performance culture	Educators as citizens and social change agents
technopoly	lifeworld
Solution: infuse technology and adopt standards/accountability measures/control technologies	Solutions: address sociocultural issues and economic disparity

What makes this approach especially useful for our purposes is that it points to issues of meaning and assessment. The ideological roots and the discursive frameworks of the debate about the role of digital technology in the reform of education invite attention to the nature of concepts that participate in the relevant debates. The indeterminacy in the role of technology makes the assessment of its usage in pedagogical and educational practices a crucial moment for the disambiguation of this role – the understanding of how digital technology can serve democratic rather than neoliberal visions of society.

The role of educators

To state that the role of educators is important is a triviality. In the politics of education, none of the political actors would deny that. A bit less trivial, however is to understand the different connotations of this role in the discourse inspired by democratic or the free-market utopia. Perhaps even less trivially nowadays, here I suggest that this role, in all its alternative ideological connotations, is fundamentally political, that is connected to and influential on the competition for the control over the future of society.

In classic sociology, roles are defined as institutionalized behavioural expectations, a technical formula that describes forms of relationship in which uncertainty, for example in education, is addressed by formal and informal rules that regulate the conduct of those involved. In professional roles, the nature of expectations reflects professional knowledge that we expect, for example, a medical doctor or a teacher to possess, but also professional rules that we expect doctors and teachers to follow when they address problems within their professional domains. To talk about the political role of the educators and its relevance in the politics of education means to talk about the relevance of the professional knowledge that educators possess and the rules they are supposed to abide by when this knowledge and these rules influence, directly or indirectly, the competition for the control over the future of society.

The professional and political roles of educators, then, have different connotations in the democratic and the capitalist discursive framework. At the origins of these differences are other, and broader, ideological differences concerning the purpose of knowledge and the nature of the social problem that professional roles are supposed to address.

In democratic discourse, educators are citizens endorsed by the knowledge, the will and the skills necessary to participate in the social construction of the democracy and to educate others to do the same. In this vision, educators are influential agents of change because the future of society depends not only on the transmission of knowledge but also on the effective socialization of participatory and egalitarian ideals. The purpose of scientific knowledge is to support the efforts to put these ideals into practice, while the concept of truth is the common communicative grounds on which different groups in society participate in these efforts.

In the neoliberal interpretation of the free-market utopia, educators are a 'delivery system' for the transmission of knowledge necessary for the process of production, but also, and most importantly, for the preservation of the structure of inequality with which it is associated. In capitalism, as Jean-Françoise Lyotard famously noted, the purpose of science is not truth but power or more precisely 'performative knowledge' and 'legitimation by power': the knowledge that serves the practical purposes of the leaders and provides them with the technological means to control the social construction of the real (Lyotard, [1979] 1982: 46–47). In the circumstances that Lyotard discusses as the 'postmodern condition', 'scientists, technicians and instruments are purchased not to find truth but to augment power' and 'universities and institutions of higher learning are called upon to create skills and no longer ideals' (Lyotard, [1979] 1982: 46–48).

While the professional role of educators is crucially important in each ideological interpretation, the political role of democratic educators, with its emphasis on democratic ideals and emancipative knowledge is subversive for the ambitions of capitalist education. Conversely, the political role of neoliberal educators, with its emphasis on production and the legitimization of inequality, is subversive of democratic education. The problem of social change and democratic legitimization of political power that is at the core of the pedagogical mission of the democratic educator is precisely what neoliberalism tries to remove from the educational agenda by reducing society to relations among individuals regulated by the market. In this vision, the mission for the neoliberal educator is to guarantee the availability of expertise for the effective management of the social order – and not to question the social order itself. Educators are thus deprived of agency, since the future of society does not depend on the actualization of democratic ideals but on the efficient administration of expert knowledge.

If the role of educators in the politics of education is looked at from the ideological binary I have suggested here, on professional grounds the challenge is complex but on political grounds the question is quite simple[4]. On professional grounds educators needs to question technology, as Ferneding suggests, and assess its educational uses in relation to competing ideological purposes and pedagogies. On political grounds, however, there is no alternative: educators can either subvert or support ideological efforts in one direction or another.

Every ideology seeks to transform society in order to assure the conditions for its survival. Every ideology therefore contains some subversive elements. Democratic utopia has been, and still is, powerfully subversive. Neoliberalism is no less subversive of democratic institutions, especially when it comes to public education, a most fundamental one among them. In the United States, for example:

> The neoliberal cuts in state services…has meant a resurgence in inequality… The earlier emphasis on public education has given way to its privatizing erosion at all levels, whether through charter schools and vouchers, through distance-learning programs for the racial poor on reservation, the dramatic privatization of higher education, or through the introduction of user fees for libraries and museums and their transformation by the culture industry model of urban branding into sites for tourist attraction. (Davidson & Goldberg, 2010: 79)

---

4 Here I have described the politics of education through the simplified lenses of an ideological binary – the democratic and free-market utopia – that is unsuitable for a lengthier discussion of the implication of postmodernism in the politics of education. If one however believes, with Lyotard, Frederic Jameson, and others that the postmodern condition is our condition and one that in fundamental ways reflects the free-market utopia and its technocentric ramifications, one has to accept also the idea that democratic educators are de facto positioned in a subversive role. On professional grounds, this role invites the reformulation of some of the concepts most affected by the postmodernist turn (truth, knowledge, technology, authority, etc.) in ways compatible with democratic values, beliefs and practices. On political grounds this role rejects the tendency of postmodernism to deny the role of ideologies and the fundamental struggle for power that is fought on the terrain of education and technology. See also (Aronowitz & Giroux, 1991).

In these circumstances, the idea of a non-political role for educators is as false and manipulative as much as the idea that in our age ideologies are dead. Both these ideas serve the ideological ambitions of neoliberalism. Those who believe that ideologies are dead, are those inclined to accept the ideals, values and practice of neoliberalism out of despair, if for no other reasons: because they think there is no alternative to the rule of the 'free market'. Educators who believe their role is a-political or non-political accept the idea that someone else can decide on their future. Most importantly, in their explicit or implicit pedagogy (Bourdieu & Passeron, 1990 (1970)), they educate future generations to accept the same ideas. Needless to say, these beliefs are also those that make educators more compliant with the managerial leadership in educational institutions, therefore contributing to the intellectual isolation of dissidents.

In a political perspective, the role of educators is a crucial one. The effective transmission of knowledge, values and beliefs associated with ideological representations of the role of technology and the future of society depends greatly on them. It can be debated if the professional ethics of educators, very broadly speaking, make them more inclined to subscribe to democratic rather than neoliberal values: to the ideas and vision of democratic education rather than those of global capitalism. What seems clear in the current stage, however, is that the effort to bring about the reform of education along technocentric and neoliberal lines deals with the role of educators in terms of compliance or removal: compliance with the prescriptions of global capitalism, or removal of their influence in education – also through the affordances offered by technocentric interpretations of digital technology. The 'politics of fear' (Robin, 2004), waged on the work-place by educational managers and administrators, can be effective against educators resisting the managerial turn and the privatization of education but also against their students when the fear of unemployment is manipulated to prevent the possibility that education may serve purposes other than the mere reproduction of the work force.

Greater effort to control education through technological or political tools, however, can be interpreted as a sign of crisis. In the ideological struggle for survival, more control is needed when consensus declines and it may not be too implausible to suggest that the neoliberal onslaught on democratic education reflects the deeper crisis of the free-market utopia itself. In fact, compliance with ideas and practices that more and more appear unsustainable to a growing number of people has to be secured through increased manipulation – and sometimes coercion. Here too, it is therefore not surprising that, quite often, the arguments in support of the re-profiling of educators' curricula and professional ethics along neoliberal and technocentric lines are wrapped up in the style of urgency, if not outright emergency. In these arguments technology evolves too quickly and schools adapt too slowly; the labour market demands new skills and competences but the teachers are too incapable or unwilling to adapt their competences and methods to the new 'learning environment'; the global economy set conditions based on 'hard' economic 'facts' but educational institutions are still too attached to 'soft' social and cultural factors, and so on.

The way educators and other potentially influential actors understand the role of digital media in education, affects the way they participate or not in the relevant debates. As an influential aspect of the politics of education, thus, this understanding is not immune to manipulation. The construing of educational 'solutions' along the predicaments of technocentric interpretations is supported by a rhetoric of emergency in which educational 'innovation' is bound up and subordinated to the fast pace of technological development and to the imperatives of the 'global economy'. As in other forms of the politics of fear, by manipulating the understanding of the digital role of education, the elites whose interests are served by global capitalism and technocentric discourse can increase their influence in society. Forcing the discussion of the problems of education in terms of technical rather than political problems, in terms of cost-effectiveness and optimal solutions rather than in those of a competition over the future of society, is a way to establish the ideological influence of the free-market utopia.

Concepts, assessments and subversion

Each of the chapters presented in this collection is a fragment of the large variety of dialogues and disciplinary expertise participating in the debate about the role of digital technology in education. In this collection, however, they have been organized in three sections to suggest that a critical understanding of the aspects relating to ideology, technology and educators in the current debate has at least three useful entry-points: concepts, assessments and subversions.

The chapters in Part One, 'Concepts' discuss some of the main notions that feature in this debate. The first contribution, by **Ulli Samuelsson** and **Tobias Olsson** is on the state of research on digital inequality: on the questions addressed and the nature of the empirical evidence supporting the current debate, as well as on important research questions in need of more systematic attention. **Daniel Chazan** and **Michal Yerushalmy** focus on the future of the mathematics 'textbook' in the digital age to invite the reader to appreciate the interplay of social forces that will presumably shape it. **Marlène Loicq** discusses the concept of pluralism to describe some fundamental requirements of democratic media and information literacy. In their chapter on curation, **Paul Mihailidis** and **Megan E. Fromm** argue for the importance of this notion as a pedagogical tool to foster media literacy education but also 'engagement, community and purpose' among students. **Filip Lab** and **Alice N. Tejkalova** discuss the concept of digital literacy and its critical relevance in the education of professional journalists. **Melissa Harness** and **Sultana A. Shabazz** examine claims concerning the educational capacity of online communities to stop the deterioration of social capital in mature capitalist societies. To look at these and other concepts that participate in the debate about the role of digital technology in education is important to understand the power/knowledge mobilized and nature of its ideological implications. It is this understanding which, following Michel Foucault (Youdell, 2011), can give us an insight into the strength but also the limits of hegemonic discourse: the productivity of power but also the indeterminacy of its discursive outcome and, consequently, the relative instability of any order. If the politics of education in this part of the century is indeed characterized by a discourse that reflects the hegemonic role of neoliberal ideology in the way both education and technology are represented (Ferneding, 2003), to challenge this hegemony one must pay critical attention to issues of meaning and question the conceptual grounds of these representations.

The chapters in Part Two, 'Assessments', discuss the features and impact of educational uses of digital technology in formal and informal education. In the politics of educational reform this dimension of the debate is important because this is where technology can be questioned and technological determinism rejected. In the technocentric culture of global capitalism, the assessment of the role of digital technology in education enforces what Antony Giddens termed 'disembedding': the "lifting out" of social relations from local contexts of interaction and their restructuring across indefinite spans of time-space' (Giddens, 1990: 21) in the effort of transforming humanity in one big market through the selective exploitation and/or elimination of differences. In the practice of education, this disembedding is brought about, for example, by reducing the complexity of incomparable experiences and diversity in education to comparable outcomes measureable in terms of efficiency in relation to the needs of the global economy. Initiatives such as the Programme for International Students Assessment-PISA are in line with this tendency and with neoliberal ambitions in the politics of education. While the precise nature of assessment practices more compatible with democratic education and a critical culture of technology is an open question, alternative possibilities may seek to evaluate the impact of this technology, e.g., on the identities, relations and practices constituting the educational process as this unfolds within the coordinates of specific cultural, political, and socio-economic contexts. The chapters in this section offer a preliminary contribution in this direction by pointing to methodological problems, particulars and ultimately the ambivalence associated with the efforts of assessing the educational role of digital technology. **Alberto Bitonti** and **Andrej Školkay** report on a European project aiming at the assessment of the best practice of informal media education in all EU countries. Using qualitative methods for the analysis of the effects of digital learning on the educational experience, **Barbara Szafrajzen** and **Karen Ferreira-Meyers** identify loneliness as a major obstacle on the way to the effective integration of this technology into the learning environment. Two separate chapters, one by **Katarina Panic, Verolien Cauberghe & Patrick De Pelsmacker,** and the other by **Rut Martínez-Borda & Pilar Lacasa** assess the role of videogames to promote health education and to develop narrative skills, respectively, among primary school children. Presenting the results of a comparative research on the introduction of lap tops in Brazil, Ethiopia and Italy, **Magda Pischetola** argues why and how teachers are a crucial interface for the success or failures of similar initiatives. The motivations and the issues behind teachers' acceptance or rejection of digital tools introduced in the classrooms through a governmental programme in Portugal and Spain are discussed in the chapters by **Sara Pereira** and **Cristina Aliagas Marín & Josep M. Castellà Lidon** respectively. Finally, **Vincenzo De Masi** and **Yan Han** introduce the reader to the role of animation as an educational tool in China, discussing how digital technology has changed a form of cultural communication that dates as far back as the 1930s.

In Part Three 'Subversions', the attention is on professional educators as influential agents in the educational usage of digital technology to oppose unwanted changes in the democratic ambitions of public education. In this part, **Judith Faifman** and **Brian Goldfarb** discuss the participative potential of digital media and the possibilities for engaged teachers to teach the 'unteacheable': knowledge and discursive practice banned by mainstream curricula. **David Elliott** and **Scott Bulfin** introduce the reader to the 'digital underlife' of a public secondary school in Australia, to reveal the pedagogical opportunities associated with the unsanctioned use of software. The chapters by **Julie Faulkner** and **Dennis N. York & Ronald D. Owston** discuss educational experiences aimed at supporting the critical appropriation of the affordances associated with digital technology in the construction and representation of self-identity among undergraduate and graduate students respectively. **Gloria Gómez-Diago** invites educators to reject the use of 'privative' software in education arguing for the pedagogical advantages associated with 'open use' software. In the meaning adopted here, 'subversion' refers to educational uses of digital technology that can resist or even oppose, in one way or another, the implementation of the neoliberal vision and the effects of technocentric culture. In a democratic perspective, the debates on this dimension are motivated by the need to identify the places of resistance associated with technologized societies (Feenberg, 2009), the opportunities available to educators, students and other non-hegemonic actors to oppose exclusion, to re-gain agency, and to effectively question the purposes and the practices inspiring the educational usage of digital technology. Rather than an alternative option to the previous two, this strategy relies on critical engagements with concepts and assessment to exploit the productivity of power in anti-hegemonic forms.

References

Adorno, T. (2006 (1975)). The culture industry reconsidered. In T. Adorno, *The Culture Industry* (pp. 98–106). New York: Routledge.

Aronowitz, S., & Giroux, H. (1991). *Postmodern education: Politics, culture and social criticism.* Minneapolis: University of Minnesota Press.

Bourdieu, P. (1991). *Language and Symbolic Power.* Cambridge: Polity.

Bourdieu, P., & Passeron, J.-C. (1990 (1970)). *Reproduction in Education, Society and Culture.* London: Sage.

Dahlgren, P. (1987). Ideology and Information in the Public Sphere. In J. D. Slack, & F. Fred, *The Ideology of the Information Age* (pp. 24–46). Norwood: Ablex.

Dale, G. (2010). *Karl Polanyi. The Limits of the Market.* Cambridge: Polity.

Davidson, C. N., & Goldberg, D. T. (2010). *The Future of Thinking. Learning Institutions in a Digital Age.* Cambridge: The MIT Press.

Ferneding, K. A. (2003). *Questioning Technology. Electronic Technologies and Educational Reform.* New York: Peter Lang.

Foucault, M. (1999 (1983)). *Discourse and Truth: the Problematization of Parrhesia* . Retrieved October 24, 2013, from foucault.info: http://foucault.info/documents/parrhesia/foucault.dt1.wordparrhesia.en.html.

Freire, P. (1985). *The Politics of Education. Culture, Power and Liberation.* Westport: Bergin & Garvey.

Gammon, E. (2008). Affect and the Rise of the Self-Regulating Market. *Millennium: Journal of International Studies, Vol. 37, No. 2*, 251–278.

Giddens, A. (1990). *The Consequences of Modernity.* Cambridge: Polity.

Haslam, A. S., Reicher, S. D., & Platow, M. J. (2011). *The New Psychology of Leadership: Identity, Influence and Power.* New York: Psychology Press.

Horkheimer, M., & Adorno, T. W. (2002 (1969)). *Dialectic of Enlightenment. Philosophical Fragments.* Stanford (new edition 1969; or.ed. 1947): Stanford University Press.

Kranzberg, M. (1985). The information age: evolution or revolution? In G. R. Bruce, *Information technologies and Social Transformation* (pp. 35–54). Washington: National Academy of Engineering.

Lasswell, H. D. (1950 (1936)). *Politics. Who Gets What, When, How.* New York: Peter Smith.

Lyotard, J.-F. ([1979] 1982). *The Postmodern Condition: A report on Knowledge.* Minneapolis: University of Minnesota Press.

MacBride, S. (1986). Foreword. In M. Traber, *ed. The Myth of the Information Revolution. Social and Ethical Implications of Communication Technology* (pp. vii–viii). London: Sage.

Marcuse, H. (2002 (1964)). *One-Dimensional Man. Studies in the Ideology of Advanced Industrial Society.* London: Routledge.

Mouffe, C. (2005). *On The Political.* London: Taylor & Francis. Newson, J. A. (2004). Disrupting the 'Student as Consumer' Model: The New Menacipatory Project. *International Relations, Vol. 18 (2)*, 227–239.
Polanyi, K. (2001 (1944)). *The Great Transformation. The Political and Economic Origins of Our Time.* Boston: Beacon Press.
Robin, C. (2004). *Fear. The History of a Political Idea.* Oxford: Oxford University Press.
Russell, B. (1932). *Education and the Social Order.* London: George Allen and Unwin.
Selwyn, N. (2011). *School and Schooling in the Digital Age. A critical Analysis.* Oxon: Routledge.
Slack, J. D. (1987). The Information Age As Ideology: An Introduction. In J. D. Slack & F. Fejes, *(Eds.). The Ideology of the Information Age* (pp. 1–11). Norwood, New Jersey: ABLEX.
Weaver, K. R. (1988). *Automatic Government: the Politics of Indexation.* Washington: The Brookings Institution.
Winston, B. (1986). *Misunderstanding Media.* London: Routledge & Kegan Paul.
Youdell, D. (2011). *School Trouble. Identity, power and politics in education.* London: Routledge.

Part One – Concepts

Digital Inequality in Primary and Secondary Education: Findings from a Systematic Literature Review

Ulli Samuelsson & Tobias Olsson

Abstract

During the last couple of decades there has been a global interest in unequal access to and use of information and communication technologies (ICTs). Without a clear state of its actual origin, the concept *digital divide* started to appear frequently in the public debate in the mid-1990s in efforts to describe and analyse disparities in ICT access. Since the mid-2000s increasing numbers of scholars have changed their research interest from a dichotomous view of digital divides – you either have or have not access – to more qualitative and contextualized notions such as digital inclusion or exclusion. This systematic literature review offers an overview of this latter, more qualitative and contextualized turn of research. It does so by looking into a specific area of research, namely research concerning digital inclusion and exclusion in the context of primary and secondary education. The literature review maps what studies have been conducted and what empirical evidence is currently available regarding digital inequality among children in primary and secondary school contexts. The review makes obvious that digital inequalities exist in several developed countries among pupils in primary and secondary education. Inequalities can most often be related to socioeconomic status, gender and ethnicity. As a conclusion, this means that any ambition to increase digital equality among young people has to struggle against well-known societal structures.

During the last couple of decades there has been global interest in unequal access to and use of information and communication technologies (ICTs). Although its origin is unclear, the concept of a *digital divide* began to frequently appear in public debate in the mid-1990s as part of the efforts to describe and analyse disparities in ICT access. Within the research field, the concept later became the very centre of ICT debates—these debates analysed how divides were delineated within social and cultural structures such as class, gender, ethnicity, and level of education (cf. Norris, 2001; Servon, 2002; Warschauer, 2003).

The early debates were often influenced by diffusion theory (Rogers, 1995), which pays specific interest to people's varying willingness to adopt innovations. As a consequence, initial digital divide research argued 'the acquisition of and access to computers and internet equipment is a fundamental for overcoming divides' (Tsatsou, 2011, p. 321) and focused mainly on access issues—i.e., who does and who does not have access to ICTs?

Since the mid-2000s, however, an increasing number of scholars have shifted their research interest from a dichotomous view of digital divides—i.e., access or no access—to more qualitative and contextualised notions, such as digital inclusion or exclusion. Helsper (2008), for instance, asks for research that examines not only access to ICTs but also how 'motivation, knowledge and skills' (p. 23) are variously distributed among people.

This systematic literature review offers an overview of this latter, more qualitative and contextualised shift. It does so by investigating a specific area of research: research concerning digital inclusion and exclusion in the context of primary and secondary education.

Background

Digital inequality could be understood 'as a hierarchy of access to various forms of technology in various contexts, resulting in differing levels of engagement and consequences' (Selwyn, 2004: 351). This statement highlights the complexity as well as the need for contextualization to be able to evaluate and understand the phenomena. Digital inequality could be viewed as both an expression and a reproducer of social inequality (Mori, 2010).

The interest in digital divide research has not only changed its focus since 2005; it has also increased. Wang, McLee and Kuo (2011) analysed references from 852 documents published between 2000 and 2009, which they found using the key word "Digital divide." They found that the number of cited documents and authors increased between the periods 2000–2004 and 2005–2009. During both periods, the same studies and authors dominate the reference lists. The ten most cited authors from the later period were (in order of citation frequency) Eszter Hargittai, Pippa Norris, Mark Warschauer, Manuel Castells, Susannah Fox, Jan A. G. M. van Dijk, Paul DiMaggio, Neil Selwyn, Sonia Livingstone and Amanda Lenhart. Castells, Norris and Warschauer were also among the ten most cited authors in the earlier period. Wang et al. found that medical journals, followed by information society and communication journals, were the most sited journals. Educational journals, however, are conspicuously absent from those most cited, although some of the most cited authors show at least some interest in educational issues.

Access to ICTs for socio-economically advantaged children versus disadvantaged children differs by only a few percentage points in Western countries, such as the Netherlands, Norway, Finland, Denmark, Iceland, Sweden, Switzerland and the United Kingdom (OECD, 2011). According to the OECD, across its countries, home Internet access increased by an average of 54 percent among disadvantaged students between 2000 and 2009. Meanwhile, there have been considerable investments in ICT resources in all 25 OECD countries. This development could be seen in the light of Yu's (2006) second category of studies, which focuses on digital divides as an economic concern and perceives governmental interference as a means to close the divides.

Nevertheless, research still shows divides in the Western world. However, these divides are less apparent in regard to access to ICTs and instead are more apparent in softer, more inclusive measurements of ICT capabilities and skills. Most of these latter studies employed an empirically broad approach, establishing a generalised view of youths' access to and use of ICTs during childhood and adolescence. Much less research, however, has analysed digital inequality within specific contexts of youths' everyday lives—in school, at home, during leisure time, etc.

Against this backdrop, this article begins to compensate for this shortcoming as a collection and overview of existing research concerning digital inequality within one specifically vital part of young people's everyday lives: school.

Aim

The aim of this systematic literature review is to determine what studies have been conducted and what empirical evidence is available on the phenomenon of digital inequality among children in primary and secondary school contexts. The following questions will be answered by this review:

- What is the nature of the evidence?
- Which theoretical foundations and scholars are predominant?
- In which countries are the studies situated?
- In which specific contexts are the studies set?
- What are the research outcomes?
- What similarities or differences could be found in the outcomes?

Search Strategy

The data was obtained from the following databases during May and June 2012:

Academic Search Elite
Communication & Mass Media Complete
Library, Information Science & Technology Abstract
Science Direct
Web of Science[1]

1 In Web of Science, limitations to the categories *Education Educational Research, Communication* and *Sociology* existed.

ERIC
SocINDEX

The main criteria for the searches was peer-reviewed academic journal articles published since 2006 that studied digital divide issues in primary or upper secondary schools, written in English or a Scandinavian language. Grey literature, such as dissertations, conference proceedings, reports and other non-peer-reviewed research, were not included.

The research area includes concepts such as digital equality or inequality, digital inclusion or exclusion, digital divide or divides and digital stratification. Thus, the following search string was entered into 'any field' in EBSCO hosted databases[2], 'Title' or 'Topic' in Web of Science and 'Abstract, Title, Keywords' in Science Direct: ((digital divide*) OR (digital inequ*) OR (digital equ*) OR (digital inclu*) OR (digital exclu*) OR (digital stratification*)) AND (school* OR educ* OR student* OR pupil*). This search resulted in a total of 1678 unique articles (Figure 1).

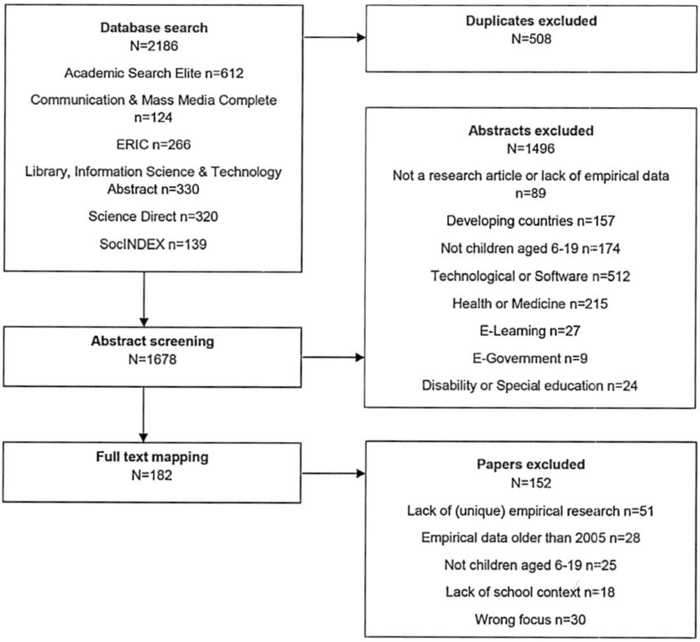

Fig. 1: The inclusion and exclusion process

2 Academic Search Elite; Communication & Mass Media Complete; Library, Information Science & Technology Abstract; ERIC and SocINDEX.

Criteria for Selection

The first step was to screen all 1678 titles and abstracts to exclude articles that clearly fell outside the research focus. Except for the demand for empirical data, no other limitations were put on the research design or data collection. The data were collected and coded for inclusion or exclusion by EPPI-reviewer[3]. Thirty articles met the inclusion criteria and were eligible for review (Appendix I, Table I).

Nature of the evidence

The majority of the studies were quantitative or combinations of quantitative and qualitative, while only five studies were solely qualitative. Consequently, most of the data were collected with questionnaires (see Appendix). Most of the studies (n=24) used only students as informants, and four studies (3; 6; 21; 28) used only teachers as informants. Two of the studies (10; 13) collected data from several different groups of informants, such as students, teachers and/or parents.

Some of the studies employed more of an evaluative approach than a research approach. There were evaluations of hardware implementations (7; 10) and software implementations (23). It must also be noted that Rosen, one author of study 23, is connected to the software company in question, according to the company's website. In some studies, it was difficult to follow the entire research process, which resulted in uncertainty concerning the method (16) and year of data collection (9; 15; 17; 21; 27). Although these studies may lack in reliability, they were included, but are marked with an * any time conclusions are drawn from them.

Predominant theoretical foundations and scholars

To determine the predominant theoretical foundations and scholars, two different approaches were used. First, the full text of the articles were analysed, and second, a meta-analysis of the articles' references, based on author(s) and title, was conducted. A total of 1163 references were analysed. The research field is multidisciplinary, which could be a reason for the lack of well-defined, predominant theories; regardless, references are mainly made to three different theoretical fields.

A majority (n=15) of the studies used the frameworks of different theories based on the relationship between *socio-economic status* (SES) and ICT access and use. Within the field of socio-economic theories, different capital theories are used,

3 http://eppi.ioe.ac.uk/cms/Default.aspx?tabid=1913.

such as Bourdieu's capital theory, bonding and bridging social capital theory[4], and knowledge gap theory[5].

The second most common theoretical foundation was studies including various takes on the concept *literacy*. Sometimes specified as digital literacy, information literacy, media literacy, computer literacy, or network literacy, this foundation was used in twelve studies. *Gender* theories were the third most common theoretical foundation; it was applied in seven studies (see Appendix II).

The most predominant scholar was Ezter Hargittai in terms of both number of references and unique publications (Table 1).

Table 1: Predominant scholars in the reviewed articles

Author	Total references	Reviewed articles referring to the author (n)	Unique publications in articles by author (n)
Hargittai, Ezter	31	12	18
Warschauer, Mark	20	11	8
Van Dijk, Jan	17	9	7
Livingstone, Sonia	13	10	7
Prensky, Marc	12	6	3
Selwyn, Neil	11	9	6
boyd, danah	11	5	8
Lenhart, Amanda	9	8	6
Knobel, Michele	9	8	4
Smith, Aaron	9	5	5

The predominance of some scholars could be explained by their clear focus on digital divide and by single articles that, despite their early publication dates, are considered key works in the research field (Appendix I, Table II). The articles refer to 537 unique scholarly journals, but the single most cited journal is *Computers & Education*, followed by *New Media & Society,* which had only half as many citations (Appendix I, Table III).

Most of the studies are conducted in one single country; the only exceptions are the studies by Tømte and Hatlevik (2011) and Zhong (2011), who compared two

4 Williams (2006). "On and off the Net: Scales for social capital in an online era". *Journal of Computer–Mediated Communication*, volume 11, number 2, pp. 593–628.

5 Tichenor, P. J., Donohue, G. A., & Olien, C. N. (1970). Mass media flow and differential growth in knowledge. *Public Opinion Quarterly*, 34, 159–170.

and sixteen[6] countries, respectively. Both these studies also used data from the OECD's Programme for International Student Assessment (PISA) studies. Other countries represented in this review are the following:

United States (1; 2; 3; 6; 7; 12; 14; 21; 22; 27; 28; 29)
Italy (5; 8; 11)
Israel (4; 23)
Germany (9; 15)
Belgium (18; 25)
Australia (13; 19)
Spain (10)
Austria (20)
Taiwan (16)
Korea (17)
Sweden (24)

Specific contexts of the studies

Digital inclusion and exclusion is often related to demographic factors, such as ethnicity, gender, socio-economic status (SES), educational orientation and residential area. The studies addressed these factors using three different sample orientations: (a) the informants constitute a representative sample or convenient sample without predefined groups, (b) the informants constitute predefined advantaged or disadvantaged groups, and (c) the informants constitute predefined groups to make comparisons.

Representative samples or convenient samples without predefined groups

Nationally or regionally representative samples (1; 11; 14; 15; 18; 20; 24; 25; 26; 28; 30)
Convenient, not nationally representative groups (2; 9; 10; 21; 22; 27)

Predefined advantaged or disadvantaged groups

Advantaged
Moderate-high SES (4; 8)
High educational achievers (4)
Disadvantaged
High poverty rates or low SES, including low socio-economic suburbs (3; 7; 13; 22; 23)

6 Belgium, Czech Republic, Denmark, Finland, Germany, Hungary, Italy, Japan, Korea, New Zealand, Poland, Portugal, Slovak Republic, Sweden, Switzerland and Uruguay.

Ethnic minorities (7; 12)
Low educational achievers (12)

Comparative studies with predefined groups according to
Socio-economic status (29)
Residential area (16; 29)
School forms[7] (5; 17; 19)
School status[8] (6)

Research outcomes

Overall, socioeconomic status (SES) is a significant factor of the use of ICTs—the higher the SES, the more advanced and advantageous the use[9]. Fourteen studies show statistically proven existing digital inequality due to SES, and two qualitative studies highlight the influence of SES on the use of ICTs. Such digital inequalities related to SES are found in twenty different countries (Table 2).

Table 2: Digital inequality related to Socioeconomic Status[10]

	Statistically proven	N	Objective
Ahn (2012)	Yes	701	Students' use of social network sites
Calvani et al.	Yes	1.056	Students' digital competence
Chapman et al.	Yes	6.230	Teachers' ICT skills and use
Gui & Argentin	Yes	980	Students' digital skills
Hohlfeld et al.	Yes	2.345	Students' use of ICTs
Lebens et al.	Yes	60	Students' computer attitudes
Liao & Chang*	Yes	1.200	Students' information literacy
Mertens & D'Haenens	Yes	1.005	Students' ICT use and ownership
North et al.	No	25	Students' use of ICTs
Parycek et al.	Yes	379	Students' internet use
Reinhart et al.*	Yes	94	Teachers' ICT use for instruction

7 Different groups, according to educational orientation.
8 High or need status.
9 Use that could lead to advantages in education and society.
10 Based on residential district, school status or individual status.

	Statistically proven	N	Objective
Robinson	No	>300	Students' information channel preferences
Tondeur et al.	Yes	1.241	Students' ICT use, competence and attitudes
Wood & Howley	Yes	514	Teachers' view regarding students computer use
Zhao	Yes	432	Students' use of different social networking services
Zhong	Yes	87.562	Students' digital skills

Digital inequality could also be related to gender, as ten studies showed statistically proven gender differences in twenty countries (Table 3). Gender differences are identified in ways of use, competence, attitudes, preferences and self-efficacy. Computer ownership is higher among boys than girls (25); boys are also more frequent users than girls (24) and score higher in general ICT interest (9). They are also less interested in social network sites than girls (1, 2), but socialise by going to Internet cafés and playing games together (17; 24). Boys are also more self-confident (9), have a more positive computer attitude (25) and perform better than girls in theoretical ICT skills (11) as well as score higher on self-reported ICT-skills (30). In regard to the effect of ICT as a tool for enhancing learning, boys tend to evaluate the improvement more favourably than girls (27). Girls are as skilled as boys in routine activities online (11), but are less interested and skilled in the technical aspects (9; 11). They prefer standard applications (9) and use ICTs for communication and socialisation (9; 17; 24).

Table 3: Digital inequality related to gender

	Statistically proved	N	Objective
Ahn (2011)	Yes	700	Students' use of social network sites
Ahn (2012)	Yes	701	Students' use of social network sites
Ertl & Helling*	Yes	90	Students' gender differences in skills and attitudes
Gui & Argentin	Yes	980	Students' digital skills
Lim & Meier*	Yes	673	Students' ICT use
Parycek et al.	Yes	379	Students' Internet use
Samuelsson	Yes	256	Students' ICT use and skills

	Statistically proved	N	Objective
Tondeur et al.	Yes	1.241	Students' ICT use, competence and attitudes
Tømte & Hatlevik	Yes	≈9400	Students' gender differences in self-efficacy in ICT
Wolsey & Grisham*	Yes	67	Students' perception of themselves as writers[11]
Zhong	Yes	87.562	Students' digital skills

Ethnicity—meaning, groups with a shared cultural heritage—is another divider for digital inequality. Three large quantitative studies found differences in use and self-efficacy in relation to ethnicity (Table 4). Ethnic differences were found within the same country (1; 2), as well as between countries (26).

Table 4: Digital inequality related to ethnicity

	Statistically proved	N	Objective
Ahn (2011)	Yes	700	Students use of social network sites
Ahn (2012)	Yes	701	Students use of social network sites
Tømte & Hatlevik	Yes	≈9400	Students differences in Self-efficacy in ICT

However, several of the studies (e.g., 2; 11; 20; 25; 26) found that SES, gender, ethnicity and other factors interact, and stereotypical assumptions must be reconsidered. This 'underpin[s] the existence of multi-facetted perspectives' (26, p. 1422).

A multifaceted perspective

The interaction of several factors on digital divides is highlighted in different ways. There could be an ethnic dimension in gender differences, as Finnish boys report a higher level of self-efficacy than Finnish girls, but Norwegian boys report a higher level of self-efficacy than Norwegian girls in only one of two areas (26). Additionally, boys' digital skills are more affected by parental education than those of girls (11).

Two U.S. studies (1; 12) claim to have found no digital divide due to SES. However, inequality due to ethnicity was found; more specifically, 'Black students were more likely to participate in social network sites [SNS] than their White

11 Pre- and post-tests after using electronic (threaded) discussion during the school year.

peers' (1, p. 159). Furthermore it was concluded that off-line social divides predict the use of different SNS's, such as Myspace and Facebook (2). Low SES Latino students were found to have the same access, confidence and use of ICTs as other American millennials, but their educational setting does not provide the opportunity to develop higher order information skills (12).

Two studies employed an approach that differs from the others. One study (10) was based on the assumption that socio-educational inequalities existed among the students and found that they could be reduced by the implementation of tablet PCs. Another study (4) found that students' use of ICTs on school related assignments was strongly dependent on traditional school practices and their valuation of the assignments—less important assignments could be completed with the help of ICTs, while more important assignments were completed using books and lesson notes.

The school factor

As presented above, several studies are made with reference to predefined groups that relate to previous research concerning advantaged and/or disadvantaged living conditions. In some studies schools with different socioeconomic status, educational orientation, location and/or governmental interference only serve as a research population. The school context itself is not used as a dependent factor for data analyses in these studies. As a result, many studies lack in deeper information about the status of the school as well as in information about the use of ICTs in relation to other schools in the country. These studies often refer to the students' individual socioeconomic status as the favoring or disfavoring factor for digital inequality.

However, almost one third of the studies (5, 6, 14, 20, 21, 28, 30) refer to characteristics of the schools as valid variables, or determinant factors, for digital inequality. Students from high schools preparing for academic studies have higher average scores on a digital competence test than students from technical institutes (5, 20). Students from schools with different educational orientation also differ in use of ICTs and software (20), something that also could be related to high and low SES schools (14). One of the studies (28) identified a specific school characteristic that was especially favorable for students' digital experience and skills: suburban affluent schools. Schools in other locations, despite the amount of poor or minority students, often fared worse. A factor strongly related to the impact of the school is its teachers. Two studies (6, 21) highlight that students at low SES schools tend to meet teachers with lower ICT competence than students at high SES schools. The conclusion is that investments in technological equipment will make little difference if the teachers themselves lack competence and technology facilitators.

The last study using school characteristics as a variable (30) is based on the international PISA survey[12]. While the other studies mainly drew conclusions from a single country, or even a single region or school, this study included 16 different countries with public as well as private schools. Several hypotheses regarding factors influencing students' self-reported digital skills were tested. According to the statistical testing there was no difference in digital skills between students from private or public schools, neither was the ICT penetration rate of the country positively related to students' digital skills. On the contrary, ICT access in school was positively related to students' digital skills, but in comparison with home ICT access it was weaker. In the 2006 data set there was a weak but significant negative relation between the ICT penetration rate at country level and school ICT access effect on the self-reported digital skills. Another hypothesis proposed that the effect of home ICT access on students self-reported digital skill would be "stronger for students studying at schools with scarce ICT access than for those studying at schools with sufficient ICT access" (p. 739). This was not supported in the data. In summary, this study shows "that the family works as a more powerful predictor of adolescents' self-reported digital skills than schools do" (p. 744).

Discussion and conclusion

This review clearly shows that digital inequalities exist among pupils in primary and secondary education in several developed countries. Inequalities are most often related to socioeconomic status, gender and ethnicity. As a result, this indicates that any effort to increase digital equality among young people must struggle against well-established structural divides. The multifaceted patterns and interactions between different factors in this finding demonstrate the need for a more complex and sociologically orientated theoretical foundation in digital divide research. The use of sociological theory in digital divide research is also strongly supported by predominant scholars, such as Selwyn[13].

Among all 1678 articles that addressed the digital divide, less than 2 percent met the selection criteria. While Wang et al. (2011) found that specific scholarly journals devoted to digital divide research have appeared and that the research has 'gained the reputation as a legitimate academic field' (p. 323), this review cannot offer a similar conclusion. Instead, it seems that articles on digital inequality

12 2003 and 2006.

13 E.g. Selwyn, N. (2012). "Making sense of young people, education and digital technology: the role of sociological theory". *Oxford Review of Education,* 38, 1.

in educational contexts are published in scholarly journals from various research fields, such as education, media and communication, sociology and human behaviour. This could be interpreted in at least two different ways: (1) as a reflection of the interdisciplinary character of the research area or (2) as an expression of little interest in the subject among education researchers. This may also explain the lack of in-depth studies on the school context's impact on digital inequality. The educational setting is mainly a framing context, not a valid variable in itself.

As digital inequalities are strongly related to current technological and societal development, it is noteworthy that several studies have been published with no indication of the time of data collection. Furthermore, most of the reviewed articles were largely based on extensive quantitative studies. However, even if they focused on qualitative aspects of digital inequality, they still lack a deeper understanding of the phenomenon. This is one of the challenges for future research.

This is arguably an important challenge for researchers within the field: to sufficiently develop and refine the theory so that research can contribute to an understanding of the phenomenon of digital inequality in not only disadvantaged groups but also advantaged groups and, particularly, in the context of compulsory education, where actual teaching efforts can be made to compensate for the divide.

References

Ahn, J. (2011). Digital Divides and Social Network Sites: Which Students Participate in Social Media? *Journal of Educational Computing Research, 45*(2), 147–163.

Ahn, J. (2012). Teenagers and social network sites: Do off-line inequalities predict their online social networks? *First Monday, 17*(1), 1–1.

Banister, S., & Reinhart, R. V., (2011). TPCK for Impact: Classroom Teaching Practices That Promote Social Justice and Narrow the Digital Divide in an Urban Middle School. *Computers in the Schools, 28*(1), 5–26.

Ben-David Kolikant, Yifat. (2012). Using ICT for school purposes: Is there a student-school disconnect? *Computers & Education, 59*(3), 907–914.

Calvani, A., Fini A., Ranieri, M., & Picci, P. (2012). Are young generations in secondary school digitally competent? A study on Italian teenagers. *Computers & Education, 58*(2), 797–807.

Chapman, L., Masters J., & Pedulla, J. (2010). Do digital divisions still persist in schools? Access to technology and technical skills of teachers in high needs schools in the United States of America. *Journal of Education for Teaching, 36*(2), 239–249.

Cotten, Shelia R., Hale, Timothy M., Moroney, Michael Howell, O'Neal, LaToya, & Borch, Casey. (2011). Using affordable technology to decrease digital inequality. *Information, Communication & Society, 14*(4), 424–444.

Delfino, Manuela. (2011). Against BibliOblivion: How modern scribes digitized an old book. *Computers & Education, 57*(3), 2145–2155.

Ertl, Bernhard, & Helling, Kathrin. (2011). Promoting Gender Equality in Digital Literacy. *Journal of Educational Computing Research, 45*(4), 477–503.
Ferrer, Ferran, Belvís, Esther, & Pàmies, Jordi. (2011). Tablet PCs, academic results and educational inequalities. *Computers & Education, 56*(1), 280–288.
Gui, Marco, & Argentin, Gianluca. (2011). Digital skills of internet natives: Different forms of digital literacy in a random sample of northern Italian high school students. *New Media & Society, 13*(6), 963–980.
Haras, Catherine. (2011). Information behaviors of Latinos attending high school in East Los Angeles. *Library & Information Science Research, 33*(1), 34–40.
Hattie, John A. (2009). *Visible learning: A synthesis of over 800 meta-analyses relating to achievement.* London: Routledge.
Helsper, Ellen. (2008). *Digital inclusion: an analysis of social disadvantage and the information society.* Department for Communities and Local Government, London, UK.
Henderson, Robyn, & Honan, Eileen. (2008). Digital literacies in two low socioeconomic classrooms: Snapshots of practice. *English Teaching-Practice and Critique, 7*(2), 85–98.
Hohlfeld, Tina N., Ritzhaupt, Albert D., Barron, Ann E., & Kemker, Kate. (2008). Examining the digital divide in K-12 public schools: Four-year trends for supporting ICT literacy in Florida. *Computers & Education, 51*(4), 1648–1663.
Lebens, Morena, Graff, Martin, & Mayer, Peter. (2009). Access, attitudes and the digital divide: children's attitudes towards computers in a technology-rich environment. *Educational Media International, 46*(3), 255–266.
Liao, Chin-Hsien, & Chang, Hsueh-Sheng. (2010). Explore the influences to Taiwan students' information literacy with the Urban-rural differences from the perspective of globalization. *Procedia – Social and Behavioral Sciences, 2*(2), 3866–3870.
Lim, Keol, & Meier, Ellen B. (2011). Different but similar: computer use patterns between young Korean males and females. *Educational Technology Research & Development, 59*(4), 575–592.
Mertens, Stefan, & D'Haenens, Leen. (2010). The digital divide among young people in Brussels: Social and cultural influences on ownership and use of digital technologies. *Communications: The European Journal of Communication Research, 35*(2), 187–207.
Mori, Cristina Kiomi. (2010). 'Digital Inclusion': Are We All Talking about the Same Thing? In Jacques Steyn, & Graeme Johanson (Eds), *ICTs and Sustainable Solutions for the Digital Divide: Theory and Perspectives*, 45–64. IGI Global.
Norris, Pippa. (2001). *Digital divide?: civic engagement, information poverty, and the Internet worldwide.* Cambridge: Cambridge University Press.
North, Sue, Snyder, Ilana, & Bulfin, Scott. (2008). DIGITAL TASTES: Social class and young people's technology use. *Information, Communication & Society, 11*(7), 895–911.
OECD. (2011). PISA 2009 Results: Students on Line: Digital Technologies and Performance. (Vol. VI).
Parycek, Peter, Sachs, Michael, & Schossbock, Judith. (2011). Digital Divide among Youth: Socio-Cultural Factors and Implications. *Interactive Technology and Smart Education, 8*(3), 161–171.
Reinhart, Julie M., Thomas, Earl, & Toriskie, Jeanne M. (2011). K-12 Teachers: Technology Use and the Second Level Digital Divide. *Journal of Instructional Psychology, 38*(3), 181–193.
Robinson, Laura. (2011). Information-channel preferences and information-opportunity structures. *Information, Communication & Society, 14*(4), 472–494.
Rogers, Everett M. (1995). *Diffusion of innovations.* (4. ed.) New York: Free Press.

Rosen, Yigal, & Manny-Ikan, Edith. (2011). The Social Promise of the Time to Know Program. *Journal of Interactive Online Learning, 10*(3), 150–161.
Samuelsson, Ulli. (2010). ICT use among 13-year-old Swedish children. *Learning, Media and Technology, 35*(1), 15–30.
Selwyn, Neil. (2004). Reconsidering political and popular understandings of the digital divide. *New Media & Society, 6*(3), 341–62.
Servon, Lisa J. (2002). *Bridging the digital divide: technology, community, and public policy*. Malden, MA: Blackwell Pub.
Tondeur, Jo, Sinnaeve, Ilse, van Houtte, Mieke, & van Braak, Johan. (2011). ICT as cultural capital: The relationship between socioeconomic status and the computer-use profile of young people. *New Media & Society, 13*(1), 151–168.
Tsatsou, Panayiota. (2011). Digital divides revisited: what is new about divides and their research? *Media, Culture & Society, 33*(2), 317–331.
Tømte, Cathrine, & Hatlevik, Ove E. (2011). Gender-differences in Self-efficacy ICT related to various ICT-user profiles in Finland and Norway. How do self-efficacy, gender and ICT-user profiles relate to findings from PISA 2006. *Computers & Education, 57*(1), 1416–1424.
Wang, Cheng-Hua, McLee, Yender, & Kuo, Jen-Hwa. (2011). *Ten Years of Digital Divide Studies: Themes, concepts and realtionships.* Paper presented at the 2011 International Conference on Social Science and Humanity, Singapore.
Warschauer, Mark. (2003). *Technology and social inclusion: rethinking the digital divide*. Cambridge, Mass.: MIT University Press.
Wolsey, Thomas DeVere, & Grisham, Dana L. (2007). Adolescents and the New Literacies: Writing Engagement. *Action in Teacher Education, 29*(2), 29–38.
Wood, Lawrence, & Howley, Aimee. (2012). Dividing at an early age: the hidden digital divide in Ohio elementary schools. *Learning, Media & Technology, 37*(1), 20–39.
Yu, Liangzhi. (2006). Understanding information inequality: Making sense of the literature of the information and digital divides. *Journal of Librarianship and Information Science, 38*(4), 229–252.
Zhao, Sherry Y. (2009). Teen Adoption of MySpace and IM: Inner-City versus Suburban Differences. *Cyberpsychology & Behavior, 12*(1), 55–58.
Zhong, Zhi-Jin. (2011). From access to usage: The divide of self-reported digital skills among adolescents. *Computers & Education, 56*(3), 736–746.

Table I: Articles selected for review and their reference numbers

Ref. no:	Author	Year	Title
1	Ahn	2011	Digital divides and social network sites: Which students participate in social media?
2	Ahn	2012	Teenagers and social network sites: Do off-line inequalities predict their online social networks?
3	Banister & Reinhart	2011	TPCK for impact: Classroom teaching practices that promote social justice and narrow the digital divide in an urban middle school.

Ref. no:	Author	Year	Title
4	Ben-David Kolikant	2012	Using ICT for school purposes: Is there a student-school disconnect?
5	Calvani, Fini, Ranieri & Picci	2012	Are young generations in secondary school digitally competent? A study on Italian teenagers.
6	Chapman, Masters & Pedulla	2010	Do digital divisions still persist in schools? Access to technology and technical skills of teachers in high needs schools in the United States of America.
7	Cotten, Hale, Moroney, O'Neal LaToya & Borch	2011	Using affordable technology to decrease digital inequality. Results from Birmingham's One Laptop Per Child XO laptop project.
8	Delfino	2011	Against BibliOblivion: How modern scribes digitized an old book.
9	Ertl & Helling	2011	Promoting Gender Equality in Digital Literacy.
10	Ferrer, Belvís & Pàmies	2011	Tablet PCs, academic results and educational inequalities.
11	Gui & Argentin	2011	Digital skills of internet natives: Different forms of digital literacy in a random sample of northern Italian high school students.
12	Haras	2011	Information behaviors of Latinos attending high school in East Los Angeles.
13	Henderson & Honan	2008	Digital literacies in two low socioeconomic classrooms: Snapshots of practice.
14	Hohlfeld, Ritzhaupt, Barron & Kemker	2008	Examining the digital divide in K-12 public schools: Four-year trends for supporting ICT literacy in Florida.
15	Lebens, Graff & Mayer	2009	Access, attitudes and the digital divide: children's attitudes towards computers in a technology-rich environment.
16	Liao & Chang	2010	Explore the influences to Taiwan students' information literacy with the urban-rural differences from the perspective of globalization.
17	Lim & Meier	2011	Different but similar: computer use patterns between young Korean males and females.
18	Mertens & D'Haenens	2010	The digital divide among young people in Brussels: Social and cultural influences on ownership and use of digital technologies
19	North, Snyder & Bulfin	2008	DIGITAL TASTES: Social class and young people's technology use.

Ref. no:	Author	Year	Title
20	Parycek, Sachs & Schossbock	2011	Digital divide among youth: socio-cultural factors and implications.
21	Reinhart, Thomas & Toriskie	2011	K-12 teachers: technology use and the second level digital divide.
22	Robinson	2011	Information-channel preferences and information-opportunity structures.
23	Rosen & Manny-Ikan	2011	The social promise of the time to know program.
24	Samuelsson	2010	ICT use among 13-year-old Swedish children.
25	Tondeur, Sinnaeve, van Houtte & van Braak	2011	ICT as cultural capital: The relationship between socioeconomic status and the computer-use profile of young people.
26	Tømte & Hatlevik	2011	Gender-differences in self-efficacy ICT related to various ICT-user profiles in Finland and Norway. How do self-efficacy, gender and ICT-user profiles relate to findings from PISA 2006.
27	Wolsey & Grisham	2007	Adolescents and the new literacies: Writing engagement.
28	Wood & Howley	2012	Dividing at an early age: the hidden digital divide in Ohio elementary schools.
29	Zhao	2009	Teen adoption of MySpace and IM: Inner-city versus suburban differences.
30	Zhong	2011	From access to usage: The divide of self-reported digital skills among adolescents.

Table II: Most cited articles in reviewed articles

Cited article	Present in (n) reviewed articles
Livingstone, S., & Helsper, E. (2007). Gradations in digital inclusion: children, young people and the digital divide. *New Media & Society*	6
Prenksy, M. (2001). Digital natives, digital immigrants. *On the Horizon.*	6
Hargittai, E. (2002). Second-level digital divide: Differences in people's online skills. *First Monday.*	5
Bennett, S., Maton, K., & Kervin, L. (2008). The 'digital natives' debate: a critical review of the evidence. *British Journal of Educational Technology.*	5

Cited article	Present in (n) reviewed articles
van Dijk J (2006) Digital divide research, achievements and shortcomings. *Poetics.*	5
van Dijk, J., & Hacker, K. (2003). The digital divide as a complex and dynamic phenomenon. *Information Society.*	4
Volman, M., Van Eck, E., Heemskerk, I., & Kuiper, E. (2005). New technologies, new differences. *Computers & Education.*	4
Hargittai, E., (2005). Survey measures of web-oriented digital literacy. *Social Science Computer Review.*	3
Attewell. (2001). The first and second digital divides. *Sociology of Education.*	3

Table III: Dominant journals in reviewed articles

Journal	Total references (n)	Articles the journal occurs in (n)
Computers & Education	32	11
New Media & Society	16	9
Journal of Computer-Mediated Communication	15	6
Computers in Human Behavior	14	7
First Monday	13	9
Journal of Educational Computing Research	11	7
Social Science Computer Review	10	6
Sociology of Education	9	7
Poetics	8	8
Information Society	8	7
On the Horizon	8	6
British Journal of Educational Technology	8	6

Research designs and methodology

			Data collection				Analyse			Year of Data collection
No:		Theoretical foundation	Question-naires	Inter-views	Observ-ations	Other…	Quantitative	Qualitative	N	
1	Ahn (2011)	SES[14], Gender		X			X		700	2007
2	Ahn (2012)	SES, Gender, Literacy, social capital	X				X		701	2009
3	Banister & Reinhart	SES, Social justice, PCK[15], TCPK			X		X		953[16]	2008
4	Ben-David Kolikant	Socio-cultural		X				X	25	2005
5	Calvani et al.	Literacy, Cognition and Socio-cultural	X				X		1.056	2009/2010
6	Chapman et al.	SES	X				X		6.230	2006–2008
7	Cotten et al.	SES, Literacy, Technology attitude	X				X		1.202	2008/2009
8	Delfino	Literacy	X		X		X	X	21	2008/2009

14 Socioeconomic status.

15 PCK stands for Pedagogical Content Knowledge and TCPK stands for Technological Pedagogical Content Knowledge.

16 82 classroom observations, 871 Quick stop protocols.

			Data collection				Analyse			Year of Data collection
No:		Theoretical foundation	Question-naires	Inter-views	Observ-ations	Other…	Quantitative	Qualitative	N	
9	Ertl & Helling	Literacy, Gender	X	X			X	X	90	> 2005
10	Ferrer et al.	SES	X	X		Debate forums	X	X	11.143[17]	2008/2009
11	Gui & Argentin		X				X		980	2007
12	Haras	Literacy, Information	X				X		290	2008
13	Henderson & Honan	SES, Literacy		X	X			X	≈50+2	2007
14	Hohlfeld et al.	SES, Literacy, Diffusion of innovation	X				X		2.345	2003–2007
15	Lebens et al.	SES, Computer attitude	X				X		60	NA
16	Liao & Chang	Literacy, Globalization	C[18]				C		1.200	2005

17 124 head teachers, 714 teaching staff, 5504 pupils and 4801 families representing 131 schools.

18 Conclusion drawn from the text, but not clearly stated.

			Data collection				Analyse			Year of Data collection
No:		Theoretical foundation	Question-naires	Inter-views	Observ-ations	Other…	Quantitative	Qualitative	N	
17	Lim & Meier	Gender, Socialization	X	X			X	X	673	NA
18	Mertens & D'Haenens	Capital, Deprivation, Differentiation	X				X		1.005	2007
19	North et al.	Capital		X		Media diaries, photographs		X	25	2006
20	Parycek et al.	Literacy	X				X		379	2009/2010
21	Reinhart et al.	Factors influencing SLDD[19]	X				X		94	NA
22	Robinson	Motivation, Information, Capital		X				X	>300	2006–2011
23	Rosen & Manny-Ikan	SES, Motivaton, Social constructivism	X				X		49+42	2007

19 Second Level Digital Divide.

			Data collection				Analyse			Year of Data collection
No:		Theoretical foundation	Question-naires	Inter-views	Observ-ations	Other…	Quantitative	Qualitative	N	
24	Samuelsson	SES, Connectivity	X				X		256	2007
25	Tondeur et al.	SES, Capital	X				X		1.241	2007/2008
26	Tømte & Hatlevik	Gender, Cognition, Self-efficacy	X				X		≈9.400	2006
27	Wolsey & Grisham	Literacy, Gender	X	X	X	Analysis of artefacts	X	X	67	NA
28	Wood & Howley	SES, Motivation[20]	X				X		514	2009
29	Zhao	SES	X				X		432	2007
30	Zhong	SES, Gender, Literacy, Information, Diffusion Theory	X				X		87.562[21]	2003+2006

20 Not clearly described.
21 PISA 2006.

The Future of Mathematics Textbooks: Ramifications of Technological Change

Daniel Chazan & Michal Yerushalmy

Abstract

As mathematics educators, the object of our research is a societal endeavor whose policies and practices are shaped by societal forces, including technological developments. Textbooks have historically played key roles in determining the mathematics curriculum by specifying the content to be taught and by providing guidelines about how this content might be taught. In this paper, we argue that technological changes pose challenges to the roles played by the textbooks and curriculum materials written by textbook authors and curriculum developers. The role of specifying what is to be taught is under challenge from centralizing forces supported by technological capacities for large-scale data mining. And, the role of providing guidance on instruction is under challenge from changes to processes for authoring and publishing books; these changes have the potential to shift the role of teachers in the curriculum development process. While we do not see these challenges as representing the death knell for textbooks, we argue that with these technological changes, textbooks may no longer play as large a role as a driver of educational change. To support our argument, we explore the historical roles of mathematics textbooks in educational systems and specify two challenges, supported by recent technological advances, to these roles that we have outlined above.

> "I predict that the word "textbook" will soon carry the same connotation as the word "scroll" does today. The word "scroll" harkens to a time when scholarly materials were produced on papyrus and stored in cool vaults, to be accessed by the few elite lucky enough to have access. Likewise, with the proliferation of scholarly works on the Internet, students and teachers are now able to create their own repositories of knowledge based upon reliable sources. Some classes are eliminating textbooks all together, opting for sites like Curriki or creating projects where students compile, authenticate, and create information based upon their research." (Davis, V. downloaded from http://coolcatteacher.blogspot.com/2009/06/are-traditional-textbooks-dead.html)

While many mathematics educators throughout the world[1] would agree that in the present in K-12 education "Textbooks represent a substantial financial investment

1 Our professional experiences have been mostly in the United States and Israel and as a result our citations and references are skewed toward experience in these countries; this paper is not an attempt to do cross-cultural work in education. While we know that there are many important differences in the nature of mathematics education in different countries, as Leung and Li (2010) observe "The increased ease of flow of information through exchange activities as well as through the internet has meant that [educational] systems are increasingly influencing each other" (p. 4). For this reason, we believe that the dynamics we point out are more widely relevant.

and strongly influence what students learn" (Reyes, Reyes, & Chavez, 2004, p. 61) and, thus, are legitimately an important focus for international comparisons of students' opportunities to learn mathematics (e.g., Haggarty & Peppin, 2002), the blog-post quoted above raises many questions: As a part of larger effects of technology on education (Christiansen, Johnson, & Horn, 2008; Collins & Halverson, 2009; Cuban, 2001; Ferneding, 2003; Selwyn, 2011), in the developed world,[2] will mathematics textbooks endure? Might other educational products come to play a more central role in communicating the mathematics curriculum than textbooks? Will mathematics teachers, in addition to textbook authors and curriculum developers, play a more central role in creating curricular materials for students? In brief, our responses to these questions are that mathematics textbooks will endure, though they may evolve and their role in the education system may become less central because common standards and assessments will play some of the roles that textbooks used to play. And, we expect that though teachers may be able more easily to edit and author documents, they will probably not take the lead in writing textbooks. The purpose of this chapter is to support those speculative answers by exploring the historical role of mathematics textbooks in educational systems and identifying challenges, supported by recent technological advances, to these roles.

Mathematics textbooks in state[3]-provided education: A historical perspective

As argued by Kidwell, Ackerberg-Hastings, and Roberts (2008), the mathematics textbooks that are so ubiquitous in schooling now were once, like public schooling itself, non-existent. Once people learned advanced mathematics by reading original mathematical texts, like Euclid (Herbst, 2002), with a tutor. When schooling became institutionalized, supported by the technological changes to printing, students began to study mathematics with teachers and grade-level textbooks provided at no cost by the school[4].

2 We are keenly aware that in many parts of the world state-sponsored compulsory K-12 education is still an unfinished project and that textbooks, let alone digital textbooks, are not as widely available as might be preferred, but we will not continue to emphasize this point in the text.

3 We will use "state" in the sense of nation, not in the sense of a unit of organization inside a federation as is the practice in the United States.

4 Initially, in the US, the decision to provide textbooks at no cost was controversial, see Westbury, 1990, "Massachusetts becomes the first state to require all communities to provide free textbooks for their students. This notion of free textbooks provided by the school, and the related "adoption" or "approval" of these texts became American institutions" (p. 7).

Historically, textbooks developed in compulsory, state-provided education as a mechanism both for outlining and specifying what it is that students should learn and in what order (Westbury, 1990). In addition, textbooks provide teachers with guidance about how students should learn that content by providing exercises and exposition, though teachers are meant to use their professional judgment in determining how to use and supplement a text, both with activities and with other resources.

Mathematics educator Gert Schubring (1987) describes, as a turning point in the development of books created as textbooks, the time not long after the French Revolution. He suggests that at this time there was an attempt to democratize access to mathematical knowledge; that the early nineteenth century was:

> … an epoch when for the first time a general and public system of education became established … This new educational system gave mathematics a considerable position… The structure of the presentation of mathematical knowledge was not prepared and adapted for the demands of this sort of teaching. A restructuration and redefinition of mathematical knowledge became necessary. (pp. 42–43).

No longer could mathematics be diffused solely through the correspondence of individual scholars (see Pearl, 2010, for example, on the role of Mersenne's correspondence in the mathematical advances of his time), the work of mathematicians, such as the Frenchman, Lacroix, in writing textbooks helped restructure mathematics in ways that made it suitable for this evolving educational system.

The development of these texts for general education in France in the early 19th century, like the later work of Bourbaki to systematize modern mathematics (Borel, 1998; Guedj, 1985), were influential throughout the world. For example, Charles Davies at the United States Military Academy at West Point helped found the nascent US textbook industry by translating French mathematics textbooks and eventually providing books to schools, as well as colleges (see Kidwell et al., 2008: 10–20). These textbooks supported the development of the mathematics research community in the United States (Parshall & Rowe, 1997).

Skipping more than a century ahead, in the mid-20th century, in the US, the mathematics curriculum is influenced by the challenge of integrated modern mathematical ideas into the pre-collegiate curriculum, concerns about pedagogy in schools, as well as continued competition between countries (Conference Board of the Mathematical Sciences, 1975). In some countries, curriculum development projects whose work is funded by the state, rather than individual mathematicians or mathematics teachers (like Lacroix or Davies), begin to produce some of the mathematics textbooks used by schools. For example, in the United States, the government, in the guise of the National Science Foundation, reluctantly, out of a fear of the political nature of curricular work (Dow, 1991), funds university-based mathematicians and scientists to play a crucial role in the updating of mathematics and science curriculum for schools (Rudolph, 2002, see Ch. 2). Thus, in the forward (1963) to *Goals for School Mathematics: The Report of the Cambridge Conference on School Mathematics,* Frances Keppel, then US Commissioner of Education, points out the ways in which this activity seemed noteworthy at the time:

> "If one were to look for the most significant development in education over the past decade, it would be reasonable to single out the wave of curriculum reform ... They [these recent curricular reforms] have been for the most part national, or at least regional, efforts. They have drawn on university scholarship and skilled teachers not only for leadership but for the immediate demands of day-to-day operation ... Almost without exception they have passed from the determination of policy and program directly into the preparation of materials for use in the schools" (p. vi).

The focus on preparing materials for use in schools was premised on the belief that simply articulating policy and program would not be sufficient. In order to have new content and ideas about teaching incorporated into classroom activity, teachers would need the guidance of new curricular materials.

The US National Science Foundation then, based on confidence in the power of curricular texts, repeats this early foray into curriculum development at the end of the 20th century, in concert with the NCTM Standards movement (Lappan, 2003). A division of labor evolves: Publishers and the marketplace provide status quo textbooks, while curriculum developers based at academic institutions, now working in concert with some publishers, create reform textbooks that are meant to move schools in the direction of the incorporation of both new content and new methods of teaching (in the sense in which NCTM advocates both principles of instruction and content standards in the 2000 *Principles and Standards for School Mathematics*). In this division of labor, teachers play a role in advocating for reform-based materials and implementing the vision of instruction that is concretized in curricular materials. As articulated by Glenda Lappan (1998), in her role as president of the North American professional organization of teachers, the National Council of Teachers of Mathematics, the role of the teacher is to work with colleagues to adopt these materials and then: "to increase the effectiveness of the materials by spending considerable time planning the lessons, listening carefully to what students are saying in the classroom, analyzing what students are learning, and consequently adjusting the mathematical tasks and the questions asked." Given the realities of teachers' work-lives, their task is not to have to search for, or create, rich mathematical tasks for their students. And, given the ways in which mathematics as a discipline grows and changes, it is not the individual teacher, or the citizenry of the country, who should make judgments about what students should learn, but people more deeply acquainted with the larger picture of what mathematics there is to know and how knowledge of that mathematics will prepare students for future education and careers.

Articulating two inter-connected roles of textbooks: What and how

The purpose of this quick recounting of key points in the history of mathematics textbooks was to illustrate the roles that textbooks play in state-sponsored education. We suggest that textbooks give teachers guidance on both *what* and *how* students should learn. On the one hand, especially initially, textbooks organized the content of what students were to learn and indicated what students needed to know at what age, grade level, or institutional track within schooling. On the other hand, by presenting instructional tasks, textbooks attempt to organize the knowledge that they present in ways that will help make this content learnable (Cohen, 2011). In playing both of these roles, textbooks support teachers by allowing them to focus their attention on modifying and customizing tasks to help their students meet the articulated goals; textbooks are a vehicle for people who are not teachers to give teachers guidance both on what, and how, students should learn.

Textbooks play these roles by virtue of what they include and what they do not, as well as how they organize content into chapters and how they distribute content over grade levels. They play these roles by dividing content into sections and providing exercises for students and teachers to assess whether or not students have acquired the knowledge that is intended. Increasingly, they also provide formative assessments and other ancillary materials that will help with remediation (For other features and descriptions of textbooks in mathematics education, see Love & Pimm, 1996).

Against this backdrop of two roles that textbooks have occupied in schooling, we see two challenges to the historical role of the textbook, each of which is gaining impetus and support from changes to today's technological environment. Our argument in the next two sections is that new technological developments potentially contribute to altering the existing balance of power between textbooks, syllabi and standards, and assessments, a balance of power that much current research assumes.

Competition to textbooks for outlining what students should learn: Technology-supported accountability and assessment

If curriculum is "what students have an opportunity to learn in school, through both the hidden and overt curriculum, and what they do not have an opportunity to learn because certain matters were not included" (McCutchean, 1982, p. 19), then textbooks, as a component of education that is provided by the state, are enmeshed in the political processes[5] that determine the intended curriculum (Seeley, 2003). Though perhaps in the early 19th century textbooks were the primary means for outlining what students should learn, these days, other documents compete with textbooks for the role of articulating the intended curriculum in the educational systems of many countries (See International Review of Curriculum and Assessment Frameworks Internet Archive, 2009).

Additionally, assessments at key educational junctures (e.g., exams at the end of junior secondary school in China; or, exams in the US that are required for high school graduation, see Center on Education Policy, 2009) play an important role in communicating expectations about what students will learn. So, textbooks do not determine curriculum on their own, rather they are a part of a system that produces the experiences students have in school. Teachers play an important role in shaping the curriculum students experience, and larger political processes shape the intended curriculum.

In our view, the rising influence of standards and assessment has a technological component. The rate of the accumulation of digital data has skyrocketed and there are robust developments in technologies to "mine" such data (as the very coining of this phrase suggests). For example, as documented in the book, "Total recall: How the E-memory revolution will change everything" (Bell & Gemmel, 2009), the MyLifeBits project at Microsoft Research (http://research.microsoft.com/en-us/projects/mylifebits/) has explored the technological changes that support collection, storage, and searching of data:

> "We are capturing so much of our lives now, be it on the date- and location-stamped photos we take with our smart phones or in the continuous records we have of our e-mails, instant messages, and tweets – not to mention the GPS tracking of our movements many cars and smart phones already do automatically… the critical technology and perhaps the least understood, is our magical new ability to find the information we want in the mountain of data that is our past. And not just Google it, but data mine it …" (Front cover).

Increasing capacities to collect, store, and search data in the developed world have influenced aspects of social policy such as community policing, and also are relevant to the data accumulated by education systems (Mosteller & Boruch, 2002). New data systems may make possible innovations in the assessment of teachers,

5 Apple, 1989, for example, articulates how in the United States, tensions between the North and the South after the Civil War, and the identification of public schooling and textbook publishers with the North, lead to the policy of state-wide textbook adoptions by southern states, rather than by individual districts within these states.

schools, and districts. For example, in the last decades scholars have begun to explore value added techniques for determining what part of the variance in student achievement may be attributed to schools or teachers, rather than to family or socio-economic status (McCaffrey et al., 2003; 2004).

Without delving into the controversies about these statistical methods (Baker, Barton, Darling-Hammond, Haertel, Ladd, Linn, Ravitch, Rothstein, Shavelson, & Shepard, 2010), these techniques require common curricula for students, common assessments given to students each year, as well as data systems that provide each teacher and student with a unique identification number that moves with them and that store student results and link them to teacher identifiers.[6] The appeal of such data systems is in enabling governments to hold educators accountable for results; proponents of the development of a greater national commonality in mathematics curriculum, see a range of benefits, including greater focus in textbooks (in the US context, see American Educator, 2010). Critics of these notions of accountability suggest that such developments are not to be applauded, that the requirements of data systems will lead to homogeneity in curriculum (e.g., Ravitch, 2010). The implication for textbooks is that their role in outlining *what* students learn might diminish; textbooks would need to reflect what other artifacts of institutional schooling outline must be taught and learned. Increasingly, textbooks or curricular materials for the same grade level or course would all cover the same content.

Technologically-supported changes to the role of teacher in preparing materials for instruction

In addition to an explosion in the accumulation of digital data, advancements in technology have also changed the nature of texts, as well as what it takes to produce and disseminate information (See Young, 2007, for a critical analysis). Who authors text materials, what it means to publish a text, and the speed at which

6 The creation of a technological infrastructure for such comparisons within states in the United States forms a substantial part of the investment of the US Department of Education's recent "Race to the Top Fund" initiative which "provides competitive grants to encourage and reward States that are creating the conditions for education innovation and reform" (Downloaded from http://www2.ed.gov/programs/racetothetop/index.html on January 4, 2011). Two of four "core education reform areas" in which states must implement ambitious plans are 'Building data systems that measure student growth and success… [and] Recruiting, developing, rewarding, and retaining effective teachers and principals …" (U. S. Department of Education, 2009, p. 2).

texts are updated are all undergoing shifts, all of which have implications for textbooks. With textbooks, these developments suggest changes to the traditional relationships between textbook author or curriculum developer and teacher.

The role of the teacher historically has been to shape the textbook for use with particular groups of students in particular places on the basis of the teacher's own professional judgment. Technological developments change what it means to supplement a textbook. In the past, supplements were done with dittos and Xerox copies; now, such curriculum supplementation can be done with digital texts written (and easily edited) by the teacher, or fetched from the web [in what some might call a web 1.0 style].[7] And, as digital composition, publication, and production become more common, beyond activities and software, these supplements can include teachers using Smartboards to add records of the work done in their classes, snapshots of the board, audiotape of classroom discussion, or perhaps even edited digital video recordings of class.

With these kinds of technologies, supplementation begins to get closer to an "open culture" concept of co-authoring a new version, rather than supplementing an existing version that remains unchanged. According to an "Open Culture" perspective, particular knowledge products or texts are not fixed; knowledge should spread freely and its growth can come from developing, altering, or enriching already existing knowledge products on a collaborative basis, without being restricted by rules linked to the legal protections of intellectual property. Licenses, like the Creative Commons License, stipulate that any product that uses a Creative Commons License resource as an input must be returned to the commons and cannot be subject to copyright. In line with this ideology, "Open Educational Resources" – web resources that can be used according to flexible copyright licenses – are created by teachers working iteratively to refine and edit the work of other teachers and posting the products of their efforts on the web for use (Morris & Hiebert, 2011, offers a related vision of teachers creating shared instructional products, but does not address issues of license).

For example, Neeru Khosla, the founder of CK12.org, a digital textbook publishing environment for schools, suggests that teachers might use the CK12 platform to create personalized parts of a book to support the learning of students with disabilities; she then uses the term "Flexing" to describe the process of adapting an existing digital book to turn what was initially created as a personalized resource

7 Sites that are used in such ways include: illuminations.nctm.org, geogebra.org, or mathforum.org/mathtools/. These sites, and others, show evidence of teachers investing time and effort both in the development and sharing of materials that reside on the web for use by others and in the use of materials developed by others.

for learning into a text that others can use (See http://www.educationnews.org/michael-f-shaughnessy/47145.html). Similarly, an Israeli site (http://www.school.kotar.co.il/Default.aspx) envisions a setting where students get a paper textbook and access to the digital format of the same book including links to interactive resources provided by the publisher. The site then encourages teachers to add their own web resources and "post" them to replace specific activities. Connexions.org is a similar site that provides users with a place to view and share educational material. With this site, authors can build up modules out of small knowledge chunks that can be organized as courses, books, or reports.

With such sites, groups of teachers coalesce initially around materials developed by others or an authored textbook. But, perhaps, over time, influenced by open culture ideas and sites like Connexions.org, as groups of teachers gain experience amending or sometimes personalizing digital textbooks, they might decide to develop textbooks as a communal endeavor. Such communal creation of products is a part of what people now associate with Web2.0 (For one set of defining principles, see http://oreilly.com/web2/archive/what-is-web-20.html), Wikipedia being a prominent example of the kind of new process of authoring that can be done with the networked technological tools now at our disposal. Wikipedia provides users with tools to write, edit and change entries; at the same time, previous versions and changes remain visible to the public. With Wikipedia, there is a commitment to a shared style of writing that makes the result a well-integrated material. Contributors strive to take a neutral view and to include sympathetically a variety of views, rather than to present a single commonly accepted as the objective truth. There are authorities that may exclude inappropriate material, but those authorities rarely use their power. The question for open textbooks initiatives (e.g., www.wikibooks.org) is whether Web 2.0 principles can be successfully integrated into a system that will have large numbers of teachers and other stakeholders collaboratively creating textbooks that are widely used.

How do the implications of the technological support for this kind of creation of public personalized versions of knowledge products sit alongside the trends to curriculum centralization outlined earlier? Perhaps, if the push toward centralization and common standards continues to gather momentum, teachers will choose to coalesce as groups around standards or curriculum documents, rather than around textbooks. This possibility is plausible especially as curriculum and standards documents flesh out their imperatives with examples meant to illustrate their intent. Thus, the NCTM provides e-examples along with its Principles and Standards (NCTM, 2000) document; the Common Core State Standards Initiative is contemplating a product that provides examples of tasks for classroom use; and in centralized systems curriculum documents are moving beyond syllabi to include examples that teachers download and use in their classrooms. For example, in Israel, the ministry's mathematics supervisor maintains a site with sample lessons for a wide variety of tasks by grade level. Thus, in addition to a relatively short document outlining "what to teach," the ministry provides digital resources that include "how to teach."

Justifying our initial speculations

Stepping back from our descriptions of the ways in which technologies support both teacher involvement in the processes of creating and supplementing textbooks and the roles of technologies in the current push toward the creation of common curricula and assessments, we now return to justify our speculative assertions that:

- Textbooks will endure, though they may evolve;
- Teachers will probably not take the lead in writing textbooks; and
- The role of textbooks in the education system may become still less central because common standards and assessments will play some of the roles that textbooks used to play.

In suggesting that textbooks will endure in the face of recent advances in technology, we find compelling Yochai Benkler's (2005) analysis of the differences between textbooks and encyclopedias. At the heart of his argument is the notion of modularity. He argues that:

> "Real textbooks appear to reside somewhere between a novel and an encyclopedia in the degree to which they can be modularized, or at least in the degree of effort required to integrate the modules into a coherent whole recognizable as a textbook. Moreover, the chunks or modules seem to be bigger. It is very hard to add a single sentence, although it may be possible to add a single example or a better-rendered equation or chart" (p. 20).

He uses these differences to argue that, even though Wikipedia has been successful, we will not see web 2.0 textbooks as dominant force in the future.[8] His key point

8 Bolstering his argument empirically, in reviewing existing wikibooks, he notes that there are not many textbooks and that the work, in general, is not of a large community; most wikibooks seem to have a single author, sometimes with minor contributions from a small group. These trends seem to be continuing, among the textbooks listed under k-12 mathematics wikibooks [retrieved January 26th 2011], there is only one featured book which is authored by a single main author and three contributors, students who edit the mathematics and the solutions. Similarly, the texts at CK12.org, which are the only mathematics

is that the lack of modularity in textbooks and their "need to be systematic, coherent, and compliant with well-defined external constraints" (Benkler, 2005: 22) intrinsically makes them a kind of document that is not as conducive to peer-creation (For an examination of this question, see Yerushalmy, 2011).

Of course, there are many who disagree with Benkler's conclusion, for example, Vicki A. Davis the teacher at Westwood Schools in Camilla, Georgia whose post opens our paper. Nonetheless, in her post, Davis conceptualizes a continued role for textbook companies in the future as "content conduits." She imagines that textbook companies will continue to have a role in making sure that experts can communicate with teachers, even if the nature of their textbook products will evolve. In her view of this future, the role of the teacher will not be to create the core text, but to augment it and connect it to lesson plans, student work, and more. Perhaps imagining a more central role for teachers seems impossible without some fundamental changes in the work-life of the teacher; the daily pressures of time and face-to-face interaction with students may limit visions, even of teacher bloggers, for the participation of teachers in the creation of curricular materials.[9]

If these observations are correct and textbooks and curriculum developers do not have to fear replacement by wikibooks written by teachers, then, perhaps textbooks and curriculum developers may face a graver threat from examples and illustrations coalescing around mandated standards. Interestingly, in the context of debates about how geometry should be taught in the Israeli middle grades, it was a group of Israeli mathematicians who were concerned about this possibility (See http://www.haaretz.com/news/national/professors-call-israel-s-junior-high-math-program-scandalous-1.330105). They argued that the curriculum documents on the ministry's website reflected a specific opinion regarding the order the unpacking of the geometrical axioms and how to teach geometry; their criticism was grounded in the view that the order of the development of ideas, as well as the examples and sample lessons, should remain the province of textbook authors and should not be provided by the Ministry of Education's committee that articulates the content of the curriculum. While their argument, and its assumption that it is possible to disconnect *what* is to be taught from *how* it is to be taught, supports

---

textbooks listed currently under the State of California initiative (http://www.clrn.org/FDTI/index.cfm), do not have large authoring communities.

9 We are not suggesting that teachers will not blog and write about their teaching; we expect that as blogging becomes even more ubiquitous more teachers will be drawn to such outlets. But, even though there are experiments at converting blog into texts, we do not see blogs becoming textbooks. For provocative experiments in this direction, consider: http://booktwo.org/notebook/wikipedia-historiography/ and http://booktwo.org/notebook/vanity-press-plus-the-tweetbook/.

an ongoing role for textbooks that is different from that of documents articulating standards, the very necessity of making the argument suggests that in a web-based environment, there are dynamics that will lead curriculum standards to encroach on what has in the past been the domain of textbooks.

Assuming for the moment that our predictions are well-grounded, are the changes to the roles of textbooks that we have described consequential? We close with one concern about the impact of current trends on the curriculum development process. As our earlier description of the important roles played by textbooks and curriculum developers in earlier eras of mathematics reform suggests, textbooks have played a role in the evolution of curriculum change over time. If textbooks and curriculum materials are tightly coupled to standards and have little leeway to experiment, particularly with new content, what remains unclear in this age of centralization is how processes of curricular change will happen. How will the mathematics curriculum grow and change to reflect evolutions in mathematics itself? How will competing curriculum visions be outlined in enough detail to understand the potential they have as alternatives to the curriculum as outlined in common standards?

References

Apple, M. (1989). Regulating the text: The socio-historical roots of state control. In P. Altbach, G. Kelly, H. Petrie, & L. Weis (Eds.), *Textbooks in American society: Politics, policy, and pedagogy* (pp. 7–26). Albany, NY: SUNY Press.

Baker, E., Barton, P., Darling-Hammond, L., Haertel, E., Ladd , H., Linn, R., Ravitch, D., Rothstein, R., Shavelson, R., & Shepard, L. (2010, August). *Problems with the Use of Student Test Scores to Evaluate Teachers. EPI Briefing Paper #278*. Economic Policy Institute: Washington, DC.

Bell, C. G., & Gemmell, J. (2009). *Total recall: how the E-memory revolution will change everything*. New York: Dutton.

Benkler, Y. (2006). *The wealth of networks: how social production transforms markets and freedom*. New Haven: Yale University Press.

Borel, A. (1998). Twenty-five years with Nicolas Bourbaki, 1949–1973. *Notices of the American Mathematical Society, 45*(3), 373–380.

Center on Education Policy. (2009). *State High School Exit Exams: Trends in Test Programs, Alternate Pathways, and Pass Rates*. Washington, D. C.: Center on Education Policy. Retrieved from http://www.cep-dc.org/.

Christensen, C., Johnson, C. W., & Horn, M. B. (2008). *Disrupting Class: How Disruptive Innovation Will Change the Way the World Learns*. New York: McGraw Hill.

Cohen, D. K. (2011). *Teaching and Its Predicaments*. Cambridge, MA: Harvard University Press.

Collins, A., & Halverson, R. (2009). *Rethinking Education in the Age of Technology: The Digital Revolution and Schooling in America*. New York: Teachers College Press.

Common Core State Standards Initiative. (2010). *Common Core State Standards for Mathematics*. Downloaded from http://www.corestandards.org/ on March 21, 2011.

Conference Board of the Mathematical Sciences: National Advisory Committee on Mathematical Education. (1975). *Overview and analysis of school mathematics: Grades K-12*. Author: Washington, DC.

Cuban, L. (2001). *Oversold and underused: Computers in the classroom*. Cambridge, MA: Harvard University.

Dow, P. (1991). *Schoolhouse Politics: Lessons from the Sputnik Era*. Cambridge: Harvard.

Editors. (2010). Common Core Curriculum: An idea whose time has come. *American Educator*, *34*(4), p. 2.

Ferneding, K. A. (2003). *Questioning Technology: Electronic Technologies and Educational Reform*. New York: Peter Lang.

Guedj, D. (1985). Nicholas Bourbaki, collective mathematician: an interview with Claude Chevalley. *The Mathematical Intelligencer, 7*(2), 18–22.

Haggarty, L., & Pepin, B. (2002). An Investigation of Mathematics Textbooks and their Use in English, French and German Classrooms: who gets an opportunity to learn what? *British Educational Research Journal, 28*(4), 567–590.

Herbst, P. (2002). Establishing a custom of proving in American school geometry: Evolution of the two-column proof in the early twentieth century. *Educational Studies in Mathematics, 49*(3), 283–312.

International Review of Curriculum and Assessment Frameworks Internet Archive, (2009, June) Curriculum documents and guidance: Results of desk research, Downloaded from http://www.inca.org.uk/thematic_probes.html.

Keppel, F. (1963). Forward. In Educational Services Incorporated (Ed.), *Goals for School Mathematics: The Report of the Cambridge Conference on School Mathematics*. Boston: Houghton Mifflin.

Kidwell, P. A., Ackerberg-Hastings, A., & Roberts, D. L. (2008). *Tools of American Mathematics Teaching, 1800–2000*. Baltimore: The Johns Hopkins University Press.

Lappan, G. (1998). Texts and Teachers: Keys to Improved Mathematics Learning. Downloaded on Wednesday, May 8, 2002 from http://www.nctm.org/news/pastpresident/1998_07_lappan.htm.

Lappan, G. (2003). The Changing Roles and Priorities of the Federal Government in Mathematics Education in the United States. In Stanic, G. & J. Kilpatrick (Eds.), *A History of School Mathematics* (Vols. 1–2, Vol. 2, pp. 897–930). Reston, Virginia: National Council of Teachers of Mathematics.

Leung, F. K. S., & Li, Yeping (Eds.). (2010). *Reforms and issues in school mathematics in East Asia: Sharing and understanding mathematics education policies and practices*. Rotterdam, The Netherlands: Sense Publishers.

Love, E., & Pimm, D. (1996). This is so: A text on texts. In A. J. Bishop (Ed.) *International Handbook of Mathematics Education*. Netherlands, Kluwer Academic Publisher: 371–409.

McCaffrey, D. F., Lockwood, J. R., Koretz, D., Louis, T. A., & Hamilton, L. (2004). Models for Value-Added Modeling of Teacher Effects. *Journal of educational and behavioral statistics, 29*(1), 67–101.

McCaffrey, D. F., Lockwood, J., Koretz, D., & Hamilton, L. (2003). *Evaluating value-added models for teacher accountability*. Santa Monica, CA: Rand Corporation.

McCutcheon, G. (1982). What in the world is curriculum theory? *Theory Into Practice, 21*(1), 18–22.

Morris, A., & Hiebert, J. (2011). Creating Shared Instructional Products: An Alternative Approach to Improving Teaching. *Educational Researcher*, *40*(1), 5–14.
Moses, R., & Cobb, C. (2002). *Radical Equations: Civil Rights from Mississippi to the Algebra Project*. Boston, MA: Beacon.
Mosteller, F., & Boruch, R. F. (2002). *Evidence Matters: Randomized Trials in Education Research*. Washington, DC: Brookings Institution Press.
National Council of Teachers of Mathematics. (1991). *Professional Standards for Teaching Mathematics*. Reston, VA: Author.
Parshall, K. H., & Rowe, D. E. (1997). *The emergence of the American mathematical research community, 1876–1900: JJ Sylvester, Felix Klein, and EH Moore*. Providence: American Mathematical Society.
Pearl, J. L. (2010). The Role of Personal Correspondence in the Exchange of Scientific Information in Early Modern France. *Renaissance and Reformation/Renaissance et Réforme, 20*(2), 106.
Ravitch, D. (2010). *The Death and Life of the Great American School System: How Testing and Choice Are Undermining Education*. New York: Basic Books.
Reyes, B. J., Reyes, R. E., & Chavez, O. (2004). Why Mathematics Textbooks Matter. *Educational Leadership, 61*(5), 61–66.
Rudolph, J. L. (2002). *Scientists in the classroom: the cold war reconstruction of American science education*. New York: Palgrave.
Schubring, G. (1987). On the methodology of analysing historical textbooks: Lacroix as textbook author. *For the learning of mathematics, 7*(3), 41–51.
Seely, C. (2003). Mathematics Textbook Adoption in the United States. In Stanic, G. & J. Kilpatrick (Eds.), *A History of School Mathematics* (Vols. 1–2, Vol. 2, pp. 957–988). Reston, Virginia: National Council of Teachers of Mathematics.
Selwyn, N. (2011). *Education and Technology: Key Issues and Debates*. New York: Continuum.
U.S. Department of Education, (2009, November). *Race To The Top Program: Executive Summary*. Washington, DC. Author.
Westbury, I. (1990). "Textbooks, textbook publishers, and the quality of schooling." In D. Elliott & A. Woodward (Eds.), *Textbooks and Schooling in the United States: 89th Yearbook of the National Society for the Study of Education, Part I*, (pp. 1–22). Chicago: University of Chicago.
Yerushalmy, M. (2011). Learning "by the eTextBook": Shifts of medium and of textbook culture. Available from The Institute For Research and Development Of Alternatives In Education, Haifa University, http://www.edu.haifa.ac.il/en/page.php?id=1930.
Young, S. (2007). *The book is dead: Long live the book*. Sydney: University of New South Wales Press.

Media and Information Literacy in the Digital Age. An Example on Exploring Pluralism

Marlène Loicq

Abstract

In the digital age, the media appears to be a powerful actor of social changes as it is seen and used simultaneously as a tool, a mean of communication, of information and of knowledge. As a consequence, it has brought the relation between school and media to a even higher level of complexity. It is therefore urgent and needed to re-think school missions and to define what it is to be media literate. This chapter aims at combining several issues brought by technological convergence and the multiplicity of media practices. To do so, it critically questions the accuracy of the Media and Information Literacy project supported by UNESCO and focuses on one of its main subject: information pluralism. Media education shouldn't be limited to the technological possibilities but should instead deeply reconnect with the actual users' experiences of media tools and contents.

Introduction

When referring to the digital age, it is necessary to point out not only the technical developments that have occurred, but also the social, economic and political changes that have accompanied this cultural upheaval in media practices. It is no longer required to demonstrate the importance of media in the lives of young people (some even mention a mediated youth culture – Hodkinson, 2007; Jenkins, 2009). However, it becomes crucial to understand media's implications in the (trans)formation of the youth's identities, their functions in citizens' participation and their ability to convoke personal expression in modern societies. By enabling the development of "smart" technologies and the explosion of social media, digital media have led to profound changes in young people's media practices, which includes the way they acquire information, entertain and communicate. The digital age then implies important modifications in how we connect to the world, in a broader, more interactive and simultaneous way (in space and time). As the UNESCO report stresses, "we live in a world where the quality of information we receive largely determines our choices and ensuing actions, including our capacity to enjoy fundamental freedoms and the ability for self-determination and development" (UNESCO, 2011: 11). Therefore, there is today no other option than to be media literate.

Being so integrated into the daily life of young people, the media have revolutionized both educational needs and opportunities. School has always been at the crossroads of information and knowledge production and diffusion. Since the emergence of communication technologies, and most of all, since the beginning of the digital age, this hegemony, however, has been challenged. School institutions have more or less succeeded in adapting pedagogical models to this new reality, and (professional) teachers have tried to overcome the paradox of being at the same time techno-enthusiasts – for the didactical possibilities offered by new media – and techno-cynics towards new contents and practices. Media education, as a project of empowerment, has arisen from this tension and is still confronted with the question of power: media industry *versus* institutional education, teachers *versus* media tools, information *versus* knowledge… these forces tend to collaborate in building a media literacy made of participation through media and critical thinking of media contents.

Media education has a unique history in many countries (Piette, 1996; Loicq, 2012), and in order not to focus on a specific national approach, we tend in this chapter to refer to UNESCO's label Media and Information Literacy (MIL[1]). Our aim is not to explore all the issues and tools of MIL, but rather to show that the media can be analyzed and understood in the digital age through one of its central issues: information pluralism.

I Media and Information Literacy: background of a permanently accurate education

Historically, young people have been too often portrayed as passive spectators and subordinated to cultural industries. However, reception studies, including cultural studies, have revealed their active attitude towards media consumption and the interpretation of texts. What has changed dramatically in the digital age is that the public is not only receiving but also equally producing messages. Ranging

1 UNESCO specialists have chosen this appellation relying on diverse experts of Media Literacy and Information Literacy. It suggests (as well as the whole MIL project) that information and media are two different things. But even if we use it as a reference in this chapter to refer to a common project despite the local specificities, this term can be problematic and could lead to a legitimisation process of one (information) over another (media) and to confusion in the understanding of media functions and issues. Instead of defining information as "news" (which is after all just a media format), we should think of it as "everything that gives facts – or representation – on the world". In that sense, every media content is a piece of information, so the distinction is no longer accurate. We have preferred elsewhere the notion of "media education" (as a reflection of "medias studies") even if it is also associated to diverse representations of the media in education (Loicq, 2011, 2012).

from one to the other, the boundary between production and reception is becoming increasingly blurred, as is the one between communication (process) and information (content). However, the active participation of young people in the media universe has nevertheless brought up once again the debate on the role of school in controlling their media environment. Past issues concerning young people's ability to demonstrate critical thinking, reflective distance and creativity are once again emerging. If each "new" media, before being supplanted by the arrival of another new one, has been accused of the same prejudices (bondage, disconnection from reality, disturbing social and educational order, etc.), then digital technologies are no exception to the rule. However, another major factor has interfered in the debate: the need to develop technical competences (often promoted by the media industry). Information and Communication Technologies (ICT) are supposed to have widened the gap between digital natives (considered to be spontaneously competent) and digital immigrants (seen as struggling to catch up with these technologies). They also renewed the confusion between media in education and media education (the first one is an educational use of a medium, the second involves an analysis of the media for itself).

The same kind of popular mythology leads the institutional debates between technophiles and technophobes who compete for the risks and opportunities of digital technologies, although all agree that school has to be associated to these technologies. For many, school can guarantee a sage and rational use of technology; for others, media is an essential issue for the social, personal and professional integration of the youth into their changing environment. The articulation of digital technologies and school processes does not refer to the same level for everyone.

Digital education is linked to the field of "computer literacy" which had arisen from debates about "information literacy" (Buckingham, 2009: 17). These approaches, which can be described as very 'technicist', were carried by an inclusion initiative aiming primarily at the participation of everyone in the "knowledge economy" or "information society". Issues of access and individual technological competences were put forward rather than understanding, collaboration and creation. Digital education is, nonetheless, offset by the skills and abilities already developed by young people according to specific needs through their experience of technologies. A relevant perspective involves understanding the communicative approach behind the use of these tools (as innovative and powerful they might be). It is the social dimension that should be apprehended in the use of digital technologies, since young people are expected to become major players in the development of a participatory web (from an educational, a social and a citizenship point of view, but also in relation to consumption, entrepreneurship, etc.).

Thus, we prefer to look at media literacy, encompassing all of these approaches without limitation, to apprehend a cross media convergence and participatory culture. Indeed, the distinction between non-digital media and digital media no longer has much relevance as media experiences now combine different modes of communication, technology platforms and practices.

I-1. Media education, information literacy: two convergent projects towards MIL

Media education is a settled project, with a strong history, and with theoretical and institutional foundations, whose aim is to comprehend these new experiences. It has been based on several theoretical concepts and movements (Piette, Giroux, 1997) which have led to specific media education projects (Anderson, 1980). Media education is a process through which students should be able to critically understand the nature, techniques, impacts and issues of media messages (their own and those produced by other individuals or by media industries). Diverse skills and competences for being media literate can be put forward, like sharing and taking part (to be full participants in the emerging participatory culture online – Jenkins, 2009), judging (ability to evaluate the reliability and credibility of different information sources), negotiating (ability to go from one community to another, discerning and respecting plural perspectives), and being motivated (to take part in public discussions – Carlsson, 2009), etc. Each of these abilities pertains to larger institutions and particular 'mediatic' systems. Furthermore, since media education is deeply rooted in socio-cultural, economic and historical concerns, the analysis has to take into account the specific educational contexts, the changes that have occurred in media industries, and the citizen expectations linked to particular national environments.

If media education has been designed differently in many countries, international bodies serve as a gateway and common place for these different approaches. In UNESCO's framework, media education has been widely investigated, promoted and even modelled at various meetings (Grunwald, 1982; Toulouse, 1990; Vienna, 1999; Sevilla, 2002; Paris, 2007; Fez, 2011; Bellaria, 2012; etc.), as well as in reports and other educational materials (Minkkinen, 1978; Morsy, 1984; Carlsson et al., 2008; Frau-Meigs, 2006). Today, these different approaches can be found under a common label – Media and Information Literacy (MIL) – which integrates the theoretical and practical achievements of media literacy on the one hand and of information literacy on the other, in a transversal perspective eminently carried by the digital.

Thus, media education ensures that people learn how to "analyse, critically reflect upon and create media texts; identify the sources of media texts, their political, social, commercial and/or cultural interests, and their contexts; interpret the messages and values offered by the media; select appropriate media for communicating their own messages or stories and for reaching their intended audience; gain, or demand access to media for both reception and production" (Vienna, 1999[2]). Key concepts for media education are: representations (media are constructions), reception (audiences negotiate meaning), media industries/producers (media have commercial implications), norms and values (media have ideological implications), languages (signs, codes and narratives), technologies (uses and social meaning), and aesthetics (cultural experience), etc. This project aims at empowering media users.

Furthermore, the idea of empowerment also brought by information literacy leads to three different levels of competences. In the first place, technical and methodological access to information should be mastered. It is necessary to be able to retrieve information, but it cannot be disconnected from evaluation since information is not a neutral good, and because the distinction between facts and opinions is not a natural process. Then, critical and creative uses of information should be taken into account when accessing information. Finally, these steps should lead to an information culture that includes ethical considerations and knowledge on media functions and uses. The development of an information literacy relies on information potentials, which are the individual capacities to increase their competences (Yoon, 2008). This perspective is crucial for the student's learning process, as she/he needs to feel confident about her/his own possibilities to adapt to the several digital environments she/he is confronted with.

Therefore, MIL as a combination of those two approaches, is concerned with "competences that emphasize the development of enquiry-based skills and the ability to engage meaningfully with media and information channels in whatever form and technologies they are using" (UNESCO, 2011: 18). It should also "emphasize the ability to understand media functions, evaluate how those functions are performed and to rationally engage with media for self-expression" (UNESCO, 2011: 18). Being media literate means being critically engaged with mass media, which includes nowadays digital technologies. It implies to encompass the personal, technological and intellectual skills that are needed to live in a digital world, including the broader social, ethical, legal and economic aspects of digital uses. Moreover, it should also take into account the diverse competences needed for playing, learning and working in a digital environment.

2 Vienna Conference on « Éducation aux médias à l'ère du numérique », April 18–20 1999. http://www.unesco.org/education/nfsunesco/pdf/VIENNA.PDF.

The MIL project is deeply rooted in digital media because, first of all, there is no longer a clear distinction between digital media and non-digital media; and, second, MIL is concerned with all media-related literacies (information literacy, media literacy, advertising literacy, news literacy, television literacy, cinema literacy, games literacy, internet literacy, computer literacy, digital literacy, FOE and FOI literacy, library literacy).

MIL aims at the understanding of how the media works as a whole, the idea of media configuration being sometimes used in that sense. MIL can participate in the understanding of processes extending from the lowest level of meaning – the study of media signs (framing, narratives, etc.) – to the largest considerations of economic and political control of the creative industries. This means questioning at the same time the production of representations in relation to issues of power, and values, etc. and particular modes of reception and patterns. MIL is mobilizing a strong theoretical background in media studies, but is also concerned with production practices connected to the reality of the audience. It is also necessary to examine the myths underlying the uses of media ownership and tools as well as the contribution of the symbolic content in the "moulding of minds" (Caronia, Caron, 2009). MIL's principal work is to break the code of the media, but also to shape it, in a process that is both theoretical and practical, as well as critical and creative, and always collaborative. Media should therefore be apprehended at the same time through a (critical) reception posture, a (responsible) production posture, and an analysis of the association of these two positions which increasingly tend to mingle.

I-2. Re-distribution of powers

This complex vision of media systems is the modern phase definition of media education. It has not always been so oriented towards the youth's media experiences, nor did it always acknowledge the public active participation. Previously, with the invention of writing, new professions, new issues, new fights for power, new hierarchies appeared, as also with the invention of printing and with the advent of electronic media. In the pre-history of mass media developments, knowledge was still constructed and built by the school and in the school. But, with an increasing number of students with a diverse experience of the world thanks to the media practice, schools had no choice but to take into account these new forms of knowledge. With the idea of introducing media into classrooms, media education was at first generally a protectionist project. This protection was operated at two levels. First, with the growth of new communication tools (press, radio and television), educators saw a risk of manipulation of the youth which had to be protected. Young people were perceived as naive and at risk, and should therefore be afforded protection against these "weapons of enslavement", through an education project built "against" the media. Secondly, these tools were perceived as a threat to the educational role of the adults, and to the institutional status of schools.

However, media cannot only be considered as tools since they have challenged this distribution of power. As school is no longer the place for dispensing a controlled knowledge, teachers are confronted with a new approach of their own functions. This is not so much that their role is abolished at the expense of another, but the roles are distributed differently, and it is necessary to reconsider the relevance and place of each in the educational process. When students bring to school a wide amount of information that they have accessed through the media, teachers have to adapt to this new reality. Information is no longer only contained in textbooks. Power is then redistributed and rivalry between institutions emerges. Education systems all over the world have been impacted by the changes brought by digital (r)evolutions. Media education has forced education systems to think differently. From a media education perspective, school should abandon its function of transmission for a more interactive vision of learning. From being the place where information is transmitted, school should become a place of (co)building knowledge.

II- Exploring pluralism in the digital age (through Media and Information Literacy)

Pluralism of news appears to be crucial for media education studies because on the one hand it refers to the historical questionings on the merging of media and school issues (which started with the development of the press), and on the other hand it is related to broader inquiries on critical and reflective thinking of citizens. Media education emerged precisely around these approaches, and these skills appeared to be central in the MIL curriculum "understanding the role of media and information in democracy" – UNESCO, 2011:30). Even if it has sometimes been used locally as a political (or marketing) argument to transfer the regulatory role of the state to individual responsibility (as is the case with Ofcom in the UK – Freedman, 2008; Livingstone, Lunt, Miller, 2007), media education is a field of study that captures the media in their complexity, and meets a vital need for adaptation to an environment largely rooted in communicative logics and information culture (Serres, 2009).

II-1. Pluralism in the digital age

The digital age has led to a more participatory culture. By being a place where everyone is able to speak up, in particular alternative voices, the Internet has been labelled a pluralistic sphere. But is it so? And what are the consequences on education? As mentioned by Cordier (2012), the formal information literacy based on the idea of learning a typical procedure to search for information and the definition of media education as a way to warn kids about media dangers are no longer accurate. Digital information is associated with a risk-taking policy, which implies to have a permanent critical view on this media practice (Serres, 2006). Being media literate means being prepared for the unpredictable. It is then more important to be aware of the process than to be able to apply strict methods for retrieving information.

While the multiplicity of information is increasing exponentially, especially in the case of news, it is becoming crucial to learn to discriminate the sources and viability of information, but it is at the same time important to seek for pluralism. In other words, it is essential for schools to give students the tools to deal with both information diversity and redundancy: "If we want media diversity to effectively contribute to opinion forming in democratic societies, communications policies should also aim at enlarging the willingness of citizens to take on their democratic responsibilities and at enlarging the cultural receptiveness in media audience to the distinctiveness of different constituent groups, ideologies, religions and life styles in society" (Cuilenburg, 2002:17). Therefore, MIL precisely aims to give citizens the competences they need to fully enjoy the benefits of this fundamental human right: "Everyone has the right to freedom of opinion and expression; this right includes freedom to hold opinions without interference and to seek, receive and impart information and ideas through any media and regardless of frontiers" (Article 19 of the Universal Declaration of Human Rights). This statement regulating information policies in numerous countries reflects a typical European approach of pluralism, or otherwise called "media diversity" in the English speaking world[3] (Cuilenburg, 2002; Rebillard, Loicq, 2013).

---

3 On the theoretical level, this terminological dichotomy is much less marked in the English speaking world, where the terms of pluralism and diversity are both employed almost indiscriminately. Both terms refer, in its most basic definition, to a state of media heterogeneity, indicative of a more assumed cultural heterogeneity (the distinction between citizenship and culture is less clear). The plurality is discussed together in the mission of the media to promote different views (using the term pluralism in French) and in identifying the origin of the voice heard (use of the term diversity in French). We can still see a difference in their use: 'media pluralism' designating more an ideal or a general orientation and 'media

Four empirical dimensions of media diversity can be distinguished: formats and issues (linked to the functions of the media), content (which is most of the time mentioned as information pluralism), people and groups (which is called media diversity), and geographical coverage and relevance (McQuail, 1992). In the American tradition, this notion is linked to the idea of media heterogeneity and is defined by three levels: source diversity (ownership and workforce), content diversity (programme type, format, genre, etc.) and exposure diversity (audience reach) (Napoli, 1999).

Pluralism is thus a major issue in democratic societies and depends on the ability of the media to support several views and voices. With the development of the Internet and related technologies, and by offering multiple areas of web publishing, some have claimed that it would allow more voices to speak up and let more people have access to information and thus have a positive impact on the public sphere. The Internet, as a wild flow of information, is consequently seen as a systematic guarantee for diversity, increasing the illusion of information multiplicity. It is then seen as a means for alternative contents to reach a larger public (more than it would with traditional media) and at the same time, as an opportunity for everyone to access any kind of information. And such an argument is based on a good reason: online markets (production, distribution, storage, etc.) have the advantage of being low-cost and of having unlimited geographical flows. But does it systematically mean that the Internet is devoted to diversity?

II-2. Pluralism and redundancy of information in the digital age

As a recent study on news pluralism suggests (Rebillard, 2012; Marty et al., 2013), we can actually admit that if pluralism and "diversity as sent" exist for online news

---

diversity' rather refers to a tangible achievement (Karppinen, 2007). The idea of pluralism is also generally associated with sources whereas diversity is often used in the description of the contents. In the European tradition, studies on access for citizens to pluralistic information prevail (information pluralism or pluralism of news). It is thus associated with media regulation and public service broadcasting. In the French speaking world, the use of the term pluralism is not equivalent to the term diversity, on the contrary, it can reveal the ongoing tensions in the Republican model. The first seems wider and may affect up to the organization of the media system, when the second would be more limited to the content of media and be seen from a social and political issue. The first would refer to the plurality of ideas in the name of freedom of expression, while the second concerns the representation of the diversity constituting a society, in the name of equality. The first affects the vision of a plurality citizen, the second of cultural plurality. In this chapter, we use pluralism in the broader sense used in the English speaking world.

(much more than television for instance), it does not represent the "diversity as received" (Van der Wurff, 2011). It shows that most of the sources publish mainstream information, and the densest online traffic is observed on those redundant websites. Therefore, on the contrary, those studies tend to reveal that the multiplicity of a news website can lead to a less original information ("more is less" theory by Paterson, 2007). This is sometimes seen as a result of an informational imperialism of a new kind. Nevertheless, we can still see that the Internet has a higher *tendency* to pluralism (than television for instance) and revives the issue of the relation between diversity of sources and diversity of contents. It appears that most of the sources give redundant information and that the less visited web sites are the ones with the most diverse content.

This means that pluralism can be applied in two different ways. Firth of all, it is a pluralism of production, or offered diversity, which is controlled by policies in certain countries, or an ethic engagement in others. Secondly, there is a consumed pluralism which results from the choice of oneself to vary one's consumption of information (source, formats, genre, etc.). As citizens, we all are supposed to be able to discriminate information, to take part in democratic debates and to actively contribute to the political and civil life of our sphere. But this perspective implies that the important problematic of pluralism in the digital age is not only the increased capacity of information production (especially from a technical point of view), but it is associated with the ability (or desire) of consumption. An important distinction can therefore be related to the exposure to diversity: content as sent and content as received (McQuail, 1992: 157). And yet, it appears that even when the content sent is diverse, the content as received might be really redundant. So consumed pluralism is not directly linked to the diversity offered, but is dependent of the capacity and desire of the individuals to seek for pluralism (Napoli, 2013). As a result, "one can hypothesize that consumed diversity of content on the web is actually lower then diversity offered" (Smyrnaios, Marty, Rebillard, 2010: 1258).

After all, the Internet is reviving the ancestral debate on media impacts on society and its issues. Such discussion usually starts with media effects theories on propaganda, accusing the powerful media industry of abusing people's interests, and then focuses on one's empowerment (as it is in reception studies for example)[4]. Despite the fact that online media consumers have a certain type of

4 Media education has always been confronted with a lot of myths around media uses and functions. Even if media studies aim at dissipating fantasies about media effects, they still occupy an important place in the field of media education. In fact, by being at a crossroad of research, educational problems and parenthood concerns, media education should link

competence in interpreting and discriminating information, school still appears to have the power (and mission) to give tools for developing choices towards diversity. In other words, education in the digital age, to be relevant, should include a reflection on the tension between what is possible with technologies and what is profitable from them. Being conscious of the necessity to seek information through different sources, to evaluate information, to compare it to others and to make our own opinion through it, can be considered as a practical critical thinking approach that can be held by MIL. As for schooling issues, it is at the same time an opportunity to teach pluralism values to future citizens and a challenge to bring them to critical thinking.

As a conclusion…

The sheer volume of media content can sometimes make us feel overwhelmed by information overload. We are all immersed in a vast array of communication networks, and we live in a world that is increasingly saturated with media images and representations. With the emergence of digital technologies, the flow of symbolic contents has exploded, putting a final end to time and space, and making it possible for everyone to create their own products. As media consumers, we are no longer only receiver/interpreter, but also producer/actor of communication. Therefore, everybody can access this new public sphere offered by the Internet, to express ideas and be at the same time confronted with someone else's ideas. But are we, as media users, aware that perhaps the more diversity of information is offered, the less we are able to see, hear and read it all?

Pluralism is a social issue that concerns not only the state in terms of regulation and public policies, but it has also become a central matter in the understanding of each and everyone's media practices. Media education has always been preoccupied by the challenges offered by pluralism, its (political, economic and social) processes, and by the role that can play individuals as media users. But to be fully relevant, it should be able to adapt to the specificities of the digital age, i.e. the portability of contents from one medium to another and multi-purpose skills. Ultimately, media education has to embed transliteracy issues. School's traditional aims are to produce literate students by teaching them how to read, write and calculate. In a time of convergent digital age, school has to encourage "the ability to read, write and interact across a range of platforms, tools and media from signing

education practices with media education researches (which is present in three different fields: media studies; education sciences; youth and media).

and orality through handwriting, print, TV, radio and film, for digital social networks" (Thomas et al., 2007). This is what we call transliteracy. It gives answers to the questions about technological improvements, economic issues, and the social, cultural and global participation of media users. It can in fact be related to the convergence culture (Jenkins, 2006). Transliteracy is being explored and studied by scholars around the world and appears to be a convergent point between media education, information culture and digital literacy. It is based on the fact that media users navigate from one tool to another with fluidity. It is motivated by the importance to clearly understand the implications of this flow (in terms of symbolic significance, responsibility and sociocultural impacts). And it is preoccupied by the necessity to be competent in handling those tools and contents, and to have equal chances to fully participate in the digital age.

References

Anderson, J. A., (1980). The theoretical lineage of critical viewing curricula, *Journal of Communication*, Vol. 30, n. 3, pp. 64–71.

Buckingham, D., (2009). The future of media literacy in the digital age: some challenges for Policy and practice, *Media literacy in Europe. Controversies, Challenges and Perspectives*, EuroMeduc Project, Bruxelles, pp. 13–24. http://www.euromeduc.eu/IMG/pdf/Euromeduc_ENG.pdf.

Carlsson, U., (2009). Young people in the European Digital Media Landscape. Challenges and Opportunities, *Media literacy in Europe. Controversies, Challenges and Perspectives*, EuroMeduc Project, Bruxelles, pp. 125–132. http://www.euromeduc.eu/IMG/pdf/Euromeduc_ENG.pdf.

Carlsson, U., Tayie, S., Jacquinot-Delaunay, G., Pérez Tornero, J. M., (2008). (eds.). *Empowerment through Media Education, an intercultural Dialogue*, Europe, ICCYM, UNESCO, Dar Graphit, Mentor Association.

Caronia, L. and Caron, A. H., (2009). Mobile learning in the digital age: A clash of cultures?, in Kleinman S. (ed.), *The Culture of Efficiency. Technology in Everyday Life*. New York: Peter Lang, pp. 191–211.

Cordier, A., (2012). Et si on enseignant l'incertitude pour construire une culture de l'information? in *Actes du Colloque COSSI, Information, Incertitudes, Intelligences* Poitiers- http://archivesic.ccsd.cnrs.fr/docs/00/80/30/91/PDF/CORDIER_Et_si_on_enseignait_l_incertitude.pdf.

Cuilenburg, J. V., (2002). The media diversity concept and European perspectives, *Media Economics, Content and Diversity Seminar*, Finnish Academy of Sciences, Helsinki, 16 December 2002.

Frau-Meigs, D., (2006). (ed.). *Media education. A kit for teachers, students, parents and professionals*, Unesco.

Freedman, D., (2008). *The Politics of Media Policy*, Cambridge: Polity.

Hodkinson, P., (2007). Youth Cultures: A Critical Outline of Key Debates, in P. Hodkinson & W. Deicke (eds.), *Youth Culture. Scenes, Subcultures and Tribes,* London: Routledge.

Jenkins, H. et. al., (2009). *Confronting the Challenges of Participatory Culture: Media Education for the 21st Century,* MacArthur Foundation, An Occasional paper on digital media and learning. www.digitallearning.macfound.org.

Jenkins, H., (2006). *Convergence Culture*, New York, NYUP.

Karppinen, K., (2007). Making a Difference to Media Pluralism: a Critique of the Pluralistic Consensus in European Media Policy, in Cammaerts B., Carpentier N. (eds.), *Reclaiming the Media. Communication Rights and Democratic Media Roles*, Bristol: Intellect Books, pp. 9–30.

Livingstone, S., Lunt, P., and Miller, L., (2007). Citizens and consumers: discursive debates during and after the Communications Act 2003, *Media, Culture and Society*, Vol. 29, n. 4, pp. 613–638.

Loicq, M., (2012). Éducation aux médias dans le monde: état des lieux et perspectives, *Jeunes & médias, les cahiers francophones de l'éducation aux médias*, n. 4, Paris: EPU, pp. 15–18.

Loicq, M., (2011). Médias et Interculturalité: l'éducation aux médias dans une perspective comparative internationale (Australie, Québec, France), Thèse de doctorat en cotutelle, Université Paris 3 Sorbonne Nouvelle, Université Laval, Québec. http://theses.ulaval.ca/archimede/meta/28807.

McQuail, D., (1992). *Media Performance: Mass Communication and the Public Interest*, Sage: London.

Minkkinen, S., (1978). *A General Curricular Model for Mass Media Education*, UNESCO, Esco édition.

Morsy, S., (1984), *L'éducation aux médias*, Paris, UNESCO.

Napoli, P.M., (1999). Deconstructing the Diversity Principle, *Journal of Communication*, Vol. 49, n. 4, pp. 7–34.

Napoli, P.M., (2013). La diversité comme principe émergent de la gouvernance de l'Internet, in Rebillard F., Loicq M., (eds.), *Pluralisme de l'information et* media diversity*: un état des lieux international*, Bruxelles: De Boeck.

Paterson, C., (2007). International News on the Internet: Why More is Less, *Ethical Space: The International Journal of Communication Ethics*, Vol. 4, n. 1, pp. 57–66.

Piette, J., (1996). Éducation aux médias et fonction critique, Montréal: l'Harmattan.

Piette, J., Giroux L., (1997). The theoretical foundations of media education programs in Kubey R. (ed.), *Media literacy in the information age*, London: Transaction publishers.

Rebillard, F., Loicq, M., (eds.), (2013). *Pluralisme de l'information et* media diversity*: un état des lieux international*, Bruxelles: De Boeck.

Rebillard, F., (ed.). (2012). Internet et pluralisme de l'information, *Réseaux*, Vol. 176, n. 6.

Serres, A., (2009). Penser la culture informationnelle: des difficultés de l'exercice…, *Les Cahiers du Numérique*, Vol. 5, n. 3, pp. 9–23.

Serres, A., (2006). Trois dimensions de l'éducation à l'information', 28–30 August 2006. http://www.uhb.fr/urfist/publics/TexteUE_Poitiers2006_A.Serres.doc.

Smyrnaios, N., Marty, E., Rebillard, F., (2010). Does the long tail apply to online news? A quantitative study of French-speaking news and websites *New Media & Society*, Vol. 12, n. 8, pp. 1244–1261.

Thomas, S., Joseph, C., Laccetti, J., Mason, B., Mills, S., Perril, S. and Pullinger, K., (2007). Transliteracy: Crossing divides, *First Monday* [Online], Vol. 12, n. 12. http://www.uic.edu/htbin/cgiwrap/bin/ojs/index.php/fm/article/view/2060/1908.

UNESCO, (2011). *Media and Information Literacy. Curriculum for teachers*, edited by Alton Grizzle and Carolyn Wilson.

Van der Wurff, R., (2011). Do audiences receive diverse ideas from news media? Exposure to a variety of news media and personal characteristics as determinants of diversity as received, *European Journal of Communication*, Vol. 26, n. 4, pp. 328–342.
Yoon, C. G., (2008). A structural model of end-user computing competency and user performance *Knowledge-Based Systems*, Vol. 21, n. 5.

Scaffolding Curation: Developing Digital Competencies in Media Literacy Education

Paul Mihailidis and Megan E. Fromm

Abstract

This chapter focuses on the concept of curation as a student- and creation-driven pedagogical tool to enhance digital and media literacy education. Specifically, it will unpack the phenomenon of curation as a pedagogical model for enhancing civic engagement, community, and purpose within social media platforms. Online curation—an increasingly common way to refer to the act of organizing various content into cohesive online stories—has taken numerous forms in recent years. Media organizations are increasingly integrating such tools into their web presence, most recently seen by the *New York Times, NPR* and the *Washington Post* utilizing *Storify* curation software for multimedia stories; and *Al Jazeera, CNN* and othersintegrating Twitter into their regular online programming. Curation is also being explored through remix—the sharing, repurposing, or re-appropriating of content online—as a function of creative commons and copyright, and in terms of cultural production and social structure. This chapter will build a framework for curation as it builds on existing models for digital and media education and remix culture. It will develop curation as a foundational media education competence to teach students about responsibility, purpose, and participation in social media spaces.

Introduction

In 2010, the Knight Foundation published a report entitled *The Needs of Information Communities.* The report explored how public communities function in information societies and recommended a series of methods for enhancing communities with online tools that enable dialog, interaction, and action-oriented behavior. More than a year later, media literacy scholar Renee Hobbs (2010) published a report titled *Digital and Media Literacy*, which explored the needs of educational bodies to integrate more structured approaches toward teaching and learning with digital and mobile media technologies.

These new reports are largely a response to a growing shift in how individuals are using information to suit their personal, political, and community needs. In light of this new information landscape, there has been much scholarship exploring how social media platforms and mobile media technologies are shifting collaboration (Shirky, 2008; 2010), participation (Jenkins, 2006, 2008; Bennett, 2008), and learning (Buckingham, 2007; Hobbs, 2010; Ito, 2010). As youth embrace participatory and collaborative technologies to facilitate a majority of their information and communication needs, how educators create dynamic approaches to teaching and learning about information online can have significant influence on the participatory culture of youth. Most notably, because today's media and communication landscape is saturated with an abundance of facts, sources, and perspectives, teaching youth a critical approach to managing—or curating—this wealth of content is paramount. Both the Knight Foundation and Hobbs's reports innovatively examine the changing communication habits of a digital culture, but sometimes to move forward we must look to the past. In this case, the longstanding art of curating serves as a tool for anchoring contemporary media literacy models, re-envisioning media education, and engendering youth participation in the digital age.

This chapter focuses on the concept of curation as a student-centered pedagogical tool to enhance digital and media literacy education. Specifically, it will reimagine curation as a pedagogical model for enhancing engagement, community, and purpose within social media platforms. Online curation—an increasingly common way to refer to the act of organizing various content into cohesive online stories—has taken numerous forms in recent years. Curation is also being explored through remix—the sharing, repurposing, or re-appropriating of content online—as a function of creative commons and copyright (Lessig, 2008; Benkler, 2005), and in terms of cultural production and social structure (Cheliotis & Yew, 2009; Dybwad, 2005; Diakopoulos, 2008).

This chapter will conclude by presenting a scaffolding approach to curation pedagogy that adds to existing models for digital and media education and remix culture (Mihailidis, 2011). It will develop curation as a foundational media education competency to teach students about responsibility, purpose, and participation in social media spaces.

Curation, engagement and digital culture

Curating—both as an art and organization method—allows the curator to tell a story across mediums. The art of curating generally refers to the selection and maintenance of records or items into a related collection, but in the case of visual communication, this often means gathering information across a multitude of mediums. In a digital culture, curation occurs when consumers scour digital media for the best or most relevant content, collecting it for their own personal and social use. As Bergdoll (1998) explains, curation happens when "arguments and insights are made with objects and images rather than primarily with words but also because collaboration is an inherent aspect of the process from conception to installation" (p. 257). Just as the museum curator addresses the negotiation between content and display, so, too, must the digital curator navigate the aggregation, presentation, and stylistic display of online content (Bergdoll, 1998). Recently, prolific use of online aggregation software has put the task of curation into the hands of the everyday digital citizen. Storify, Reddit, and other online tools allow users to make sense of a multitude of information sources in a flexible, personal manner. In doing so, we see how online curation is now, in the digital age, an ongoing endeavor that is constantly recreated, remixed, and re-appropriated (Lessig, 2008).

While the digital age makes curation an exciting and potentially endless exercise, the abundance of data from news and social media requires users to internalize their own story narrative before communicating online. This mimics responsible forms of literacy, as Hobbs explains (2010): "[P]eople need to have a good understanding of how knowledge is constructed and how it represents reality and articulates a point of view" (p. viii). Curators, just like journalists, must juggle audience expectations and demands with obligations regarding the authenticity and accuracy of content. In doing so, "the act of curating creates not only the narrative, but also the conversation" (Mihailidis & Cohen, 2013).

Online participation, whether as digital curator or consumer, facilitates increased awareness and civic voice. As social media becomes a more significant part of daily information and communication needs, educators at all levels are tasked with helping students negotiate their digital and real time efforts so that traditional skills of critical inquiry, evaluation, and analysis are applied across all mediums (Jenkins, et. al., 2009). Similarly, as media use increasingly requires exploration and organization of myriad data across websites and platforms, the task of curating information is paramount to learning.

Why curation matters for digital and media education?

Youth today enter the classroom with a heightened sense of digital familiarity (Prensky, 2001; Rosen, 2010). While this familiarity has been challenged in terms of its value for youth (Thomas, 2011; Bayne & Ross, 2007; Bennett et al., 2008; Bowman et al., 2010; Brown & Czerniewicz (2010), and does not necessarily mean that youth will be more competent media users, (Hargittai, 2005; Jones et al., 2010; Kennedy et al., 2008), it does reflect a shifting approach to how we think about teaching and learning in a digital age. At the same time, as digital media increasingly grow central to learning competencies of contemporary society, models for teaching and learning must now incorporate more diverse, integrated, and dynamic models for social and digital media platforms. These models, placed in the context of media literacy, can enhance the value of curation for youth empowerment in a digital culture (Kuiper & Volman, 2008; Sanchez et al., 2006; Taboada & Guthrie, 2006). By emphasizing thoughtful selection and circulation of information, curation supports a higher order of media consumption that embraces media literacy's basic ideals while also predicating the overall experience on an expectation for significant citizen engagement. Put more simply, when curating becomes a central focus in media literacy education, the impetus for citizen action and response is reinforced.

The emerging media literacy landscape is one that is more fully integrated into the competencies needed for digital learners of an information age. Media literacy is premised on promoting critical thinking skills through the ability to access, evaluate, analyze, and produce information. (Aufderheide & Firestone, 1993; OFCOM, 2005; Potter, 2010; Silverblatt, 2001; Thoman & Jolls, 2005). Media literacy outcomes alternate between and among informed decision-making, individual and social agency, critical analysis of mediated messages, savvy consumption and production skills, and participation in local, national and global dialogue (Frechette, 2002; Gaines, 2010; Hobbs, 2010, 2011; Livingstone, 2004; Tisdell, 2008). Media literacy scholar David Buckingham (2003) writes:

> [Media Literacy is] A critical literacy that involves analysis, evaluation, and critical reflection, that is possible only through the 'acquisition of a metalanguage—that is, a means of describing the forms and structures of different modes of communication; and it involves a broader understanding of the social, economic and institutional contexts of communication, and how these affect people's experiences and practices (Luke, 2000). Media literacy certainly includes the ability to use and interpret media; but it also involves a much broader analytical understanding. (38)

Media literacy, in this context, applies a series of core competencies around critical inquiry and analysis of media messages. These abilities are rooted in a need to make sense of the world around us as portrayed through media systems. To approach media literacy education in a digital age, Henry Jenkins identifies "a set of core social skills and cultural competencies that young people should acquire if they are to be full, active, creative, and ethical participants in this emerging participatory culture" (Jenkins, 2006b).

1. **Play** — the capacity to experiment with your surroundings as a form of problem-solving
2. **Performance** — the ability to adopt alternative identities for the purpose of improvisation and discovery
3. **Simulation** — the ability to interpret and construct dynamic models of real world processes
4. **Appropriation** — the ability to meaningfully sample and remix media content
5. **Multitasking** — the ability to scan one's environment and shift focus as needed to salient details.
6. **Distributed Cognition** — the ability to interact meaningfully with tools that expand mental capacities
7. **Collective Intelligence** — the ability to pool knowledge and compare notes with others toward a common goal
8. **Judgment** — the ability to evaluate the reliability and credibility of different information sources
9. **Transmedia Navigation** — the ability to follow the flow of stories and information across multiple modalities
10. **Networking** — the ability to search for, synthesize, and disseminate information
11. **Negotiation** — the ability to travel across diverse communities, discerning and respecting multiple perspectives, and grasping and following alternative norms.

Fig. 1: Jenkins's Core Media Literacy Skills for Participatory Culture

Jenkins's media literacy skills emerge from his development of a participatory culture that promotes active, inclusive, and collaborative social and online behaviors. The abundance of new platforms that foster collaborative production, social advocacy, and interactive dialog necessitates a new look at how young citizens today learn to not only critically analyze information, but also to critically express and socialize as public participants. Yochai Benkler (2005) develops this need in his formulation of a networked information economy:

> The Internet allows individuals to abandon the idea of the public sphere as primarily constructed of finished statements uttered by a small set of actors socially understood to be "the media" (whether state owned or commercial) and separated from society, and to move toward a set of social practices that see individuals as participating in a debate. Statements in the public sphere can now be seen as invitations for a conversation, not as finished goods (p. 180).

What Benkler, in his vision of a participatory media conversation, and Jenkins, in his construction of transmedia navigation in the model above, both imply but fail to articulate is exactly how that communication unfolds across a digital spectrum. That is, while new approaches to media literacy must "make sure that digital citizens are well-informed citizens in both understanding information and in their ability to evaluate and analyze what they are seeing" (Swiggum, 2008, p. 16), they must also centralize the user within this experience. Curation does exactly this, requiring with almost every media interaction the application of a broad range of the media literacy skills Jenkins outlines. This approach reflects the need for youth to understand how to effectively analyze and critique media messages, but also to build participatory, expressive, and collaborative competencies for mindful online contributions to daily life: connections that are increasingly present in contemporary media literacy scholarship (Rheingold, 2012; Hobbs, 2011; Hobbs & Cooper Moore, 2013; Share, 2009; Schiebe & Rogow, 2011).

Curation, in this sense, can provide a way to approach teaching and learning about information in digital contexts that incorporates active audiences, integrated information landscapes, and the fast-paced media environment (Hobbs, 2011). Using curation to improve digital competency and goal-oriented online learning has the potential to create more analytical, participatory, engaged, and interactive youth in both online and offline life. (Kahne et al., 2012; Rheingold, 2008; Ito, 2009).

These learning competencies are now just emerging, but they must be implemented with proper learning processes and goals attached. If the focus around new digital tools in the classroom is primarily about the tools themselves and not about the human capacities to create, critique, share and express with these tools, they may not fulfill the potential of these tools to enact strong and lasting engagement and learning in youth. Civic media scholar Eric Gordon (2013) writes about the risks associated with technological determinism in digital culture:

> The digital tools we have available to us can be used to demonstrate that we *have* digital tools; but that is a short-lived thrill. Digital tools are a means to an end. If they are treated as an end in themselves, they threaten to subvert the community engagement process, sublimating the potential human connections and learning to the flashy functionality of a digital billboard.

To mitigate these risks, this chapter proposes a set of competencies for curation as a digital and media literacy outcome. We utilize scaffolded learning to approach four curation competencies—critique, contribute, collaborate, create—that collectively offer a path to digital and media literacy education competencies. This approach is positioned as an efficient framework for teaching about multimedia consumption, intertextual analysis, framing and perspective, agenda setting and bias, sources, voices, and credibility online (Leu et al., 2011). It also positions the classroom as a space that can integrate "the media habits and networks that students use outside of the classroom within a formal setting…to better engage a generation of digital learners" (Mihailidis & Cohen, 2013).

Scaffolding for curation

By providing incremental instruction and tools for further development, scaffolding provides students with structured learning design while at the same time propelling them on their own journeys of self-edification. While scaffolding is often conceptualized via rote skills development (vocabulary, math computation, etc.), we use the construct here to better understand the learning implications of online curation presented in our model (see Figure Two).

Scaffolding any concept or skill demands students approach learning in graduated intervals–they start with the basic idea and move deliberately through a layered process until they have mastered not only the skills but also the critical disposition to meaningfully execute those skills. This is not unlike the process of developing media literacy. However, while core concepts of media literacy are often learned and practiced simultaneously, students should master individual processes before practicing the holistic exercise so that the overwhelming nature of the end task–curating potentially infinite data–is a cumulative and practiced effort.

The figure below presents a scaffolded approach to curation and media education. We offer four key competencies for developing a critical approach to curation in digital culture. First, students learn to *critique* the abundance of information available online. What is truthful? What is misleading? How do we know? This first step lays the critical foundation for both curation and media literacy. Second, students learn to *contribute* to online culture in meaningful and appropriate ways. Sharing information and personal experiences online should be a reflective but audience-based process. Third, students learn to *collaborate* in online spaces by developing cooperative skills that are both platform-specific and platform-agnostic. If Facebook is the dominant medium, students should understand what it means to curate and collaborate in this space while also applying those skills to new social media as they develop. Fourth, students learn to *create*. Creation fuels the collaborative culture of today's online and social media, and our youth have tremendous creative capacity for producing and re-imagining media content.

The steps of this model prepare students to critically *curate* the multitude of online content for personally and socially engaging purposes. The act of curating on its own might simply imply collecting information across sources. However, curating in a media literacy context and within the scaffolded model here implies a critical, civically valuable activity that positions students to better engage in the world around them. Because "the web now mandates curation as a default for users navigating its exponential content, the ability to curate information is central to media literate competences in collaborative spaces" (Mihailidis & Cohen, 2013).

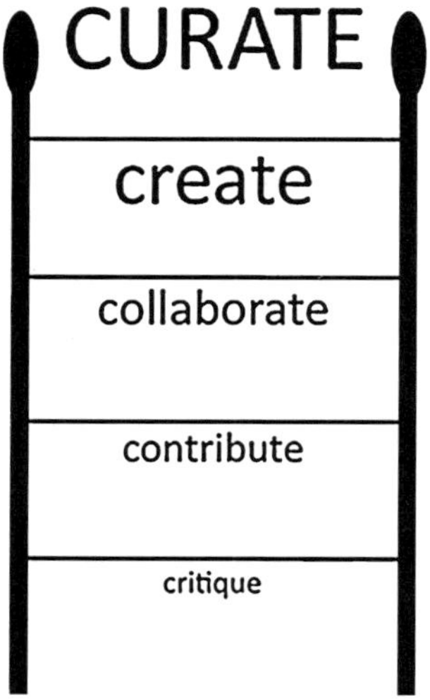

Fig. 2: A Scaffolded Approach to Curation

1. CRITIQUE – Media literacy education rests on the foundations of critical thinking (see Alvermann & Hagood, 2000; De Abreu & Mihailidis, 2014; Kellner & Share, 2005, 2007; Livingstone, 2004). The abundance of information online has made available more valuable, balanced, critical, and independent information. It has also brought the possibility for the uncritical consumer to collect mistakes, mistruths, and misinformation (Bartlett & Miller, 2011). Helping young citizens become critical thinkers empowers them to interact with traditional and new media in an increasingly productive, civic-minded way. The first step in the scaffolding approach to curation entails teaching students to think critically about the value of information they consume, and the manner and context of delivery establishes a foundation from which core media literacy competencies can flourish.

2. CONTRIBUTE – Youth primarily use social networks, aggregators, and mobile apps for information needs today. In turn, social networks have provided new functions that help users share information in meaningful and productive ways. Social networks, writes Shirky (2008),

> ...operate as both amplifiers and filters of information. Because information in the system is passed along by friends and friends and friends (or at least contacts and contacts of contacts), people tend to get information that is also of interest to their friends. The more friends you have who care about a particular piece of information—whether gossip or a job opening or a new song they like—the likelier you are to hear about it as well (p. 221).

Contributing, the second competency in the scaffolding model for curation, approaches the act of contribution as a self-reflective, audience-based experience, where individuals are able to "produce effective and responsible media messages" (Silverblatt, 2001, p. 120). In the digital age, producing messages is as simple as tweeting, posting, or sharing. For the networked crowd, contribution is a default–without contributions, the network will dissipate. Media literate crowds understand their contributions to public spaces as helping to define narratives, dialog, and topics of interest for a large group. They see the value of their contributions—whether humor, insight, or escape—as adding to a dynamic and eclectic group of voices collectively fueling the group's position, connectivity, and vibrancy. They are also aware of the potential harms of filter bubbles (Pariser, 2011), monitoring behavior online, and location-based data tracking.

3. COLLABORATE – The third rung on the curation scaffold is collaboration, which involves the behavioral shift from simply contributing meaningful and valuable content to an *active* form of cooperation. Participatory approaches to media literacy can be seen in the rich examples of collaborative spaces that exist today. *Kickstarter, Groupon, Carrotbmob, Charity Water*, and *Ushahidi* are only a few of the platforms that exist entirely around the collaborative capacities of citizens. Supporting great ideas, finding ways to benefit local organizations, or to voice opinions and track violence all take coordinated and collaborative effort between members of the network. Media literacy competencies must advocate for these "collaborationists," a term Jenkins (2006) coins, because they represent the nexus of participation and media culture.

4. CREATE – Lastly, the media literate curator must be able to create context to build a sense of connectedness and place in digital culture. We have to look no further than *YouTube* to see the creative potential for young citizens today. Over 100 hours of content are uploaded to this space every minute[1]. Citizens can now compete with networks for creativity, creation, and appropriation. Uploading diverse content—some original, some remixed—shows the development of an ecosystem of civic creations that provide a collective narrative about any range of searchable issues. In *Remix*, Lawrence Lessig (2008) writes that "using the tools of digital technology—even the simplest tools, bundled into the most innovative modern operating systems—anyone can begin to "write" using images, or music, or video. And using the facilities of a free digital network, anyone can share that writing with anyone else" (p. 69).

---

1 For Statistical details on YouTube, please see: http://www.youtube.com/yt/press/statistics.html.

Creation, in the context of media literacy, is about the capacity that youth have to produce, share, and appropriate "media" content in public spaces. Creation does not necessitate starting from scratch—as it may have been deemed in a pre-digital age—but includes the new ways in which media and information are repackaged, appropriated, and distributed. Creation also allows youth to take ownership of their capacity to produce and to understand foundations in critical message construction, distribution, and reception. "By creating their own productions," writes media literacy scholar Belinha De Abreu (2011), "[students] must now learn to conceptualize and critically think while being reflective of how audiences view texts" (p. 37). From memes to remixing, the media literate citizen takes advantage of their ability to create and share contributions, and recognizes the power that such relationships have for civic voices online (Erstad et al., 2007).

Conclusion: curation and learning in digital culture

> The future of digital culture—yours, mine, and ours—depends on how well we learn to use the media that have infiltrated, amplified, distracted, enriched, and complicated our lives. How you employ a search engine, stream video from your phonecam, or update your Facebook status matters to you and everyone, because the ways people use new media in the first years of an emerging communication regime can influence the way those media end up being used and misused for decades to come. – Howard Rheingold, *Net Smart*, 1.

In today's digital culture, youth have greater autonomy of their information and communication habits. In turn, as Rheingold notes above, this will dictate how new social platforms, tools and technologies are used and misused for time to come. As mobile platforms and peer-to-peer technologies increasingly facilitate the daily information and communication needs of youth today, educators must incorporate new models for critical navigation, inquiry and expression online.

This chapter positions curation as a core competency for digital and media literacy education. The four specific steps in our framework that lead to meaningful curation are not meant to be prescriptive, but rather offer different entry points and ideas for teaching about curation in a media literacy context. Students may be skilled online organizers but struggle with ways to collaborate. Others may be savvy creators of information but less understanding of the avenues for sharing information in mindful or thoughtful ways. Curation, in this sense, is not an end to a means, but rather a structured, methodical entry point for real engagement with digital media and personalized content today. Past models for media education that were premised on critical thinking as a response mechanism to media messages are no longer enough. In today's digital culture, media literacy must necessarily incorporate critical navigation and expression as parallel to analysis and evaluation. Curation is one way to approach this new landscape, and one increasingly relevant to a generation that is creating, sharing, and expressing more than ever before.

References

Alvermann, D. E., & Hagood, M. C. (2000). Critical media literacy: Research, theory, and practice in "New Times". *The Journal of Educational Research, 93*(3),193–205.

Aufderheide, P., & Firestone, C. M. (1993). *Media literacy: A report of the national leadership conference on media literacy*. Cambridge, UK: Polity Press.

Bartlett, J., & Miller, C. (2011). Truth, Lies and the Internet: A report into young people's digital fluency. *Demos*. Retrieved: http://www.demos.co.uk/files/Truth_-_web.pdf.

Bayne, S., & Ross, J. (2007). The 'digital native' and 'digital immigrant' debate: a dangerous opposition. Annual Conference of the Society for Research into Higher Education (SRHE), Brighton, UK, December, 2007.

Benkler, Y. (2005). *The wealth of networks: How social production transforms markets and freedom*. New Haven, CT & London, UK: Yale University Press.

Bennett, S., Maton, K., & Kervin, L. (2008). The 'digital natives' debate: A critical review of the evidence. *British Journal of Educational Technology, 39*(5), 775–786.

Bennett, W. L. (2008). *Civic life online*. Cambridge, MA: MIT Press.

Bergdoll, B. (1998). Curating history. *Journal of the Society of Architectural Historians, 57*(3), September, 257–366.

Bowman, L. L., Levine, L. E., Waite, B. M., & Gendron, M. (2010). Can students really multitask? An experimental study of instant messaging while reading. *Computers & Education, 54*, 927–931.

Brown, C., & Czerniewicz, L. (2010). Debunking the 'digital native': beyond digital apartheid towards digital democracy. *Journal of Computer Assisted Living, 26*, 357–369.

Buckingham, D. (2003). *Media education: Literacy, learning and contemporary culture*. Cambridge, UK: Polity Press.

Buckingham, D. (2007). Digital media literacies: Rethinking media education in the age of the Internet. *Research in Comparative and International Education, 2*(1), 43–55.

Cheliotis, G., & Yew, J. (2009). An analysis of the social structure of remix culture. In *Proceedings of the Fourth International Conference on Communities and Technologies* (pp. 165–174). University Park, PA: ACM.

De Abreu, B. (2011). *Media literacy, social networks, and the web 2.0 environment for the k-12 educator*. New York: Peter Lang.

De Abreu, B. & Mihailidis, P. (Eds.) (2014). *Media literacy education in action: Theoretical and pedagogical perspectives.* London: Routledge.

Diakopoulos, N. (2008). *Remix culture. Mixing up authorship*. Retrieved from www.cc.gatech.edu/~NAD.

Dybwad, B. (2005). *Approaching a definition of Web 2.0*. Retrieved from: http://socialsoftware.weblogsinc.com.

Erstad, O., Gilje, O., & de Lange, T. (2007). Re-mixing multimodal resources: Multiliteracies and digital production in Norwegian media education, *Learning, Media and Technology, 32/2,* 183–198.
Frechette, J. D. (2002). *Developing media literacy in cyberspace: Pedagogy and critical learning for the twenty-first-century classroom.* Westport, CT: Praegar.
Gaines, E. (2010). *Media literacy and semiotics*. New York: Palgrave.
Gordon, E. (2013). Beyond Participation: Designing for the Civic Web. *Journal of Digital and Media Literacy, 1*(1).
Hargittai, E. (2005). Survey measures of web-oriented digital literacy. *Social Science Computer Review, 23*, 371–379.
Hobbs, R. (2010). *"Digital and media literacy: A plan of action,"* A white paper on the digital and media literacy recommendations of the knight commission on the information needs of communities in a democracy. Washington DC: The Aspen Institute.
Hobbs, R. (2011). *Digital and media literacy: Connecting culture and classroom*. Thousand Oaks, CA: Corwin Press.
Hobbs, R., & Cooper Moore, D. (2013). *Discovering media literacy: Teaching digital media and popular culture in elementary school*. Thousand Oaks, CA: Corwin Press.
Ito, M. (2009). *Living and learning with new media: Summary of findings from the digital youth project.* Cambridge, MA: MIT Press.
Ito, M. (2010). *Hanging out, messing around, and geeking out*. Cambridge, MA: MIT Press.
Jenkins, H. (2006). *Convergence culture: Where old and new media collide*. New York, NY: New York University Press.
Jenkins, H. (2006b). Confronting the challenges of a participatory culture (part seven). Retrieved: http://henryjenkins.org/2006/10/confronting_the_challenges_of_6.html.
Jenkins, H. (2008). *Combating the participation gap: Why new media literacy matters* [Distinguished lecture]. UC Berkley School of Information. Retrieved from http://www.ischool.berkeley.edu/newsandevents/events/dls20080206.
Jenkins, H., Purushotma, R., Weigel, M., Clinton, K., & Robinson, A. J. (2009). Confronting the challenges of participatory culture: Media education for the 21st century, *A Report for the MacArthur Foundation,* Cambridge, MA: MIT Press.
Jones, C., Ramanau, R., Cross, S., & Healing, G. (2010). Net generation or digital Natives: Is there a distinct new generation entering university? *Computers & Education, 54*(3), 722–732.
Kahne, J., Lee, N., & Feezell, J.T. (2012). Digital media literacy education and online civic and political participation. *International Journal of Communication, 6*, 1–24.
Kellner, D., & Share, J. (2005). Towards critical media literacy: Core concepts, debates, organizations, and policy. *Discourse: Studies in the Cultural Politics of Education 26*(3), 369–386.
Kellner, D., & Share, J. (2007). Critical media literacy, democracy, and the reconstruction of education" In D. Macedo & S. R. Steinberg (Eds.). *Media literacy: A reader*. (pp. 3–23). New York: Peter Lang.
Kennedy, G., Dalgarno, B., Bennett, S., Judd, T., Gray, K., & Chang, R. (2008). Immigrants and natives: Investigating differences between staff and students' use of technology. In *Hello! Where are you in the landscape of educational technology?* Proceedings ascilite Melbourne 2008. Retrieved:http://www.ascilite.org.au/conferences/melbourne08/procs/kennedy.pdf.
Kuiper, E., & Volman, M. (2008). The Web as a source of information for students in K– 12 education. In J. Coiro, M. Knobel, C. Lankshear, & D. J. Leu (Eds.). *Handbook of research on new literacies.* Mahwah, NJ: Lawrence Erlbaum Associates, 241–266.

Lessig, L. (2008). *Remix: Making art and commerce thrive in a hybrid economy*. New York, NY: Penguin Press.

Livingstone, S. (2004). Media Literacy and the Challenge of New Information and Communication Technologies. *The Communication Review*, *7*(1), 3–14.

Leu, D., McVerry, J. G., O'Byrne, W. I., Kiili, C., Zawilinksi, L., Everett-Cacopardo, H., Kennedy, C., Forzani, E. (2011). The New Literacies of Online Reading Comprehension: Expanding the Literacy and Learning Curriculum. *Journal of Adolescent & Adult Literacy 55*(1), 5–14.

Mihailidis, Paul. (2011). (Re)Mix, (Re)Purpose, (Re)Learn: Using Participatory Tools for Media Literacy learning outcomes in the Classroom. *Action in Teacher Education, 33/2*, 1–12.

Mihailidis, P. (2014). *Media literacy and the emerging citizen: Youth, participation and engagement in the digital age.* NY: Peter Lang Publishers, *in press.*

Mihailidis, P., & Cohen, J. (2013). Exploring curation as a core digital and medialiteracy competency. *Journal of Interactive Media in Education,* Vol. 2, Spring.

OFCOM. (2005). *Media literacy audit. Report on media literacy amongst children*, Office of Communication. London. Retrieved: http://www.ofcom.org.uk/advice/media_literacy/medlitpub/medlitpubrss/children/children.pdf.

Pariser, E. (2011). *The filter bubble*. London: Penguin.

Potter, W. J. (2010). *Media literacy, 5th edition*. Thousand Oaks, CA: Sage.

Prensky, M. (2001). Digital natives, digital immigrants. *On the Horizon, 9*(5), 1–6.

Rheingold, H. (2012). *Net smart: How to thrive online.* Cambridge, MA: MIT Press.

Rheingold, H. (2008). Using participatory media and public voice to encourage civic engagement. In W. Lance Bennett (Ed.). *Civic life online: Learning how digital media can engage youth.* Cambridge, MA: MIT Press, 97–118.

Rosen, L. (2010). *ReWired: Understanding the igeneration and the way they learn.* New York: Palgrave Macmillan.

Sanchez, C. A., Wiley, J., & Goldman, S. R. (2006). Teaching students to evaluate source reliability during Internet research tasks. In S. A. Barab, K. E. Hay, & D. T. Hickey (Eds.). *Proceedings of the seventh international conference on the learning sciences*. Mahwah, NJ: Lawrence Erlbaum Associates, 662–666.

Schiebe, C., & Rogow, F. (2011). *The teacher's guide to media literacy: critical thinking in a multimedia world.* Thousand Oaks, CA: Corwin Press.

Share, J. (2009). *Media literacy is elementary: Teaching youth to critically read and create media.* New York: Peter Lang.

Shirky, Clay. (2008). *Here Comes Everybody: The Power of Organizing Without Organizations.* New York, NY: Penguin.

Shirky, C. (2010). *Cognitive surplus: Creativity and generosity in a connected age*. New York, NY: Penguin.

Silverblatt, A. (2001). *Media literacy: Keys to interpreting media messages*, 2nd edition. Westport, CT: Praeger.

Swiggum, K. (2008). Hyperworlds: The merging of generation "M," information and communication technologies, online safety, and medial literacy. *PNLA Quarterly, 72*(2), 14–18.

Taboada, A., & Guthrie, J. (2006). Contributions of student questioning and prior knowledge to construction of knowledge from reading information text. *Journal of Literacy Research, 38*(1), 1–35.

Thoman, E., & Jolls, T. (2005). Media literacy education: Lessons from the center for media literacy. *Yearbook of the National Society for the Study of Education, 104*(1), 180–205.

Thomas, M. (Ed). (2011). *Deconstructing digital natives*, New York: Routledge.

Tisdell, E. (2008). Critical media literacy and transformative learning. Drawing on pop culture and entertainment media in teaching for media diversity in adult higher education. *Journal of Transformative Education, 6*(1), 48–67.

Journalist Education and Truth in the Digital Age: Why We Need Critical Digital Literacy

Filip Lab, Alice N. Tejkalova

Abstract

The chapter deals with the importance of the concept of digital literacy in media education. Under digital literacy we understand a skill necessary for survival in the digital era, cognitive skills needed for solving problems connected with digital media production and existence in the online environment. The digital era has brought a wide spectrum of potentially problematic areas for media consumers as well as media producers. Our text illustrates these topics on a wide range of examples from current media, visual and social landscape. We address the issues connected with digital media, topics related to usage of social networks, alternative and counter-culture practices, etc. We try to illustrate potentially problematic issues of digital environment on the side of media producers, such as copyright and authorship protection, sources of information, its gathering, etc. The aim of this chapter is to show how the things surrounding us have radically changed in the last two decades and why this issue of digital literacy is important for the ability to orientate oneself in everyday life and why it should become the integral part of (not only journalistic and media) education.

Introduction

The purpose of this chapter is to introduce the importance of the concept of digital literacy in media education. With the rapid development of digital technologies and media there is a rising need for each individual to be able to use these technologies, to understand a wide range of new practices and to continually adapt to new features and functions of these innovations. Digital literacy concerns not only the everyday use of computers, cell phones and other digital devices, but a far more significant and complex existence online within different social networks. Contemporary practice not only involves abilities such as the construction of knowledge from non-linear information, but also more complex and complicated skills.

This literacy is particularly important in the field of journalism where most of the production of news content is more or less digital. Working with information sources, the ways of gathering, retrieving, sorting and evaluating information has changed completely. Education in the area of digital literacy is one of the basic demands of people working in the news industry, including journalists, photojournalists as well as media scholars.

Within the term, digital literacy, we understand the skills necessary for survival in the digital era, cognitive skills essential to solving problems connected with digital media production and existence in an online environment. We take for granted that digital literacy should be a part of contemporary regular media related curriculum. The digital era has brought a wide spectrum of potentially problematic areas for media consumers as well as media producers. Because we are also lecturers of journalism and media studies, we will illustrate these topics with a range of examples from current Czech media, visual and social landscapes.

The aim of this paper is to show the important connection between digital literacy and the ability to orient oneself in everyday life and why it should become an integral part of (not only journalistic and media) education.

Media literacy in the education of 21st century journalists

With the rise of digital electronic media we are witnessing new ways of production, distribution and reception of an unimaginably large amount of media content. Hand in hand with the rapid proliferation of media content comes the question of quality of information, sources and channels. These changes significantly influence our everyday media consumption experience, but even more problematize the area of media production. Media consumption is becoming an integral part of our everyday lives as the rate of consumption is higher than ever before. The importance of visually represented information and communication is increasing as well. The problem now is not the access to information, but the ability to effectively use it. Media literacy is a useful umbrella concept covering a wide range of disciplines, using research methods, approaches and concepts from sociology, political science, psychology, gender studies, cultural studies as well as aesthetics and art.

A wide range of definitions of media literacy exists, bringing diverse perspectives. Defined as, "critical autonomy relationship to all media," by Aufderheide in her well known definition, media literacy specifies the ability to decode, evaluate, analyse and produce media of all kinds. The possibility to become a media literate person should be accessible to everyone. Media literacy is defined as a movement designed to help understand, produce and negotiate meaning in cultural production (Aufderheide, 1992). A very close view is shared by the European Commission, which stresses the critical aspects and also acknowledges media production as well as reception (European Commission, 2007).

Media literacy in digital environment is usually understood as digital literacy, under which we understand a set of skills required to solve problems and perform tasks in digital environments (Gilster, 1997; Lenham, 1995; Tapscott, 1998). The centrality of technologies in literacy is another important aspect of media literacy research (Kress, 2009; Snyder and Beavis, 2004). A wider survey of media literacy definitions and approaches was conducted by Koltay (2011) with focus on media literacy as well as information literacy and digital literacy.

For our purposes, the relationship between media literacy and education is the most interesting. The definition of media literacy by the National Association of Media Literacy Education emphasizes the educational aspect:

> Media literacy: The ability to ACCESS, ANALYZE, EVALUATE, and COMMUNICATE information in a variety of forms-is interdisciplinary by nature. Media literacy represents a necessary, inevitable, and realistic response to the complex, ever-changing electronic environment and communication cornucopia that surround us. To become a successful student, responsible citizen, productive worker, or competent and conscientious consumer, individuals need to develop expertise with the increasingly sophisticated information and entertainment media that address us on a multi-sensory level, affecting the way we think, feel, and behave. (NAMLE, 2013)

According to other definitions oriented toward education, media literacy should help students understand how media produce content, how are media organized and how they construct reality, but also to increase students' enjoyment and understanding of the media. This all should go together with obtaining the skills and knowledge needed in media content production process (Gutiérrez Martin and Hottmann, 2001). New digital aesthetics and the new social effects of digitalization and the necessity to include them in media literacy educational programs are subjects of interest to Pollard and Olason (2004).

In a Czech context, media literacy is a long term subject of interest to our colleagues, Jan Jirak and Radim Wolak, also focused on media literacy in general, the relationship between media literacy and general education, and functions of media literacy and media practice (2007).

The importance of digital literacy in the education of a 21st century journalist has several significant aspects. First, because of the omnipresent electronic technologies in our lives, there is the necessity to master the quickly appearing new technologies, to adopt the new digital environments and networks and to adapt to new tools, which are all the fundamental conditions for journalists to be able to perform their jobs. This is also the most common aspect of media literacy in journalism education. This technocentric approach to educational process in general is often criticised as economically and technologically driven, elitist and repurposing education toward functionalist ends (Ferneding, 2003; Selwyn, 2011). The second aspect, often overshadowed by over attention to the importance of mastering the new technologies, involves the legal and ethical issues that have risen under new digital conditions. Since the beginning of the digital era, journalists have been facing whole new sets of problems, such as brand new possibilities of manipulation of information, for example in photojournalism (e.g. Newton, 2001; Wheeler, 2002; Munro, 2006) and new fields of journalism such as data journalism (Gray, 2012). Legal aspects go hand in hand with these technologically enabled new fields, covering an entire new range of issues, questioning traditional concepts of copyright protection, privacy policy, protection of personality, dissolving the border between private and public. All these examples are challenging the traditional aspects of journalists' everyday work.

Changing of working patterns and routines

Although the technocentric approach in media research has been repeatedly challenged, we cannot deny that changing technology (along with social changes) has had several implications for the work of journalists. Within the past two decades journalists all over the world have been changing their working routines and patterns under the influence of digital media. They have been both creating those media and influenced by the digital environment. It does not matter whether the journalists work for online media or for print or audio-visual ones that have their websites or 24/7 news channels, it is unimaginable they would write or broadcast just one piece of news per day as used to be standard in the past. They have to write or broadcast a couple of them.

The impact of financial recession is also strongly tied to changing work patterns, as for example Picard (2013) reminds:

> All the companies expanded and some commercial firms, particularly in North America, took on heavy debt on the expectation the good times would continue (Picard 2006). They did not, of course, and the structures and costs developed in the wealthier era can no longer be maintained; hence, the cutbacks and downsizing. (Picard 2013: 21)

It is definitely also the problem of media companies in the Czech Republic. In some cases, for example in audio-visual media, this leads to the consolidation of positions, as journalists have to be able to also take pictures and edit the reports with specialized software, another trend we need to consider in journalism education.

Nevertheless, the pressure on journalists to be as quick as possible to publish their stories to succeed in the competition and at the same time being overloaded by the tasks (a lot of journalists complain about their staff being undersized) bring a number of issues that need to be further discussed in the context of needed innovation in journalist education. These issues include problems of information literacy, dealing with social networks and theft of content.

Problems of information literacy

The problem facing today's journalist is not having access to information but, quite the opposite, being able to find and select quality information from a wealth of information, being able to decide which sources are to be trusted and which not. The digital environment changed the nature and character of information and media business as well. Access to media is now much easier than ever before, as we can see in the phenomena of citizen journalism, hyperlocal journalism and media activism of different kinds, but also in very simple media hoaxes, fake information and fake articles. Social networks can work as both watchdogs of these phenomena as well as channels of their wide distribution.

The Czech media landscape is not very often subject to the attempts of media activists as other western countries are used to (e.g. actions of media activists known as TheYesMen). However one instance occurred during the summer of 2007 when the group of Czech artists and activists, Ztohoven,[1] made an intrusion into the live broadcasting of national Czech Television and its weather report programme, Panorama. Using basic office equipment (a laptop, video-editing software) they were able to change the official broadcasting with their own content, so instead of a panoramic view of Czech landscape, viewers watched an explosion of an atomic bomb on their TV sets.

> On June 17th 2007 our group invaded media and television territory, intruded and impeached its trueness as well as its credibility. Pointed out the possible confusion of the media presented picture of our world for the real one. Is everything that our media such as newspapers, television, internet offer on a daily basis real truth or reality? It is this idea that our project is to introduce to the general public, a sort of reminder to everyone. We truly believe that the independent territory of television governed by public law is that kind of media which can handle such a thing even at the cost of self impeachment.[2]

This provocative act did open questions about how the media is protected against such acts, and how we can trust the media This example was part artistic action and part attack on the media, but raised discussion about the standards of Czech journalism.

In 2010 there was the case of a fake presidential letter written by a group of political activists called Hradni Particka (Prague Castle Posse).[3] This congratulation by former Czech president Vaclav Klaus to director of Czech National Gallery Milan Knizak has been republished by several Czech media outlets. Another fake presidential letter from

---

1 www.ztohoven.com.

2 Ztohoven. The Media Reality. http://www.ztohoven.com/?page_id=45&lang=en. Cit. 2013-04-30.

3 Prof. Klaus blahopreje prof. Knizakovi k 70. narozeninám. http://www.hradniparticka.cz/2010/04/prof-vaclav-klaus-blahopreje-prof.html. 20th April 2010. Cit. 2013-04-30.

a parodic website was republished by several mainstream media (e.g. news portal www.parlamentnilisty.cz, or conservative right wing magazine www.fragmenty.cz), despite the fact that the letter contained very explicit and provocative expressions. Both of these examples were kinds of tests to determine how the mainstream media works with sources and fact checking (quite similar to the practice of TheYesMen – www.gatt.org).

A more serious mistake happened in September 2012 during reportage on the so called "assassination" of Czech president, Vaclav Klaus, when a protester shot the president with an airsoft gun. This in fact innocent incident was largely covered by the media, and an item of the exclusive material broadcast a day after the incident (29th September 2012 on the biggest private national station, TV Nova) included a video of the incident with a recording of bodyguard communication. Later it was revealed that it was faked and none such material existed (the communication between bodyguards is crypted, making it impossible to record).[4] In all three of these cases, the media published the inaccurate content without any problems, later blaming external factors for their own failure.

Another interesting example, which we use as an exemplary case study during our lectures, is the case of politician, Jaromir Petelik. On 27th October 2012 the Czech tabloid newspaper, Blesk, published an article with the title, "Red Man in Town Hall – Hang the Rightists", with a screenshot of the politician's alleged Facebook profile.[5] In the following hours another tabloid news server, Novinky.cz, republished the article and then several "serious" media followed suit as well (iHned.cz, CT24.cz, Tyden, etc.). A day after this incident, it was revealed that the screenshot was faked.

> I suppose that in times when social networks are becoming more and more the only sources of information, it is quite alarming that journalists are not able to reveal these kinds of hoaxes, especially, when it is so obvious and trivial as this one. I am glad that the media reacted to this situation after publishing this article, and I hope they will pay more attention to internet information sources,

comments media journalist, Michal Zlatkovsky, on the situation.[6]

---

4 Zaznam Klausovy ochranky je mozna falesny, rika inspekce. http://www.tyden.cz/rubriky/domaci/zaznam-klausovy-ochranky-je-mozna-falesny-rika-inspekce_247711.html. 1st October 2012. Cit. 2013-04-30.

5 Pravicaky povesit a podnikatele vyvlastnit, pise se na facebooku pod jmenem komunisty Petelika. http://www.blesk.cz/clanek/zpravy-politika/184260/pravicaky-povesit-a-podnikatele-vyvlastnit-pise-se-na-facebooku-pod-jmenem-komunisty-petelika.html. 27th October 2012. Cit. 2013-04-30.

6 Michal Zlatkovsky. Jak dlouho trva zmanipulovat media? Necelych pet minut. http://www.mediar.cz/jak-dlouho-trva-zmanipulovat-media-necelych-pet-minut/. 28th October 2012. Cit. 2013-04-30.

Social networks as sources of information

Social networks are quite often used as sources of information by Czech journalists, as they are by many all over the world. Social networks can accelerate the work of a journalist and lead to exclusive information. "Even though I was not in London, but in Prague, I knew personal and interesting information for my comments from Facebook profiles of Czech athletes," says a 26-year-old sports journalist covering the Paralympic Games 2012 for Ceska televize (Czech Television).

Although Czechs have used Facebook extensively for several years, it was not common until last year to see, for example, quotations of athletes referenced as having been got from Facebook in the media. It is hard to say why this acceptance of Facebook by the media has occurred so recently. Perhaps it stems from the fact that in the beginning, the media covered the Facebook phenomenon as some weird thing that steals people's time they should be better committing to their work.[7] So it was hard to admit that those who criticized were actually also doing the same thing. Later the atmosphere changed and more Facebook-friendly articles were printed[8] and references to Facebook began to appear. On one of the five main Czech news servers www.ihned.cz we can even find a new section called "Sportovci na sitich" (Athletes within networks) that contains only information published on social networks by famous athletes from all over the world.

Twitter is not very popular in the Czech Republic, especially in comparison with Facebook. While Facebook is used by more than 3.5 million Czechs, there are just slightly over 165 thousand Twitter users in our country together with our neighbouring Slovaks[9]. So Twitter still generates the potential of bringing something "surprising" to the "mainstream" media audience. It proved the case when the Thursday supplement of the main Czech non-tabloid daily, Mlada fronta DNES, at the beginning of this year published an interview with the host of one of the political debates during the presidential campaign in the format of tweets.[10] It was meant to demonstrate the importance that was attributed to social networks during the presidential campaign (it was the first time the president of the Czech

7 E. g. Kvita, Milan. Facebook – pojdme zabijet cas spolecne. Ovsem.net. http://www.ovsem.net/ruzne/facebook-pojdme-zabijet-cas-spolecne/. 7th June 2009. Cit. 2013-04-30.

8 E. g. Bednar, Vojtech. Facebook umi byt uzitecny. Pomaha hledat krev dobrovolnych darcu. iHNed.cz. http://tech.ihned.cz/c1-52043490-facebook-umi-byt-uzitecny-pomaha-hledat-krev-dobrovolnych-darcu. 8th June 2011. Cit. 2013-04-30.

9 http://www.klaboseni.cz/vyvojpoctu.php, cit. 2013-04-27.

10 Polacek, Tomas. Volby ve 140 znacich. Magazin Mlade fronty DNES. Praha: MAFRA, a. s. 31st January 2013.

Republic could be elected directly by all voters, not just by members of parliament) by many political analysts and journalists.[11]

There still are, however, journalists in the Czech Republic who have not yet joined social networks or have joined them because they have to, but do not feel comfortable with it. A 47-year-old editor of a TV news programme for children, who used to work also as a foreign correspondent and the editor of the main news programme, says:

> I created a Facebook page for our programme because we were looking for some regular, frank feedback from the audience, and for almost 2 years had just random emails. When I made the webpage, the feedback started to be slightly better, but it was Facebook that gave it the spin, regularity and better quality for us. But I have to admit I am too old for Facebook, I see it as a waste of time, for me it is just a tool to connect with the audience to get better feedback for my work.

What we always stress when speaking with our students about social networks and using them as a source for news and articles is that they cannot be the only source of information. This is simply because things do not really happen there, things happen in the "real" world. We highlight "critical autonomy" as accented by Aufderheide (1992). Some campaigns and events can start online, but you need to track them in "reality", however socially constructed it is.

We also try to show students that their fascination with the novelty and rapidness of the communication that is almost always associated with so called new media is just a matter of interpretation. Take, for example, David Morley (2007) and other sceptical media oriented scientists who highlight the fact that when the era of writing came everyone was fascinated and it was the same with book printing, the telegraph, telephone, photography, radio, television, internet, etc. Every time period has its new media, but it continues to be used for the very oldest purpose – to transmit a message. But what each new communication invention brings is a quicker and more precise transmission over longer distances.

That said, it is far easier now than it was, for example, 50 years ago, to cause some affair or mischievous misunderstanding when "posted" information is picked and published without verification (due to rapid time pressure and online intermedia competition).

---

11 E.g. Kasik, Pavel. Za uspech Schwarzenberga mohou socialni site. Karla je plny Facebook. idnes.cz. http://technet.idnes.cz/internet-volby-prezidenta-d03-/sw_internet.aspx?c=A130112_184201_sw_internet_pka. 12th January 2013. Cit. 2013-04-30. Lidovky.cz, CTK. Ovlivnil Facebook a Twitter výsledky voleb? Lidovky.cz. http://www.lidovky.cz/cesky-internet-rezonuje-vysledky-prvniho-kola-prezidentske-volby-1f4-/media.aspx?c=A130113_133855_ln-media_hm. 13rd January 2013. Cit. 2013-04-30.

Legally OK?

Authorship of information "published" on social networks is also a frequent topic we discuss with our students. One can never know for sure who the author is of anything published online without "real" verification of it. The issue of online authorship is connected with the issue of copyright law, which is another problematic field in current Czech journalism.

One of the projects that highlighted this topic in recent months in the Czech Republic was a weekly, Agenda[12]. It was published twice by the publishing house, Sanoma, and their creators (almost all of them journalists specializing in topics connected with media) later admitted it was meant as a test of other journalists' reactions from other media and a demonstration of how stealing media content works in the Czech Republic, usually not publicly declared. Some journalists later published their doubts as to the creators' intent and thought the authors really meant it, claiming that after the wave of criticism they withdrew and tried to mask it with the "project".[13] Nevertheless, what is important for us is that it really shed light on this matter often discussed in academic circles (e.g. Trampota and Necas, 2007), but practised without hesitation in the media.

Following the publication of the two issues of Agenda in question, a conference was held by the authors of the magazine at the beginning of April 2013. It was called Pravne je to OK (Legally OK) and focused on how topics and news are copied from both Czech and international media by Czech journalists. The media analyst and journalist, Ondrej Aust,[14] opened the conference by declaring that thanks to monitoring the Czech media he had found the 10 most common ways content is stolen. According to his research, the Czech media publish daily just 15 % of their exclusive content, while all other content is found somewhere else and more or less modified. News servers, for example, reword news from other Czech servers, sometimes with a short credit to the server or translate news from foreign servers (and do not cite them). Thus the same quotations and sentences can be found in different types of media.[15] But legally it is OK.

---

12 Agenda should have been a weekly, inspired by the British, The Week, the motto of which was: "The best of media: from print to Facebook." It was filled with information from other media that was "quoted there", fulltext versions of articles with pictures. More information: https://www.facebook.com/TydenikAgenda, cit. 2013-04-28.

13 E.g. Slizek, David. Tydenik Agenda byl pry viralem, ktery ma vzbudit diskusi o citacich v mediich. Lupa.cz. http://www.lupa.cz/clanky/tydenik-agenda-byl-pry-viralem-ktery-ma-vzbudit-diskusi-o-citacich-v-mediich/, 25th March 2013, cit. 2013-04-30.

14 He is the editor-in-chief of www.mediar.cz, a server oriented toward what is going on in the media.

15 Hutnik, Matous. (2013). Ti, kteri kradou, a ti, kterym to nevadi. In *Fles*, vol. 20, no. 9. Prague: Faculty of Social Sciences, p. 2. (in Czech)

We mentioned above that social networks can generate exclusive information, but it remains harder and harder to get any as more and more people are interconnected. This is especially so in the Czech Republic, inhabited by slightly over 10 million people, with 5 nationwide dailies and 1 nationwide but regionally oriented daily, 1 big public radio broadcaster and 2 more private news radios and 1 public and 3 commercial nationwide TV companies. The number of journalists is quite low[16] as is "V.I.P." sources of information. Further, it is clear that politicians who actively use their Facebook or Twitter accounts want to have "friends" among as many journalists as possible and vice versa. So then the publication of "exclusive" information merely depends on the ability of the journalist to copy something as quickly as possible to his or her article. And it is not much, according to our opinion.

Resume

Today the biggest problem of a journalist is no longer access to information, but exactly the opposite – how to choose from the immense variety of information available what is relevant, how to select trusted sources of information. With various cases from the contemporary Czech media landscape we have tried to show how important these issues are as a part of journalism curriculum. We are trying to give our students at least a basic introduction to the very complex area of media literacy, not limited only to the examples shown here, but also in the areas of visual literacy, digital literacy and information literacy.

There are several problems to consider within the digitalized Czech media landscape, the most striking one being orientation in the inordinate amount of data available. Additional problems include sources of information and their credibility. Czech journalists very often republish articles from other media sources without paying closer attention to their content. „Stealing" of topics and sometimes even parts of texts among journalists is another intimately linked issue.

In other potential areas of media literacy the Czech media landscape remains a bit behind other countries, e.g. citizen journalism is not a very common practice in the Czech Republic. This was clearly visible during a huge explosion in Prague on 29th April 2013, which also strongly hit the building of our faculty in the centre of the city. The only citizen journalism contribution about this event was created

---

16 From research on the population from which we sampled for the Worlds of Journalism Study (www.worldsofjournalism.org), in 2012, we found the total number of people who work both full time and more than 50% of their working time in political news departments to be 1191.

by a colleague of ours, new media guru and journalist, Milos Cermak, who posted an image from the moments after the explosion on his Twitter account just a few minutes after the blast[17].

References

Aufderheide, P. (1992). *Media Literacy: A Report of the National Leadership Conference on Media Literacy*. Washington, DC: Aspen Institute. Available online April 2013 at: http://www.medialit.org/reading_room/article356.html.

Boorstin, D. J. (2012). *The Image: A Guide to Pseudo-Events in America.* New York: Vintage Books, ISBN 978-0-307-81916-1.

Das, R. (2011). Converging perspectives in audience studies and digital literacies: Youthful interpretations of an online genre. *European Journal of Communication*, 2011, 26: 343.

European Commission (2007). *A European Approach to Media Literacy in the Digital Environment*. Available April 2013 online at: http://ec.europa.eu/avpolicy/media_literacy/docs/com/en.pdf.

Ferneding, K. A. (2003). *Questioning Technology: electronic technologies and educational reform*. Peter Lang.

Hutnik, Matous. (2013). Ti, kteri kradou, a ti, kterym to nevadi. *Fles*, vol. 20, no. 9. Prague: Faculty of Social Sciences, p. 2. (in Czech)

Gutiérrez Martín A. G. and Hottmann, A. (2006). *Media Education across the Curriculum*. Kulturring in Berlin e.V. Available online April 2013 at: http://www.mediaeducation.net/resource/pdf/downloadMEACbooklet.pdf.

Gilster, P. (1997). *Digital literacy*. New York: Wiley.

Lenham, R. (1995). Digital literacy. *Scientific American*, 273, 253–255.

Tapscott, D. (1998). *Growing up digital*. New York: McGraw-Hill.

Gray, J., Chambers, L., Bounegru, L. (2012). *The Data Journalism Handbook*. O'Reilly Media.

Hull, G., and Schultz, K. (2001). Literacy and learning out of school: A review of theory and research. *Review of Educational Research 71*(4): 575–611.

Jirak, J, and Wolak, R. (ed.). *Medialni gramotnost: novy rozmer vzdelavani*. 1. vyd. Praha: Radioservis, 2007. 152 s. ISBN 978-80-86212-58-6. (in Czech)

Koltay, T. (2011). The media and the literacies: media literacy, information literacy, digital literacy. In *Media, Culture &Society*, 33: 211.

Kress, G. (2009). So what is learning, actually? Social change, technological change and a continuing place for the school? In Livingstone S (ed.) *Digital Literacies: Tracing the Implications for Learners and Learning*. ESRC Seminar Series: The Educational and Social Impact of New Technologies on Young People in Britain. Bristol: ESRC.

Livingstone, S., and Haddon, L. (2009). *Introduction*. In Livingstone S and Haddon L (eds.). *Kids Online: Opportunities and Risk for Children*. London: Policy Press.

Messaris, P. (2001). Visual culture. In J. Lull (Ed.), *Culture in the communication age.* London: Routledge.

17 https://twitter.com/cermak/status/328781940834586624.

Morley, D. (2007). *Media, Modernity and Technology: The Geography of the New*. New York: Routledge.
Munro, N. (2006). Real or fake?, *National Journal*, 4/8/2006, vol. 38 issue 14.
National Association For Media Literacy Education (2013). *Media Literacy Defined*. Available April 2013 online at: http://namle.net/publications/media-literacy-definitions/.
Newton, H. J. (2001). *The Burden of visual truth: the role of photojournalism in mediating reality.* Mahwah: Lawrence Erlbaum Associates, 2001.
Olson, S. R., and Pollard, T. (2004). The Muse Pixelope: Digitalization and Media Literacy Education. *American Behavioral Scientist*, 48: 248.
Picard, R. (2013). Killing journalism? The economics of media convergence. In Nienstedt, H.-W. – Russ-Mohl, S. – Wilczek, B. (eds.). *Media Convergence/Medienkonvergenz*. Berlin, Boston: Walter de Gruyter. pp. 19–27.
Selwyn, N. (2011). *Education and technology. Key issues and debates*. Continuum.
Snyder, I., and Beavis, C. (2004). *Doing Literacy Online: Teaching, Learning and Playing in an Electronic World*. New York: Hampton Press.
Trampota, T., and Necas, V. (2007). Intermedialni agenda ceskych medii. *Nase spolecnost*, vol. 5, no. 2, pp. 24–32. ISSN 1214-438X. (in Czech)
Wheeler, H. T. (2002). *Phototruth or Photofiction? Ethics and Media Imagery in the Digital Age.* Mahwah: Lawrence Erlbaum Associates, 2002. ISBN 0805842616.

Bowling Online: A Critical View of Social Capital and Virtual Communities

Melissa Harness & Sultana A. Shabazz

> *Trust is the expectation that arises within a community of regular, honest, and cooperative behavior, based on commonly shared norms; on the part of other members of that community ... Social capital is a capability that arises from the prevalence of trust in a society or in certain parts of it. It can be embodied in the smallest and most basic social group, the family, as well as the largest of all groups, the nation, and in all the other groups in between.*
>
> (Francis Fukuyama: 1996)

Abstract

In 1995, Robert Putnam introduced his theory of social capital in *Bowling Alone: America's Declining Social Capital.* Furthering his research, in 2000, he published *Bowling Alone: The Collapse and Revival of American Community*, in which Putnam attempts to explain how and why Americans' social capital has consistently declined in the wake of the 1960's era. Putnam's uses his main argument to demonstrate how the United States, historically recognized as a leader in democratic civic engagement, is in danger of reaching critically deficient levels of social capital, thus leading to a society that no longer trusts or knows its own members. This chapter seeks out a modern relevance for Putnam's concept of social capital in a nation increasingly defined by hyper-realism and virtual lives. In engaging some of the critiques of this particular iteration of social capital, we engage with hidden discourses of marginality and historical contextuality, the effect of dis-association and individualism on the development of communal bonds, and implications for virtual social capital. In the end, we suggest the possibility of a paradigm shift that is reflective of the faceted selves we embody today – where identities lie along a continuum from communal to virtual and technology facilitates choices about engagement and responsibility.

Introduction

In 1995, Robert Putnam introduced his theory of social capital in *Bowling Alone: America's Declining Social Capital.* Furthering his research, in 2000, he published his book *Bowling Alone: The Collapse and Revival of American Community*, in which Putnam attempts to explain how and why America's social capital has consistently declined in the wake of the 1960's era. Putnam's uses his main argument to demonstrate how the United States, historically recognized as a leader in democratic civic engagement, is in danger of reaching critically deficient levels of social capital, thus leading to a society that no longer trusts or knows its own members.

However, much controversy has surrounded Putnam's work in the last decade. Some critics point to Putnam's negligence of interpersonal networks outside of more traditional organizations, as well as the sometimes ambiguous logic and use of the term *social* capital (Fischer, 2001). Other critiques come from within a post – modernist and feminist framework, calling attention to the social reality and marginalized discourses in Putnam's work. Additionally, many disagree with his categorization of technology as anathema to the development of social capital and a civic populace.

Our purpose, with Putnam's particular construction and application of social capital in mind, is to address those arguments by bringing the core of Putnam's research into a modern historical context focused on the nexus of 1) social capital as structured within spaces of power – recognizing those discourses marginalized in Bowling Alone; 2) the effect of dis – association and individualism on the development of communal bonds; and 3) the emergence of virtual communities (specifically Massively Multiplayer Online Roleplaying Games – MMORPG) as new arenas for social connectivity pushing the boundaries of what is meant by community. Further, by investigating whether these new digital environments add to a sense of social engagement or operate as hyper – realism – simulacra replacing *in vivo* the real – we hope to establish if social capital itself has become a relic of a post- modern virtual world or if it has been replaced by a type of *virtual social capital*, one that bleeds over into the real world creating a new definition of community.

The foundations of social capital

According to Putnam (1995: 19), social capital 'refers to connections among individuals – social networks and the norms of reciprocity and trustworthiness that arise from them'. Putnam contends that social capital is of great importance for both communities and society in general, acting as a force that those within particular societies can draw upon to solve problems within their own communities. Underlying this centrality is the realization that '... social networks have value. Just as a screwdriver (physical capital) or a college education (human capital) can increase productivity (both individual and collective), so too social contacts affect the productivity of individuals and groups' (1995: 18). Putnam holds that social capital is the oxygen that keeps the organism of community alive and vibrant.

Putnam provides evidence for the decline of social capital over the course of the last several decades by using traditional social organizations, such as bowling leagues and the girl scouts, as his historical touchstones. Since the 1960's, the decline in political knowledge, voting and memberships in various organizations is alarming in American society. Instead of bonding together to demonstrate unity and camaraderie, what Putnam (2000: 82) calls the 'cult of individual' has developed.

However, any discussion of social capital becomes complicated when its value is constructed in a segregated pre- 1960's American landscape, where many women and most people of color were not allowed to join unions or fraternal organizations. Social capital – especially its manifestations linked to economic gains – does not favor those who are excluded or marginalized in the social sphere. Measurement in Putnam's pre – 1960's America then becomes analogous to giving an assessment of academic performance to the college – track students in a school, and then reporting on how well your student population is doing, which at the time consisted primarily of white middle – class males.

This concern is reflected in Putnam's discussion of two types of social capital: *bonds* and *bridges*. Bonding social capital includes associations between persons who are already similar to one another, and it has the effect of reinforcing identities. On the other hand, bridging social capital characterizes connections between individuals from different stations of life. Putnam indicates the greater desirability of the latter, in comparison to the former: it is bridging social capital which allows individuals to generate broader identities and connect with others who may not be like them. Although bridging social capital is lauded by Putnam, it is necessary to acknowledge the structural forces that affected such implementation in the 1960's.

According to Fischer (2001: 7), 'Putnam's distinction between "bridging" and "bonding" types of social capital (better phrased as bridging versus in-bound social networks) reinforces a contrast between public and private rather than a contrast between social and asocial.' While Fischer marks a valid distinction, we have to go further to look at how that public/private contrast gets performed in social spaces.

The public/private divide, as noted by many feminist scholars (Lather, 1987; Martin, 1982), becomes gendered in popular discourse to connote male/female, and this gendered rendering of the female presence in Putnam's work (acknowledged by the author) does not fully engage with who gets to name and/or claim social capital. It is not a distinction addressed by Putnam, although he does review the position of women in reference to their effects on participation in typical women's organizations. However, once he concludes that women are not the root cause of the decline in social capital within America, the conversational focus is swiftly shifted back to men. This gender – neutrality hides the position of women/wives on the private side of the divide as their identities become subsumed in their public partners' place in the social and roles as citizens (Prokhovnik, 1998).

Further, people of color in a pre – 1960's America had a very different social experience as well. Many of the social organizations and activities examined by Putnam – for example, voting and union membership – were highly prohibitive, if not directly illegal, for people of color (Oldendorf, 1990). Although there was much in the way of community interaction in segregated Black neighborhoods – like adult education programs in the South that focused on literacy, health, and job training for a generalized social betterment (Franklin, 1990; Williams, 1990; Neverdon – Morton, 1990) – marginalization within the greater society troubles Putnam's usage of bridging social capital. A closer reading of Putnam's description helps to explain how this contention should be understood.

Referring to 'individuals from different stations in life' demarcates class distinctions – a distinction more easily made in the absence of race (with white females already subsumed into the male). This lays the groundwork for inter – class bridging and community building without troubling the segregationist discourse of the times. If nothing else, combining a feminist critique with a critical race studies frame (Delgado and Stefancic, 2001) would open space for recognizing the need to restructure the parameters of social capital to reflect the totality of the social base.

The rise of dis-association and the cult of individualism

After establishing that social capital has been in decline for several decades now with the use of empirical data, Putnam then shifts to determining contributing factors. He considers a number of possible culprits, including the entrance of women into the workforce, pressures associated with time and money, as well as the effects of increased mobility and urban sprawl. A growing number of women, adding work time outside the home to their regular domestic responsibilities, would seem to imply fewer available resources left over for civic engagement or participation in social organizations. Men, too, were finding themselves spending longer hours at work and in commutes, as the upwardly mobile moved out into suburban neighborhoods. However, none of these prove to be the primary cause of the decline. In the end, Putnam settles upon two explanations for the decline of American social capital: generational change and the rise in television viewership.

Essentially, Putnam argues that our grandfathers' and grandmothers' generation was, in a certain sense, very special. They were forced to endure many hardships, including the Great Depression and WWII. And, as a result of these extreme tribulations, they developed into a generation of individuals who appeared to be very civically oriented. The children of the Baby Boomers' and subsequent generations have grown up with the ideas of materialism and corporatism firmly implanted into their psyches, which has led to the deterioration of community life in America. This argument, however, requires us to quantify concepts such as hardship, tribulations, and extreme duress. Could we not argue that historical moments like the Civil Rights' era, the Vietnam War, or 9/11 also had jarring impacts on people's lives and influenced their perceptions of others, society, and their role in society? Additionally, research by Fischer (2001) questions whether levels of civic engagement have actually decreased or simply changed forms.

Indeed, it may be this changed representation that is at the heart of Putnam's second explanation. He surmises that increased television viewership leads to less of almost every form of civic participation and social involvement. Why is this the case? Putnam provides three possibilities: television vies for limited time, television could have psychological effects which cause civic isolation and programming content could weaken civic participation. As already mentioned, time (specifically leisure time) quickly became a shrinking commodity by the 1970's. Shifting patterns of mobility not only led to longer commutes but also added distance between families and more traditional forms of social engagement, from lodge halls to neighborhood watering holes and churches. Television, with its explosion of content, became a powerful competitor for limited leisure time. Putnam claims that television causes civic isolation and that it has a deleterious effect on civic participation, which are both indicative of dis-association and the rise of the cult of the individual.

Once again, we find it helpful to contextualize the situation. John Brehm and Wendy Rahn (1997) in *Individual – Level Evidence for the Causes and Consequences of Social Capital* claim that individuals in America face incentives for acting selfishly in society. They examine in this article social capital based on an individual level, and examine issues concerning democratic institutions and issues pertaining to hegemony within American society.

Dis – association rises when individual citizens in America essentially ask for the benefits of social capital without paying the costs or actually wanting to engage in activities that would create social capital in the first place; thus, creating 'inescapable conflict between the interests and desires of individuals and the requirements of society' (Brehm and Rahn: 999). This claim of individual unregulated self-interest is the problem that the authors say is the major issue at play, not the decline in the amount of social capital within America that Putnam had originally proposed.

This unregulated self – interest is what is leading many in American society to be distrustful of others around them. It is fostered by competition among members of society over economic pursuits and wealth attainment – competition that has increased dramatically as individuals face the increased pressure of globalization. Thus, Brehm and Rahn (1997: 1009) hypothesize that 'income inequality and levels of unemployment diminish individual levels of interpersonal trust' and thus individuals in society begin to see others that they may have trusted as competitors. Essentially, when society's rewards become inequitably dispersed, 'people may begin to feel exploited by others, thus diminishing their faith in their fellow citizen' (1997: 1009).

For Brehm and Rahn, the reciprocal relationship is what most directly represents the social capital idea. Citizens who participated in their communities outside of their individual neighborhoods and became part of a broader picture beyond themselves, had very positive outlooks about helpfulness, trustworthiness and equity among their peers and fellow human beings. However, Brehm and Rahn struggle with the ideas that social capital is the main contributing factor to a decline in communal relations in American society.

Toward a paradigm shift: virtual social capital and beyond

David Kong and Marqus Theodore (2011) in *Competitive Video Games and Social Capital: New Frontiers of Community Formation* introduce the way competitive video games or more specifically Massive Multi-player Online Role Playing Games (MMORPG) are changing the ideas of the type of social capital that Putnam wrote of in *Bowling Alone*. The authors contend that the 'mechanisms that encourage social connectedness exist in new technologies, and comprise a new frontier for community formation' (2011: 5). They further claim that unlike television, which Putnam contends has been the downfall of social capital in America, the internet, or more specifically, games that are played in community formation online, have had a positive impact on social capital which has caused a community unto itself – leading to a communal expression with a 'shared cultural identity through various forms of art, language (slang), fashion, merchandise, and electronic media' (2011: 4). Kong and Theodore's sole contention is that social media does not create a counterfeit community, as many scholars claim happens within the online realm; but it is the impetus that is perpetuating a new and better type of social capital within not only America, but the world.

The idea of the counterfeit community comes from Freie (1998: 3) who claims that it is the 'disjunction between the longing for community and the reality of separation that makes us vulnerable to counterfeit claims of community'. The decline in real world connections is what makes the counterfeit community so appealing. The underlying value of Freie's claim is that counterfeit communities are an outcome of weakened community bonds across society. The conclusion is that we have essentially changed the way we interact with each other in response to changes in our social milieu.

Scholars, including Freie have asserted that the internet is a double-edged sword. Most claim that internet communities, although they do tend to open up new horizons and let people interact who might not do so otherwise, in the most simplest terms, do not foster a sense of *true* community; they do not imply any real sense of obligation, trust or commitment between members. To this effect, Freie understands cyberspace and the internet to be one of the biggest breeding grounds for the falsification of social capital and hence the counterfeit community. He further asserts that the relationships that are formed via online, specifically those in community gaming situations, do not lead to lasting or real relationships and only provide a temporary psychological satisfaction to those involved in them. Freie writes that:

> when difficult problems arise that threaten one's involvement in the cyberspace community, it is far too easy to either avoid or withdraw. The community thus fails to provide a genuine and lasting group of relationships. This temporariness is a fundamental characteristic of the structure of cyberspace communities and makes it inevitable that communities on the Internet will be counterfeit. (1998: 154)

In addition, Freie also contends that it is quite easy to manipulate a person's true identity, so that even if one claims to know or trust someone online, it does not necessarily follow that the person is who they say they are, or would act in a certain way toward the other individual in real life. It is because of these contentions that Freie maintains in no uncertain terms that the internet and gaming communities do not foster a sense of social capital, and in fact may be adding to its decline within America society.

As a counterpoint, Felicia Wu Song (2009) writes in *Virtual Communities Bowling Alone, Online Together* about the rapid generational changes that have taken place over the last two decades in American society – changes that Putnam saw as instrumental to the decline in social capital. Specifically, for Song, how we define social capital must adjust due in large part to technological transformations within our world. She claims that:

> after the novelty of computer-mediated communication wore off, it is arguable that the appetite for online communities may not have been so much about having an experience that was completely "other" or removed from what was known in our face-to-face, physically bound settings. Instead, the success of [online communities] may serve to crystallize the fact that we still enjoy being in relations with the people that we know and that we still grant credibility to our friends and loved ones, being prone to trust their contacts, interests,

> and commitments. What this technology gives us, then, is a means of adapting our existing relationships to challenges posed by the social realities of geographic distance and the task-cluttered lives that contemporary Americans seem to have. (2009: 136)

Further, it is Song's (2009: 130) contention that virtual communities 'do not so much introduce a completely new dynamic of membership to the public sphere' but that they actually serve to enhance and reinforce what has already been transforming over time. Putnam insists that even in light of new technological innovations, he hopes that social capital will become important to us once again. He hopes that the internet becomes like the telephone, something that improves social capital in America, and not like the television that has seemingly lowered how we feel about our communities. It is also Song's ultimate hope that online communities, including game play, will enhance the idea of social capital in American society. What her research adds to the discussion is a view into a new take on causality. Whereas, Putnam may view the decline of traditional notions of social capital as a result of a rise in technological integration and generational shifts, we might see Song's view as seeing the formation of new technology driven forms of social capital as the result of changes within our larger social structure. A new system emerges to allow us to adapt to a new social landscape.

Within this new social landscape, the prevalence of virtual communities constitutes another major shift in social reality. We earlier challenged the legitimacy of Putnam's construction of social capital because it ignored the social realities of women and people of color. The intention, however, was not to discard the concept completely. Social capital in its genesis is a function of the way individuals relate to each other to create and maintain the whole. Traditional conceptualizations of social capital, however, do not reflect the modern, technologically advanced society we inhabit. On the other hand, virtual social capital – by dint of its digital nature – lacks the presence to reinforce real world communal bonds. The real issue, then, is whether social capital still exists in a form which can reproduce the positive functions put forward by Putnam. Replacing one formation with the other is therefore insufficient. What remains is to appreciate what happens when we accept their strengths and limitations … and keep both formations.

This requires a paradigm shift. A modern version of social capital reflects the mobile, technology driven, multifaceted lives of people today. It acknowledges our continued connections to family, neighborhoods and communities while recognizing that the ways we interact have changed. Additionally, it accepts the fluid nature of identity – the different selves we present as we interact with others and engage with different sections of our world (Barker, 2008).

This shift re – conceptualizes social capital along a continuum – marked on one end by traditional institutions and on the other by virtual representations.

A single individual inhabits identities that fall along the continuum – reproducing a need for community, yet reflecting varying degrees of engagement and obligation. We coordinate a neighborhood yard sale to raise money to buy laptops for an afterschool program. The success of this event relies on a sense of responsibility and obligation for the communal well – being as well as the ability to exercise social networks for a common cause. We sign the Greenpeace petition online, occasionally read the campaign newsletters they email, and send a donation once a year (Davis, 2003). For some, this might be an example of how dis-association leads to a breakdown in communal responsibility. However, such a participatory option increases the range of communities that individuals can now connect to – no longer bound by space or time – with the format allowing them to define their level of attachment while balancing the needs of the social and the individual. And, twice a week, our avatars on Guild Wars join a dozen or so virtual comrades online and stretch the possibilities of who we are. In virtual space, we get to challenge the social markings that influence our communal experiences and see what it is like to be a part of something bigger than us. In an age where communities do not always inhabit defined physical spaces as they did during Putnam's golden age, the flexibility to create multiple connections across the continuum stands in for a less desirable situation where no connections are made at all. It then becomes the cumulative effect of these connections – real and virtual – that help societies flourish.

Conclusion

In the end, it is the bigger picture that Putnam is most concerned about: what will a marked decline in social capital mean to the way our society functions, our communities are structured and our citizens treat each other? Traditionally defined, social capital functioned as a key element in the creation and maintenance of stable, flourishing communities. In these communities, reciprocal relationships were centered on mutual commitment to communal goals for the greater good. For many, these relationships were manifested in communal identities fostered through social organizations – lodges, women's societies, bowling leagues. In order to engage with this concept in a modern context, however, it is necessary to fully situate it in its original milieu. This means understanding the sociocultural parameters that engendered Putnam's construction – a mostly segregated American landscape where access to communities and institutions was highly proscribed.

After reaching its heyday in the years following WWII, traditional representations of social capital were challenged by emerging social realities linked to the

Civil Rights era which began in earnest in the 1960's. Social capital, as traditionally conceptualized, did not question the marginalization of women's roles in society or the exclusion of people of color from most social organizations. This reality directly challenged the idea of social capital as an essential element in the representation of America as a leader in democratic civil engagement. In addition, changes in the social fabric brought on by urban sprawl, rising numbers of women entering the workforce, new patterns of mobility, diminishing leisure time and the heightened presence of television drastically altered patterns of civic engagement.

As levels of dis – association rose and people found it more convenient to engage from a distance, the social shifted toward an individual focus. The resultant individualism, fostered by unregulated self-interests and economic pressures, presaged a climate of distrust and the breakdown of communal bonds. However, such dire predictions about the complete demise of social capital andcommunity are being challenged by the increasing presence of technology in our lives. The question then becomes whether *virtual social capital* is analogous to Putnam's social capital – providing basic functions of reciprocity, networking, and trust.

MMORPG's create community in virtual space. Here people come together to establish a community with a recognized, agreed upon, purpose. In these counterfeit communities, hyper-real replicas of the world, players build mutually beneficial relationships and extensive networks. As technology becomes integrated into our everyday lives and physical connections are hampered by the hectic pace of modern life, these virtual communities can serve to replace the connections that traditional communities provided. We might even argue that they do a better job representing democratic ideals as anonymity removes the superficial markers that foster marginalization and discrimination. Yet, we have to question the substance of what is being offered.

Virtual social capital replicates in name only. In a MMORPG, membership is based on a fantasized self – outside the boundaries of real-life obligations or expectations. The democratic ideals of Putnam's social capital required a common element that – when threatened – strengthened the communal bonds as individual survival depended on the whole. In the virtual world, we can just log off, suffering no consequences for our disconnection. However, we caution against a wholesale denouncement of the way technology is changing the way we connect and communicate: the change has already occurred and understanding the cyborg allows us to see how we can use the system to inform a new sense of community.

In the final analysis, we would argue that Putnam's basic vision of social capital has fractured to reflect multiple realities in our modern society. Just as scholarship has helped us to understand that we all embody different identities in multiple contexts, our complex lives require multiple avenues for communal connection and social networking. In this new imagining, social capital becomes a factor set along a continuum from traditional manifestations to virtual realities. Technology meets us at different levels of engagement and commitment – allowing us to create multiple communities to support and nourish a complex world.

Putnam concludes *Bowling Alone* by declaring that, 'We should do this, ironically, not because it will be good for America – though it will be – but because it will be good for us as a whole' (2000: 414). Ultimately, the discussion on how the concept of social capital can find synergy with our modern, virtually enhanced perceptions of self and community is relevant because it helps us to understand how we cope with changes in our social environments and recognize the possibilities for reshaping the ways we relate to each other.

References

Brehm, John and Wendy Rahn, (1997). Individual-Level Evidence for Causes and Consequences of Social Capital, *Journal of Political Science 41/3*, 999–1023.

Barker, Chris, (2003). *Cultural Studies: Theory and Practice.* London, Sage.

Davis, Joseph E., (2003). The Commodification of Self, *Hedgehog Review 5/2*, 41–49.

Delgado, Richard, and Jean Stefancic, (2001). *Critical Race Theory: An Introduction.* New York: NYU Press.

Fischer, Claude S., Bowling Alone: What's the Score? Presented to "Author Meets Critic: Putnam, *Bowling Alone*" session of the meetings of the American Sociological Association, Anaheim, California, August 2001.

Franklin, V. P., Education for Life: Adult Education Programs for African Americans in Northern Cities, 1900–1942, in H.G. Neufeldt & L. McGee, eds., *Education of the African American Adult: An Historical Overview*. New York: Greenwood Press 1990, (pp. 113–134).

Freie, John F., (1998). *Counterfeit Communities: The Exploitation of Our Longings for Connectedness.* Lanham, Maryland: Rowman and Littlefield.

Fukuyama, Francis, *Trust: Social Virtues and the Creation of Prosperity.* New York: Simon and Schuster, 1996.

Kong, David S. and Marqus Theodore, (2011). Competitive Video Games and Social Capital: New Frontiers of Community Formation (D. o. Sociology, Trans.). Los Angeles: University of California Los Angeles (UCLA).

Martin, Jane Roland, (1982). Excluding Women from the Educational Realm, *Harvard Educational Review 52/2*, 133–148.

Neverdon-Morton, Cynthia, (2009). African American Women and Adult Education in the South, 1895–1925, in H.G. Neufeldt & L. McGee, eds., *Education of the African American Adult: An Historical Overview.* New York: Greenwood Press, pp. 163–178.

Oldendorf, Sandra B., (2009). Literacy and Voting: The Story of the South Carolina Sea Island Citizenship Schools, in H.G. Neufeldt & L. McGee, eds., *Education of the African American Adult: An Historical Overview.* New York: Greenwood Press, 191–210.

Prokhovnik, Raia, (1998). Public and Private Citizenship: From Gender Invisibility to Feminist Inclusiveness, *Feminist Review 60*, 84–104.

Putman, Robert D., (1995). Bowling Alone: America's Declining Social Capital, *Journal of Democracy 6/1*, 65–78.
Putnam, Robert D., (2000). *Bowling Alone: The Collapse and Revival of American Community.* New York: Simon & Schuster.
Seligman, Adam B., (2003). *Modernity's Wager: Authority, the Self, and Transcendence*. New Jersey: Princeton University Press.
Song, Felicia Wu, (2009). *Virtual Communities Bowling Alone, Online Together*. New York: Peter Lang Publishing, Inc.
Williams, Lillian S., (2009). Black Communities and Adult Education: YMVA, YWCA, and Fraternal Organizations, in H.G. Neufeldt & L. McGee, eds., *Education of the African American Adult: An Historical Overview.* New York: Greenwood Press, 135--162.

Part Two – Assessments

Informal Media Education in Europe: An Analysis of the Best practices[1]

Alberto Bitonti[2], Andrej Školkay[3]

Abstract

This chapter maps and proposes an analysis of European best practices in informal media education. Our study is based on an extensive research in all EU countries. The research included three different and increasingly complex stages of selection and analysis, and allowed us to tackle important methodological issues concerning the evaluation itself of informal educational activities. We have categorised best practices in media education according to the most often used definition of media literacy: fostering access to and analysis of the media and their contents, raising evaluation skills and awareness on the use of media, and fostering creative production of media content. In addition to this, the study suggests a method for the evaluation of hundreds and hundreds of projects and programmes in informal education in Europe – something that is currently by and large missing.

Introduction

In the last two decades digital technologies and EU/EC as well as national government initiated and supported programmes and policy initiatives have substantially changed and expanded the world of education in Europe, also in the field of informal education. However, there has been little attention paid to the impact of these initiatives on actual learning, as well as on financial efficiency and possible wider (including cross-border) extension of these projects.

By 'informal education' we refer to all those educational paths which take place beyond regular school curricular activities, and that involve other intermediating subjects (such as NGOs or media), often relying on processes of self-learning and social acquisition of knowledge. Digital technologies heavily affected this kind of

1 This essay is a product of a research made jointly by Eurispes (Italy) and Skamba (Slovakia) as part of the European project EMEDUS (www.emedus.org), which involved a consortium of research institutions and universities from different European countries, under the Lifelong Learning Programme of the European Commission.

2 Alberto Bitonti is Research Analyst at Eurispes (Rome, Italy), Adjunct Professor at IES Abroad Rome and Fellow of the School of Public Affairs at American University (Washington DC, USA).

3 Andrej Školkay is the director of Skamba – School of Communication (Bratislava, Slovakia).

processes by providing a much wider audience with direct access to educational resources, by allowing an easy and fast distribution of contents, and most importantly by lowering the costs and the obstacles to the independent creation of digital products potentially by everybody.

A crucial role in this situation is played by the education to digital technologies themselves and to media in general, i.e. by those processes which contribute to cultivating digital literacy and media literacy. Media literacy refers to the individual competencies of users, which – in a frame of citizen participation to social and political life – must be able to critically read (in a broader sense), understand and use the media (and particularly digital media). This is why we believe our research is relevant in this regard: it focuses at the same time on two fundamental aspects of the impact of digital technologies on the world of education. On the one hand we consider the idea of informal learning and informal education as enhanced by digital technologies; on the other hand we focus on media (especially digital media), both as objects of study and as channels/providers of media education.

Our study is part of a wider project on media education in Europe: when we were asked to formulate some policy recommendations to the European Commission concerning media literacy and informal media education, we decided to undertake an extensive research in all European Union countries, looking for best practices to learn from and for good ideas to spread. Of course, we had to overcome several theoretical difficulties and methodological problems, as well as face actual research obstacles and objective limits to our ambitions of research.

This chapter aims at giving a synthetic account of our study (concluded at the end of 2013), by tackling the idea of informal media education (par. 1), exploring the methodological issues arisen in the collection and the evaluation of cases (par. 2), developing an analysis of some good practices as well as some less positive experiences (par. 3), and drawing some selected conclusions useful for policy goals too.

The informal dimension of media education

Digital technologies greatly enhanced and enriched the world of informal education on many levels, both cognitive and factual; but what precisely do we mean when we refer to informal education? Despite a wide terminological variety, reflecting different views and highlighting different features of the concept (Knowles, 1975; Simkins, 1977; Marsick and Watkins, 1990; Lave and Wenger, 1991; Reber, 1993; Jeffs and Smith, 1996; Eraut, 2000; Gee, 2004; Drotner, Jensen and Schroeder, 2008), informal education can be described as the mix of experiences, processes and educational itineraries that one or more subjects construct through the dynamics of cooperation or virtual collaboration, as well as through the exchange of knowledge and experiences, and through the participation of one or several subjects to one or more activities with educational aims. In other terms it is the education which occurs beyond formal contexts (such as school classes or traditionally structured courses).

Informal education usually does not use standard methods or strategies like the ones characterising formal courses in or outside school; it is not necessarily founded on a specific correspondence between a planned or expected didactic (or educational) objective and the structured educational itinerary that leads to the achievement of that objective. Most often, it does not include standard evaluation systems either (this is one of the sources of major methodological problems, as we will see later). In other words, the "informal" context refers to those spontaneous processes that an educator cannot always predict. Different individuals learn differently from these processes depending on their cultural and educational background, as well as on their individual cognitive and emotional potential. From the didactic point of view, although an educational mediation is planned in order to increase the competences, it is difficult to include and define precisely some standard procedures to be used by educational mediators. From a methodological point of view, the informal dimension of media education is difficult to analyse, because due to its heterogeneity it is a challenge to use some reference criteria and indicators capable of strictly defining its educational profile and impact. In addition, various important indicators needed for proper scientific evaluation of pedagogical impact and cost efficiency are usually missing or not easily available.

However, by applying the idea of informal education to the specific context of media education, we can try to articulate the concept more in detail. If we were to reflect on and synthesize the basic ingredients of informal media education, the first factor would certainly be the emphasis on the development of cognitive and meta-cognitive processes of the individual. The elaboration of media education plans is often pragmatic and participative.

The second factor that characterizes the informal dimension of media education derives from the approach of learning by doing and by using. It refers not so much to the educational strategies as to the tactics of appropriation of the inputs, knowledge and competencies that learning individuals observe, transmit or share. In comparison to older media, what characterizes digital media specifically is that the vast majority of users learn to use digital tools and new media on their own, *by doing* indeed.

In conclusion, informal media education can also be characterised by a process of post-alphabetization or new alphabetization. Informal media education should be a life-long learning process. The digital dimension of media literacy refers to the traditional objectives of media education that oscillate between the basic alphabetization and the ability of creative production of media contents. Still present is also an important more traditional part of media literacy that tackles the critical analysis and evaluation of media messages or self-regulation of media experiences by the user (Celot and Tornero, 2009; Ceretti, Felini and Giannatelli, 2006).

To sum up, at an analytical level education can have three basic forms: formal, non-formal and informal (but see also Zaki Dib, 1997–1998). Earlier approaches regarded formal, non-formal, and informal education as distinct categories. For example, Coombs and his colleagues distinguished between informal and non-formal education, defining informal education as learning in daily life situations, and non-formal education as planned educational activities taking place outside the classroom (Coombs and Ahmed, 1974). Nevertheless, the two terms have been used interchangeably throughout the literature.

Indeed, in contrast to Coombs and Ahmed, more recently Rogers (2004) proposes that all three analytically separate parts should be viewed as part of a continuum, with fine gradations between them and blurred boundaries. According to Rogers, the key analytical and practical distinction between these three categories of education would lie in the individualization of learning. While formal education would be highly de-contextualized, standardized, and generalized, informal learning would be highly contextualized and non-formal learning would be a hybrid that would include informal learning as well as formal learning. But there is a great uncertainty in the current context as to what constitutes non-formal/informal education, what the term refers to, what its meaning is (see Kamil, 2007). Non-formal education as we understand it today would cover flexible schooling, while informal education would have to do with highly participatory educational activities. This is precisely where media literacy education by and about digital tools fits.

Evaluation and methodological considerations

As may be evident from what we wrote in the previous paragraph, the major problem with informal media education is that its heterogeneous character, lack of (self-)evaluation of its pedagogical effectiveness reports and lack of revealed financial data make its scientific evaluation a challenge. A wide variety of actual experiences fall under the domain of informal media education, and that does not allow easy comparisons, for instance between the educational activities of a local community media centre and an educational web portal managed by a big

TV company or by a public agency. In the context of informal media education we necessarily had to deal with diverse and original practices, managed by media companies (TV broadcasters, newspapers, radios, social networks), by public organizations (regulatory authorities, Ministries of Culture, Media or Education) or non-governmental organizations (small associations, councils of users, as well as international private organizations). This is why we had to tackle a number of methodological issues, the main one indeed being making comparison between cases possible, useful and logical, naturally using some objective and general criteria in order to formulate impartial evaluations. We had two different teams of research (Slovak and Italian): as a result, on the one hand, we could rely implicitly on an international perspective and on the independence of evaluations; on the other hand, though, the need for objective and impartial criteria was even stronger, because we had to coordinate the work of research of several people with different cultural and linguistic backgrounds. As mentioned, our objective was to select a number of best practices to analyse in depth, in order to take them as examples of success and draw useful insights to formulate policy recommendations.

Considering everything said so far, we designed our path of research articulating three moments of evaluation, following different criteria and procedures:

1) research and first selection from all available cases (made individually by all researchers involved), finally collecting more than 110 cases from all over Europe; although preference was given to the most recent cases, by the design of the study we had to select at least one case study from each of EU27 countries[4].
2) further selection of good practices (made assembling the positive evaluations of four independent evaluators), finally getting to 36 best practices (a sample which could be manageable for more detailed analyses), by applying an objective scheme of evaluation, including specific criteria and indicators;
3) a final selection and analyses of 10 best-ranked practices (a sample which could be subject to a very detailed analyses).

In the first phase, the two teams of research worked independently, looking for good practices of informal media education, across all sectors, in EU countries. The methods used for our search were mainly three: a) email and phone interviews to various experts, teachers and government officials working in the field of media education; b) searching the web, consulting organizations' websites and following links on portals of media education; c) questionnaires to specific subjects (both individual educators and organizations). At the end of the first phase, putting

4 Our study started before Croatia joined EU.

together all the cases collected individually by all the researchers, we assembled more than 110 cases targeting all categories of informal media education.

In the second phase, we needed to restrict our field of observation. As a result, we had four independent evaluators (all working in the field of media education) selecting around 36 cases (out of the total list), which most closely resembled key criteria (whenever data were available) such as

- project innovativeness level,
- cost efficiency
- project logical structure (introduction, definitions, key terms, organization of tasks, etc.)
- support for development of key competencies in ML (media literacy)
- support of cooperation between teachers and students
- potential of the sustainability
- interactive and effective delivery methods.

Even if the selection was somehow arbitrary (we could not carry detailed and time-consuming research on all these criteria in all 36 cases), we were able to achieve a higher degree of impartiality by overlapping the four independent evaluations, keeping in our selection only the ones that had been positively assessed by at least two evaluators. In other words, we used our experience from the experimental phase when we attempted to use both a questionnaire and a qualitative evaluation of selected very heterogeneous projects. Following this procedure, we got to exactly 36 cases (resulted from the addition of the cases that received four "votes", three votes and two votes).

In the third phase we had to select our final best practices, trying to achieve as much objectivity as possible in the selection process. This is why we developed a more sophisticated procedure, creating an evaluation scheme composed of various indicators and of a scoring system for every element considered. The scheme was based on three main criteria:

1. pedagogical effectiveness
2. economic efficiency
3. impact

By pedagogical effectiveness, we referred to the presence of: ideally, learning assessment or, at least, customer satisfaction tools (we are aware of the fact that these are different and irreducible categories), *ex-ante* and *ex-post* analyses of needs and performance, a clearly stated methodological approach, target and objectives clearly identified, innovative pedagogical strategy (bringing new added value regarding methods, tools and approaches).

By economic efficiency, we referred to the cost per unit of the pedagogical initiative, resulting from the relation between the budget of the project and the number of people reached by it. We were unable to identify economic efficiency in all cases, including some of the best projects according to overall criteria (the project managers simply did not reply to our repeated written or phone requests).

By impact, we referred to the extension of the project (local, national or international) and to the number of people reached (we had three different groups: less than 100, between 100 and 1000 and over 1000). Every element of the three criteria in our scheme had a pre-assigned score, which allowed us to assign a precise score (and rank) to every case, thus selecting the best practices among them.

Naturally, the process we followed is far from being perfect. It can only be considered an original attempt to deal with the two-fold problem outlined in the previous paragraphs: evaluate a variegate and diversified pool of cases all falling under the category of informal media education, without giving up a sufficient degree of objectivity and impartiality in the selection of the best practices. Ideally, one can achieve all three major goals – pedagogical effectiveness, economic efficiency and impact. This, in fact, happened in the case of some of the best projects presented below. Thus, the measurement tool, by definition arbitrary, can be used in the future by others – or may be adjusted to other criteria, e.g. if one prefers the pedagogical impact over all other aspects.

For example, we compared our methodological approach with that used in a similarstudy: Parola, Ranieri and Trinchero (2010, 138–140) in their study used an in many aspects different approach both in selecting criteria used for evaluation as well as in their ratings of particular criteria (scale, with "1" = Low and "5" = High). Thus, they considered:

- Educational Relevance: significance of the educational objectives, integration into the curriculum, impact on the school, involvement of extra-school educational agencies
- Teaching Approach: planning appropriateness, effectiveness of methods, content accuracy and appropriateness to level, students engagement
- Media Use: added value for the project/experience, appropriateness for topic/skills, variety and integration of media used in the project/experience, ease of use both for students and teachers
- Sustainability: time manageability, sustainability of the staff, equipment affordability, cost effectiveness
- Product (if any): originality, content accuracy and communication effectiveness, graphics appeal, ease of use)
- Documentation Quality: documentation completeness, appropriateness of methodological tools used to document the process (e.g. log book, observation

grid, checklist etc.), appropriateness of media used to document the process (e.g. text, audio, video etc.)
- Dissemination.

Each topic was to be completed with a comment, and finally with an overall evaluation of the experience in an open-ended question.

Clearly, the above-mentioned methodological approach does not differentiate sufficiently enough among variables which have equal value (not in reality, but in the approach they are used). For example, involvement of extra-school educational agencies is much less important or indeed irrelevant compared to a definitely important criterion such as Students Engagement (learning by doing). However, in the assessment process they had equal value. If we focus only on criteria in the same category, for example on Educational Relevance, then it seems clear that significance of the educational objectives again is a key criterion but Involvement of extra-school educational agencies may be a by and large irrelevant criterion. In her response, Maria Ranieri responded to this criticism as follows:

> "When talking about criteria there is always a certain degree of subjectivity. Therefore, what I estimate as relevant in my context could seem irrelevant in other context. Criteria are values-based, so they are strongly influenced by the social and cultural context. From our point of view, it makes sense to consider as a relevant factor the "Involvement of extra-school educational agencies" since in many documented (unfortunately in Italian) experiences this variable has been a key factor for the success and the continuity of the project. Moreover, considering other theoretical works on innovation, it's clear that different levels of analysis must be taken into account to assess educational projects: we can distinguish at least three levels, i.e. micro/meso/macro levels: the role of extra-school agencies would be relevant at the meso level"[5].

It remains questionable in this category what the criterion "Impact on the School" means and how it can be evaluated. Perhaps it would be more proper to use "*Impact on Quality of Testing Graduates' Results*"? Maria Ranieri responded to this criticism in the following way: "*we refer to whether the school changed its practices towards the media or not, which is quite relevant from our point of view, if media education must enter into the school*".

Finally, while we mentioned that the authors Parola, Ranieri and Trinchero (2010) did not differentiate sufficiently among various evaluation variables (criteria) at the same time they used too many variables (some of them very vague) which would be very difficult to compare – at least in our case study.

5 Email from May 18, 2013.

The above-mentioned discussion on methodology represents only a small part of all methodological and research issues we had to deal with. This discussion will hopefully help future researchers in the area of evaluation of various projects in informal media education.

Best practices in Europe in informal media education

As mentioned, we have focused on the most typical categorizations of media literacy competencies (Tornero, 2004; Celot and Tornero, 2009; Jenkins, 2009; Calvani, Fini and Ranieri, 2009). Therefore, in this paragraph, we will analyse and present some of our best practices according to the different media literacy competencies on which each practice focuses. We first deal with three cases of projects fostering access to media and their contents (par. 3.1). Secondly, we deal with two cases fostering analysis of media and their content (par. 3.2). Then, we present three projects which aim to raise evaluation skills and awareness on the use of media and their contents (par. 3.3). Lastly, we present two cases of projects fostering creative production of media content (par. 3.4). Obviously, some projects covered more aspects and media literacy competencies at the same time, but we categorized them here according to the prevailing one.

Fostering access to the media

One of the most interesting European cases of projects promoting access to media we have identified is Communities 2.0, a project created by the Welsh government through a partnership of public and private organizations active in the Welsh region of Convergence.

Through training, mentoring, technical support, ICT-related business support, research and sharing of best practice, the programme was able to reach around 20.000 people in four years (2009–2012), providing assistance *in loco*, organizing courses and training sessions, providing suggestions on line on the best ways to get someone acquainted with digital technology (pushing towards an "intra-family" training, for example with parents or grandparents, or with friends), and offering "How to" manuals, video-guides and links related to basic operations with computer as well as more complex uses of software (such as video and audio editing, digital photography, etc.), or the creation of a website and cloud computing.

The programme was designed to reach different targets in various contexts of stronger or weaker digital exclusion, and carries on different activities (they also run their own blog, in addition to the presence in all main social networks), ensuring a high level of involvement of users and – what is even more important – of the people around the final users. In fact, their "appeal" to contact them and benefit from their services is mainly directed to community organizers, social housing landlords, group leaders and voluntary association managers, among others. The impact factor of the programme is even bigger thanks to the "train the trainers" courses, which teach people (such as social operators or simple voluntaries) how to teach about the digital world.

The aforementioned characteristics allow us to make three positive considerations about the programme. a) The project ensures a higher level of participation and involvement in comparison to programmes conceived as one-direction activities of knowledge transmission (typical of formal media education), thus fully developing the potential of informal media education directly in the place where education is needed (enterprises, social centres, communities). b) The strategy of the programme is evidently based on the awareness of the close relationship between digital inclusion and full citizenship, because digital competencies are not presented and taught as a learning outcome *per se*, but as effective tools directly connected and pragmatically tied to the everyday life of people, associations and enterprises. In fact, the programme is implemented through networks and structures that exist independently from the programme, this way overcoming the potential barrier that sometimes can be created between a learning environment and what is seen as "real life". c) The programme strongly supports the economic development and the growth of the region, because digital technologies allow enterprises and organizations as well as single users to improve their business profiles and their attitudes towards everyday problems, making people save time and money (economic capital) and stay "connected" (social capital) in their communities and beyond. The only negative side of the project resides in the very high cost of the programme (around 13 million euros for the period 2009–2013), which hardly makes the programme scalable or reproducible without the involvement of public governmental authorities. Yet, their innovative approach, structural organization and strategic conception make Communities 2.0 one of the European best practices to look at when we discuss informal media education.

Our second case in this category is Wiener Bildungsserver ("Vienna Education Server"), a non-profit organization active in Vienna (Austria). It is a network of individuals and representatives of various educational institutions and branches in the Vienna City School Board (Wiener Stadtschulrat), aiming to promote media activities in school and in non-school related fields and to provide access to information and communication technologies to all population groups. There were different "independent" websites specifically designed for various target groups, each providing media education materials and further links: www.netbridge.at (coordination and trends), www.ideen-kiste.at (elementary school teachers and parents of 0–6-years-old children), www.lehrerweb.at (teachers), http://kidsweb.at (children) and http://eltern web.at/ (parents). Overall, this Austrian multidimensional project contains many useful ideas and links on various aspects of media literacy. These are somehow not so well centralised, so it may take effort to find all of them and, furthermore, access is often limited by the need to register. However, it is still a good example of a project which succeeds in reaching the target – groups over 1,000 people – and articulating the right strategy.

Our third best practice is represented by Kennisnet, a Dutch public organization which provides educational content and support in the use of information and communication technology, targeting mainly teachers, pupils and parents. Of special educational importance seems to be their project *IT competency framework for teachers*. In this project, Kennisnet describes which skills teachers need to integrate IT in such a way that it makes their education more attractive, more efficient or more effective. The Framework applies to teachers in primary, secondary, and vocational education. Within the framework developed by Kennisnet, the approach to ICT is explored and explained specifically from the point of view of the teacher, describing how IT can support each key task. It is an excellent and science-based tool, and a very good example in the scenario of a fully digitalized educational environment.

Fostering analysis of media and their content

One of two best practices in this category appears evident if we consider the success and the diffusion of the format in various EU countries (in summer 2013 the programme was present in nine countries: the UK, Germany, the Netherlands, Belgium, Sweden, Finland, Hungary, Portugal and France). The format has in most cases been developed by local advertising sector associations and by various companies and corporations: the programme is in most cases named *Media Smart*. Of course the various national versions of the programme may show slight differences of quality or organization, but the core-format is the same in all the cases. This format derives from an educational programme which was started in Canada in 1990. Media Smart develops and provides (free of charge and on request, through simple agreements with schools) educational material to primary schools. The learning material is developed, reviewed or approved by teams of independent experts of media literacy. This is an actually quite famous and already known project, whose effectiveness continues to appear quite evident, considering the increased number of schools and countries adopting it.

The aim of our second best practice in this category, *Project Evvoluce* (it was active in the Czech Republic between 2011 and 2012, with a one year preparatory phase), was to develop cross-curriculum activities by merging environmental studies with multicultural, multimedia, social, and European studies. The project was run by an NGO (Centrum ekologické výchovy). The total budget was around 800.000 euros. It reached about 8.000 pupils, with a relatively high production cost of 100 euros per unit. We appreciated the creativity, cross-curricularity and adaptability of this project on, but not only on, media education. A very important aspect was that all materials were extensively tested. In the end, this is a very good example of integration of media-educational content with other disciplines, according to the interpretation that we exposed in the previous paragraphs, which considers implicitly cross-curricular life-long learning.

Raising evaluation skills and awareness on the use of media and their contents

The first project in this category is the Slovak cartoon series *Sheeplive*. This project was actually evaluated as the best project among all informal media education projects we have studied.Since every episode can be replayed and easily localized for different languages, the project has a high cost efficiency. The project, including various side-productions, costed about 400.000 euros.This seems to be an outstanding informal initiative focusing on the media/digital literacy of young children. The cartoon series for children goes back to the traditions of original cartoons for children and youth traditionally created in the former Czechoslovakia. In particular, the project focuses on the safety of children and youth, especially the risks related to the Internet, mobile phones and new media technologies. The project serves as a prevention tool for children: it wittily shows teenagers a mirror of their improper behaviour, and gives adults an opportunity to learn too. A civic association has been producing this series of cartoons already since 2008, with the support of various domestic donors and the Safer Internet Programme of the European Union. The NGO produced 601 episodes of Sheeplive cartoons within different linguistic versions. Sheeplive Cartoons have been seen on the YouTube channel 1.761,084 times until the end of 2012 (in various linguistic versions). The high numbers of viewers and the fact that the authors have been producing new episodes every year, prove the popularity of this series. Since every episode can be replayed and easily localized in 21 different languages, the project shows a high economic efficiency. The programme can still be seen as basic, from the point of view of innovation level (a traditional fairy tale), yet, it also offers interactive tools to test the gained knowledge. Episodes are independent and cover different aspects of mobile and internet communication. They are very logical, simple and always contain a "lesson learnt". The multi-level content communicates different messages for various age groups and thus it is attractive to all of them. This programme is very supportive for development of key competencies in ML, since it shows real life examples and sets them in the non-probable environment of a sheep farm. Every episode is based on a simplified real example and clearly shows wrong and right behaviours in handling the media. In summary, its pedagogical – educational evaluation of impact suggests that it managed to attract (in a sense of getting attention or awareness, at least) quite large target audiences. Further, the programme fared well at international festivals too[6]. In conclusion, it seems that some old-fashioned pedagogical-educational approaches – cartoons/fairy tales – still can work relatively well in media education today.

The second initiative is Finnish *Mediakasvatusseura* (Media Education Centre). It runs a web portal directed to professional educators and workers, researchers, students, voluntary organizations and parents. The mission of the portal is to increase the awareness as to media education and provide material resources for users in three languages. Around 20.000 visitors every month use the portal to look for material useful for their activities. The website also includes news and information about events and conferences, a massive collection of material for different target groups, information about research and statistics, online forums as well as a survival kit for parents. *Mediakasvatusseura* proved to be a precious initiative, also as an "aggregation point" for all those who work with or are interested in the field of media education, although many contents could be promoted with more innovative strategies in order to catch younger generations more easily, even when not explicitly interested in the issue of media education.

Our third project in this category, *Abeceda* ("Alphabet"), was produced in the Czech Republic by an NGO. The project was supported by the European Social

---

6 The cartoons received various international awards in 2009–2011. In 2011: Special Recognition, European Award of Excellence, City for Children, Stuttgart, Germany; Best Motion Picture at European Prevention Film Festival for project Sheeplive, Székesfehérvár, Hungary; Professional Audience Award at European Prevention Film Festival for project Sheeplive, Székesfehérvár, Hungary. In 2010: Prix Danube Award at the 20th Film Festival, Bratislava, Slovakia; the Official Selection in the TV Series category at the International Animated Film Festival in Annecy, France; Rainbow Marble Award for responsible approach at the International Advertising Festival, which is part of the Zlín International Film Festival for Children and Youth, Czech Republic. In 2009: International Jury Award at the 36th Ekotopfilm Festival, Slovakia; ITAPA International Congress Special Award, Slovakia; First Prize in Slovakia in the European Crime Prevention Prize competition, Slovakia.

Fund in total value about 580 00 euros. It reached about 12 000 people, so cost per unit can be estimated relatively high 50 euros. The project aimed at promoting reading and media literacy at primary schools in three areas: readership and reading literacy, reading literacy and media education, and reading literacy and creative writing. For this purpose, four materials, freely downloadable from the web (after registration), are available. These materials have been downloaded between 120–200 times as of May 2013. Considering these materials were already sent by regular mail on DVDs to 2000 Czech primary schools, and that in order to download one must register first, this shows a relatively high interest among the target audience. The general portal (www.ctenarska-gramotnost.cz) offers short know-how focused at innovative approaches to teaching (each seen between 400 and 6.500 times). The e-learning courses on reading literacy (seen by about 1800 times) is more for the self-evaluation of teachers. There are many other guides focusing on creative writing or analysis of films. There are also links to educational videos on YouTube (e.g. describing the use of electronic/digital textbooks or video monitoring of experimental teaching). In a playful form a special portal for children (www.sotkoviny.cz) offers advice on how to write reports, interviews, commentaries and comics. The final output also includes a full-format school magazine. There are many other tips and bits of advice, e.g. recommended journals and magazines for children. However, there are some limitations since everyone must first sign in, in order to get full advice. These pieces of advice have been seen by between 2.000 and 10.000 pupils. The innovation level of this project can overall be seen as advanced. The positive factor is that the project is operating even after the funding has expired.

Fostering creative production of media content

In this category, we have identified *Média Animation*, an education resource centre in Bruxelles (Belgium) among our best projects. The principal activities carried out by *Média Animation* focus on the teacher's training and the creation of new tools and methods to facilitate and support teaching overall through innovative strategies such as new audio-visual techniques and multimedia equipment. A strong methodological awareness is evident in the various programmes of the centre, which certainly is an example of excellence in several fields of digital literacy.

Our second best practice in this category is represented by Mediální škola/ Mediálna škola ("Media School").These are actually two independent projects which originally were co-organised by a Salesian Youth Centre in Brno (Czech Republic), in cooperation with another Salesian Youth Centre in Bratislava (Slovakia). The target group includes youth (15–20 years old), in the Czech case especially Salesians and those working with youth; in the Slovak case, schools, centres for extra-school activities and parishes. They offer four to six basic courses delivered in the form of a practically oriented workshop led by professional media lecturers. In the Czech case there is also a final international festival of media production. The project costed about 3.200 euros and reaches about 20 people per course. The initial cost per unit was thus relatively high, about 160 euros. Currently the Czech Centre charges participants with some 15 EUR fee each, while Slovak project charges 20 euros per participant.

These two cases, as well many of the previously analysed ones, present the advantage of being examples of fully integrated and situated learning environments in a social context, be they educational institutions or private associations, so that they implicitly show the relevance of digital and media literacy in a frame of real social life, thus actuating the potential of informal media education.

Conclusion

What may we conclude from our research? Firstly, it is necessary to continue to work on the fine-tuning of the assessment tools of media literacy projects and of informal media education in particular. The fact that informal processes are fairly hard to conceptualize and categorize does not mean that researchers must not try to always elaborate new theories and new tools in order to frame, evaluate and compare them.

In fact, curiously enough, in spite of a flourishing of informal media educational initiatives, there is not a sufficient number of studies at national level (Tomková 2010) or comparative research at international level focusing on that (Nóvoa and Yariv-Mashal, 2002; Livingstone, 2003). Despite all the methodological problems we mentioned, evaluation and assessment tools are necessary for impact analyses of educational projects, as well as performance management tools for educational mediators. It is urgent to create evaluating tools to "measure" what students learned, allowing consideration of the efficiency of training courses or other educational activities.

Our study provides a contribution for future research in this area, firstly, by making the methodological limits of researching the informal domain of media education more evident and secondly, by proposing some criteria (which may be developed into indicators after further conceptual and practical elaboration) to assess projects of informal media education.

Secondly, life-long learning cannot help increasingly relying on a closer integration of formal and informal education, since digital technologies definitely contributed to make the distinction between different learning environments increasingly blurred. This does not mean that we are uncritical technological supporters, but clearly, modern technologies are being used by children and youth in general, thus increasing media literacy is an imperative.

Third, there is a need to include the analysis and the assessment of the actual pedagogical – educational impact of projects (both *ex ante* and *ex post*) in all projects. This should be done at least initially, for example by analysing the educational needs of the target group, targeting the messages, or testing whether a project can really bring expected educational achievements. In the case of larger projects (e.g. TV programmes) these should be done on a smaller experimental sample. Parola, Ranieri and Trinchero (2010, 17) explicitly warn that a kind of unawareness of the relevance of a proper assessment of what students learn seems to prevail. They urge to create evaluating tools to "measure" what students learned, allowing consideration of the efficiency of a training course. For example, Ashley, Maksl and Craft (2013) have developed and assessed a measurement scale focused specifically on critical news media literacy (in formal education, but this can be adapted to informal education too).

We have welcomed some examples (in countries such as Austria, Czech Republic, Germany and Slovakia) of competitions (regional or national), either ad hoc or on annual basis, aimed to evaluate various media literacy/educational programmes. It is urgent to create evaluating tools to "measure" what students learn, allowing the consideration of the efficiency of training courses or other educational activities.

Our study provides a contribution for future research in this area, firstly, by making the methodological limits of researching the informal domain of media education more evident, and secondly, by proposing some criteria (which may be developed into indicators after further conceptual and practical elaboration) to assess projects of informal media education.

In the end, life-long learning cannot help increasingly relying on a closer integration of formal and informal education, since digital technologies definitely contributed to make the distinction between different learning environments increasingly blurred.

References

Ashley, S., A. Maksl and S. Craft (2013). *Developing a News Media Literacy Scale, Journalism & Mass Communication Educator* 2013 68: 7 originally published online, DOI: 10.1177/1077695812469802.

Calvani, A., A. Fini and M. Ranieri, (2009). Assessing digital competence in secondary education. Issues, Models and Instruments, in M. Leaning, *Issues in Information and Media Literacy. Education, Practice and Pedagogy*, Informing Science Press: Santa Rosa (CA), pp. 153–172.

Celot, P. and J.M. Tornero (2009). *Study on assessment criteria for Media Literacy Levels*, Final Report, European Commission, Brussels.
Ceretti, F., D. Felini and R. Giannatelli (2006). *I primi passi della media education*, Trento: Erikson.
Coombs, P. H. and M. Ahmed (1974). *Attacking Rural Poverty: How non-formal education can help,* Baltimore: Johns Hopkins University Press.
Drotner, K., H.S. Jensen and K.C. Schroeder (2008). *Informal Learning and Digital Media*, Cambridge Scholars Publishing: Newcastle.
Eraut, M. (2000). Non-formal learning and tacit knowledge in professional work, *British Journal of Educational Psychology*, No. 70, pp. 113–136.
Gee, J. (2004). *What video games have to teach us about learning and literacy*, New York: Palgrave Macmillan.
Jeffs, T. and M.K. Smith (1996). *Informal Education: Conversation, Democracy and Learning*, Derby: Education Now Books.
Jenkins, H. (2009). *Confronting the Challenges of Participatory Culture: Media Education for the 21st Century*, Cambridge (MASS): MIT Press.
Kamil, M. (2007). *Appeal Of Non Formal Education Paradigm. Looking Again At Non-Formal And Informal Education Towards A New Paradigm*, Center for Research in International Cooperation in Educational Development, University of Tsukuba. *http://file.upi.edu/Direktori/FIP/JUR._PEND._LUAR_SEKOLAH/196111091987031001-MUSTOFA_KAMIL/nonformal%20education%20alan%20rogers%202.pdf.*
Knowles, M.S. (1975). *Self-Directed Learning: A guide for learners & teachers*, New York: Association Press
Lave, J. and E. Wenger (1991). *Situated Learning: Legitimate peripheral participation*, Cambridge: Cambridge University Press.
Livingstone, S. (2003). On the Challenges of Cross-National Comparative Media Research, *European Journal of Communication,* 18(4), 477–500.
Marskick, V.J. and K.E. Watkins (1990). *Informal and Incidental Learning in the Workplace*, London: Routledge.
Nóvoa, A. and T. Yariv-Mashal (2002). Comparative Research In Education: A Mode Of Governance Or A Historical Journey? *Comparative Education*, vol. 39 (4), pp. 423–438.
Reber, A.S. (1993). *Implicit learning and tacit knowledge: An essay on the cognitive unconscious*, Oxford: Oxford University Press.
Parola, A., M. Ranieri, R. Trinchero (2010). *Guidelines for the Assessment and Evaluation of Media Education Paths,* Project Number 142299–LLP–1–2008–1–IT–COMENIUS–CMP, On Air Project.
Rogers, A. (2004). Looking again at non-formal and informal education – towards a new paradigm, in *The encyclopaedia of informal education*, www.infed.org/biblio/non_formal_paradigm.htm.
Simkins, T. (1977). *Non-Formal Education and Development. Some critical issues*, Manchester: Department of Adult and Higher Education.
Tomková, Jarmila (2012). *Mediácia bezpečného používania Internetu. Ako k nej prispievajú projekty OZ ESLOVENSKO? Záverečná správa z prieskumu. (Mediation of Safe Internet Use. How the NGOs contribute to this. The Final Research Report).* http://www.zodpovedne.sk/download/Prieskum_Mediacia.pdf.
Tornero, J.M. (2004). *Understanding digital literacy*, European Commission.
Zaki Dib, C. (1997–1998). *Formal, Non-Formal And Informal Education: Concepts/Applicability.* http://www.techne-dib.com.br/downloads/6.pdf.

Critical Review of an e-Learning Tool

Barbara Szafrajzen & Karen Ferreira-Meyers

Abstract

The article is based on a recent doctoral research in communication and information sciences which set out to compare two teaching methods (the same training given in a face-to-face setting and at a distance) in order to analyze and understand the influence of a technological tool (Szafrajzen, 2010). It attempts to establish a critical assessment of e-learning, with respect to actual practices and actors' "points of view in a given situation" (Parsons, Schütz, 1978) of learning. For this, the research tries to highlight the meanings for the actors, meanings that are the key to their understanding and thus learning (Depover, Giordana and Marton, 1998). This study allows us to understand and analyze a few of the meaningful learning experiences of e-learning education students (3rd year Bachelor's Degree), hosted by a university in the south of France.

Introduction

The place of communication and information technology in the current academic landscape is indisputable. E-learning and e-education has grown significantly in many universities, thanks to various factors (technological, pedagogical, psycho-social, cognitive, socio-economic, etc.). The integration of computer science tools in this new type of learning device (Choplin, 2002) has led to learners greatly modifying their learning experiences in a meaningful way, forcing the university to adapt to these changes. In addition, new problems inherent to the students' needs to "tame distance" (Jacquinot, 1993) have thus emerged.

In human and social sciences, many researchers have been interested in cyber-space, especially the emergence of an "ideology" community within it. In the early 1990s, science education literature concerned with models of collaborative work and distributed cognition is already abundant (Resnic, Levine, Teasley, 1991). In anthropology, research on collective intelligence and virtual agora offers, at the same time, a cyberspace anthropology as "public service" and "collective intelligence" (Levy, 1994). More recently in sociology the work of Maria C. Papadakis summarizes the main characteristics specific to these communities (Papadakis, 2003).

To understand the place of ICT in learning environments, we base our comments on some of the meaningful learning experiences from the concrete example of an e-learning education program in communication and information sciences[1]. We investigate how a communicative study helps to understand and analyze meaningful learning experiences of learners in this type of training.

To understand how the social actors, specifically the learners, co-construct their collective learning reality in their e-learning environment, we choose to first adopt an epistemological position which follows a "constructivist convention" (Le Moigne, 2003). The methodology involves two main qualitative methods of data analysis: the method of qualitative content analysis and the method of qualitative systemic analysis (Mucchielli, 2004). In a third step, we describe the device as well as the e-learning learning situation. Finally, we look at how students bridge the distance through the emergence of a learning community.

The epistemological framework

We wish to determine the meaning that each learner gives to his or her learning situation[2]. For this, we make our first assumption[3] that meaning is only constructed in situations and in interactions with the learning device (whether human entities, material and/or ideational). Situational semiotics focuses on the idea of emerging meaning in situations and interactions. The genesis of shared meaning is the issue at the heart of this research method. Moving away from compartmentalised representations which the actors have of their situation, this method offers a new vision of a much broader and more complex situation. We also assume that there are collective learning situations within this distance e-learning learning[4]. To understand

1 This article reiterates and elaborates some of the results obtained in one of the authors' recent doctoral research in communication and information sciences, entitled « Etude communicationnelle de deux dispositifs d'apprentissage mis en place au sein d'un même département universitaire. Le cas de la Licence en sciences de l'information et de la communication », PhD obtained on 10 December 2010 in Montpellier (France).

2 We understand the term "learning" in the sense of Etienne Wenger: Learning has a social dimension and manifests itself in social interactions of actors engaged in a common practice (Wenger, 1998).

3 We seek to confirm these assumptions in our field study.

4 As part of the doctoral research, we tried to explore some meaningful learning experiences of students in distance education. Our study also observed the emergence of a learning community born of a collective approach to knowledge sharing. However, we do not want to consider construction and sharing of knowledge in a limited way, namely as an exclusively collective dynamic. This is why we specify that we are interested in players (specifically learners) situations and interactions with their learning device, so that they understand the representations of their distance learning.

how the learners co-construct their collective learning reality, we choose to adopt the constructivist epistemological position (Le Moigne, 2003).

Jean-Louis Le Moigne proposes the term "constructivist convention" to scientific communities: "In presenting itself as an alternative convention, constructivism also reveals the conventional positivist epistemologies"(*ibid.*: 61). The term "constructivist convention" also highlights the possible nuances in the different ways of understanding the constructivist posture and "allows a 'generally accepted' representation of "the classic or institutional epistemological convention" (*op. cit.*: 45).

Within this convention, learning is seen as an active mechanism; the learner seeks the meaning of his action with regard to the meaning[5] that can be grafted to this action. To better understand this, our approach is based on constructivism as described by Alex Mucchielli (Mucchielli, 2003). This author postulates that knowledge is constructed, unfinished, plausible, suitable and contingent, purpose-oriented, dependent on the actions and experiences of the knowing subjects, structured by the process of knowledge while also and at the same time structuring it, and, finally, forged in and through the interaction of the knower with the world (Mucchielli, 2004). We take the term constructivism to the extent that we construct the meaning given by the actors in a situation through a contextualization of their words and actions, without reading grids or *a priori* considerations of data. It is therefore a progressive construction of signification. Other authors, such as Peter Ludwig Berger and Thomas Luckman (2006) also developed the idea of collective construction of social reality. "Construction" then is only the reality constructed by those involved in the situation. Therefore, a constructivist learning device would be a device offering construction of knowledge routes to each of the actors present in the learning situation. The search for meaning is therefore based on items deemed relevant and interesting for the actors. Then, taking the precepts of Paul Watzlawick, we can say that *the actors then produce "secondary realities"* (Watzlawick).

Knowledge is not an acquired given but rather something that is constructed. Thus, the researchers consider that reality in itself does not exist; there are only representations co-constructed by the actors: "Under this assumption the path of knowledge does not exist *a priori*, it is constructed along the way" (Thiétart,

5 Etienne Wenger speaks of "negotiation of meaning" to define the concepts of community of practice (Wenger, 1998). For him, the negotiation of meaning during the action which is taking place is the most relevant stage to analyze the collective practices. It is precisely within this idea, mentioned by Etienne Wenger, of negotiation of meaning that we situate our discussion, or even "sense-making" (creative meaning) as Karl Weick understands it: The dynamic process of creating sense in construction (Weick, 1995).

2007: 24).Therefore, we choose to think of learning situation as built by the actors while present. In this sense, we try to find the meanings they give from their point of view; this is precisely why we speak of "point of view of the actors in a situation", to borrow a phrase previously used by Talcott Parsons and Alfred Schütz (Parsons, Schütz, 1978).

What interests us here are the points of view of individual and collective actors in educational systems: their projections, their visions, in other words what they think, what they are, or what they claim to do. It is through different questionnaires but also simple participant observations that we focus on the vision they have of their learning, whether classroom based or at a distance. Indeed, to highlight the views of stakeholders, also equates to bringing out the meanings for the actor, "meanings" that are key to understanding and therefore to learning (Depover, Giordana and Marton, 1998).

In addition, each player has its mode of operation, method of thinking, experience, knowledge, and it is within social interaction that s/he will give them meaning. In this regard, Anne-Nelly Perret-Clermont considers that these are "[...] interactions that require the subject to coordinate its actions with those of others, as the result of a process of decentering that engages in a conflict between his point of view and that of its partners" (Perret-Clermont, 1979: 136). In this sense, the idea of socio-cognitive conflict refers to "cognitive restructuring" (*ibid.*) and implies the existence of different points of view which have to be taken into consideration.

The construction of knowledge is an iterative phenomenon as it occurs gradually, individually, but also collectively (we will also discuss collective construction of meaning in this article). This idea echoes that of recursion loops; a role player from the situation's point of view is ultimately the result of a constant interaction between the individual, the surrounding environment, and all other involved individuals.

In view of this "constructivist agreement", knowledge is regarded as inherent in human constructions. Therefore, a learning device, whether face-to-face or at a distance, offers knowledge construction that the learner should own (so we also position ourselves in the idea of action, or the learner taken as an actor of his learning). Many educationalists, also in pedagogics, studied and demonstrated the importance of distinguishing the terms "knowledge" and "expertise". To understand the distinction we make between these two terms, we take the two definitions recently proposed by Renald Legendre. According to him, knowledge includes "facts, information, concepts, principles we acquire through study and experience" (Legendre, 2005: 274), while expertise is "to have in mind a set of information, ideas and data, which are knowledge of a field of activity, an object or a person" (*ibid.*). These two definitions correspond to our point of view and it is precisely because we are interested in the construction of this knowledge that we prefer to invoke the term knowledge.

Following these epistemological precepts we chose to do our fieldwork first, anchoring our methodology on a qualitative approach.

The methodological framework from a qualitative approach

Our research problem leads us to construct a methodology in terms of practices and perspectives of actors in a given situation. We formulate our problem statement as follows: "How can a communications study allow us to understand and analyze meaningful learning experiences of students in a distance e-learning setup?". This statement highlights our commitment to focus on the construction of knowledge among students. However, the research problem can be considered in three parts: first, we seek to understand the meaning given by the role players of their learning situation. This understanding will enable us, secondly, to understand the functioning of e-learning. Finally, through the understanding of how this works, we question the idea of sharing knowledge in a process that we see as collective and shared by the community of learners.

To avoid the "critique of the arbitrary choice of data" (Matthey, 2003: 39) collected and analyzed, we choose to use methodological triangulation, which refers to crossing different data gathering techniques, so as to "improve the validity of the proposed results"[6] (Mangenot, 2006).

We therefore prefer a qualitative approach bringing together four main data collection techniques: observations (made during monthly face-to-face meetings), interviews (centered non-directive and active directive interviews), keeping of a diary (technique used throughout our study), as well as the analysis of several conversations on the discussion forum. This qualitative methodological approach led us to mobilize two main methods of data analysis: the method of qualitative content analysis and the method of qualitative systemic analysis (Mucchielli, 2004).

The method of qualitative content analysis, also called method of categorization, enabled us to deal with three main themes with our learners (having induced the questions during the interviews, with various sub-categories such as the relationship system, the organization of work, etc.): the learners' profile, their meaningful learning experiences and their views on their learning paths. After completing each interview, we inserted all the comments gathered in a reading

6 We understand the concept of practice (just like learning) within the meaning proposed by Etienne Wenger, namely in terms of a social approach.

grid. We then compared each of these opinions, in order to bring out differences, recurrences, etc. (Szafrajzen, 2010).

The second method is called the method of qualitative systemic analysis. By combining conventional techniques (interview and observation, thematic content analysis and graphical representation), the so-called systemic qualitative analysis method wishes to understand and analyze the meaning given by role players in a given situation. Complemented by an analytical commentary showing the circular causalities, the method also highlights the system's logic (implicit and latent rules directing the role players) and "game rules" of the present role players, or repetitive scenarios (Mucchielli 2006). It is to highlight the encompassing system, that is to say, the environment for a pre-defined framework and then to understand the existential and secondary benefits that role players take from their interactions.

In line with the comprehensive approach, the qualitative systemic method adds six reading and interpretation principles of any communication:

- The systemic principle: a phenomenon has to be analyzed in conjunction with a range of other phenomena;
- The framework principle asking the role players to look at and define the environment of any phenomenon;
- The principle of the primacy of systemic context: a phenomenon exists and has meaning only in conjunction with the given context created by the system itself;
- The principle of circular causality: a chain of cause and effect acting through feedback to enhance or inhibit the mechanism;
- The homeostatic principle: a phenomenon system develops an internal force that holds it together;
- The principle of emergence of paradoxes: "*in a system, each phenomenon is both autonomous and forced, organized and organizing, informing and informed*" (Mucchielli, 2004).

It is in line with the work of the school of Palo Alto in the sense that the researcher highlights the significance of the interaction between the different actors. This method interprets the operation of communicational phenomena by attempting to explain the meanings of the exchanges between the different actors involved in the situation (Mucchielli, 2004). Alex Mucchielli (2004) affirms that it is qualitative in that it allows the emergence of the meanings of the exchanges in a communicative system. It is also scientific as it is the researcher with his/her epistemological intellectual, analytical and methodological referents who makes the meanings emerge. Finally, it is part of constructivist paradigm insofar as it highlights the construction of meaning in emerging situations: "The systemic theory of communication is a constructivist theory of the meaning of communications (and of the remainder of communicational phenomena)" (Mucchielli, 2006: 54–55).

Having clarified our epistemological and methodological coordinates, we now propose to introduce e-learning in the field of communication and information sciences.

E-learning in communication and information sciences

The definitions stemming from the learning device typology now distinguish "enriched face-to-face" situations: situations of education or training in which there is multimedia usage in the presence of students, and "enhanced face-to-face" situations: teaching or training situations carried out upstream and/or downstream at a distance with a face-to-face component. They must also be distinguished from so-called mixed situations (or blended learning), situations where education or training activities take place outside the physical presence of the teacher and can lead to "light", "reduced" or "almost nonexistent" face-to-face components.

This plurality of denominations supports all our research, whether bibliographical or web-related, having made us encounter a large amount of names to define distance education, depending on the amount of face-to-face and distance: embedded learning, distance learning, blended learning, full e-learning, mix learning, etc.

According to some authors, we have now arrived in the era of integrated learning: "After "distance learning" and "blended learning", this is the era of the "integrated learning""[7].

The term "Integrated Learning" was proposed by Pierre Dillenbourg to explain the current development of blended learning with complementary face-to-face teaching and distance learning, making the link between different pedagogical and technological strategies:

- integration of an educational strategy to develop both individual, group and classroom work,
- integration of classroom teaching (lecture, exercises, practical work, etc.) and distance teaching (forum, exercises, etc.), the so-called the pedagogical scenario,

7 During the fourth edition of the Forum des TIC held at the Université du travail de Charleroi (Belgium), Pierre Dillenbourg proposed, in a visioconference, an intervention provocatively entitle "The end of e-learning" ("La fin du e-learning").

- integration of different technologies,
- integration of theoretical and practical knowledge/skills.

> Therefore, instead of speaking of CSCL in such a broadened sense of the concept, we tend to use the notion of **integrated learning**, i.e. integration within a coherent pedagogical scenario of activities that occur across multiple social planes (individual, group and class) and places, and can be supported with multiple tools. In formal and informal learning settings, CSCL activities are embedded in more comprehensive sets of activities. (Dillenbourg, Fischer, 2007).

Therefore it is necessary to talk about integrated learning to discuss learning devices bringing together face-to-face and distance modalities, such as the ones we studied.

The presentation of the field of study inevitably leads us to begin by distinguishing two frames of research: that of the learning tool and that of the e-learning situation. In this sense, our approach can be described as "tool-oriented", seeking to bring out the meaning of the communication through its interaction with components of the learning tools (Wilhelm, 2010). To define the term learning device or learning tool, we choose to use Georges Le Meur's definition, the "educational provision" (Le Meur, 2002):

> A learning tool can be defined as a set of services, organized in time and in space, to allow students to perform learning [...]. The online learning tools are characterized from a technological point of view by a strong digital instrumentation of the act of learning (*Ibid.*: 185).

Thus, a learning (or training) tool can be considered as a set of components (in terms of resources/learning tools) available to students to learn. It is also "a body, a place of social interaction and cooperation with its intentions, its material and symbolic functioning and, finally, its own modes of interactions" (Peraya, 1999: 153).

Our research focuses on the third year Bachelor's degree, called Licence 3 in France (a National Diploma accredited by the Ministry of National Education) provided in face-to-face format (over a year), but also at a distance, as e-learning (over two years). The main difference between e-learning and classroom training lies in the components of each of the two learning systems. Classroom training is usually provided by a trainer to learners in the same specialized environment, relying on a direct teaching relationship and in a lecture mode, for a predetermined period.

The studied e-learning environment here is only open under the Continuing Vocational Training format and has a limited number of spaces for about thirty students (called student interns) and it does this because it wants to be a successful educational program in which teachers and student trainees or interns are committed[8]. The students engaging in such training are required to sign a learning contract between the two parties (students and teachers). By signing this document, the student intern agrees to be present at all face-to-face sessions and perform the required work in a timely manner. More symbolically, the learning agreement means the student interns are "responsible for their training": the system leads them to take responsibility for the success or failure of their training.

The program is based on "a specific support tool" whose components are:

- Monthly gatherings: a meeting is organized by the teaching staff every month. Students emphasize the importance of these meetings, allowing them to meet, to encourage each other, to materialize and individualize relationships.
- An educational site: a platform provides for the organization of activities and access to online resources. The intern (student) also has access to a discussion forum; these forums are free and organized by theme and everyone can participate by writing a message at any time and reading the other posts. The written and asynchronous aspects of the forum allows for the "sharing of experiences" (Develotte, Mangenot, 2004).
- Telephone tutorials: Every week, teachers (who then take the role of tutors) provide individualized assistance in answering direct questions from students. The telephone tutorials, an integral part of the learning environment, offer students the opportunity to get in touch with their teachers (synchronous mode). They can then ask any question directly, ask for help and advice.
- Online appointments ("Chat"): students and teachers have the opportunity to meet regularly to discuss and apply technological knowledge by discussing a particular topic.

All components of this learning tool allow the researchers to assume from the onset of the study that there are collective learning situations, as we shall see in the following description of the learning situation.

The actual operation of these components is what we call the learning situation. We are interested in actors and their *actions*, 'actual actions': what the stakeholders are doing (effective actions or informal practices), saying (remarks) and the visions they have of their actions and words (depending on how they perceive the learning tool). It is also about the ways of organizing work under the constraints

8 The learners have to pay for this programme. In general, businesses support them as most of the learners are employees.

inherent to their non-academic life (personal and professional constraints of the student)[9]. We use "learning situation" to describe the concrete and real actions, the various components of discretionary learning that we just described. In this study, we look at "how they – the learners – do" or the actual concrete actions of the learners.

During the investigation, 19 people were registered for the course: the average age of these students is thirty years (we see a very large majority of women in this training: one man only per eighteen women). Half of the students[10] are married, one quarter are single and the last quarter are people who are cohabiting. More than one in two has at least one dependent child. Over three-quarters of them are employees and provide various functions depending on their areas of activity: journalist, assistant manager, administrative manager in an engineering school in computer science, communication assistant in the metalworking sector, medical assistant in a pharmaceutical laboratory, a person in charge of a logistical team. They come from various educational backgrounds (Accounting and Management, Communication-advertising, Graphics, Business Communication, Services and communication networks). This description raises the primary characteristic of these students: they work while studying.

The reasons that led students to choose this type of course are very diverse and range from the fact that this type of training offers the opportunity to learn in an institution without having to move from home (and especially without having to change their personal and professional organization), an interest in the content of the training itself, the desire to grow professionally, the desire to obtain a Bachelor's Degree recognized by the state, the opportunity to be able to grow and to enrich oneself intellectually as well as the department's theoretical position.

After having identified the different student profiles and the reasons for their enrollment in distance education, we wanted to investigate their views on the relations they had with each other and with the teaching team. With these, the opinions of students[11] indicate a strong need to "tame distance" (Jacquinot, 1993) and to overcome geographical distance between them: "We are really waiting for an immediate return from the teaching staff in terms of information, certainly, but also and especially in terms of relationships, support and counseling", two students noted. Indeed, since they see the pedagogical staff on very limited occasions,

---

9 These factors inevitably single out the actor in a particular situation as we consider his tastes, choices and personal opinions, values, past, culture, challenges, positioning. This set of elements is what is called the system of relevance.

10 To be clear, we have chosen to quantify the given information, even if the sample is small.

11 Three quarters of the surveyed students.

students say they expect ongoing support and high reactivity when sending messages to their teachers, or when asking questions during the telephone tutorials. The main criticisms of students emerge from the technical tools, and more specifically the platform, which is not as good as they would like it to be (connection problems or disconnections without apparent reasons, etc.).

However, more than half of the students surveyed said that the platform, including the discussion forum, help to maintain close relations between them, giving them the opportunity to recreate links, to comfort themselves and others, to situate themselves as compared to others, to feel supported and understood by other people sharing the same learning situation[12].

In addition, students also use, on a regular basis, other means of communication, especially online conversations on servers like Msn Messenger or on social networking sites like Facebook. Thus, they argue that their exchanges are more "individualized", more "discrete" and more "friendly". Just like the forum discussions, telephone tutorials are components of the course appreciated by students for availability and demonstrated commitment of tutors, for the psychological support they represent, or for the informational assistance provided.

We propose now to look back on this situation from a communicational viewpoint and thus better understand how students bridge the distance through the emergence of a learning community.

Bridging the gap/distance through the emergence of a learning community

Whatever the reasons for the student interns to choose e-learning rather than traditional classroom training, this choice is meaningful and relevant to the personal/professional projects of the actors concerned and emphasizes the indisputable motivation they have to complete their project. These student interns allow a new meaning to emerge around this action related to the choice of training; this new meaning is intrinsic to the actor himself, his challenges, his personal objectives related to his identity, his professional objectives and, finally, the objectives of his university.

Through the description of the learning tool as well as the situation of e-learning, we were able to check our own postulate of the existence of collective learning situations. Indeed, whether at monthly face-to-face meetings, in

12 This is precisely why we often find, on the discussion forums, personal and/or professional information, showing inherent constraints in their learning situation.

their discussions on social networks or on the discussion forum, these students share their personal, psychological and academic problems but also try to create opportunities to study together outside of the framework provided by the training system(despite the distance between them). These practices emphasize a strong need to address the latent lack induced by this type of learning tool. In fact, a student cannot be an isolated actor alone in the course and must be considered in interaction with others of the same learning tool. At the onset, when the learner enters the course, s/he does not know the other learners (whom s/he never meets often anyway). To counter this, the students will get to know each other through various technological media: "Education and training are ways to build and assert oneself, against oneself, but also to be recognized in a community, the small community of peers and the wider community of professional and social relationships" (Glikman, 2002: 253).

Students build these relationships through the different technological tools; this is how a learning community is constructed. In this sense, the digital space "can be conceptualized as community support, shared space of the collective" (Wilhelm, 2010: 98).

In 1991, in a study conducted by Jean Lave and Etienne Wenger (*Situated Learning: Legitimate Peripheral Participation*), the term community of practice appears for the first time. This concept initially refers to various social groups setting up places and times allocated to learning and incoming students. They then hypothesized that learning is a process of participation in social practices, or "communities of practice". They then sought to understand the process of acquisition of knowledge/expertise in a way of belonging to social groups rather than in terms of cognitive construction. Thus the act of learning becomes a way to participate in social practice or a way of belonging to a community.

In 1998, Etienne Wenger continues his ethnographical study by developing the theory of communities of practice. He then proposed a mapping of communities of practice, including 3 features which enable these communities to be identified: mutual engagement, joint enterprise and shared repertoire. Mutual commitment ensures the existence of shared practice and points to ordinary relationships between members of a community within a social entity (which we found in our study, especially during the observation of the face-to-face sessions).

The joint enterprise is between what the organization requires in terms of objectives and activities and what the role players actually do in the organization.

Finally, the shared repertoire refers to tools (documents, etc.), gestures, codes, routines even becoming elements of practice (as we have observed in the analysis of the conversations on the discussion forums in particular).

As such, students say they can refer to other students who share the same problems, the same needs, and have the same definition of the learning situation: "We know it is not enough to develop communication tools for people to communicate, but it is important that they can co-build a dynamic exchange" (Paquelin, in Le Meur, 2002: 181, our translation). The observations made in the discussion forum and the outspoken freedom of speech observed lead us to analyze this collective exchange approach as an emerging trend within a learning community.

Many authors from the field of educational technology have analyzed the different types of online communities to highlight classifications or typologies. Thus, France Henry and Beatrice Pudelko (2006) define four types of virtual communities: the community of interest, the community of intellectual interest, the community of learners and the community of practice. According to their definitions, the community of learners that we present here corresponds to a community of practice characterized by the identification of the flow of knowledge, mutual assistance, exchange of information, building relationships, sharing of know-how.

Scientific literature on the concept of community establishes distinction and demarcation levels of practices, according to the strength of the social ties developed between the community members and the didactic intent (Henry Pudelko). Thus the notion of community of practice can sometimes be used in conjunction with other theories such as epistemic communities (Hass, 1992), professional communities (Vaast, 2002) or virtual communities (Rheingold, 1995)[13].

While initially the communities, in the traditional sense of the term, are characterized by a certain geographic proximity[14], the virtual learning communities compensate for this distance through sharing of common interests, common projects, but also common values. Without a doubt, in the present study, the creation of this learning community is facilitated by the participants' own cultural and identity backgrounds[15]: "For there to be a sense of belonging to a community, the scene of the interactions (in face-to-face or electronically) must bring together to persons who own or build common bonds between them and whose interactions are reciprocal, sustained, long lasting" (Proulx, 2004: 4).

---

13 It is also worth noting that some researchers and theorists radically question the very notion of community developed by Lave and Wenger in particular: we think of James Gee who, in 2005, proposed the notion of "affinity space", but the present paper chooses not to develop this theory.

14 We refer to the notion of territorial anchoring of a community.

15 As such, it should be noted that virtual communities may reflect a social structure reproducing some characteristics of the structure, rules, norms, implicit or explicit codes of conduct, sanctions of a face-to-face society.

Indeed, these commonalities undoubtedly facilitate the establishment of common and ritualized type of frequent informal conversations outside the university with other means of communication than those available to them in the learning device (conversations via Msn or Facebook) as we have seen in our research.

By engaging in this course, students sign a learning agreement; this demand for commitment reflects an autonomous operating injunction (Wilhelm, 2010) made by the learning device. Especially as we have seen in the analysis of conversations on the discussion board, students try to recreate a true learning community, transcending the boundaries of distance in their training by finding cues and spaces of acceptance in this new device training, instilling a group dynamic, thus overcoming latent loneliness (students work remotely). In doing so, they remind everyone that they have the same goal of a successful training, and they must help each other, regardless of how they operate and consider the various components of the device.

Christine Develotte and François Mangenot cite Barry Wellman, who, in 2001, defines learning communities as follows: "Communities are networks of relationships between people who contribute to conviviality, help, information, a sense of belonging and social identity" (Develotte, Mangenot, 2004, our translation). This definition takes into account the socio-emotional dimension, as well as the cognitive and stresses the importance of social ties, particularly through the "help" that can be given by tutors.

Through these means of communication, students can then overcome the problem of the distance between them, "tame the distance and delete the absence" (Jacquinot, 1993).The spontaneity of online interactions in small groups of learners […] having a common activity and animated appropriately produces a feeling of closeness and solidarity between students and a spirit of cooperation and mutual encouragement. A familiarity between online learners is thus created, despite the age, culture, initial training and professional differences, despite the distance or thanks to it and the differences between the learners. And in this climate of sympathy, spontaneity and mutual support, the relationships of the online learners with their trainer quickly lose their hierarchical nature (Bates, 1995: 209–210, quoted by Develotte and Mangenot, 2004: 331). Students try to move beyond the boundaries of distance; they have to find back references in this new learning environment, to instill group dynamics, thus overcoming latent loneliness (of the student in an e-learning environment). The creation of this learning community (virtual or real) becomes a challenge for each of them, placing them in a collective intellectual practice and inspiring a motivational dynamic of participation[16].

---

16 This social phenomenon is at the heart of the dialectical process that Wenger called "participation" and "reification": by participating, each member of the group seems to be involved

We speak of a collective approach to knowledge sharing to the extent that we observe that these student interns share their responses to their difficulties, as well as their knowledge. This idea of collaboration allows them to reach a common goal, a common interest, namely the successful completion of the course, or more concretely work together on a joint project to submit thereafter (group work).

Thus, students have completely transformed their relationship to knowledge, now evolving into a whole new work environment, with practices very different from the traditional face-to-face set-up. The insertion of an information tool within the learning environment leads the learners to change their environment; learning is more of self-centered, autonomous and brings learner empowerment.

Conclusion

The presentation of an e-learning course in communication and information sciences has enabled us to highlight some of the meaningful learning experiences for students using the learning tool. In particular, we found that loneliness – very present in the training – induced the emergence of a learning community, with students venturing on a collective and shared path. This understanding of the stakeholders' views in a learning situation is only possible given the meaning that each student gives to his/her learning situation, experiencing and interacting with other components of the course (be these human entities, material or ideational).

This study highlighted that students were forced to change their position of learning alone at a distance to that of a learner belonging to a learning community. Their respective behaviors in the group then take on new meanings, revolving mainly around identity recognition of shared interests and objectives (to the extent they deal with other students sharing the same situations, needs, issues, problems, and thereby the same meaning).

We can then assume that the creation of this community is a way for them to move beyond the virtual group and to project, in an imaginary or symbolic way, social and relational characteristics inherent to any physical and real community. It now remains to be examined what the scope, importance or social and cultural engagement, of such communities can be in the implementation of social projects.

---

in this community and the meaning given to this action becomes that of identity construction (Wenger, 1998).

References

Choplin, H., (dir.), (2002). Les TIC au service de nouveaux dispositifs de formation – *Éducation permanente*, n. 152.

Depover C., Giardina M., Marton P., (1998). *Les environnements d'apprentissage multimédia*, Paris: l'Harmattan.

Develotte C., Mangenot F., (2004). Tutorat et communauté dans un campus numérique non collaboratif, *Distances et savoirs*, vol. 2, n. 3, p. 309–333.

Dillenbourg P., Fisher F. (2007). Basics of Computer-Supported Collaborative Learning, in *Zeitschrift für Berufs- und Wirtschaftspädagogik.* 21, p. 111–130.

Glikman V., (2002). *Des cours par correspondance au 'e-learning', panorama des formations ouvertes et à distance,* Paris: Presses Universitaires de France.

Jacquinot G., (1993). Apprivoiser la distance et supprimer l'absence? Ou les défis de la formation à distance, in *Revue Française de Pédagogie*, Paris, INRP, n. 102, p. 55–67.

Lave J., Wenger E., (1991). *Situated Learning: Legitimate Peripheral Participation*, Cambridge: Cambridge University Press.

Legendre R., (2005). *Dictionnaire actuel de l'éducation*, 3ème édition, Montréal, Éditions Guérin.

Le Meur G., (dir), (2002). *Université ouverte, formation virtuelle et apprentissage : communications francophones du cinquième Colloque européen sur l'autoformation*, Paris: l'Harmattan.

Le Moigne J.-L., (2003). *Le constructivisme. Modéliser pour comprendre,* Tome 3, Paris: l'Harmattan.

Lévy P., (1994). *Intelligence collective*, Paris: La Découverte.

Mangenot F., (2006). Analyser les interactions pédagogiques en ligne, pourquoi, comment? *Intercompreensão*, 13 (décembre 2006), Comunicacão electronica em contextos de educacão linguistica. Teorias e praticas, p. 11–28. Editions Cosmos/Escola Superior de Educacão de Santarem, Portugal.

Matthey M., (2003). *Apprentissage d'une langue et interaction verbale*, 2èmeédition, Bern: Peter Lang.

Mucchielli A., (dir), (2004). *Dictionnaire des méthodes qualitatives en sciences humaines,* Paris: Armand Colin.

Mucchielli A., (dir), (2003). La place du constructivisme pour l'étude des communications, *Actes du colloque de Béziers*, Béziers, Centre d'étude et de recherche sur l'information et la communication, Avril.

Mucchielli A., (2006). Un nouveau domaine des sciences info-com : la formation à distance, *Distances et savoirs*, vol. 4, n. 2, 2006, p. 223–229.

Papadakis M. C., (2003). People Can Create a Sense of Community in Cyberspace, *Revue en ligne*, Arlington, SRI International, URL: www.sri.com/policy/csted/reports/sandt/it/Papada kis IT virtual communities issue brief.pdf consulté en février 2010.

Parsons T., Schütz A., (1978). *The Theory of Social Action*, Bloomington: Indiana University Press.

Peraya D., (1999). Médiation et médiatisation : le campus virtuel. Le dispositif. Entre usages et concepts, *in* Jacquinot G., Montoyer L., (dir.), *Le Dispositif. Entre usage et concepts,* Hermès, CNRS, n. 25, p. 153–167.

Perret-Clermont A.-N., (1979). *La Construction de l'Intelligence dans l'Interaction Sociale*, Genève: Peter Lang.

Proulx S., (2004). Les communautés virtuelles construisent-elles du lien social?», *Actes du colloqueL'organisation média. Dispositifs médiatiques, sémiotiques et de médiations de l'organisation*, Université Jean Moulin, Lyon, 19–20 novembre 2004, 8 p.
Resnick, L.B., Levine J.M., Teasley S.D., (eds.), (1991). *Perspectives on Socially Shared Cognition*, American Psychological Association, Washington, D.C., 1991, p. 1–20.
Szafrajzen B., (2010). *Lecture communicationnelle de deux dispositifs d'apprentissage au sein d'un même département universitaire. Le cas de la licence en sciences de l'information et de la communication*, thèse de doctorat, Université de Montpellier.
Thiétart, R.A., (2007). *Méthodes de recherche en management*, Paris: Dunod.
Watzlawick P., (dir), (1988). *L'invention de la réalité. Contributions au constructivisme,* Paris: Seuil.
Weick, K. E., (1995). *Sensemaking In Organizations*, Thousand Oaks: Sage.
Wenger E., (1998). *Communities of Practice: Learning, Meaning and Identity*, New York: Cambridge University Press,.
Wilhelm C., (2010). Emergence d'une culture communicationnelle au sein d'un dispositif international en ligne, Distances géoculturelles et proximité axioliogique, *Distances et savoirs*, n.1, vol. 8, p. 79–107.

Social Health Education Programs at School: Investigating the Integration of Serious Games in the Curriculum

Katarina Panic, Verolien Cauberghe, Patrick De Pelsmacker

Abstract

To date, studies conducted on the effectiveness of games as learning tools often show mixed results, making it difficult to generalize about their overall impact on learning. Therefore, this study investigates the relationship between technology and education, more specifically the potential of educational games as a tool to enhance the effectiveness of traditional health education programs in school. First, we investigate whether including a serious game into a traditional school health education program can potentially increase the effectiveness of this program, increasing children's awareness of the health issue and improving their behavior. Second, we consider how these games should be integrated into health education programs to maximize their potential. We investigate the impact of two integration strategies (a game as pre-instructional versus post-instructional strategy) to maximize the learning (and persuasive) process of the health education program. The results show that integrating a serious game into a traditional classroom lesson appears to be an effective tool to increase children's classroom attention, although it does not directly lead to behaviour change. Second, the results reveal that games are better played before the lesson than afterwards. In sum, this study shows that digital games can provide an additional value to the educational program but in domains like health education where actual behavioural changes are pursued, the transfer from game to behaviour change is neither automatic nor guaranteed.

Introduction

Every year, new public health campaigns are launched in an attempt to shape people's attitudes, increase awareness, and improve changes in personal or collective behavior. In general, these campaigns can be labeled as social marketing campaigns, as they use marketing principles and techniques to advance a social cause, idea or behavior (Kotler & Zaltman, 1971). When it comes to social marketing campaigns targeting children, a large portion of the education is provided through the school system. Schools are important outlets to reach millions of children, and school-based education programs allow social marketers to educate children on key topics like health problems (e.g. unhealthy nutrition) and promote lifelong healthy behaviors (e.g. physical activity). Today, however, traditional school health education programs and other behavior-change interventions targeted at children are facing a big challenge as they seem to be limited in their effectiveness (Baranowski et al., 2002; Summerbell et al., 2005; Waters et al., 2011). Although the specific reason behind this decline is unknown, various authors attribute these findings to changes that the current generation is facing (e.g. Baranowski et al., 2008), basing themselves mainly on Prensky's (2001) 'digital natives' theory.

According to Prensky (2001), people born in the last two decades are substantially different from earlier generations because they are always surrounded by, and interacting with, new technologies such ascomputers, videogames, cell phones, and so on. For this reason, this generation is often labeled as 'digital natives' (Prensky, 2001) or the 'net generation' (Tapscott, 1998). While previous generations may learn to use new technologies along the way, digital natives are supposed to be 'native speakers' of the digital language as they have been immersed in this technology all their life (Helsper & Enyon, 2009). As a result, it is argued that pupils from the net generation process information in a fundamentally different way. Digital natives are said to be so used to technology and active, collaborative learning that the way they think and learn has changed (Prensky, 2001; Tapscott, 2008). If this is the case, however, there are some profound implications for education as our current educational system is unprepared for these 'new ways of learning' (Oblinger & Oblinger, 2005; Rainie, 2006; Underwood, 2007; Gibbons, 2007; Bennett, Maton & Kervin, 2008). This is echoed by Prensky's (2001: 1) claim that: '*our students have changed radically. Today's students are no longer the people our educational system was designed to teach*'. A powerful new teaching method, according to Prensky and other advocates of game-based learning, would be to use computer games to teach the digital natives. As games combine learning with fun, challenge and interactivity, they are expected to appeal more strongly to youngsters of the net generation than traditional education (Clarke & Dede, 2007; Dede, 2009). Baranowski and colleagues (2008: 74) also confirm the potential of games for traditional school health education, arguing that '*new channels are needed to reach children that offer promise of promoting substantial health-related behavior changes. One such new channel is the video game.*'

Although the concept of the net generation has been widely adopted in literature, recent work argues that Prensky's theory is overly simplified and lacks empirical support, as most knowledge has been derived from anecdotal accounts or based on untested assumptions (see Bennett, Maton & Kervin (2008) or Bennett & Maton (2010) for a review). For example, recent empirical research has questioned the validity of the generational interpretation of the digital native concept (Helsper & Eynon, 2009). While some support the natives / immigrants dichotomy proposed by Prensky, reporting significant differences between their use of (and preferences for) technologies(e.g., Facer & Furlong, 2001; Dutton & Helsper, 2007; Livingstone & Helsper, 2007; Cheong, 2008; Hargittai & Hinnart, 2008), other studies fail to find results predicted by the digital native rhetoric(e.g., Conole et al., 2006;

Kennedy et al., 2008, 2009; Czerniewicz & Brown 2010; Jones & Healing, 2010; Jones et al., 2010). Also, while traditional studies assume that the digital natives are a homogenous group characterized by a wide experience and advanced skills in using information and communication technologies (Prensky 200;1 Oblinger & Oblinger 2005; Tapscott, 2008; Bekebrede, Warmelink &Mayer, 2011), recent studies indicate that the Net Generation is actually a diverse group when it comes to technology use and experience (van Dijk 2005; Barzilai-Nahon 2005; Helsper & Enyon, 2009; Kennedy et al., 2010; Hargittai, 2010). In sum, we can conclude that more and more authors are questioning Prensky's concept of digital natives, which in turn relates to a broader and possibly critical debate on the educational role of digital games. If the notion of a new, digital generation is exaggerated, should we also question the potential of digital games as a means to teach this new generation? Today, although various authors support the potential of games as learning tools (Squire & Steinkuehler, 2005; Garcia-Barcena, & Garcia-Crespo, 2006; Vasiliou, & Economides, 2007; Tuzun et al., 2008; Echeverria et al., 2011; Yang, Chien, & Liu, 2012), others appear far less enthusiastic about this new approach to learning.Ferneding (2003), for example, argues that there is a need for a more critical attitude toward the adoption of technological innovations in education. Other authors even label Prensky's work as 'misplaced technological determinism', arguing he attributes too great a role to technology, and thereby questioning the importance of digital technology for younger generations, as well as its value in educational practices (Selwyn, 2009; Koutroloulos, 2011).

In order to contribute to this debate, the first and main goal of this study is to investigate the relationship between technology and education, more specifically the potential of educational games (also referred to as serious games) as a tool to enhance the effectiveness of traditional health education programs in school. As mentioned above, studies conducted on the effectiveness of games as learning tools often show mixed results, making it difficult to generalize about their overall impact in improving learning. Also, most research is focused on the effectiveness of games as learning tools, but games are rarely studied as a part of an overall health education program. As a consequence, empirical research on the explicit integration of games into the pedagogical process of the class is lacking (Echeverria et al., 2011). In this study, we investigate whether including a serious game on dental hygiene into a traditional school health education program can potentially increase the effectiveness of this program, increasing children's awareness of the health issue and improving their behavior.

Second, next to research explaining *whether* serious games can be effective learning tools, it is also essential to consider *how* these games should be integrated into health education programs to maximize their potential (Van Eck, 2006).

Games can be integrated in various ways and previous research shows that different ways of implementation may lead to different learning outcomes, but their effects on behavioral outcome are unknown. Today, however, an important factor inhibiting the use of serious games in health education programs at school is the teacher's lack of knowledge about how to implement these games in traditional teaching (Baek, 2008). Therefore, the second aim of this study is to investigate the impact of two strategies to integrate games into the traditional lesson to maximize the learning (and persuasive) process of the health education program. The impact of a game as *pre-instructional versus post-instructional strategy* in relation to a traditional lesson is examined.

Theoretical framework and hypotheses development

Games as learning tools

One of the main aspects of social marketing is to increase and improve children's health-related knowledge and behavior and avoid or reduce health risks. Although today, health information is mainly communicated to children through traditional media, the substantial growth of new interactive game technology raises new opportunities for health education. Indeed, an increasing amount of research suggests that computer games can also be powerful learning tools (Klopfer & Squire, 2008; Mitchell, Dede, & Dunleavy, 2009). When used for purposes other than mere entertainment, these games are referred to as serious games, defined as:

> a mental contest, played with a computer in accordance with specific rules, that uses entertainment to further government or corporate training, education, health, public policy, and strategic communication objectives (Zyda, 2005 p. 26).

Besides being a fun activity, serious games also involve pedagogy, thereby offering a new and interactive learning experience based on learning by doing (Schaffer et al., 2005).The benefits of video games as learning tools have been extensively documented in various studies. Among others, due to their fun and engaging nature, games are said to attract and maintain attention, increase player engagement and interest in the subject, promote a more positive attitude towards learning and enhance behavior change through enhanced motivation (Ryan, Rigby & Przybylski, 2006; Bourgonjon et al., 2009). Therefore, digital games could potentially be interesting new communication tools to integrate in health education programs at schools, making the educational activities more enjoyable and increase engagement while fostering better behavioral outcomes (Baranowski et al., 2003).

To date, however, most games used in a classroom context focus on traditional disciplines such as mathematics, science or language (Papastergiou, 2009), aiming to increase children's knowledge rather than change children's behavior. Although there are games which have proven to be effective in changing children's behavior, these are often advergames designed to change children's behavior in a commercial sense (e.g. Mallinckrodt & Mizerski, 2007). Nevertheless, a few games have been found to change children's health-related behavior, but these are rarely suited for general health education programs at school, as these games often focus on specific health issues such as teaching children with type 1 diabetes to use insulin (Brown et al., 1997) or enhancing self-management skills for children with asthma (McPherson et al., 2006). To our knowledge, only a few general health education games can be found (e.g. for improving dietary outcome), but these are investigated in simple effect studies (play versus no play), rather than evaluated as a part of a health education program (see Baranowski et al., 2003; Pempek & Calvert, 2009). As educational games should be integrated *in* the school curriculum, rather than being an add-on (Mitchell & Savill-Smith, 2004), the main goal of this study is to investigate whether integrating serious games into the traditional lessons could potentially bring added value to health education programs at school.

Learning in a state of flow

Integrating educational games in traditional lessons has the advantage that teachers can combine education with entertainment and playfulness. This playfulness, supplemented by high challenge, clear goals, multimodal representation and continuous feedback triggers an experience of flow during game play (Csikszentmihalyi, 1990). Flow is an optimal state of enjoyment where people are completely absorbed in the game, feeling as if they were actually part of the game, also referred to as immersion, forgetting their surroundings (Gentile, 2009). As argued by Adachi and Willoughby (2012), a positive outcome of video game play is that it may induce flow since the player may experience extreme focus, lose track of time, and find the activity intrinsically rewarding. The combination of the flow experience and the active participation allows games to encompass and capture a player's full attention (Baranowski et al., 2012). In addition, research in the domain of integrated marketing communication shows that a multiple-source condition engenders higher attention compared to a single-source condition (Peltier, Schibrowsky &Schultz, 2003). Therefore, we expect that integrating games into the traditional lesson may lead to increased attention and concentration with children, increasing their attention to the game, but also to the traditional lesson in which the game is integrated.

H1: *Compared to a traditional teacher-centered lesson, a combined teaching method (where an educational game is included in the lesson) will result in a higher attention to the traditional lesson.*

Next to increasing children's attention, a feeling of flow (evoked by the game) is believed to be a component of intrinsic motivation. This claim is supported by the findings of Baranowski et al. (2008), proving that games may be intrinsically motivating, which may in turn promote a more positive attitude towards learning and enhance behavior change. Indeed, Finneran and Zhang (2005) state that during flow, people are so absorbed in an activity that they show high performance without being aware of their environment. In addition, research shows that interactivity raises the comprehension and retention rate of players, which may enhance learning as well (Lindstrom, 1994).

Furthermore, feelings of flow have been proven to support a positive user experience (Inal &Cagiltay, 2007). Therefore, it can be expected that integrating serious games into the educational programs at school may lead to a 'transfer' of positive feelings, leading to a more enjoyable, more interesting and thus more effective learning environment than traditional learning modes. This means that children do not only like these games, but their increased attention during game play may also boost the educational impact of games. This is confirmed by Dowey (1987), who found that a combination of traditional teaching and game-based learning is the best way to transfer health-related knowledge to children. Based on these findings, we expect that a combined teaching method of a traditional lesson with a game will be an effective way to increase children's awareness and thus improve their health related behavior:

H2: *Compared to a traditional teacher-centered lesson, a combined teaching method (where an educational game is included in the lesson) will result in more favorable <u>behavioral intention</u> (improve dental hygiene).*

Integrating games in the classroom – comparing different integration strategies

Although a lot of attention has been devoted to the effectiveness of games as learning tools, research has overlooked the practical aspect of integrating computer games in a classroom setting. However, additional investigation is necessary to determine how games should be integrated into the education program at school (Read & Shortell, 2011). The fact is that developing effective games is not enough. Educators or schools should also know what to do with them. And while the majority of students play video games, this is, however, not the case for teachers (Schaffer et al., 2004). Therefore, the next challenge for game designers and educators is to understand how to integrate games into the predominant arena for learning: schools. If we are to bring computers into the classroom, it is essential to know how these games can be integrated most effectively to improve student learning.Therefore, we try to find an answer to this question by testing to what extent different lesson/game sequences can influence the desired outcomes. In sum, two different types of strategies can be distinguished, based on when the game is integrated into the traditional lesson. In the *pre-instructional strategy,* the game is played before the lesson in order to evoke interest in the topic. In the *post-instructional strategy*, however, games are played after the lesson for synthesis and to enhance memory (Van Eck, 2006).

To date, however, only one study has examined the effect of integration strategies on learning outcome, but this study dates from 1985 and uses a game designed to teach children mathematics, rather than improve their health behavior (Bright, Harvey & Wheele, 1985). According to the 'bin model' theory (Wyer & Srull, 1986), children are only able to process a limited amount of information, which is why the order in which information is presented affects children's processing. According to this model, information encountered last will have a higher probability of recall, following the last-in-first-out principle. Also relevant here are the mechanisms of the *primacy* and *recency effects*, two types of order effects identified by researchers in risk communication, marketing and psychology (Hogarth & Einhorn, 1992; Buda & Zhang, 2000; Petty, Tormala, Hawkins & Wegener, 2001; Murphy, Hofacker & Mizerski, 2006; Chiou, Wan & Lee, 2008). A primacy effect occurs when learning is more heavily influenced by early experience than by later experience or by the first presented information. The recency effect, on the other hand, occurs when the last presented information generates a stronger effect than earlier presented information (Luhmann, 2011). Impression formation research showed that low motivation to process is linked with primacy effects and high motivation to process information is associated with recency effects (Eingar et al., 2012; Petty et al., 2001). The reasoning behind this is that it asks more motivation to withhold judgment until all information has been processed (Ein-gar et al., 2012). As playing a game is a typical situation which evokes high motivation to process information among players (Papastergiou, 2009), we expect recency effects to occur.

As the aim of this study is to increase children's attention to – and enhance the effectiveness of – traditional education programs at school, the main goal is to enhance the learning outcome of the traditional lesson. Taking both the bin model theory and the primacy and recency theory into account, the best way to obtain this effect is to precede the traditional lesson with the game. This is in line with an advertising study on message sequence by Loda and Coleman (2005), who found that preceding traditional advertising with multimedia publicity leads to more message acceptance and more message response, increasing advertising effectiveness. Therefore, we expect that playing an educational game *before* attending the lesson will raise curiosity and interest, resulting in more attention paid to the subsequent traditional lesson:

> ***H3:*** *When the educational game precedes the lesson, children's attention to the lesson will be higher compared to the condition where the game is played after the lesson.*

In addition, we expect that playing an educational game *before* attending the lesson will raise curiosity and interest, leading to a deeper processing of the subsequent traditional lesson and hence more impact on attention and behavioral outcome.

> ***H4:*** *When the educational game precedes the lesson, children's behavioral intention will be higher compared to the condition where the game is played after the lesson.*

Materials and methods

To test the hypotheses, 3 different experimental conditions were set up in which children 1) played the game before the traditional lesson, 2) played the game after attending this lesson or 3) only attended the lesson but did not play the serious game (control group). In total, 5 classes from different primary schools across Belgium were examined and pupils were randomly divided across conditions. In total, 136 children from the third grade (mean age = 8 years, 53% boys) participated. Children between the age of seven and nine are chosen because at this age children are capable of reading information and they also have the skills to play the computer game properly. Prior to data collection, institutional approval and parental and child informed consent were obtained.

At the start of the experiment (expect for the control condition), the pupils were informed that they were about to attend a lesson and play a computer game, and that they would be asked a few questions afterwards. The educational topic was dental care since this is a part of the third-grade curriculum and a current health problem among young children. In the lesson, the importance of dental hygiene, healthy food and frequent visits to the dentist were discussed.

In the first two conditions, each child individually played the serious game either before or after attending the same collective lesson. The game was especially developed to teach third grade children the importance of dental hygiene. Throughout the game, children are challenged to brush teeth correctly using the mouse, visit the dentist and distinguish between healthy and unhealthy food (see appendix 1). In the third (control) group, the children did not play the educational game, but only attended a traditional teacher-centered lesson. As there is no game play, this lesson lasts approximately 10 minutes longer than the lesson in the first and second experimental conditions in order to keep the 'total learning time' equal between all groups. This is important because the total time the children are exposed to the topic can have an important effect on the learning process. Further, we made sure that all the children received the same amount of information (whether they played a game or not), only presented in a different way (through the game or via the teacher).

Afterwards, all participants were asked to complete the same standardized questionnaire measuring self-reported attention to the lesson (Hart & Staveland, 1988) and behavioral intention to brush teeth better and more frequently (based on the scale by Marin, Lee & Yang, 2004). Given the young age and limited reading skills of the target audience, existing scales were simplified into one item, 4 point Likert scales. A few days after the experiment, the parents of each participant received a survey asking them to indicate on a 5-point scale (never – very often) whether they have noticed any increased engagement concerning dental hygiene with their child ('*Since the study, is your child more consciously engaged with his or her dental care?*'), or any improvement in their dental care ('*Since the study, does the child ask to brush his or her teeth more often than before?*').

Results

To test the first two hypotheses, the results of the children who played the game before attending the lesson are compared to those of the children who did not play the game (control group). Independent t-tests show that children from the combined condition (game + lesson) pay significantly more attention to the lesson (M= 3.73) than children who only attend the (longer version of the) lesson (M = 3.34, $t(60)= 2.750$, $p = .008$). This shows that integrating a game into the lesson can increase the amount of attention children pay to this lesson, supporting H1. However, the results show no difference in children's intention to improve their dental hygiene between the combined condition (M = 2.73) and children who only attended a lesson (M= 2.60, $t(58)= 1.344$, $p = .185$). H2 is not supported. A follow-up survey conducted among the parents reveals that children from the combined condition showed more conscious engagement with their dental hygiene (M= 3.33) than children from the control group (M= 2.47; p = .034). However, there appears to be no difference in the amount of behavioral change parents had noticed between these two groups (p = .138).

To test the third and fourth hypotheses, the results of the children who played the game before the lesson were compared to those of the children who played the game after attending the lesson. The results show that when the game is played before the lesson, children paid more attention to this lesson (M = 3.73) than when it is not preceded by game-play (M= 3.48, $t(67)$= 1.945, p = .056). This supports H3. Further, children's intention to improve their dental care is significantly higher when the educational game is played before the lesson (M= 2.73), than when it is played afterwards (M= 2.48 $t(66)$= 2.579, p = .012). H4 is supported. Furthermore, the results of the follow-up survey show that parents noticed a higher increase in both children's engagement (p= .003) and their dental care (p= .029) in the game-lesson compared to the lesson-game condition.

Conclusion: what is the use of games in traditional education?

When it comes to the debate of the educational role of digital games, both ardent proponents and techno-cynics can be found. While some argue that shifting our current educational system towards a more digital approach is necessary, others describe this notion of digital natives or "new millennium learners" who need to be approached with renewed educational formats as overrated and unrealistic (Bennett, Maton & Kervin, 2008). As to date, empirical research on the explicit integration of games into the in-class pedagogical process is lacking, the goal of the present study was to shed light on *whether* games should be used and *how* they can be implemented in traditional school-based health education, in order to increase children's motivation to adjust their behavior and reconnect them with traditional health education programs at school.

The present study contributes to the literature on game-based learning in several ways. First, the results show that integrating a serious game into a traditional classroom lesson does not improve children's intention to adjust their behavior in a favorable way. However, implementing computer games in the classroom does appear to be an effective tool to increase children's classroom attention. This suggests that although games could potentially be an effective way to reconnect today's children with the educational system, it does not directly lead to behavior change. This is in line with previous research which suggests that games may be very appealing to children, but may also distract children from learning (Jaruratanasirikul, Wongwaitaweewong & Sangsupawanich, 2009).

Second, when educational games are integrated in traditional education, this study provides a first step towards a practical guideline for educators on how to best implement computer games in the classroom. The results reveal that games are better played before the lesson than afterwards. This way, through recency effects, the last presented information generates a strong learning effect, generating interest in the topic and making children pay better attention to the subsequent lesson, which even results in a higher behavioral intention. Consequently, these results provide a guideline for those digital immigrants (teachers) who wish to integrate serious games into their traditional teaching methods.

In sum, this study provides some evidence in support of a more nuanced interpretation of the popular assumption that games are indispensable tools in the current educational system. The results show that digital games can provide an additional value, but they are not essential or omnipotent as educational tools. Although children seem to be attracted by the game, and integrating a game in the educational program has the power to increase children's classroom attention, the results show that in domains like health education where actual behavioral changes are pursued, the transfer from game to behavior change is neither automatic nor guaranteed.

Finally, we end this chapter with some directions and suggestions for further research. First, it would be interesting to investigate the effect of these games after repeated exposure, since repetition could affect both learning and attention once the players get more confident with the game. Secondly, further research could, for example, use recall methods to measure attention in addition to the self-reported measures used in this study. Finally, as not all games will be equally effective at all levels of learning, further research should look into different types of serious games discussing different educational topics.

References

Adachi, P.J.C & Willoughby, T. (2012). Do Video Games Promote Positive Youth Development? *Journal of Adolescent Research*, 28(2), 155–165. DOI: 10.1177/0743558412464522.

Baek, Y.K. (2008). What Hinders Teachers in Using Computer and Video Games in the Classroom? Exploring Factors Inhibiting the Uptake of Computer and Video Games, *CyberPsychology & Behavior*. December 2008, 11(6): 665–671.

Baranowski, T., Baranowski, K., Cullen, K.W., Marsh, T., Islam, N., Zakeri, I., Honess-Morreale, L. & DeMoor, C. (2003). Squire's Quest!: Dietary outcome evaluation of a multimedia game. *American Journal of Preventive Medicine*, 24(1) 52–61.

Baranowski, T., Buday, R., Thompson, D. & Baranowski, J. (2008). Playing for Real: Video Games and Stories for Health-Related Behavior Change, *American Journal of Preventive Medicine*; 34(1): 74–82.

Baranowski, T., Baranowski, J., O'Connor, T., Lu, A.L & Thompson, D. (2012). Is enhanced physical activity possible using active videogames? *Games for Health Journal*, 1(3), 228–232.

Baranowski, T., Cullen, K.W., Nicklas, T., Thompson, D. & Baranowski, J. (2002). School-based obesity prevention: a blueprint for taming the epidemic. *American Journal of Health Behavior*, 26, 486–93. [PubMed: 12437023].

Barzilai-Nahon, K. (2006). Gaps and Bits: Conceptualizing Measurements for Digital Divide/s. *The Information Society: An International Journal*, 22(5). DOI: 10.1080/01972240600903953.

Bekebrede, G., Warmelink, H.J.G & Mayer, I.S. (2011). Reviewing the need for gaming in education to accommodate the Net generation. *Computers & Education*, 57(2), 1521–1529.

Bennett, S. Maton, K. & Kervin, L. (2008). The 'digital natives' debate: A critical review of the evidence. *British Journal of Educational Technology*, 39(5), 775–786.

Bennett, S. & Maton, K. (2010). Beyond the 'digital natives' debate: Towards a more nuanced understanding of students' technology experiences. *Journal of Computer Assisted Learning*, 26(5), 321–331.

Bourgonjon, J., Valcke, M., Soetaert, R. & Schellens, T. (2009). Students' perceptions about the use of video games in the classroom. *Computers & Education*, 54(4), 1145–1156.

Bright, G., Harvey, J.G. & Wheele, M.M. (1985). Learning and Mathematics Games. *Journal for Research in Mathematics Education*, Monograph, 1, i+1-189.

Brown JS, Liberman DA, Germeny BA, Fan YC, Wilson DM, Pasta DJ. (1997). Educational video game for juvenile diabetes: results of a controlled trial. London: Medical Informatics.

Buda, R. & Zhang, Y. (2000). Consumer product evaluation: the interactive effect of message framing, presentation order, and source credibility. *Journal of Product & Brand Management*, 9 (4), 229 – 242.

Cheong, P.H. (2008). The Young and the techless? Investigating Internet use and problem – solving behaviors of young adults in Singapore. *New Media and Society*, 10(5), 771–791.

Chiou, W.B., Wan, C.S. & Lee, H.Y. (2008). Virtual experience vs. brochures in the advertisement of scenic spots: How cognitive preferences and order effects influence advertising effects on consumers. *Tourism Management*, 29 (1), 146–150.

Clarke, J. & Dede, C. (2007). in The 2007 Computer-Supported Collaborative Learning (CSCL) Conference, C. A. Chinn, G. Erkens, S. Putambekar, Eds., New Brunswick, NJ, (International Society for the Learning Sciences, New Brunswick, NJ, 2007), pp. 141–144.

Csikszentmihalyi, M. (1990). *Flow: The Psychology of Optimal Experience*. NY: Harper and Row.

Czerniewicz, L. & Brown, C. (2010). Born into the Digital Age in the south of Africa: the reconfiguration of the "digital citizen". Proceedings of the 7th International Conference on Networked Learning, 859–865.

Dede, C. (2009). Immersive Interfaces for Engagement and Learning. *Science 2*, 323(5910), pp. 66–69, DOI: 10.1126/science.1167311.

Dowey, J.A. (1987). Computer games for dental health education in primary schools. *Health Education Journal* September 1987, 46(3), 107–108.

Dunleavy, M., Dede, C. & Mitchell, R. (2009). Affordances and Limitations of Immersive Participatory Augmented Reality Simulations for Teaching and Learning. *Journal of Science Education and Technology*, 18(1), 7–22.

Dutton, W.H. & Helsper, E.J. (2007). The Internet in Britain: 2007. Oxford (UK): Oxford Internet Institute, University of Oxford. Available online at, http://www.oii.ox.ac.uk/microsites/oxis/.

Echeverría, A.,García-Campo, C. Nussbaum, M., Gil, F., Villalta, M., Améstica, M. & Echeverría, S. (2011). A framework for the design and integration of collaborative classroom games. *Computers & Education*, 57(1), 1127–1136.

Ein-Gar, D., Shiv, B. & Tormala, Z.L. (2012). When Blemishing Leads to Blossoming: The Positive Effect of Negative Information. *Journal of Consumer Research*, 38 (5), 846–859.

Facer, K. & Furlong, R. (2001). Beyond the Myth of the 'Cyberkid': Young People at the Margins of the Information Revolution. *Journal of Youth Studies*, 4(4), 451–469.

Ferneding, K.A. (2003). Questioning Technology. Electronic Technologies and Educational Reform. In *Counterpoints: Studies in the Postmodern Theory of Education*. Vol. 159. Eds: J.L. Kincheloe and S.R. Steinberg. Peter Lang, NY.

Finneran, S. & Zhang, P. (2005). Flow in computer-mediated environments: promises and challenges. *Communications of the Association for Information Systems* (15), 82–101.

Garcia-Barcena, J. & Garcia-Crespo, A. (2006). Game Based Learning: A Research on Learning Content Management Systems. Proceedings of 5th WSEAS International Conference on Education and Educational Technology. pp. 541–592.

Gentile, D. A. (2009). Pathological video-game use among youth ages 8 to 18: A national study. *Psychological Science*, 20, 594–602. doi: 10.1111/j.1467-9280.2009.02340.x.

Hart, S. & Staveland, L. (1988). Development of NASA-TLX (Task Load Index): Results of Empirical and Theoretical Research. Human Mental Workload, Amsterdam: North-Holland, 139–183.

Hargittai, E. (2010). Digital Na(t)ives? Variation in Internet Skills and Uses among Members of the Net Generation. *Sociological Inquiry*, 80(1), 91–113.

Hargittai, E. & Hinnart, A. (2008). Digital Inequality: differences in Young adults use of the Internet. *Communication Research*, 35(5), 602–621.

Helsper, E. & Enyon, R. (2009). Digital natives: where is the evidence? *British Educational Research Journal*. pp. 1–18. DOI: 10.1080/01411920902989227.

Hogarth, R.M. & Einhorn, H.J. (1992). Order effects in belief updating: The belief-adjustment model. *Cognitive Psychology*, 24 (1), 1–55.

Inal, Y. & Cagiltay, K. (2007). Flow experiences of children in an interactive social game environment. *British Journal of Educational Technology*, 38, 455–464.

Jaruratanasirikul, S., Wongwaitaweewong, K. & Sangsupawanich, P. (2009). Electronic Game Play and School Performance of Adolescents in Southern Thailand. *CyberPsychology & Behavior*. October 2009, 12(5), 509–512.

Jones, C. & Healing, G. (2010). Net generation students: agency and choice and the new technologies. *Journal of Computer Assisted Learning*, 26(5), 344–356.

Jones, C., Ramanau, R., Cross, S. & Healing, G. (2010). Net generation or Digital Natives: Is there a distinct new generation entering university? *Computers & Education*, 54(3), 722–732.

Kennedy, G., Judd, T., Dalgarno, B. & Waycott, J. (2010). Beyond natives and immigrants: exploring types of net generation students. *Journal of Computer Assisted Learning*, 26(5), 332–343.

Kennedy, G., Dalgarno, B., Bennett, S., Gray, K., Waycott, J., Judd, T., Bishop, A., Maton, K., Krause, K. & Chang, R. (2009). *Educating the Net Generation: A Handbook of Findings for Practice and Policy*. Australian Learning and Teaching Council, Sydney.

Klopfer, E. & Squire, K. (2008). Environmental detectives – the development of an augmented reality platform for environmental simulations. *Educational Technology Research and Development*, 56(2), 203–28.

Kotler, P. & Zaltman, G. (1971). Social Marketing: An Approach to Planned Social Change. *Journal of Marketing*, 35(3), 3–12.

Koutropoulos, A. (2011). Digital Natives: Ten years after. *Journal of Online Learning and teaching*, 7(4). http://jolt.merlot.org/vol7no4/koutropoulos_1211.htm.

Lindstrom, R. (1994). *The Business Week Guide to Multimedia Presentations: Create Dynamic Presentations That Inspire*, New York: McGraw-Hill.
Livingstone, S. & Helsper, E. (2007). Gradations in digital inclusion: children, young people and the digital divide. *New Media & Society*, 9(4), 671–696.
Loda, M. & Coleman, B.C. (2005). Sequence Matters: A More Effective Way to Use Advertising and Publicity. *Journal of Advertising Research* 45(4), 362–372.
Luhmann, C. (2011). Integrating spatial context learning over contradictory signals: recency effects in contextual cueing. *Visual Cognition*, 19 (7), 846–862.
Mallinckrodt, V. & Mizerski, D. (2007). The Effects of Playing an Advergame on Young Children's Perceptions, Preferences, and Requests. *Journal of Advertising*, 36 (2), 87–100.
Marin, B., Lee, C. & Yang, F. (2004). The influence of ad model ethnicity and self-referencing on attitudes. *Journal of Advertising*, 33(4), 27–37.
McPherson AC, Glazebrook C, Forster D, James C, Smyth A. (2006). A randomized, controlled trial of an interactive educational computer package for children with asthma. *Pediatrics*, 117, 1046–54.
Mitchell, A. & Savill-Smith, C. (2005). *The use of computer and video games for learning. A review of the literature*. Learning and Skills Development Agency, London.
Murphy, J., Hofacker, C. & Mizerski, R. (2006). Primacy and Recency Effects on Clicking Behavior. *Journal of Computer-Mediated Communication*, 11: 522–535.
Oblinger, D. & Oblinger, J. (2005). Is It Age or IT: First Steps Toward Understanding the Net Generation | EDUCAUSE.edu.
Papastergiou, M. (2009). Exploring the potential of computer and video games for health and physical education: A literature review, *Computers & Education*, 53(3), 603–622.
Peltier, J.W., Schibrowsky, J.A., and Schultz, D.E. (2003). Interactive integrated marketing communication: combining the power of IMC, the new media and database marketing. *International Journal of Advertising*, 22 (1), 93–115.
Pempek T. & Calvert, S. (2009). Use of advergames to promote consumption of nutritious foods and beverages by low-income African American children. *Archives of Pediatrics and Adolescence Medicine*, 163 (7), 633–637.
Petty, R., Tormala, Z., Hawkins, C. & Wegener, D. (2001). Motivation to Think and Order Effects in Persuasion: The Moderating Role of Chunking. *Personality and Social Psychology Bulletin*, 27 (3), 332–344.
Prensky, M. (2001). *Fun, play and games: what makes games engaging. Digital game-based learning*, New York: McGraw-Hill.
Rainie, L. (2006). Digital "natives" invade the workplace. Pew Internet & American Life Project. Retrieved from http://pewresearch.org/pubs/70/digital-natives-invade-the-workplace.
Read, L.J & Shortell, S.M. (2011). Interactive Games to Promote Behavior Change in Prevention and Treatment. *The Journal of the American Medical Association*. 2011; 305(16): 1704–1705. doi:10.1001/jama.2011.408.
Ryan, R., Rigby, S. & Przybylski, A. (2006). The Motivational Pull of Video Games: A Self-Determination Theory Approach. *Motivation and Emotion*, 30(4), 344–360.
Schaffer, D.W., Squire, K.D., Halverson, R., & Gee, J.P. (2005). Video games and the future of learning. *In Phi Delta Kappan*. October, vol. 87, no. 2, 105–111.
Selwyn, N. (2009). The digital native – Myth or reality? Aslib Proceedings, 61(4), 364–379.
Shaffer, D. W., Squire, K. R., Halverson, R., & Gee, J. P. (2004). Video games and the future of learning, Retrieved from http://www.academiccolab.org/resources/gappspaper1.pdf.

Squire, K.D. & Steinkuehler, C.A. (2005). The genesis of "CyberCulture": The case of Star Wars Galaxies. In D. Gibbs & L. Krause (Eds.), *Cyberlines: Languages and cultures of the Internet* (2nd ed.). Albert Park, Australia: James Nicholas Publishers.

Summerbell, C., Waters, E., Edmunds, L., Kelly, S., Brown, T. & Campbell, K. Interventions for preventing obesity in children. (2005). Cochrane Database of Systematic Reviews, 3 (No. CD001871). DOI: 10.1002/14651858.CD001871.pub2.

Tapscott, D. (1998). Growing Up Digital: The Rise of the Net Generation. New York: McGraw-Hill.

Tapscott, D. (200.) Grown Up Digital: How the Net Generation Is Changing Your World. New York: McGraw-Hill.

Tuzun, H., Yilmaz-Soylu, M., Karakus, T., Inal, Y. & Kizilkaya, G. (2008). The effect of computer games on primary school students' achievement and motivation. *Computers & Education* vol. 52, Issue 1, January 2009, 68–77.

Underwood, J. (2007). Rethinking the Digital Divide: impacts on student tutor relationships. *European Journal of Education*, 42(2), 213–222.

Van Dijk, J. A. G. M. (2005). *The deepening divide: Inequality in the Information Society*. Thousand Oaks: Sage.

Van Eck, R. (2006). Digital game-based learning: it's not just the digital natives who are restless. *Educause review*, 41(2), 1–16.

Vasiliou, A. & Economides, A. (2007). Game-based learning using MANETs. Proceedings of the 4th WSEAS/IASME International Conference on Engineering Education, Agios Nikolaos, Crete Island, Greece, July 2007.

Waters, E., de Silva-Sanigorski, A., Burford, B.J., Brown, T., Campbell, K.J., Gao, Y., Armstrong, R., Prosser, L. & Summerbell, CD. (2011). Interventions for preventing obesity in children. *Cochrane Database of Systematic Reviews*, 12 (No.: CD001871). DOI: 10.1002/14651858. CD001871.pub3.

Wyer, R. & Srull, T. (1986). Human cognition in its social context. *Psychological Review*, 93(3), 322–359.

Zyda, M. (2005). From Visual Simulation to Virtual Reality to Games. *Computer*, 38(9), 25–32.

Children and Video Games: Oral and Written Narratives

Rut Martínez-Borda & Pilar Lacasa

Abstract

This chapter traces the development of a multimedia workshop that took place at a Spanish public school and the work of twenty-one third-year girls and boys (aged 8–9) who wrote narratives based on their use of video games in the classroom. The analysis scrutinizes the role of video games as educational tools and examines how these, supported by classroom discussions, can contribute to the development of narrative thought as present in written compositions available in different contexts. The findings indicate that the children manage to write their own stories based on their interactions with the video games and that their reconstructions of computer games stories are dependent on specific contexts. Moreover, the video game plays an important role in the development of narrative thought because it serves as a vehicle of symbolic contents that enables the child to sequence and specify his or her own experience.

Introduction

Commercial video games are instruments designed originally for entertainment that allow players to share their experiences, both real and virtual, in interactive contexts (Ito, 2010). However, considering these media as educational tools can be controversial due to their content, the values they transmit and the interaction with the players.

The bitterest detractors claim that video game contents have the potential to negatively influence the players' attitude and behaviour. Studies have targeted possible links to addiction, aggression, violence, social development, and a variety of stereotyping and sexual morality issues (Dziewanski, 2011; Bickham, 2004; Horton, 2011). The results of these studies do not always coincide. For example, within the realm of aggression studies, some analysts have found that exposure to violent video games correlates with at least a temporary increase in aggression and a decrease in pro-social behaviour (Anderson & Bushman, 2001), whereas other authors have concluded that video game violence is not related to engaging in aggressive behaviour (Ferguson & Kilburn, 2009). However, some experts have based their work on the potential positive effects of video games (Kushner 2007; Kenyota, 2010), which is a view that we share. In this article, we treat video games as "cultural emergent forms" in the global context that affect the leisure time of children between the ages of 8 and 18.

It is true that the use of commercial video games in the school context is not easy. Video games do not educate by themselves, nor does television or other media; it is the audience's interaction with those media and the role of a "mediator" that transforms them into educational tools. In this case, the role played by adults becomes essential in the transformation process of the game as an educational resource to create constructive and meaningful learning situations related to the acquisition of new literacies. (Berger, 2002; Lacasa, 2013)

Following this approach, we focus on how video games, supported by conversations in the classroom, contribute to the development of narrative thought as present in written compositions, available in different contexts. This paper analyzes the evolution of children's narratives, working in small-group and large-group situations after playing commercial video games in the classroom. Adopting an ethnographic and action research perspective, we anticipate our results will inspire specific practices of using commercial video games as educational tools when children learn to elaborate and build stories in specific multimedia contexts in which the educational use of video games is combined with watching movies and acting out a theatrical play.

Gamers and game interaction: signs and meaning

Video games play a meaningful and natural role in the everyday life of children and young people and provide them with new experiences, interesting stories, social events, fun, challenges, excitement and many moments of learning. They make it possible for players to participate in valued communities of practice and, as a result, to develop the ways of thinking that organize those practices by creating meaningful experiences for the players (Lacasa, 2013; Cortés, 2011). The games become cultural objects that have value in specific contexts when the user faces problems and challenges before making decisions (Gee, 2008).

Focusing on the concept of game, Salen and Zimmerman (2006) consider the presence of rules as a fundamental aspect in its definition:

> "A game is a system in which players engage in an artificial conflict, defined by rules that results in a quantifiable outcome." (Katie Salen & Eric Zimmerman, 2006. p. 96)

The value of the rules and the presence of an imaginary world or playful creation are fundamental to the concept of the game (Steinkuhler, 2012). The interaction with video games allows the players to live meaningful experiences, face continuous challenges, learn by doing in worlds of rules and feel part of them thanks to the characters. This aspect is closely related to the presence of "virtual" contexts and spaces.

However, the objects are not valuable in themselves, it is the activities and practices that emerge from the interaction which make them meaningful. For this reason, we must observe the players and their interaction with the game to be able to determine how they generate new knowledge and forms of expression.

Moreover, we must not forget an important element in the game world that connects the player directly with the game – the character or hero (Popper, 2013). Recent studies on the narrative of games have highlighted the character function, which allows the narrative to go forward. This is important, since the player adopts an identity and the possibilities for action, spatial relationships and connecting with other characters multiply. From this perspective, Egenfeldt et al. (2008) consider the character as the necessary link between the player and the narrator, i.e. the junction between the interactive options chosen by the player and the narrator's response. The player needs the character, but he/she has the ability to become the author of his/her own adventures, which will be reflected in the narratives.

Adopting this approach, we consider that video games allow gamers to learn and think differently than they are used to and provide very suitable material to create constructive and meaningful learning situations related to the acquisition of new literacies. When combined with other media, video games contribute to the development of digital literacy, a necessary competence to engage young people in society through different means of communication. By literacy, we understand the process by which people become aware of the discourses they use and, in doing so, gain control of the communication situations using a reflective and critical manner in order to achieve a certain goal. It is a process that allows people to control the languages they use and thus transform them into more complex models to enable new and more elaborate activities in communicative and interactive contexts (Mitchell, 2002; John-Steiner, 1994; Olson & Torrance, 1991). Currently, research is being conducted in the same direction (Dobson & Willinsky, 2009), which takes into account new communication tools that generate different forms of literacy and thinking. Thus, new media in digital environments allow users to become creators of information and knowledge builders able to control the discourses they use to convey their messages to remote audiences – something that was limited to the mass media professionals until very recently. By controlling their discourses, users' experiences in the game become personalized and specified, both individually and collectively.

As mentioned above, at the time of playing the player discovers the logic of the game (rules) while experiencing a story based on his/her actions. Henry Jenkins (2003, 2004) understands the relationship between video games and narrative from a spatial perspective, in which space is the key element for narrative possibilities. The construction of complex plots and characters is not as crucial as the space to be explored, controlled and mapped. This is how stories and multiple endings can be invented. In computer games, the players must interact with the story, which is opposed to the linear structure of narrations (Carlquist, 2002). Both the game and the narrative situation move in a world that only comes to life as long as there is someone to interpret the signs that appear in those contexts. By inviting the player to become involved in the sequence selection process, the narrator opens a transitional space that allows the reader/player to participate in narrative creation. For example, the player becomes a narrator who chooses paths, and the game plot becomes a detached and almost unique experience. The decisions made by each player are different stories. Space generates narrative in video games and, by making these choices, the reader "moves the focus away" from him/herself and feels "as if" he/she is the one creating the story. This way, narratives in video games generate an affective, cognitive involvement that gives way to an immersion process in the plot, and we can understand the concentration and interest generated by the game (among other skills) and reject the argument of a lack of concentration of the users. Xavier Berenguer defines the connection between the player and the choice of history as an interactive dilemma between "the author's need to control history and the freedom of the interaction to change" (Berenguer, 1998). Video games and, more specifically, the adventure game analyzed in this chapter, are built around this dilemma. The game designer creates a storyline and a set of rules that should allow the story to progress but, in turn, offers a certain degree of freedom and motivates the player to act in the game. These games in which the player must advance through predetermined sequences are known as "progression games" (Juul, 2009).

We have chosen to address these ideas because, by introducing video games in the classroom as a game element, we offer students moments of interaction and decision-making, turning them into the "authors/writers" of their own adventures. As we will see later on, the data obtained in the research have allowed us to analyze how students develop their creative skills, especially related to the way in which they build stories based on the video games' contents.

Narratives and adventure video games

Some game theorists who have approached the question of games and narrative from various perspectives have also inspired this work. Gee (2006) and Jenkins (2004) both discussed the creation of narrative via spatial exploration and episodic play in video games. Murray (2000) describes games and narrative in relation to the concept of 'procedural authorship', while Pearce (2004) develops the notion of 'emergent narrative' to describe narrative-like event sequences that emerge during play. Alternatively, Zagalo et al. (2005) incorporate embodiment, emotion and cognition into their analysis of narrative in games. Our idea of narrative coincides with that of classical authors such as David Olson (1990: 99 and 101):

> "In the classical tradition, dominant in our literate society, narrative is taken as antithesis of thought (…) There is nothing natural about narrative (…), narrative form, when applied to experienced or imagined events, create a story. These stories are constructed and interpretative in nature, memorable, functional and entertaining. Narratives, then (…) can be seen as forms of thought-devices for interpreting experience and informing action."

These ideas come from an old book, but we can find similar concepts in many other sources, for example, Bruner (2002):

> "Narrative is organized around the dialectic of expectations supporting norms and the possibility of evoking transgression. It requires a cast of characters who are free agents with minds of their own; they are recognizable by expectations about the ordinary state of the World, even if it is somewhat enigmatic." (Bruner, 2002)

We are interested in narratives relating to the use of technologies in educational settings. Looking for new models of interpreting school settings, we focus on some authors such as Ferraro (1994), who believes that *"the narrative form constitutes a basic tool for meaning construction and event interpretation. It could be said that, more than language, narrative should be considered the primary modelling system."* In this case, the narrative is a tool that interprets and constructs one process. Based on this idea, we can consider narrative not just as a formal discourse issue, but also as *"a cognitive construct, or mental image, built by the interpreter in response to the text"* (Ryan, 2004). Focusing on our connection between the narrative and the video game world, we can say that the reader (or player, in this case) moves to the world of the writer (game designer) when living the adventures that take place in the virtual world of the game (the experience).

In addition to the hidden action and resolution of problems, the video game features contents (space, time, actions and characters) that offer the perfect space for the player's action (Gretchen Papazian, 2013). It is for this reason that adventure games are more related to the ability to create narratives. In this type of game, the player makes a narrative reconstruction of events planned by its creator, in some cases across platforms, by testing, achieving goals, etc. The decisions made by the player determine the path to follow in order to achieve the ultimate goal of the game. Adventure games present one method that starts out from a specific story world and inserts possibilities of user action to make it interactive. This is the approach in games such as Tomb Raider: since the plot of these games must be adapted to the possibilities of action offered by game controls, they are usually fairly different from their literary or cinematic sources. Many of the games based on a pre-existing story tend to become stereotyped shooters and quests with weak integration of the player's actions into the storyline. These games attract players for the spatial and visual pleasure of finding themselves in a familiar fictional world and encountering well-known characters rather than for the temporal pleasure of enacting a specific sequence of events (Grove, 2013). In this kind of design, the story world takes precedent over the story. Let's see how the game is introduced in the instruction manual of the video game:

> Lara Croft is presumed dead and several of her colleagues and friends are holding a memorial service in her honour. This service leads to a sort of vigil, where the gathered recall some of Lara's past exploits. These stories make up the adventures, and there are four unrelated episodes. Each of these finds Lara searching for some mythical artefact in some mystical land, usually against some European adversary. Descriptions of the episodes sound like variations on Clue solutions: You have the Frenchman with the Philosopher's Stone in the Roman Coliseum and the German with the Spear of Destiny in the Russian submarine. Lara will also have to hunt demons in an Irish moor and find an Egyptian artefact in a high-security skyscraper.

This description shows that, right from the beginning, the player faces two essential elements that define the game: on the one hand, the adventures Lara Croft is going to go through and, on the other, the problems the player will have to solve in order for the story line to advance. This combination of the problems presented and the fictional experience ended up being determining factors for what happened during the workshop, and we will see it reflected in the children's narratives. These simple instructions embody both representational and ludic designs; they continue the narrative events, characters, unresolved conflicts and episodic trajectory, while also issuing a ludic imperative, which provides the object of the game. From this point of view, we analyse the productions written by the children on Lara Croft, where we are able to observe the use of space as the context in which the action takes place and the predominance of time as students reconstruct the actions experienced in the game as a narrative (Klaus Bredl, 2013).

Case study: Lara Croft's world in the children's written compositions

The methodology on which our analytical process is based consists of our own case study techniques combined with the use of some ethnography practices and an ecological approach, which explores what happens in natural situations (Atkinson, Coffey, Delamont, Lofland & Lofland, 2001; Lacasa & Martínez, 2013).

Its validity is based on a detailed description of the cases in which we can explain how people make sense of their activities in defined socio-cultural contexts (Bazeley, 2013). A micro-ethnographic analysis of multimodal discourses is also carried out. We have presented in detail the steps followed in the generation of information and data analysis (Del Castillo, García-Varela & Lacasa, 2003).

In this case, as can be seen in the data, we are exploring the role of video games as educational tools to examine how adventure games, supported by discussions in the classroom, can contribute to the development of narrative thought as present in children's written compositions.

Context: participants and phases

Participants

The data collected and analyzed for this research were gathered at a public school in the Madrid region. We worked in a multimedia workshop and the students were in their third year of primary education *(8–9 years old)*. In this context, we worked for a total of *six one-hour sessions*, in which *11 boys, 10 girls and their teacher* participated, as well as the *researchers* themselves. We were participant observers (McNiff, 2013; Tracy, 2013).

Regarding who chose the game to be played, the children told the adults that Lara Croft was the game they played the most at home. The adults decided to take the opportunity to teach them to be critical of the violent messages of the game.

For this reason, the aim of the workshop was to develop critical and narrative thinking in the children by using video games as educational tools in the classroom with the goal of acting out a play. Several reasons justify the joint introduction of computer games, theatrical representation and the Internet as educational resources. First, the workshop development demanded the combination of different resources that are not mutually exclusive but rather, complementary; besides, the fact of introducing different symbolic codes helped to generate a critical consciousness, bearing in mind that the children needed to take into account a close audience, in the case of the theatre, and a distant one when posting on the Internet.

We expected the children to approach the narrative dimension of an adventure game, supported by the teacher and the researchers, by working together using new technologies in the classroom. Moreover, the fact that they were playing a violent video game in this workshop created educational situations that would allow for critical reflection. The aim of the adults was to situate the children critically in front of the screens of the game by means of consecutive reconstructions of the game and by supporting specific processes of meta-reflection.

Workshop Phases

This workshop was organized around three main phases that developed over six sessions:

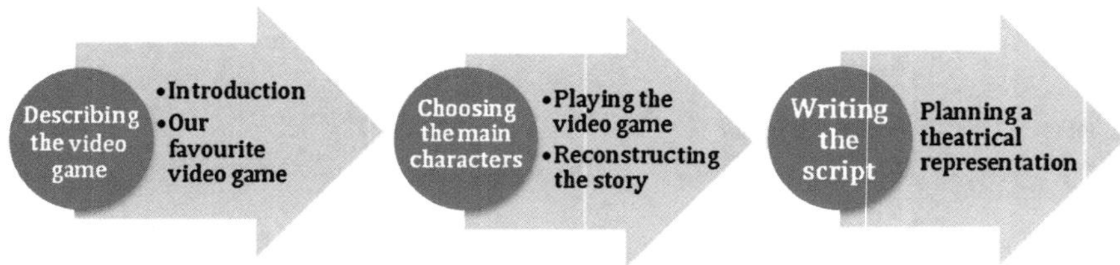

Fig. 1: The workshop sessions

- *First moment: Learning to co-exist with video games in the classroom.* During this first meeting (first session), the participants decided what they were going to do in the workshop. The idea was to play the video games they played at home and come up with a story for a play. The children told the adults what their favourite video games were and how each of them was played. We then drew up a list of all the video games the children suggested and took a vote. "Tomb Raider" was the game most children voted for.
- *Second moment: What happens in the video game.* During the second and the third sessions, the children started playing the video game in groups of two or three for approximately twenty minutes and then began to reconstruct the story of the video game helped by different strategies adopted by the adults as they developed the story. The strategy that turned out to be most useful was that of playing the video game via a video projector that allowed all the students to continue playing while writing the story because this made it easier for them to organize their ideas.
- *Third moment: How we adapted the video game for theatrical representation.* The rehearsal of the script and the scene took place in the fourth session of the workshop. At this moment, in order to motivate her students, the teacher suggested they produced a dramatization of the video game story they had just written. To do so, the students adapted the story they had made up in order to be able to represent it in groups of six. The children thought of how they would

interpret it and how they would dress up to stage it. Sessions five and six were devoted to representing the story and discussing it from an educational values perspective.

Analysis: writing, thinking and playing

Defining Categories

To explain how video games, supported by classroom discussions, can contribute to the development of narrative thought as present in written compositions available in different contexts, we used the narrative reconstructions of each session using AtlasTi.[1] By focusing on specific conversations, we explored the dialogues among participants in order to show how the children were writing narratives at different phases of the workshop using computer games as educational tools.

In order to explore the narrative structure of the video game, a set of categories was defined following the models of Pearce (2004), Siegel (2001), and Vogler (1998). Some categories present in the video game structure served to analyze the children's narratives in relation to the video game. In this case, the first aim was to explore the relationship between two perspectives: on the one hand, a more traditional idea related to the study of literature (Bakhtin 1982/1988, Greimas 1996/1999 (4th ed.) and, on the other hand, a perspective related to the idea of "video games as a narrative gender" (Carlquist 2002, Vogler 2001, Siegel 2001, Jenkins 2004).

Looking for concepts common to these two perspectives, we defined four dimensions (time, action, space and characters) to be linked directly to the nine acts according to Siegel. These dimensions appear in the game structure, and in this case we considered them of great interest since they are the categories we took as a reference for the analysis of our texts.

---

1 ATLAS. Ti is software used in qualitative and quantitative research. It works with large volumes of data, i.e. text, images, notes, video and audio. It allows analyzing and visualizing all documents and opening new interpretative views on the material.

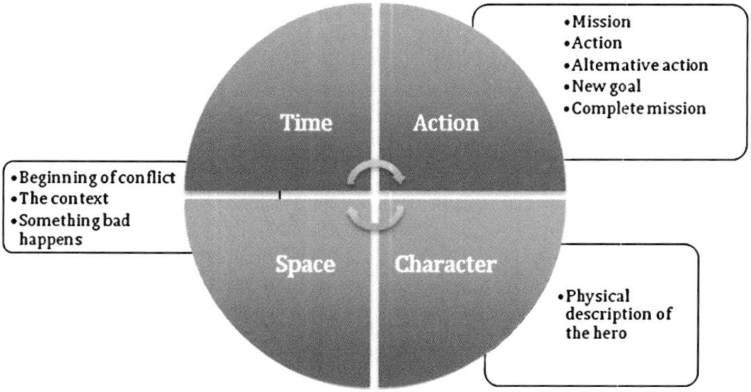

Fig. 2: Dimensions and categories used for the interpretation of narrative of the video game (Siegel, 2001)

Additionally, constructing a narrative required us to focus on the analysis of its structure. From a literary perspective, we should refer to organization and consider Aristotle's classic notion (beginning, middle and end). More recent authors such as Syd Field (1984) divide stories into three acts: context, confrontation and resolution. But what happens in the case of video games? Is the game structure similar to that of a story? Following Siegel's studies, we could make a connection between the nine acts listed above in relation with the four dimensions (time, action, space and character) and the moment in the story in which they appear, thus resulting in a linear form present in video games. The following figure shows this relationship:

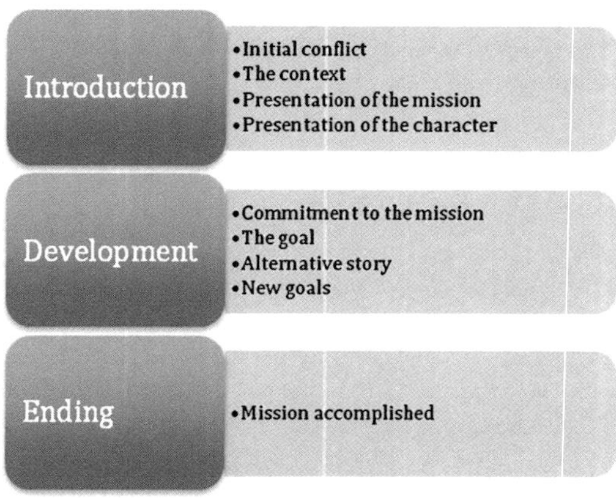

Fig. 3: Relationship between categories and the narrative structure of stories and video games

As can be seen, the categories we have defined for the analysis of the data are based on the theoretical models of Siegel and Vogler. Starting from the designed pattern, we analyzed the presence of these categories in the texts that the children wrote.

Categories	**- Context of the video game story** Determined by four elements: The conflict, the space, the time and the facts. The first one refers to the general context of the story in which the adventure is framed; it describes the challenge from the moment the mission is assigned to the character. The time and space elements are usually interrelated, since they appear in a short film at the beginning of the game. While the images that situate the story in a specific scenario are shown, the narrator's voice situates the facts in time. Finally, the player receives the information through which the whole plot of the game is to develop.
	- The mission The starting point of the mission is the moment in which the hero accepts the challenge. The player decides whether to go ahead with the adventure or not. If he does, his objective is to achieve it, losing is not an option.
	- The character He must fulfil the mission which has been assigned to him. In most of these video games, he becomes the main character of the adventure. The information received by the player about him is usually very brief.
	- Alternations in the action They are all the setbacks or address changes which are presented to the player along his adventure. For example, at a specific moment in which one doesn't know how to beat a rival, a character appears, giving us information about his weak point.
	- The action It is the succession of chained facts that take place to reach an end. The player will be in charge of overcoming the obstacles or facing the characters that will try to hinder the development of his mission.
	- Fulfilled mission After overcoming all the obstacles, the main character reaches the game's final stage in which all the tools gathered to win the final battle and to be able to reach the game's goal should be used.

The stories about Lara Croft's video game

Taking Siegel and Vogler's models as a starting point, we can make a link between the children's texts and the narrative present in adventure video games.In these pages, the data to be analyzed are the end products of each of the phases in which the workshop was divided:

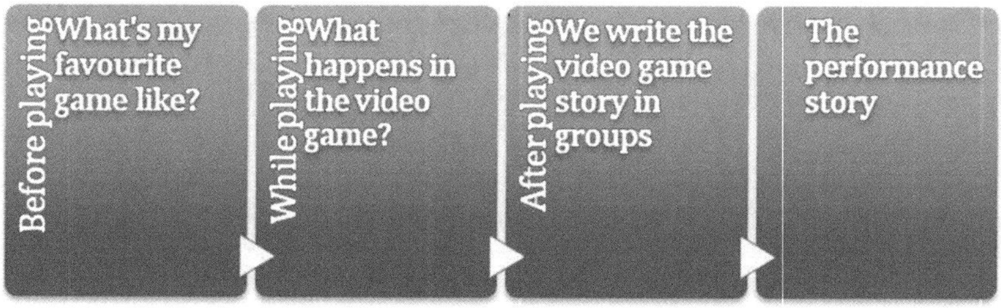

Fig. 4: Key moments of the workshop for the construction of narratives

In each of these phases, the children wrote a text related to the work that had been done during the session. The tasks were usually to answer the question that either the teacher or the researcher posed to guide the children through the activity. In this sense, the different narratives that the children constructed in the workshop following the teacher's instructions defined the analysis unit. Before analyzing each of these documents in detail, let us look at the following table. The information is the presence-absence of the category in that document, and the number represents the number of works that reflect this category[2].

MAIN PHASES	BEFORE PLAYING	WHILE PLAYING	AFTER PLAYING	
CATEGORIES/ TASKS	What's my favourite video game like?	What happens in the video game?	We write the video game story in groups	The performance story
Context of the video game story	1	14	X	X
The main character	2	6	X	X
The mission	3	9	X	X
The action	1	12	X	X
Alternative in the action	1	4	X	X
Mission accomplished	–	–	X	X

Fig. 5: Presence of categories in the children's texts

2 Total number: 22.

The presence of those categories in the children's texts depends fundamentally on the relationship the child has with the video game. Later, we analyse each of the documents in a specific way, but first consider the information in this table:

- In the first place, we can see that, out of 22 texts, only 3 talk about the game focusing on the description of the mission, on what you have to do if you play.
- Secondly, all the children have played in class and, when they write the history individually after discussing it with the teacher, the most frequent categories are those that refer to the context of the story and the actions of the main characters. We should bear in mind that, in this case, they were "telling" what happened in the video game. In this case, we see how the information transmitted by the media is not as relevant to some. Most of them focus on the contextualization of the story of the game in action and leave aside the mission and information related to the character. When the story is written in groups with the help of an adult, all categories appear.
- Lastly, in the case of the performance story, when they write the theatre script in small groups, all categories appear except for the main character, because the children think that the main character's information in a dramatization story is intrinsic to the setting and the attire.

The children focus the information on some category or other depending on the situation in which their text is written. This is an example of how the mission's category was presented in the different documents.

The mission	" (...) has to kill the baddies (...)" What's my favourite video game like?
	"(...) Lara Croft wants to kill the baddies (...)" What happens in the video game?
	"(...) goes to the cave for the eye of the triangle and fights a tiger." We write the video game's story in groups
	"(...) was preparing to avenge her father's death, who had been murdered by his best friend (...)" The performance story

But what happens when we focus the analysis on the texts written by the children over the workshop? What are the differences? We now focus on several narrative productions as present in the children's writings. We need to point out that the use of video games was a very interesting tool to introduce narrative telling and thinking into the classroom. Now, we see two examples of these after they played. The first example is in relationship to what happens in the video game; it is the children's first experience with the game. Then, we focus on the analysis of two theatre scripts considered as the highest level of complexity reached in the workshop.

a. What happens in the video game? Write the game's story game in groups. This is the story that the children constructed together with the teacher while they were playing the video game.

Working on a play-writing	Lara is training in the house that her father left her. She enters the house looking for a weapon and finds the closed cupboard. She enters the labyrinth for the flares, returns to the house and opens the cupboard. She takes her SUV and goes to the cave for the eye of the triangle and fights a tiger.
	Characters which might appear in the play: dinosaurs, the butler, a ninja, the tiger, the villain (the madman) and Lara Croft.

The second part refers to several characters that were really present in the video game, as considered and analyzed by the research team. However, what were the main features of this text?

Present Tense	"Lara is training (...)" "She enters (...)" "She takes (...)"
The parts of a story	"Lara is training in the house (...). (...) She enters the labyrinth (...) (...) She takes her SUV and goes to the cave for the eye of the triangle and fights a tiger."

We can see that the parts of any story are not differentiated as introduction, development and ending. The text is written in the present tense, and not all who want to appear in the play actually do so.

b. The performance story: Theoretical script

Once upon a time, a girl was training to avenge the death of her father. Her father had been murdered by his best friend. After training, she went to her parents' mansion looking for weapons. After finding some, she took a car and went to a cave. There she found a tiger and fought it. She shot him. Then she left the cave and faced a ninja and killed him too. Finally, a dinosaur came out and went behind Lara and she knocked it over with a stone. It fell to the ground and Lara shot him. Then, her father's friend showed up and Lara killed him.

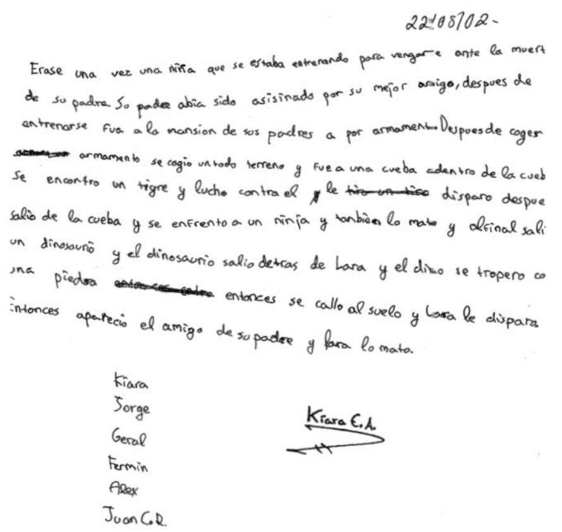
22/08/02-

Erase una vez una niña que se estaba entrenando para vengarse ante la muert
de su padre. Su padre abia sido asisinado por su mejor amigo, despues de
entrenarse fue a la mansion de sus padres a por armamento. Despues de coger
armamento se cogio un todo terreno y fue a una cueba adentro de la cueb
se encontro un tigre y lucho contra el y le ~~tiro un tiso~~ disparo despue
salio de la cueba y se enfrento a un ninja y tanbien lo mato y al final sali
un dinosaurio y el dinosaurio salio detras de Lara y el dino se tropero co
una piedra entonces se callo al suelo y Lara le dispara
entonces aparecio el amigo de su padre y Lara lo mato.

Kiara
Jorge
Geral
Fermin
Alex
Juan C.R.

Kiara C.A.

Fig. 6: Theatrical script by Group 2

We can see that, unlike the previous one, the parts of the story differ since it has an ending and begins like any other tale: "Once upon a time…". It is written in the past tense and features all the characters in the story. Something that seems important to us is the fact that the children use adverbs of time to arrange their ideas and that the action develops in time.

Moreover, it is interesting to pay attention to the scripts written by the children. Two aspects stand out: first, the reference to the kind of actions that the actors must represent; second, the way in which these actions are distributed among the main characters. Both aspects introduce the children to a symbolic world that is also expressed by means of oral and written discourses (Schechner, 2013). There are important differences between the scripts of each of the groups regarding these points.

If we focus on the script that appears in Figure 7, we can see how the children have organized the main characters and actions: every action is assigned to a specific character, which is also clearly identified numerically. For example, Lara is always the first one and the actress who plays this role is Irene. In the case of the characters that represent the tigers, the actresses are Laura and Ester and are always identified as "2nd". This numerical reference that the organization of the script facilitates refers to the order in which the roles were distributed and written down by the teacher. The children were able to use these and turn them into an instrument that helped them organize the activities of the play. On the other hand, it should be noted how the children were able to attribute an action expressed in a verb to every character. Even just observing the form in which the script is written we see that a line is assigned to every action, only on one occasion is there the concept of "1st Lara-Irene both attacking and defending herself."

1st Lara-Irene: She runs

2nd Tigers: Laura and Ester: They attack Lara.

1st Lara-Irene: She attacks and defends herself.

3rd Dinosaur-Juan Carlos Sánchez: He follows Lara and stumbles.

1st Lara-Irene: She takes the opportunity and shoots.

2nd Tigers-Laura and Ester: They attack again.

1st Lara-Irene: She defends herself.

5th Loco-Cristina Martínez: He acts stupidly and attacks Lara.

1st Lara-Irene: She defends herself.

6th Butler-Yolanda: He chases Lara.

1stLara-Irene: Lara shoots him.

1° Lara-Irene: corre.

2° Tigres-Laura y Esther: Atacan a Lara

1° Lara-Irene: Ataca y se defiende.

3 Dinosaurio-Juan Carlos Sánchez: Sigua a Lara y tropieza.

1° Lara-Irene: Aprovecha la ocasión y dispara.

2° Tigres-Laura y Esther: Atacan de nuevo.

1° Lara-Irene: Se defiende.

4° Ninja-Juan Carlos Garcia: Lucha con Lara.

1° Lara-Irene: Se defiende.

5° Loco-Cristina Martinez: Hace el tonto y ataca a Lara.

1° Lara-Irene: Se defiende.

6° Mayordomo-Yolanda: Persigue a Lara.

1° Lara-Irene: Lara le dispara.

Fin

Fig. 7: Theatrical script by one of the groups

The other groups did not demonstrate this level of complexity. If we look for example at the script written by Group 2 (Figure 6), we can see that this was more of a "story" than a play. The text shown in Figure 7 reproduces many of the discussions that had already taken place in the classroom. In any case, only the first part of the text explains Lara's motivation, something really difficult to represent (Lara was training to avenge the death of her father).

In conclusion, we believe that a key to the process of construction of the story could be that, while the first one was written while they played, the second time round the students already had the history in their heads and they narrated it as fact, since this time they found it easier to shape the story.

Conclusion and new perspectives

Violent and non-violent video games may become *the future of how people teach and learn as a society*. Unlike other media available today, video games can be an enormously motivating learning tool. However, when introduced into the classroom and turned into an educational tool, they manage to have the players' full attention by immersing them in a virtual world.

Numerous researchers have proposed potential *positive effects of video games on aspects of social and cognitive development and psychological* well-being (Jenkins, Lacasa, Gee). In this case, it has been shown that the video game has played an important role in the development of narrative thought, as it serves as a vehicle of symbolic content that enables the child to sequence and specify his or her own experience. We have considered the narrative text as a means by which speakers represent real life as events of fiction in which the player was presented as well as his or her social and cultural world.

The use of gaming has the ability to actively involve students in learning. From this perspective, the video game recreates a mythical environment, but with the advantage that it allows the player to participate in the ritual that develops in the course of the game. The very fact that the player interacts with the multimedia experience enables him/her to believe his/her own story. At the same time, it facilitates the development of symbolic thought for which the child is able to reconstruct those contents with a critical focus. In this line, adventure video games have narrative values with certain particularities typical of computer formats. The game consists of a simple story and it is the player's action which, through his/her logic and behaviour, develops and tells the story. Narrating the experience is not only about telling it, discussing it and imagining it, but also about acting it out. Furthermore, the fact that the children participated in these "games of fiction" (by playing the video game and dramatizing it) helped them to reconstruct their own experiences.

References

Anderson, C.A., & Bushman, B.J. (2001). Effects of violent video games on aggressive behavior, aggressive cognition, aggressive affect, physiological arousal, and pro-social behavior: A meta-analytic review of the scientific literature. *Psychological Science*, 12, 353–359

Atkinson, P., Coffey, A., Delamont, S., Lofland, J., & Lofland, L. (Eds.). (2001). *Handbook of Ethnography*. London: Sage.

Bakhtin, M. M. (1982/1988/2003). *Estética de la creación verbal*. Mexico: Siglo XXI Editores.

Bazeley, P. (2013). *Qualitative Data Analysis: Practical Strategies*. London: Sage.

Berger, A. A. (2002). *Video games: a popular culture phenomenon*. New Brunswick, N.J.: Transaction.

Bickham, David S., (2004). Video Games Foster Violent Behavior. *Media Violence*. Ed. Louise I. Gerdes. San Diego: Greenhaven Press.

Bredl, K. & Bösche, W. (2013). *Serious Games and Virtual Worlds in Education, Professional Development, and Healthcare*. Herskey: IGI Global.

Bruner, J. (2002). *Making stories. Law, literature, life*. Cambridge, MA & London, UK: Harvard University Press.

Carlquist, J. (2002). Playing the story. Computer games as a narrative genre. *Human IT, 6*(3), 7–53.

Cortés Gómez, S., Martínez-Borda, R. & Lacasa, P. (2011). Learning Narratives with Harry Potter. Manuel de Falla's The Prophet newspaper. *Serious Games and Edutainment Applications.* London: Springer. p. 309–327.

Del-Castillo, H., García-Varela, A. B., & Lacasa, P. (2003). Literacies through media: identity and discourse in the process of constructing a web site. *International Journal of Educational Research, 39*, 885–891.

Dobson, T. M., & Willinsky, J. (2009). Digital literacy. In D. R. Olson& N. Torrance (Eds.), *The Cambridge handbook of literacy* (pp. 3–22). Cambridge: Cambridge University Press.

Dziewanski, D. (2011). Popular Culture Promotes Gun Violence. *Gun Violence*. Ed. Louise Gerdes. Detroit: Greenhaven Press.

Egenfeldt, N. et al. (2008). Understanding video games. New York: Routledge

Ferguson, Christopher J. (2004). Video Games Have Become a Scapegoat for Violent Behavior. *Media Violence*. Ed. Louise I. Gerdes. San Diego: Greenhaven Press.

Ferraro, G. (1994). Percorsi virtuali nella formazione d'immagine. In R. Grandi (Ed.), Semiotica al marketing (pp. 155–172). Milano: Franco Angeli.

Gee, J. (2008). Video Games and Embodiment. *Games and Culture, 3*(3–4), 253–263.

Gee, J. P. (2006). Semiotic domains: Is playing video games a "waste of time"? In K. Salen & E. Zimmerman (Eds.), *The game design reader: A rules of play Anthology* (pp. 228–267). Cambridge, Massachussetts: MIT Press.

Gee, J., & Hayes, E. R. (2011). *Learning and language in the digital age*. New York: Routledge.

Greimas, A. J. (1996/1999 (4ª ed.)). Elementos para una teoría de la interpretación del relato mítico. In R. Barthes, U. Eco, T. Todorov & y otros (Eds.), *Análisis estructural del relato* (pp. 39–76). Mexico D.-F.: Ediciones Coyoacan.

Gretchen Papazian, J. M. S. (2013). *Game On, Hollywood! Essays on the Intersection of Video Games and Cinema*. Jefferson: McFarland.

Grove, N. (2013). *Using Storytelling to Support Children and Adults with Special Needs: Transforming lives through telling tales*. New York: Routledge; 1 edition.

Horton, Joseph J. "A free speech challenge for parents." *The Humanist* Sept.-Oct. 2011: 9+. *Gale Opposing Viewpoints In Context*. Web. 20 Sep. 2012.

Ito, M. et al. (2010) *Hanging out, messing around and geeking out*. Cambridge: MIT Press.

Jenkins, H. (2003). Transmedia Storytelling. *Technology Review Published by MIT http://www.technologyreview.com/Biotech/13052/.*

Jenkins, H. (2004). Game design as narrative architecture. *http://web.mit.edu/21fms/www/faculty/henry3/games&narrative.html#1*, Access November 22.

John-Steiner, V., Panofsky, C. P., & Smith, L. W. (Eds.). (1994). *Socio-cultural approaches to language and literacy. An interactionist perspective*. New York: Cambridge University Press.

Juul, J. (2009). *A Casual Revolution: Reinventing Video Games and Their Players.* Cambridge, Massachusetts: MIT Press.

Kenyota, G. (2010) Video Games Should Not Be Regulated by Legislation. *Video Games*. Ed. Laurie Willis. Detroit: Greenhaven Press.

Kushner, D. (2010) Violent Video Games Do Not Cause Aggression. *Video Games*. Ed. Laurie Willis. Detroit: Greenhaven Press.

Lacasa, P. (2013). *Learning in real and virtual worlds: commercial video games as educational tools*. New York: Palgrave McMillan.

Lacasa, P., Martínez-Borda, R., & Méndez, L. (2013). Media as practice: Narrative and conceptual approach for qualitative data analysis in *Studies in Media and Communication.* North America: Redfame Publishing.

McNiff, J. (2013). *Action Research: Principles and practice*. New York: Routledge

Mitchell, C., & Reid-Walsh, J. (2002). *Researching children popular culture. The cultural spaces of childhood.* New York: Routledge.

Murray, J. H. (2000). *Hamlet on the Holodeck; The Future of Narratives in Cyberspace* (3rd ed.). Cambridge: The MIT Press.

Olson, D. (1990). Thinking about narrative. In B. K. Britton& A. D. Pellegrini (Eds), *Narrative thought and narrative language* (pp. 99–113). Hillsdale: Lawrence Erlbaum Associates.

Olson, D. R., & Torrance, N. (Eds.). (1991). *Literacy and orality*. Cambridge: Cambridge University Press.

Pearce, C. (2004). Towards a Game Theory of Game. In N. Wardrip-Fruin & P. Harrigan (Eds.), *First Person: New Media as Story, Performance, and Game*. Cambridge: MIT Press.

Popper, S. P. (2013). *Rethinking Superhero And Weapon Play*. New York: Open University Press.

Ryan, M.-L. (2004). *Narrative across media: the languages of storytelling*. Lincoln: University of Nebraska Press.

Salen, K., & Zimmerman, E. (Eds.). (2006b). *The game design reader: A rules of play Anthology*. Cambridge: MIT Press.

Schechner, R. (2013). *Performance Studies: An Introduction*. London: Routledge.

Siegel, D. (2001). The Nine-Act Structure. A story-structure class for writers and film buffs. In Steinkuehler, C., Squire, K., & Barab, S. (Eds.) (2012). *Games, learning, and society: Learning and meaning in the digital age*. New York: Cambridge University Press.

Syd Field, F. (1984). *The Screenwriter's Workbook*. New York: Dell Publishing.

Tracy, S. J. (2013). *Qualitative Research Methods: Collecting Evidence, Crafting Analysis, Communicating Impact*: Chichester: Wiley-Blackwell; 1 edition.

Vogler, C. (1998). *The Writer's Journey: Mythic structures for writers*. Los Angeles: M. Wiese Productions.

Zagalo, N., & Branco, V. (2005). Storytelling and Interactivity in Videogames, from MYST to ICO. *Deliverable 3.1.1 of INSCAPE, project 004150*, 19–36.

Teaching With Laptops: A Critical Assessment of One-to-one Technologies

Magda Pischetola

Abstract

In recent years Information and Communication Technologies (ICT) have become the main keyword for school innovation. There has been an increasing amount of literature on how traditional teaching methodologies should be redesigned in order to include the use of technology. However, few studies have recognized that school innovation especially requires investments in human capability – not technology – to respond to the demands of the information age. The chapter presents a comparative qualitative research carried on between 2009 and 2012 in primary schools in Italy, Ethiopia and Brazil. The examined programs – *One Laptop Per Child* in Italy and Ethiopia; *Um Computador por Aluno* in Brazil – provided children with low-cost and low-power laptops, designed both for didactical and personal use, with the purpose to actively involve them in knowledge construction. The findings illustrate how difficult it is for teachers to deal with a new setting of didactics, and how important is to provide them with the necessary training and institutional support, in order to enhance a meaningful process of school innovation.

Introduction

The question of how to bring about a real transformation of teaching and learning touches one of the most relevant issues in the debate about the use of technology in education. On the one hand, it is generally agreed upon that traditional educational practices should be redesigned through ecological approaches that include the possibilities given by the interaction with the digital media and the engaging dynamics of web 2.0 (Bucy & Newhagen, 2004; Buckingham &Willet, 2006). On the other hand, there has been relatively little research regarding the influence of the situational contexts on digital technology integration, or on the importance of values and habits intrinsic to the local school and community culture (Pischetola, 2011; Warschauer, 2003).

Launched in 2005 by the Massachusetts Institute of Technology, the *One Laptop Per Child* (OLPC, on the Internet at the URL: http://one.laptop.org) initiative and its design of a $100 laptop for developing countries has popularized the concept of "one-to-one" technologies, which are essentially low-cost personal digital devices to facilitate learning for school-aged children. Using different devices – a PC, laptop, handheld, or tablet PC – many other projects around the world reproduced the OLPC pedagogical idea over the past years. One of them is the

Brazilian *Um Computador por Aluno* (UCA, on the Internet at the URL: http://prouca.comunidades.net) which, except for the use of a different laptop, is an exact reproduction of OLPC.

The key pedagogical intention behind the design of these projects is the Activity Theory framework, which argues that students can generate new knowledge from their direct experience of the world (Cole, 1991; Engeström, 1987; Leontiev, 1981; Vygostky, 1978).

The approach has its roots in Vygotsky's theory of collaborative learning (1978), which points out the need to provide a space for interaction between student and teacher where learning occurs. By introducing the concept of "Zone of Proximal Development", the author analyzes the development of skills from the interaction with others and concludes that the construction of knowledge is an interactive process. In this perspective, learning should be considered a social activity. This not only requires the development of the individual, but also the presence of the community to which he belongs.

Ever since Vygotsky's foundational work, the Activity Theory has to deal with questions of diversity and dialogue between different traditions or perspectives (Engeström, 1987, 6). The basic premise of this theory is that knowledge is first constructed in a social context and is then taken up by individuals, influenced by their background, culture or embedded worldview (Cole, 1991). In this sense, the Activity Theory considers every kind of human activity as object-oriented, collective and culturally mediated. Stating that all knowledge is the result of an active construction endorsed by the subject, it claims that "instead of just individual transformation, development should be viewed as collective transformation" (Engeström, 1987).

The purpose of the research here presented was to identify what the rationale of this educational trend is, what the first observable students' achievements through the access of one-to-one technologies are, and what could be considered positive and negative aspects that make a difference in a classroom where every child owns a connected computer.

Activity Theory and one-to-one technology

The pedagogical stance promoted by the OLPC and the UCA projects holds that students should learn by doing, while the teacher's role is to mentor the learner, as a facilitator of the whole process. The idea is inspired by the Activity Theory approach, and it argues that students generate new knowledge from their direct experiences, building it on the notions and information they already hold (Papert, 1983). On these grounds, every child who has access to a mobile digital device is expected to become an active participant in a learning community, and contribute to a substantial change of the traditional school environment, where students are generally passive consumers of knowledge (Greeno et al., 1996). According to the OLPC mission statement, "it is an educational project, not a laptop project" (OLPC website: http://one.laptop.org). Giving children direct access to a personal technology will involve them actively into knowledge construction processes, improve their learning approach and broaden their opportunities for social inclusion.

This study is an attempt to address the issue of students' and teachers' engagement with technology. Three areas of skills development are identified as crucial in the purpose of the one-to-one initiatives: *digital literacy*, *collaboration*, and *problem solving*. The figure below illustrates their core elements.

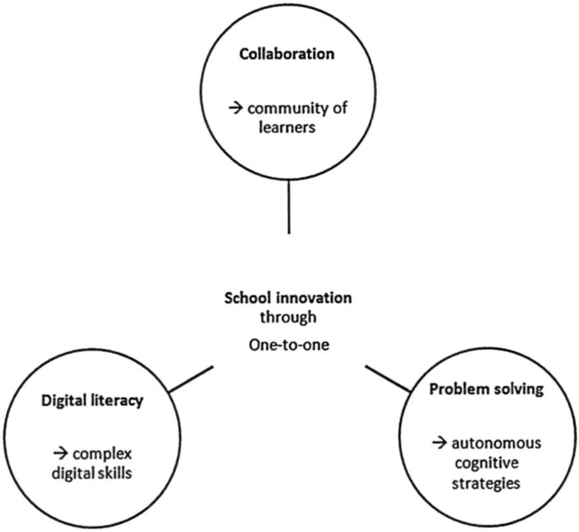

Fig. 1: Expected skills development with one-to-one technology

1) Digital literacy

ICT has changed the landscape of information access, and made a framework integrating various kinds of literacy necessary. What is required nowadays is *the ability to understand information and – more importantly – to evaluate and integrate information in multiple formats that the computer can deliver* (Gilster, 1997). Hence, if the ability to construct information from multimedia tools is lacking, then however good the operational skills are, information will not be capitalized on effectively. In a one-to-one perspective, teachers have to guide their pupils towards the development of meaningful and complex digital skills, which comprise the ability to use the media strategically (Jenkins, 2006; Van Dijk, 2005).

2) Collaboration

According to constructivists, the process of sharing other persons' points of view results in learners building understanding together that would not be achievable alone. This process is known as collaborative elaboration (Brown & Campione, 1994) and allows learners to discover principles, concepts and facts that make sense for them (Mills, 2010). Central to collaborative learning is Vygotsky's concept of "Zone of Proximal Development" (1978), where learners are challenged within close proximity to, yet slightly above, their current level of development. The ultimate goal of this approach is the embodiment of a method of learning that makes the subject progressively autonomous in their cognitive acts. Transferred to the one-to-one programs, the model is that of the community of learners in which *each member is at the same time apprentice and teacher* (Ligorio, 1994).

3) Problem solving

The logical-mathematical intelligence – as Gardner (2006) points out in his major work – not only has to do with numbers and abstractions, but also with reasoning, critical thinking, and the capacity to understand the underlying principles of some kind of causal system. In an evolutionary perspective, this intelligence is available to the individual as a means to enhance his or her adaptation to the environment, finding the best solution to the problems that could be offered (Fabio, 2002). This results in the cognitive ability to respond to these demands autonomously, as well as in openness to divergent thinking in the future (Robinson, 2001). As a consequence of a new learning setting, teachers have to adapt to the role of facilitators, paying attention to both content and cognitive strategies (Vattimo, 2002). Instead of didactic lectures that cover the subject matters, the teacher has to support the learner to get his/her own understanding of the content, through a process of heuristic problem solving.

The present research was designed to examine if school-aged children engaged in laptop immersion programs are more likely to learn how to learn, in a perspective that includes the three mentioned skills areas. It centers on the relationship between these skills and the evidence of a change in the learning environment, drawing upon the assumption that technology represents only one of the aspects that will promote school innovation. The foregoing discussion aims at identifying what the elements of a successful program implementation are. The main issue under scrutiny is the teachers' reaction to the laptop presence in the classroom.

Three comparative case studies: Italy, Ethiopia, and Brazil

This section introduces a comparative research on three case studies. The first two were conducted in Italian and Ethiopian primary schools, where OLPC was implemented, during the school year 2008–2009. The third one was carried out in Brazil with the same methodology, on the parallel UCA program, in 2012. The research question that drives them is whether a one-to-one technology approach can bring about the envisaged educational change, and what the key elements of success are. It starts from the initial hypothesis that the expected change in a learning environment will mainly relate to the teachers' attitude towards the didactical use of the new device.

Research methodology

The fieldwork research followed a qualitative methodology, based on three different tools:

- Participant observation in the classrooms throughout the school year (10/country);
- Focus groups with children at the end of the school year (10/country);
- Intensive interviews with teachers and coordinators throughout the school year (20/country).

In all three contexts the sample was composed by schools equally distributed in rural and urban areas.

In Italy, the area for fieldwork research was the province of Brescia, where the regional school board had distributed 300 laptops in 10 different primary schools. In terms of availability and access to ICT, 84% of children of the sample already had a computer at home before they received the OLPC laptop. Those who did not have access to technology were mainly children of immigrant families, which compose 18% of the examined classrooms.

In Ethiopia the Engineering Capacity Building Programme (ECBP website: http://www.giz.de/Themen/en/14270.htm) was in charge of distributing 5000 XO laptops, of which 300 were donated by Italy as a result of the 2007 *Give One, Get One* promotion[1], to Ethiopian primary schools. In the sample the research included

1 Give 1 Get 1 Program information can be found at the URL http://laptop.org/en/participate/ways-to-give.shtml.

all three primary schools that were part of the project: two schools located in the capital of the country, Addis Ababa, and one in the rural area of Mullo Sayyo (Oromia region). None of them were connected to the Internet. The infrastructure for Internet connection in the whole country is still very limited and this is the main reason why the service is very expensive. Even among children of the urban area, coming from a higher socio-economical background, only 6% had seen a computer before the OLPC project.

The last fieldwork research, held three years later on a different one-to-one program, the Brazilian *Um Computador por Aluno*, could not include all the primary schools that received laptops in the sample. This led us to select four of them: two situated in the South of the country, in Santa Catarina state, and the other two located in Bahia, in the north-east region of the country. While Santa Catarina is a state with a generally high socio-economical level, Bahia is one of the Brazilian states with the highest rates of school drop-outs and the worst educational infrastructures (IBGE, 2010).

The overall data collection involved 30 classrooms, and led to a total of 30 focus groups with pupils and 60 interviews with the teachers/coordinators. The study was based on a set of questions:

- What is the impact of a one-to-one technology introduction in the local educational system?
- How was technology integrated into the existing teaching methodologies?
- How does the laptop influence both children's and teachers' skills development?
- Does the development of new skills result in a change of the learning environment?
- If there was a change, can it be considered towards school innovation, and why?

The study involved discovering how the whole community reacted to the introduction of a new didactic tool in a traditional educational setting, considering both advantages and disadvantages. It is premised on the awareness of the difficulty of isolating one variable – such as technology – in a complex concept such as student achievement, especially considering that the data were gathered in the relatively short time of a school year.

The method used for data analysis is the one suggested by the authors of Grounded Theory (Glaser& Strauss, 1967). The transcribed texts are read with an inductive approach, in which individual events, situations and personal opinions are grouped to form general categories of interpretation. The analysis of the data collected gives some interesting information.

Main findings

In all three contexts, the findings suggest that technology certainly does have a role in encouraging discovery learning and knowledge sharing.

In Italy, the study shows the beginning of a culture of "disseminated leadership" (Pischetola, 2010), which highlights an increased active participation in school activities among less-motivated students. Teachers underline how the laptop helped socially excluded children – especially the second generation immigrants – to become the most respected students in the class, after being recognized by the group of peers as the "experts" in technology. This links up to personal motivation as the real key for change and innovation. In fact, as literature has often pointed out (Maslow, 1954; Glasersfeld, 1989; Van Dijk, 2005), motivation to learn is strongly dependent on the learner's belief in his/her potential for learning.

In Ethiopia, the results call for placing value on the role of active students, and their initiative in innovative uses of technology in education. The outcomes identified that one-to-one technology embodies an ethos, in which social support acts as the core of the learning process. Among the three researched contexts, Ethiopian children were the most creative users of the laptop. They employed effective search strategies to access new information, texts, images, and videos, facing the absence of an Internet connection through the construction of an impressive social network among them. They collaborated to provide each other technical support and were able to produce interesting and esthetically beautiful graphic contents.

In Brazil, one of the most striking results to emerge from the data is that older students, who also received the laptop, imposed to themselves a self-regulating frame about the use of the Internet at school. Whenever the rules for the use of the laptop were not clear and led to distraction (or web addiction), teenagers reacted by building their own set of rules, basically looking for self-discipline. Another issue that is worth commenting on is the very positive result given by collaboration between children and teachers, in those schools where the direction asked students to contribute to laptop integration. The correlation between these results is interesting because of the value that pupils' help represents for teachers, weather they accepted it explicitly or not.

It is clear from the above that collaboration and problem solving skills were comprehensively detected in different proportions in all the examined contexts. However, it must also be noted that digital literacy was not attained by many: the skills achieved by students and teachers are mainly technical, operational competences. In fact, technology was considered by the majority simply as a new *tool*, more than a new *space* for work. This finding has important implications for reflecting on the general meaning of school innovation. The most crucial point which arose in the research is that the integration of a new technology at school represents an enormous challenge to teachers' established methodology. The OLPC/UCA constructivist approach expects the teacher to support the children's spontaneous desire to discover, and turn the class into a *learning community* (Brown & Campione, 1994). It is important to stress this, assuming that the teacher's attitude has an impact on the class attitude and on the perception that children – and families – have of the new tool.

One of the most interesting results of the research in the schools of Italy, Ethiopia and Brazil concerns the approach of teachers to a new teaching situation. In the cross-analysis of the data, we can identify methodological differences among the teachers that we have grouped into four categories (Pischetola, 2011).

1. Traditional method. Some teachers have received the laptop with caution. Their manner of using computers in teaching has been the traditional way, where the children were asked to follow the steps outlined by the teacher. This prevented the children from learning by discovery and, in general, increased dispersion in the classroom. Whenever this approach has not changed during the school year, a gradual loss of control and authority was observed among teachers, with a feeling of frustration and disappointment that turned into a negative perception of the project.
2. Interactive method. The attitude of the teacher is rather open to dialogue with the students, with the results of much greater participation than the traditional frontal method. Children are often called to the blackboard and there is always an involvement of the class, with competitive dynamics that act as a positive stimulus to the attention. The computer is partially integrated in teaching, although more as a tool to support education than as an element of structural change.
3. Driven experimentation. Instead of waiting for the teacher's instructions, pupils are encouraged to direct the desire for discovery to solve specific tasks. Their assignment concerns not only searching for new information, but also using their existing knowledge to build new skills. It goes without saying that a methodology of this kind encourages collaboration between students, joined in the search for a solution or in the advancement of a task. As for what concerns the teacher, he/she controls the progress of activities by giving constant feedback to the pupils and reinforcing their motivation.
4. Free experimentation. The teacher leaves full freedom for learners to experience individual paths of discovery, and assumes that the child possesses a greater curiosity than the adult, as well as better technological expertise. Moreover, the teacher puts himself/herself at a peer level with the pupils, sharing the learning

process with them, both of the laptop features and their application in didactics. Interestingly, observations have demonstrated this methodology to result in distraction more commonly than in focused work practices, as the students often perceived the free experimentation of the laptop as simple recreational activity.

A comparison of these results reveals that the approach that can be considered closest to the constructivist model of teaching is the one we called *driven experimentation*. However, it is also the teaching methodology that was least observed in the surveyed classes. In fact, most of the interviewed teachers pointed out the difficulty of managing the role of facilitator of a discovery process, and explained their resistance to this methodology with three main reasons.

Firstly, there is a challenge related to the class size and student-teacher ratio. In Brazil the classes of primary schools can consist of 40 students. In Ethiopia the number of pupils sometimes reaches 60 per class. Moreover, we should consider the socio-cultural issues that make the teachers' work conditions even more critical. In Italy, for example, in a class of 25 children 20% are immigrants, which represents a problem in communication and mutual comprehension (ISMU, 2007). In Ethiopia, students start school with different ages, which results in classes that are very heterogeneous (Hartel, 2008). And in Brazil, schools face challenging structural problems, given the unequal access to education and its quality, and the excessive drop-out rate (EFA, 2000).

Secondly, giving space to collaboration concretely means that the teacher has to face a setting where children move in the classroom, compare their results and help each other. Many teachers experience this as a very difficult situation to handle, both in terms of time and space. They often shared their worries during the interviews, about the use of the laptop not being compatible with the requests from the school system, where lessons are 45 or 50 minutes long, which is not even enough time to give the students a clear task, switch on all the computers (facing all kind of very frequent technical problems), and start working. And teachers still have to cover all contents of their subject, give evaluations, and comply with the lesson plans.

Thirdly, OLPC states that the laptop should be transversal to all disciplines. This means teachers should collaborate to design the contents and build interdisciplinary projects. But the way schools structure teachers' time does not give them any spare time to meet and discuss their didactics together. They hardly find the time for training, and only if the management of the school cares about it. The one-to-one technology programs implicitly expect teachers to work in their free time to learn about the use of the laptop in didactics. A minority of teachers (10 to 20% of the researched samples) do, and the findings show that these are also the ones who achieved the best results in building a learning community in their classes. The question is then: do we expect school innovation to happen spontaneously, as a result of teachers' personal motivation?

To sum up, teacher motivation and his/her methodology– as well as the personal conviction of the importance of the technology– are critical issues for the integration of a new tool in teaching and learning. And yet, they are not always spontaneous elements: they depend on the teacher's socio-cultural background, the working context and conditions, the school administration, the technical support, the exchange and collaboration with colleagues.

Lessons learned and future work

In the constructivist model of learning which is at the base of one-to-one initiatives around the world, the teacher's role is to mentor the learner by enabling quested problem solving and allowing creation of new knowledge (Calvani, 2001; Glasersfeld, 1989). Nevertheless, the evidence of the OLPC/UCA deployments in Italy, Ethiopia and Brazil suggest teachers often do not have the required capability to adapt their methods to participatory learning. That is because the one-to-one formula brings into focus the need of a change of the traditional hierarchal relationships between teachers and pupils. It calls for a new learning paradigm, but at the same time it does not consider how teachers will coordinate the use of a new device in their overcrowded classrooms without receiving any methodological assistance. One major drawback of this approach is that a connected laptop on every student's desk is obviously not only a tool, but more – as in the words of a Brazilian teacher – *as giving children the world.* The great majority of the interviewed teachers recognized the importance of technology for school innovation, but also expressed their frustration over a new classroom setting which is difficult for them to manage. They universally agreed on the need for more assistance in incorporating technology into the curriculum, and for a slower assimilation in their didactics through training.

Further analysis revealed that the OLPC approach failed to take cultural and methodological aspects into account. In some cases, as it happened in Ethiopia, fostering cooperation and exchange of knowledge between teachers and pupils would mean to completely change established didactic methods towards a child-centered approach, which is not acknowledged as effective in the local culture. The lack of a needs analysis before the implementation of laptop programs might result in a distortion of the innovation concept and lead to a reproduction of the same traditional teaching methodology, which merely substitutes an old tool (the textbook) with a newer one (the laptop). That is to say that rather than being an innovative solution, one-to-one laptop programs may simply amplify what is already occurring in schools, for better or worse.

These observations suggest that the provision of technology alone will not change education. Not only are the tools needed in the knowledge culture, but also the motivation, the enthusiasm for taking initiative, and the satisfaction of achieving goals (Ferneding, 2003). Certainly, for school innovation to occur, it is necessary to disrupt the teacher-centered approach, and place the learner at the center of the learning process. However, it should be considered that it is challenging for teachers to adopt this approach, as it involves a change, sometimes radical, in their work. Moreover, there are cultural aspects to take into account when implementing a project with technology in a new reality. Many initiatives addressing school innovation through technology expect positive results without enough preparation of the teachers, adequate planning and a sufficient infrastructure. On the contrary, it is our belief that a systemic strategy for school innovation will position technology as an assistant tool for teachers, rather than the other way around. It will provide a more comprehensive cultural approach, particularly taking into account the teachers' needs, including technical support and systematic cycles of training. That is to say, transformation of learning environments is unlikely to happen by itself in a spontaneous process. A systemic approach is needed, if the program is to achieve some of the desired educational goals.

References

Brown, A. L., & Campione, J. (1994). Guided discovery in a Community of Learners. In: McGilly, K., ed., *Classroom Lessons: Integrating Cognitive Theory and Classroom Practice*. Cambridge (MA)-London: MIT Press.

Buckingham, D., Willett, R. (2006). *Digital generations: children, young people and new media*. Mahwah (NJ): LEA.

Bucy, E. P., Newhagen, J. E. (2004). *Media access: Social and psychological dimensions of new technology use*. Mahwah: LEA.

Calvani, A. (2001). *Educazione, comunicazione e nuovi media. Sfide pedagogiche e cyberspazio*. Torino: UTET.

ECBP-Engineering Capacity Building Programme website: http://www.giz.de/Themen/en/14270.htm.

Education For All. *Country Reports: Brazil*. EFA 2000.

Engeström, Y. (1987). *Learning by Expanding: an Activity-Theoretical Approach to Developmental Research*. Helsinki: Orienta-Konsultit.

Fabio, R. A. 2002. *L'intelligenza potenziale. Strumenti di misura e di riabilitazione*. Milano: Franco Angeli.

Ferneding, K. A. (2003). *Questioning Technology: Electronic Technologies & Educational Reform*. New York: Peter Lang.

Fosnot, C.T. (2005). *Constructivism: Theory, Perspectives and Practices*. New York and London: Columbia University.

Gardner, H. (2006). *The development and education of the mind*. London-New York: Routledge.

Gilster, P. (1997). *Digital Literacy*. New York: John Wiley & Sons.

Glaser, B., Strauss A. (1967). *The Discovery of Grounded Theory*. New York: Aldine.

Glasersfeld, E. (1989). Constructivism in Education. In Husen, T., Postlethwaite, N. *The International Encyclopedia of Education. Research and Studies*, vol. 1. Oxford: Pergamon Press.

Gonnet, J. (1997). *Éducation et Médias*. Paris: Presses Universitaires de France.

Greeno, J. G., Collins, A. M., Resnick, L. B. (1996). Cognition and learning. In D. Berliner and R. Calfee. *Handbook of Educational Psychology*. New York: MacMillian.

Hartel, H. (2008). *Low-cost devices in educational systems: The use of the "XO-Laptop" in the Ethiopian Educational System*. GTZ: Addis Ababa.

ISMU. (2007). *L'immigrazione straniera nella Provincia di Brescia, Osservatorio Regionale sulla Multietnicità*. Milano: Iniziative e Studi sulla Multietnicità.

Jenkins, H. (2006). *Convergence Culture: Where Old and New Media Collide*. NYU Press: New York.

Leontiev, A. *Problems of the development of mind*. English translation. Moscow: Progress Press (Russian original, 1947).

Ligorio, B. (1994). Community of learners. In *TD – Tecnologie Didattiche*, 4 (1).

Maslow, A. H. (1954). *Motivation and personality*. New York: Harper & Brothers.

Mills, K. A. (2010). A review of the "digital turn" in the new literacy studies. *Review of Educational Research* 80.2, pp. 246–271.

OLPC – One Laptop per Child website: http://one.laptop.org.

Papert, S. (1983). *The children's machine, rethinking school in the age of the computer*. New York: Basic Books.

Pischetola, M. (2011). *Educazione e divario digitale. Idee per il capacity building*. Milano: Unicopli.

Pischetola, M. (2010). One-to-one technology: students leading change. *Research on Education and Media*, v. 2 N. 1

Robinson, K. (2001). *Out of Our Minds: Learning to be Creative*. Oxford: Capstone.

UCA – Um computador por Aluno website: http://prouca.comunidades.net.

Van Dijk, J. (2005). *The Deepening Divide. Inequality in the Information Society*. London-New Delhi: Sage Publications.

Varisco, B. (2002). *Costruttivismo socio-culturale: genesi filosofiche, sviluppi psico-pedagogici, applicazioni didattiche*. Roma: Carocci

Vygotsky, L.S. (1978). *Mind and society: The development of higher psychological processes*. Cambridge (MA): Harvard University Press.

Teachers and the Challenges of Digital Technologies in Education: The Portuguese 'e.escolinha' Programme

Sara Pereira

Abstract

The media, old and new, are today a significant presence in the lives of children and youth, playing an important role in the way they learn and understand the world. Several studies show how the media are influential agents of socialization for the new generations, often more than family or school. Despite the recognized importance of the media in children's lives, educational institutions are frequently closed to the media culture of the students, who leave their experiences and media practices outside the school walls. Based on the results of a survey of a group of primary school teachers, this paper aims to present and discuss the teachers' perspectives on the place of digital media in education and its impact on educational practices. The questionnaires were distributed to 80 teachers from the third and fourth grades of basic education (8–10 years old), teaching in 30 primary public schools in the municipality of Braga, a city in the northern Portugal. Based on the Portuguese programme 'e.escolinha' whose aim is for every child in the 1st cycle of basic education to have access to a laptop named 'Magalhães', this paper aims to understand the uses of digital media, and in particular the uses of this computer, in school. The study highlights the motivations and the issues that underlie teachers' acceptance or rejection in engaging with digital technologies in the classroom setting. In so doing, this chapter shows that teachers recognize the importance of the media and communication technologies in education, but their integration into teaching activities is not yet a usual and rooted practice The chapter concludes by considering the difficulties and the constraints indicated by teachers in using digital media, namely the 'Magalhães' computer, and some ways to overcome them.

Introduction

In 2000, the European Council (EC) of Lisbon defined a strategy for the European Union (EU)[1] that aims "to make Europe the most competitive and dynamic economy of knowledge, capable of generating sustainable economic growth with

---

1 This strategy was known as "Lisbon Strategy" or "Lisbon Agenda" and was launched in 2000 following a meeting of the European Council, in the Portuguese capital, as a response to the challenges of globalization and ageing. This Strategy was re-launched in 2005 and this renewal helped clarify its scope and aims. It was in the scope of this revision that the Technological Plan was born in 2005, giving rise to the Technological Plan for Education in 2007. This included four programs: "e.escola" (e.school), "e.professor" (e.teacher), "e.portunidades" (e.opportunities), e "e.escolina" (e.little school). The latter was launched in 2008 and is the main focus of analysis in this chapter.

more and better jobs and greater social cohesion" (http://www.dges.mctes.pt). To achieve these goals, in 2005 it was agreed that each Member State would prepare a National Reform Plan and present a National Strategy in line with the objectives of the Lisbon Strategy. Following this agreement, several countries designed and implemented programmes to equip schools with digital technologies and to promote the use of these technologies by students at various levels of education. In the case of Portugal, in 2007, the XVII Portuguese Government launched the Technological Plan for Education, which intends "to place Portugal among the five most advanced European countries in technological modernization of education" (www.pte.gov.pt). This Plan was presented as "the largest programme of technological modernization of Portuguese schools" representing "a unique effort to equip schools with technological infra-structures, provide online content and services and strengthen students' and teachers' ICT skills " in order "to prepare the new generations for the challenges of the knowledge society" (www.pte.gov.pt).

A year later, in 2008, the 'e.escolinha' (e.little school) programme was launched within the Technological Plan for Education. The main target of 'e.escolinha' was children aged between 6 and 10 years old attending the first cycle of basic education (primary school). The most visible side of this programme was the distribution of a laptop (named 'Magalhães', a tribute to Fernão de Magalhães, a Portuguese navigator from the XVI century) to all primary school pupils, free of charge or at an extremely low price.

Although this measure has allowed many children to have access to a personal computer (and also access to the Internet for those who bought it), it received some criticism from teachers, parents, opposition parties and the society in general. The excessive concern with delivering technology, overlooking media literacy or digital literacy goals, as well as the disregard for pedagogical practices and the need for teacher-training were some of the main criticisms raised and also the main reasons for the limited success of the initiative. This means that the programme was a lot more centred on the equipment than on the child, the teacher or the teaching-learning process. The purpose of distributing computers to schoolchildren was not accompanied by a training plan for the use of technology aiming to empower children to use it in a critical, responsible and secure way, which would also require the training of teachers.

However, computers were distributed to approximately 500,000 children (for three school years), which means theywere introduced into schools as a part of children's daily lives. As a result, what happened, and what did not happen, at school? How were those computers used? Were they incorporated in the pedagogical practices of teachers and in the teaching-learning process? What are the gains and the main difficulties faced by teachers when digital technologies enter the classroom setting? What are the main problems in using digital technologies at school? Are teachers resistant to or enthusiastic about the use of digital technology? These are some of the main questions that this paper intends to discuss based on a critical media education approach.

Making sense of digital media in education

Since the programmes set up in the 1980s and 1990s aimed at getting computers into schools did not produce the expected revolution in the educational system, other kinds of initiatives have since been launched and implemented during this decade all over the world. In Portugal, these initiatives respond to a public policy that intends to modernize schools and give the opportunity to all students to have a personal computer and a broadband connection.

This kind of technological plan for education, reflecting a tendency that seems to be present in contemporary society, assigns technology the power to change and boost education as well as other areas in society. This enthusiastic view of the great potential of technology is based on a "techno-romantic" or "techno-utopian" (Selwyn, 2011) perspective. Policy-makers believe that technology, more specifically the computer, will revolutionize schooling and will transform the way students learn. This was also the point of view that was behind the launch of the 'e.escolinha' programme.

Alongside these arguments, negative discourses emerge that condemn technology in education. We agree with Buckingham (2007) when he states that this debate "has often been conducted in quite absolutist terms" (p. 48). The author is also right to consider that this polarization does not imply that "we should seek to arrive at a 'happy medium' between them [both positions]" (p. 49). Nevertheless, more nuanced perspectives could be possible to reach if we assume that advantages and disadvantages of using technology cannot be separated.

The polarization of this debate focuses much attention on one side or on the other, but ignores some key issues. As Buckingham (2007) argues "fundamental questions about what teachers and students might want to use technology for, and about what we might need to know about technology, tend to be marginalized" (p. 49). In addition, the competences children need to acquire in order to deal effectively with digital technologies are an issue that is not usually addressed.

Between these dichotomous arguments, it is important to listen to the main players, i.e., teachers, students and parents. Often the arguments about the use of technology in education do not echo the perspectives of the main actors of the whole process, and it is fundamental that they are not left out, particularly because, as Buckingham stated "there is frequently a significant gap between the imagination of policy-makers and of more academic accounts of educational technology – and the realities of teaching and learning" (Buckingham, 2007: 30).

In our opinion the main question is not the use of digital media in school or its importance for the educational process. Our lives are surrounded by media and it is essential that students develop critical approaches to using these means. The main points have to do with the principal focus of these policies, the way they are translated into practice and how the everyday realities of schools and classrooms are considered.

Linda Phipps (2000), from the St William's Foundation, United Kingdom, analysed over 40 projects carried out by public authorities, private agencies and community groups. These projects were considered positive examples of applications of new technologies to reduce the disadvantage experienced by the more excluded groups in our society (Phipps, 2000: 39). Phipps concluded that such projects have centred on access and hardware. According to the author, these projects are based on a belief in equality of access and on a belief in the potential of ICT to solve the inclusion of disadvantaged people in the information society. Phipps recognises that the lack of information access may lead to cumulative disadvantage and, therefore, access could create opportunities in several areas. But she questions if this "is effective enough for ICTs to have a real and significant impact on the lives and opportunities of disadvantaged groups" (p. 47). In this sense, she emphasizes "*relational* more than *distributional* measures" (id.) which means more a focus on people and community than on distribution of technology because "new levels of empowerment will not come about without strategies for community involvement and basic capacity-building among community groups" (p. 45). In the case of the Portuguese programme we are focusing on, the community would be the school community, namely, students, teachers and parents. Previous analyses of this programme (Pereira & Melro, 2012) confirm, however, that the community was not its centre or a concern. The community was not involved; they were seen more as recipients than active agents. Herein lies one of the critical points of the programme and that may have contributed to it not having achieved the expected success.

In the same line of thought as Phipps, Mark Warschauer (2003) states that the technology programmes around the world "too often focus on providing hardware and software and pay insufficient attention to the human and social systems" adding that "meaningful access to ICT comprises far more than merely providing computers and Internet connections" (p. 6). This seems to be one of the problematic aspects of the programmes within the Portuguese Technological Plan for Education. In the case of 'e.escolinha' the access dimension was taken into account but other factors pointed out by Warschauer as significant, such as physical, digital, human and social resources, relationships and also content and language, literacy and education, community and institutional structures (p. 6), were undervalued dimensions or even ignored.

Another significant issue, referred to by Buckingham (2007), is "that the use of technology is often mandated from the top down: it is a decision made by administrators or other outsiders that is then imposed upon the teaching profession" (p. 51). Indeed, in the case of 'e.escolinha', the programme was imposed by central authorities and the teachers were not enlisted as collaborators. There was not even an organized training programme for the teaching staff. Training is clearly crucial for enhancing technology in schools and it has been fundamental for the implementation of this governmental initiative. Therefore, some teachers appeared to be reluctant in using the laptop. As a result, there was a significant gap between the euphoric discourses of the policy-makers about the potential of the 'Magalhães' laptop and the realities of classroom practices, as can be seen in the following sections.

Methods

This study is part of a broader research project which seeks to examine the policies that comprise the Portuguese governmental programme 'e.escolinha' (little school) and get to know how children use the 'Magalhães' computer at home and at school. The first objective was achieved by collecting and examining documentation produced within the framework of the Technological Plan for Education (TPE) and, more specifically, within the 'e.escolinha' programme. In addition, interviews were conducted with policy-makers and with companies connected with the setting up and implementation of the TPE. In order to fulfil the second objective, questionnaires were distributed to children attending schools of the 1st cycle of basic education in the Braga municipality (a city in northern Portugal) as well as to their teacher and parents.

This paper is based on the analysis of the teachers' questionnaires. Between May and June 2012, 80 teachers from 30 schools of the 1st cycle of basic education answered the questionnaire, which had the following objectives:

1. Get to know the teachers' perceptions about the importance and the place of the media in school.
2. Ascertain whether the teachers use the media and the new technologies, particularly the 'Magalhães' computer in the teaching-learning process.
3. Establish whether years of teaching service and ICT training are factors that influence teachers' perceptions and their use of ICT in school.

4. Determine how the 'Magalhães' computer was used in school and how the teachers integrated it in their pedagogical practices.
5. Register the teachers' opinions on the 'Magalhães' computer and on the public policy which set out its distribution.
6. Identify the challenges, problems, advantages and difficulties in implementing the 'e.escolinha' programme in the classroom.
7. Ascertain whether the teachers require specialized training in the use of digital technologies in education.

The Computer programme IBM-SPSS Statistics v21 was used to conduct the statistical analysis of the data collected from the "Teacher Questionnaire – Navigating with 'Magalhães', focusing on the first four objectives mentioned above.

The descriptive analysis of the data was carried out taking into account the nature of the variables being studied. The following measures were calculated: absolute frequencies; relative frequencies (percentage of valid cases %); central tendency (mean); dispersion (standard deviation); and the maximum and minimum values. In the multiple choice questions, the percentages of answers presented are in relation to the total number of valid cases.

For the inferential analysis, we resorted to the application of non-parametric tests since, on the whole, the conditions of applicability of parametric tests were not met. To compare independent or unconnected groups the Mann-Whitney and Kruskal-Wallis tests were used. When there were two groups to be compared, the former was used, and if there were more, the latter was employed. Whenever significant differences were detected, these were identified by a pair-by-pair comparison using the Mann-Whitney test. To check the independence between two categorical variables, Chi-square tests were used (Marôco, 2011).

All the tests were applied with a confidence level of 95% unless otherwise stated.

Brief description of the Portuguese education system and characterization of the respondent group of teachers

Compulsory schooling in Portugal lasts 12 years and covers two levels: basic education and secondary education. Basic education is divided into three cycles: the first cycle is four years long and is attended by children aged between 6 and 10; the second cycle takes two years and is attended by 10 to 12-year-olds; the third cycle lasts three years, and is attended by children between the ages of 12 and 15. Secondary Education takes three years and is for students aged between 15 and 18. Before compulsory schooling, children may attend pre-school from the age of 3 to 6.

This study focuses on the 1st cycle of basic education, which corresponds to primary school. It is the only level of education where the students have only one teacher who teaches all the subjects. There are four main subjects: Portuguese, Mathematics, Social and Physical Environment Studies, and Artistic and Physical Expression. The curriculum matrix for this level of education also includes three areas that do not have the status of subjects: project work, guided study and citizenship education. Since 2008, 1st cycle schools have also offered Curricular Enrichment Activities, which include a foreign language (English) and, depending on the schools, Music, Physical Education and Information and Communication Technologies. These activities are held outside class time, are not compulsory and are taught by teachers hired by the local city councils.

In order to conduct this study, 80 teachers from 30 schools of the 1st cycle of education in the Braga municipality answered the questionnaire, which equates to 42% of the total number of schools of this level of education in the municipality. Only teachers who had 3rd and 4th year classes were requested to complete the questionnaire since they were the ones who would have the most experience using the 'Magalhães' computer. The overwhelming majority (94%) of the teachers are female, which seems to reflect the overall scenario of the teaching profession in Portugal as far as gender is concerned. In terms of age, 80% of the teachers are 40 years of age or older, while only 20% are younger than 40 with the mean being 47 (standard deviation= 7.9 years).

Regarding academic qualifications, the overwhelming majority has a degree in the field of education while only 5% have a post-graduate qualification or master's degree.

In terms of years of teaching service, the vast majority (75%) has been teaching for more than 20 years, underscoring the experience of this group of teachers. Only 25% have been in the profession for less than 20 years, with the mean being 25.6 (standard deviation = 8.4 years) years of service.

Most of these teachers (N=63) stated that they underwent training in the use of information and communication technologies in schools. Only 15 mentioned they did not get any training. It should be noted that 88% of the teachers (N=76) stated that they have access to the Internet at school, while 12% do not. Of those who do, 54% have access in the classroom and 46% do not.

Listening to teachers: how they face the challenges of digital media in education

In this section we present the results from three topics taken from the teachers' questionnaires: (1) perceptions of the importance of digital media in children's lives and in education and the use of these means in teachers' daily and professional lives; (2) using the 'Magalhães' computer, and (3) views on the main contributions and constraints that 'Magalhães' has for education practice and the teaching–learning process.

Perceptions and uses of the media in school

The vast majority of the respondents (N=78) thinks that media and digital technologies have an important or very important role in children's lives (99%) besides considering them also as important or very important for curricular activities (98%).

However, as can be seen in the graph in Fig. 1, most of the means are rarely or never used by the teachers in their pedagogic activity. The computer and the Internet are the means they state as using most often in their pedagogic practice, although, as other data collected from the questionnaire confirm, they may not use them when interacting directly with the children but rather when planning classes or preparing materials for them.

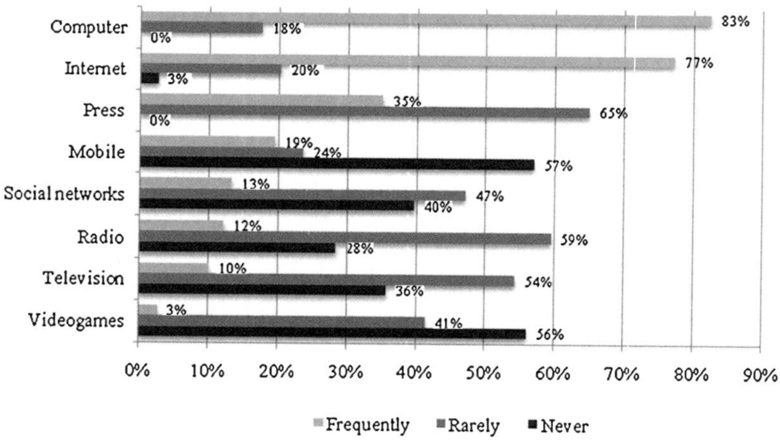

Fig. 1: Uses of the media in teachers' pedagogical practice

In fact, of the 77 respondents to the question on the day-to-day use of the computer at school and/or at home, only one stated she did not use a computer. Sending emails, searching on the Internet, preparing classes and making PowerPoint slides are the activities the teachers mention they do most often on their computer.

As far as the use of the computer for pedagogic activities is concerned, only four teachers stated they do not use it. Those who do, use it to prepare classes (73); to carry out activities in the classroom (67); communicate with other teachers (60);

communicate with students (26); make materials available to students (24) and to communicate with parents (22). As mentioned before, the computer appears to be more of a resource that is used to plan and manage school activities than a means to enhance the teaching-learning process.

One of the aims of this study is to determine the connection between the teachers' years of practice and how they use the computer. On the whole, the results indicate that the teachers who have been teaching longer use the computer less often in their pedagogic activity (mean= 26; SD= 8.4 years of teaching service)

Besides this, the use of the computer to prepare and carry out class activities is more significant among the teachers who have been teaching for fewer years. This may suggest that teachers who have begun their educational activity more recently are more open to integrating ICT in the classroom; they may be younger as well, they could have acquired ICT teaching skills through their initial training and, therefore, be more used to and aware of technologies. Teachers who have been teaching for longer appear to use the computer mostly as a communication tool, i.e., what stands out is the use of email to communicate professionally. This result leads us to question whether newer teachers from 'digital native generations' are a little more aware and sensitized to integrate technology into the classroom curriculum because of their own engagement with ICT or because they were taught how to use technology in initial teacher training[2].

The study also sought to determine the relation between ICT training and the teachers' use of the computer. On the whole, no difference can be seen between teachers who underwent training and those who did not, as far as the frequency of computer use is concerned. The only case where there appears to be statistical evidence to establish a dependency connection between computer use and ICT training is "editing images and photographs" ($p<0.05$), since this feature is clearly more often used by teachers who have ICT training. With regard to the relation between ICT training and computer use in pedagogic activities, it was found there is practically no difference between teachers with ICT training and those without when it comes to using the computer for pedagogic purposes. The main activities undertaken are: "Preparing classes" (94%); "Carrying out classroom activities" (86%) and "Communicating with other teachers" (77%).

---

2 In Portugal, initial teacher training is the responsibility of Higher Education Institutions. As mentioned in the Portugal Report on ICT in Education (European Schoolnet, 2013), "In Portugal, institutions have autonomy in this area [ICT in initial teacher training] and are therefore free to decide whether or not to include ICT in initial teacher education. Nonetheless, most institutions that are responsible for initial teacher training provide ICT as a basic study" (p. 9). ICT in-service training is not compulsory.

Although most of the other means play an important role in children's daily lives, when it comes to their use in pedagogical practice they are rarely explored and analyzed by teachers. The mobile phone, for instance, which is today a convergent technology allowing children access to a variety of resources through an internet connection, is not explored by more than half of the teachers. Even newspapers and magazines, which could be more readily used in the classroom due to the ease with which this sort of material can be collected, are seldom objects of analysis. This study shows how the media seem to be far from being a common feature of school practices, despite playing a significant part in the younger generation's daily activities. Various authors have drawn attention to the fact that there is a mismatch between how children and young people use media and ICT at home and in their daily lives, and how they use them in the school context (Selwyn, Potter and Cranmer, 2010). The results of this study, based on the teachers' questionnaire as well as on the children's and parents' questionnaires administered within the same project, show this gap as well, demonstrating that informal or formal learning takes place outside school and does not get much attention in this context. A reading of the results of the study undertaken by Selwyn, Potter and Cranmer (2010) in primary schools in the London area may suggest that the contradiction between the value teachers assign to the media and the actual work they carry out with them in class could be connected with the fact that they feel neither competent nor confident enough to bridge the gap between the uses and the practices children have at home and the experience they have with ICT at school and explore the children's interests and capacities in the classroom. This interaction would require, however, teachers to be familiar with the experiences children have with these technologies at home, which, according to the abovementioned study, is something teachers are in fact aware of but not so familiar as to be able to make full use of them in the classroom.

Uses and non-uses of the 'Magalhães' computer

As mentioned previously, the 'e.escolinha' programme sought to distribute a laptop to every child in the 1st cycle of basic education. The computer cost no more than €50, but in the case of children who benefitted from the School Social Services, it could be purchased for €20 or even obtained free of charge. At first the programme did not make provision for the laptops to be handed out to teachers, which for many meant a constraint on their using it.

Only 12 of the respondents received the 'Magalhães', although 58 mentioned having had the chance to explore the computer and its content. Teachers who had not stated it was precisely due to the fact that they did not have one, but there were others who said they had not done so because the computer was for the students and not for the teachers, which is rather surprising considering the laptop was meant to be used within educational practice.

When asked about specific training on the 'Magalhães' computer, of the total number teacher respondents (77), more than half (53) report they had not done any. The reasons given were lack of training sessions (66%), lack of information and funding (both with 23%) and lack of time (11%).

When it comes to the use of the 'Magalhães' computer, what the results show is that it is mostly infrequently (43%) or not at all used (36%). Only 21% mentioned using it frequently. The reasons given by the 36% of the teachers who stated never having used or not currently using 'Magalhães' are damaged computers, the fact that not all students have them, the lack of electrical outlets in the classroom and students forgetting to bring the computer to class are mentioned by more than 50% of the teachers. Technical and logistical reasons seem, therefore, to be the main reasons hindering the use of the computer in the classroom. Less frequently, the respondents also reported difficulties that arise from work organisation and management and from training.

Turning now to the 64 % of the teachers (N= 39) who stated that they use the computer, be it sporadically or frequently, they were asked about the way they use the laptop and what their objectives were.

Of the teachers who use the computer in the classroom, only one said it was on a daily basis. Nineteen teachers stated they used it once or more a week while 19 others mentioned they used it only on a monthly basis. In other words, the use of the computer in educational activities is still sporadic, being a resource to carry out specific tasks. It is an auxiliary tool used occasionally and not one which is integrated in the teaching-learning process. The activities teachers say students carry out most often on the 'Magalhães' computer in the classroom,shown in Table 1, are indicative of this sporadic practice. Among the activities pointed out as most frequent, two pertain to tasks which are usually carried out with a pen or pencil: "do exercises" and "read and write texts". Although they are mentioned as being carried out most frequently, they are not yet a regular and daily activity in pedagogical practice. Power Point presentations are also frequent but just as sporadic, being used mainly for the presentation of assignments or school projects. As far as games are concerned, these are educational in nature. Some of them were originally installed on the computer and are mostly used when students have finished the planned work or when they have completed their individual tasks and are waiting for their colleagues to finish theirs. Although conducting a search on the Internet is among the five most frequent activities, it is still an underused practice in the classroom. The use of the computer at home to carry out activities connected with education, namely to do school assignments, is also low, in line with what is reported in the "Key Data on Learning and Innovation through ICT at School in Europe" (EACEA, 2011).

Taking into account these results, it can be said that, in their educational practice with their students, teachers still do not take much advantage of the potential of digital media. They are not very innovative as far as their use is concerned and do not use them much to provide active and collaborative learning. This is why it is important for teachers to receive technology skill training.

Table 1: The five activities teachers say students either never do or frequently do on the 'Magalhães' computer in class

Never	Frequently
Go to social networks (96%)	Do exercises (57%)
Send emails (83%)	Play games (50%)
Produce videos and films (79%)	Make Power Points (43%)
Watch the news on the Internet (72%)	Search on the Internet (23%)
Produce videos and films (44%)	Read and write texts (16%)

It is important to point out that there appears to be a dependency connection (at a confidence level of 95%) between the use of the 'Magalhães' with students and whether or not the teachers had specific training for that computer. This information suggests that training teachers may step-up the use of digital media in education and be the way to prepare and enable teachers to integrate media into educational practice. However, as was discussed above, the relation between ICT training and the use of computers by the teachers, whether for personal purposes or for pedagogical activities, was not considered to be significant. How can this difference be accounted for? One explanation may reside in the fact that teachers respond better to a more specific training plan with the purpose of addressing a particular situation they are going through at the time and for which they would like to find action strategies.

In general, it can be said that the number of years of teaching service does not influence how students use their 'Magalhães' computers in the classroom. In fact, the most and the least frequent activities match the ones presented in Table 1.

Using the 'Magalhães' computer at school: contributions and constraints

In this last section we sought to determine what the teachers' opinions were on the main contributions made by the 'Magalhães' as well the main factors which constrain its use, regardless of whether it is used or not.

On the whole, there was significant agreement among the teachers as to the contributions brought by the 'Magalhães' to school (Fig. 2). An exception was the item "Increase in indiscipline in the classroom" since 74.5% of the respondents disagreed with it, while 25.5 % agreed. The items "Facilitate communication within the school community" and "Improve the relationship between school and family" also stood out, as the percentages were evenly split between the two opinions.

It should be pointed out that there is a number of items on which over 90% of the teachers agreed. These are connected with the promotion of skills, access to knowledge, student motivation, co-operation and participation, as well as with the diversification of activities. Thus, it seems clear that, according to the teachers, the 'Magalhães' computer brought significant benefits to school, students and teachers.

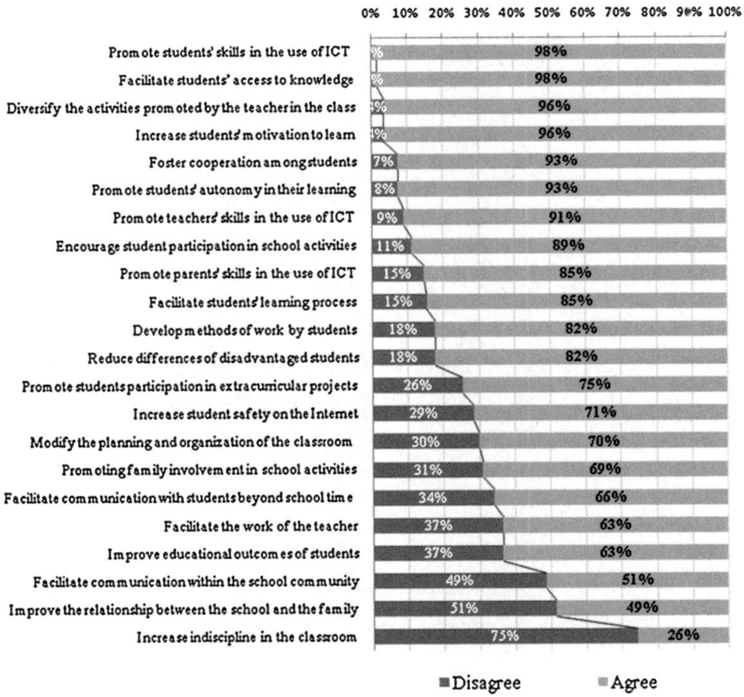

Fig. 2: Main contributions of the 'Magalhães' computer

In terms of the main factors which constrain the use of the computer (indicated by at least 2/3 of the teachers), these pertain to "practical" and technical aspects connected with computer malfunctions, lack of computers or infrastructures (power outlets or Internet connections) (Fig 3).

It is interesting to note that the teachers' lack of pedagogical knowledge is the constraint they assigned the least importance to, as only 12% stated they agree it was in fact one. Concerning their shortcomings in terms of technical knowledge, opinions were almost equally divided: 39% agreed and 33 % disagreed.

Although it was found previously in this study that specific training appeared to have a positive impact on the use of 'Magalhães', teachers reported external issues, i.e., technical and infrastructure issues as constraining factors rather than their training or pedagogical knowledge.

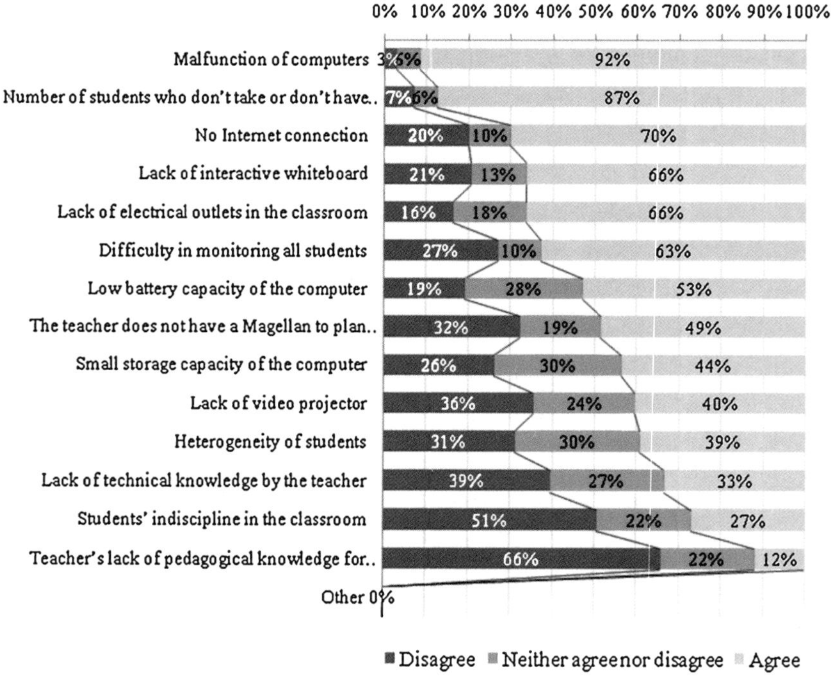

Fig. 3: Factors which constrain the use of 'Magalhães'

The teachers were also asked to say what they would change in the distribution of the 'Magalhães' computer if it were still operational. It was our intention to determine those features the teachers regarded as critical in this initiative which would require changing in order to ensure its success. The teachers' answers reveal some of the main problems that have already been pointed out, both by this group of teachers and by public speeches on this governmental measure, some of which were covered in the media (Pereira, 2010).

It is, therefore, clear thatamong the suggestions made by the teachers are the main constraints to the implementation of the measure in schools and in classrooms: constant computer malfunctions and a lack of a technical support centre to help solve this problem; the fact that the computer was not distributed to the teachers (its retail price was six times the maximum price paid by a child, which made it difficult for teachers to purchase); the lack of training sessions to prepare teachers to integrate the technology in the classroom; the limited availability of contents/software to teach and learn specific issues; the fact that the computers were taken home instead of staying at school which is connected with the fact that they could be reused the following year. These are some of the suggestions put forward by the teachers if they could change the programme, which are simultaneously some of the critical factors underlying its implementation.

The 'e.escolinha' programme was discontinued in June 2011 when the XIX Constitutional Government took office, which meant that the huge political and economic investment in this initiative and all the promises of change in the teaching–learning process were put on hold.

However, these teachers' voices show how important it would have been for the government to have taken the teachers on board as partners in this programme, instead of creating this top-down initiative and imposing it on the teachers and the whole of the education community without paying much attention to the idiosyncrasies of the school environment.

Discussion of the results

The evidence from the Portuguese Ministry of Education statistics clearly shows that there has been a significant improvement in the ratio of students per computer. Before the implementation of the 'e.escolinha' programme (2005–2006), the ratio of students per computer in the 1st cycle of basic education was 15:9 in public schools and 9:5 in private schools. This number decreased substantially in the school year 2008–2009, in which the 'Magalhães' computer was distributed, having fallen to 1:1 and 1:2 in public schools and in private schools, respectively. Only one year after the implementation of the initiative, the ratio of students per computer reached the maximum rate of 1:1 in both schools systems. The same scenario is present in the number of students per computer with Internet connection, but with a major difference: from 26:5 in public schools and 13:8 in private schools in 2005–2006, to a ratio of 1:1 and 1:2, in 2008–2009, respectively (Gabinete de Estatística e Planeamento da Educação & Direcção de Serviços de Estatística, 2011).Thanks to this programme and to the Technological Plan in general,

Portugal took the lead in Europe as far as children's access to computers and the Internet was concerned, exceeding the European average of three to seven students per computer (European Schoolnet & University of Liege Psychology and Education, 2013). In a country with low schooling rates among the adult population, this governmental programme democratized laptop ownership by making it possible for families, especially those with low incomes, to possess one. This feature is also made clear by the number of families who joined the 'Magalhães' initiative: 98% of the 1,517 students surveyed had acquired this computer.

However, despite this enthusiastic response, the results suggest that the use of this computer in school has generally been sporadic and piecemeal, since it is not embedded in classroom practice. Although teachers assign importance to digital media in children's lives and teaching practice, they report they do not use these means much for enhancing and enriching learning.

According to a study conducted for the European Commission on ICT use in Education (European Schoolnet & University of Liege Psychology and Education, 2013), "school heads and teachers consider that insufficient ICT equipment (especially interactive whiteboards and laptops) is the major obstacle to ICT use" (p. 9). However, in the case of this group of teachers, the fact that each student had a laptop did not mean ICTs were more widely used in school and in the classroom, which may explain another of the conclusions of the abovementioned study that states "no overall relationship was found between high levels of infrastructure provision and student and teacher use, confidence and attitudes" (id.).

As far as computer use by the teachers is concerned, it was established that although they use it more frequently outside the classroom, its use is connected with pedagogical practice. In a study that sought to characterize ICT uses in educational contexts, Ponte, Oliveira e Varandas (2003), from the Faculty of Sciences of the University of Lisbon, Portugal , mention three categories of use: (i) an additional educational aid to assist students in their learning, (ii) a personal productivity tool to prepare materials for classes, to carry out administrative tasks and to search for information and materials, and (iii) an interactive medium to interact and collaborate with other teachers and educational partners (p. 3). When applying this typology to the present study, the results point mainly to the uses mentioned in the second and third categories, while the first is the least frequent, especially concerning the use of the computer to develop activities with students in the classroom. In fact, many teachers used the computer for administrative tasks, preparing materials for classes and communicating with other teachers, students and parents. Some other studies have also indicated that teachers equipped with computers use them first and foremost for administrative functions (Mundy, Kupczynski & Kee, 2012) and to prepare their teaching (European Schoolnet & University of Liege

Psychology and Education, 2013), which is in agreement with the conclusions of our study.

As regards the frequency of use, only a small proportion (N=9) was using 'Magalhães' in the classroom more than once a week, and 27 were not using it at all. Thus, the use of the computer was very limited, and even for those who use it frequently it was not a central aspect of their pedagogical practice and their students' learning process. There was some use of the computer for word processing, making power points, Internet searches and playing (educational) games, but its use was very limited for creating and producing content, such as producing videos or writing on blogs.

Therefore, we can conclude that 'Magalhães' was not effectively integrated in the classroom and has not changed teachers' practices, as the policy-makers and the companies had enthusiastically announced and expected. However, these findings are not exactly a novelty. Similar conclusions are echoed by other studies. Buckingham (2007), after having presented some studies on the uses of ICT in classroom states that, in general "it seems fair to conclude that classroom teaching and learning have been far from transformed through the advent of technology" (p. 59). Based on those studies, the author puts forward another conclusion which is common to the results of this survey: "most teachers are quite ready to use computers at home and in other areas of their professional lives: they tend to 'resist' only when it comes to using them in the classroom" (p. 59).

The most common reasons cited by teachers for the computer underuse were structural or logistical. The fact that students left the computer at home, the computer hardware and software, constraints pertaining to school premises and infrastructure were, to some extent, the teachers' most apparent difficulties in using the computer. It was interesting to note that teachers considered these obstacles more relevant than their skills and knowledge to handle the equipment and to use its resources to support learning in the classroom, and then the training provided for teaching staff. It is true that the relationship between computer use and training in ICT was not statistically significant; however, there was a positive relationship between the 'Magalhães' use and specific training on the use of this computer.

Moreover, in the open questions in the questionnaire about the teachers' perspectives on the 'e.escolinha' programme and the distribution of the 'Magalhães' computer, they expressed other reasons for not using the computer, or for not using it frequently, and emphasized precisely the lack of training and the fact that the programme focused mainly on access and neglected educational purposes. They also advanced some proposals to ensure a greater success of this initiative.

72% of the teachers (N= 74) consider the 'e.escolinha' important or very important, highlighting, for instance, the fact that this programme gave equal opportunities to all primary school children to have a computer, thereby reducing social disadvantages among them. Despite this positive opinion, they point out some weaknesses too. Limitations of the training provision and the lack of an educational project were identified as significant factors affecting teachers' capacity in using the computer. The maintenance of the computers was another aspect that teachers found particularly hard to control given the frequent breakdowns of computers. A further problem relates to the way children use the equipment. In the opinion of a large number of teachers, the computer was used by children mainly as a toy and to play games; it was not seen as a resource for schooling. Teachers also believe that the computer should have stayed in school and not been taken home. Constraints related to the number of students per class (25 on average) are another factor indicated by some teachers. The quotations below could illustrate some of these arguments:

> I think this programme was important but with few benefits for children because they should have invested in the initial training of teachers in this area to develop good pedagogical practices with children (Female, 32 years old, teaching the 4th year, 8 years of service).

> The teachers were not properly informed and had no initial training. For children, in general, the 'Magalhães' computer was a toy (Female, 46 years old, teaching the 3rd year, 19 years of service).

> Some students just spoiled the computers. They took them to play games at home (Female, 54 years old teaching the 4th year, 32 years of service).

> I think they did not create conditions in schools for their use. Adequate training was not given to teachers either. (Female, 45 years old, teaching the 3rd year, 23 years of service).

> The initiative was interesting but the computer in the hands of the children lasted a very short time. My understanding is that schools should be equipped with computers (Female, 51 years old, teaching the 4th year, 29 years of service).

> It's not always easy to use the 'Magalhães' in a pedagogical context because some students have damaged them. As there is no Internet in the rooms, it's impossible to carry out some tasks (Female, 50 years old, teaching the 4th year, 28 years of service).

> Computers should not be given to children because most children use 'Magalhães' as a toy and when I ask students to bring their computer to school I see that most of them are already broken. Schools should have a room with computers (desktop or portable), where students would move to have specific computer classes with specialized teachers. The teacher of the 1st cycle has already a very extensive curriculum to work throughout the school year (Female, 42 years old, teaching the 3rd year, 18 years of service).

Based on the results of the research, we can conclude that, despite the many advantages of the programme also recognized by teachers, there are many reasons why this initiative has failed to transform learning in the manner that many of its advocates have envisaged. The centralized and top-down nature of this initiative could perhaps explain the gap between the government policy and the local schools' constraints and the teachers' professional skills and needs as well. In fact, the idea of distributing the 'Magalhães' computer comes from the government and from the industry rather than from teachers or from the school community. This policy focused mainly on access and hardware, which turned out not to be as effective as to have a significant impact on the lives of children and their families and on school life in general. In line with Phipps (2000), it could be argued that what is fundamental is a "movement from a technical, technology-centred perspective to an application- and user-oriented perspective, to support demand and the needs of users" (p. 48). The provision of a digital literacy programme would have been essential because, by extending to the "e.escolinha" programme the conclusion that the abovementioned author reached on the ICT application projects she examined, the promise this programme made to increase levels of digital empowerment "will not come about without strategies for community involvement and basic capacity-building among community groups".

On the whole, it can be said that this programme, aimed specifically at primary school children as well as the other programmes comprising the Portuguese Technological Plan for Education, allowed for the social inclusion of families, particularly underprivileged ones, insofar as the lack of access to means of communication increasingly used in society may accelerate exclusion. However, if we consider that the concepts of inclusion and exclusion are multidimensional (Phipps, 2000), and are connected with each individual's situation and life opportunities, it may be said that this governmental programme provided a positive response to the social inclusion dimension (access to digital media), but inclusion is not only about providing equal opportunities in terms of access. In other words, the programme was important as far as access was concerned, but it was not very significant in terms of usepractices or in boosting interaction with and participation in the community, which are other dimensions of social inclusion. Using Phipps' terminology, the programme addressed 'distributional' issues (resources at the disposal of an individual or household) more than 'relational' issues (for instance, social participation, realization of social rights)[3].

3 Phipps argues that poverty is primarily focused upon distributional issues and the notion of social exclusion focuses primarily on relational issues (Phipps, 2000: 43).

Final remarks

David Buckingham (2007) argues that "the idea that digital technology will fundamentally transform education is obviously part of a bigger story" (p. 31). And it is, indeed. Contrary to the politicians in charge of the 'e.escolinha' programme, and even the former prime minister, who advocated it, the 'Magalhães' computer has not transformed learning nor has it revolutionized the institution of the school. This is not to deny the importance of this programme and its success in terms of students' access to a personal computer, nor is it to deny that some teachers are using it and are taking educational advantage of it. But, the schools' reality is much more diverse and complex than was pictured by the programme's policy-makers. Democratizing access to the computer, especially for low-income families, was, indeed, the most positive impact of this policy. It should, however, be noted that the strong enthusiasm generated by this governmental programme was also due to the expectations families have with regard to the educational value of the new technologies.

An aspect that seems evident is the gap that is being created between how technology is used in school and what children are doing with it outside school. As Buckingham (2007) states,

> If most schools have remained relatively unaffected by the advent of modern media technology, the same cannot be said of children's lives outside school. On the contrary, childhood is now permeated, even in some respects defined, by the modern media – by television, video, computer games, the internet, mobile phones and popular music, and by the enormous range of media-related commodities that make up contemporary consumer culture (p. 75).

Similar results were revealed by other studies, namely the research project carried out by Selwyn, Potter & Cranmer (2010) and the study prepared for the European Commission about benchmarking access, use and attitudes to technology in European schools (European Schoolnet & University of Liege Psychology and Education, 2013). Not only are students' ICT-based activities at home more frequent compared to ICT activities at school, but there is also a divide between children's media home experiences and their school experiences. In our study, there is also a mismatch between teachers′ opinions about the importance of the media in children's lives and their use in pedagogical activities. As commented before, this could be due to the difficulty in working with children's home experiences and to a lack of confidence in how to explore these means in a critical away. In some cases, this could also be explained by the scepticism of some teachers regarding the educational value of some media (for instance, mobile phones and videogames).

In our perspective, teachers' training is clearly crucial for promoting the use of (digital) media in schools and for implementing media literacy. We consider media literacy a fundamental means to approach technology at school and a way to respond to the increasing role of media in children's lives. Media literacy challenges teachers to go beyond access and promote creative opportunities and critical media uses. Through in-service training, teachers could become more confident in using media and ICT, participate more in professional development,and be more enthusiastic about ICT use in the teaching and learning (T&L) process. After all, "teachers' confidence and opinions about ICT use for T&L affect the frequency of students' ICT use for learning: boosting teacher professional development makes a difference, and appears to be a condition for an effective and efficient use of the available infrastructure" (European Schoolnet & University of Liege Psychology and Education, 2013: 14).

But this training, as well these kinds of technological policies for education, need to be realistic about the primary school realities and their diversity, the nature of this education level and its organizational constraints. They must also take into account that primary school teachers, as indeed teachers from other grades, have external pressures and must follow some priorities. The transforming technology practices inside the school cannot be done in a flash, since these kinds of changes are progressive, not radical. It is true that the technological policies and programmes, such as 'e.escolinha', are already having an effect on teachers' thinking about ICT, but they can be better suited to the realities of schools and the experience of teachers and pupils. There are also at least two aspects that were overlooked by the 'e.escolinha' programme and which deserve to be considered: one concerns the development of children's media literacy, helping them to think critically about their uses and engagement with media and ICT, promoting critical and creative practices and understanding of these means to make the best use of them in their everyday lives. The second concerns the importance of involving teachers in the definition of these policies. As was seen earlier, teachers were able to give suggestions on what they thought worked in the 'e.escolinha' programme , what did not work and could have worked better. Therefore, why not listen to teachers and take their perspectives on these issues into account? This could be the contribution of this research project for policy-makers, teachers staff, and society in general, in other words, giving voice to teachers (and children and their parents as well) showing the importance of involving them in this kind of decision-making.

Acknowledgements

This study is an integral part of a three-year project titled "Navigating with 'Magalhães': Study on the Impact of Digital Media in Schoolchildren" directed by the author of this paper. The research project is being carried out at the Communication and Society Research Centre, University of Minho, funded by the Portuguese

Foundation for Science and Technology [PTDC/CCI-COM/101381/2008] and co-funded by the European Regional Development Fund [COMPETE: FCOMP-01-0124-FEDER-009056].

References

Buckingham, D. (2007). *Beyond Technology. Children's Learning in the age of digital culture*. Cambridge: Polity Press.

EACEA (2011). *Key Data on Learning and Innovation through ICT at School in Europe*. Brussels: Education, Audiovisual and Culture Executive Agency (EACEA) P9 Eurydice. Retrieved from http://eacea.ec.europa.eu/education/eurydice).

Estratégia de Lisboa [Lisbon Strategy]. (n.d.). Retrieved from http://www.dges.mctes.pt/DGES/pt/Reconhecimento/Uni%C3%A3o+Europeia/Estrat%C3%A9gia+Europa+2020/Estrategia+Lisboa.htm.

European Schoolnet & University of Liege Psychology and Education (2013). Survey of Schools: ICT in Education. Benchmarking Access, Use and Attitudes to Technology in Europe's Schools. Final Study Report prepared for the European Commission DG Communications Networks, Content & Technology. Belgium: European Commission.

European Schoolnet (2013). Portugal – Country Report on ICT in Education. Brussels: European Schoolnet. Retrieved from http://insight.eun.org.

Gabinete de Estatística e Planeamento da Educação (GEPE) & Direcção de Serviços de Estatística (2011). *Educação em Números – Portugal 2011*. Lisboa: GEPE.

Marôco, J. (2011). *Análise Estatística com o SPSS Statistics [Statisitcs Analysis with SPSS Statistics]*. Pero Pinheiro: ReportNumber.

Mundy, M.-A., Kupczynski , L. & and Kee, R. (2012). Teacher's Perceptions of Technology Use in the Schools. SAGE Open 2: originally published online 13 March 2012. Retrieved from http://sgo.sagepub.com/content/2/1/2158244012440813.

Pereira, S. & Melro, A. (2012). As políticas tecnológicas para a educação e a literacia digital: o caso do programa governamental 'e.escolinha'. *Estudos em Comunicação*, nº 12, 287–317.

Phipps, L. (2000). New Communications Technologies. A conduit for social inclusion. *Information, Communication & Society,* 3:1, p. 39–68.

Plano Tecnológico da Educação [The Technological Plan for Education]. (n.d.). O PTE, Missão e Objectivos [The Technological Plan for Education, mission and objectives]. Retrieved from http://www.escola.gov.pt/pte.

Ponte, J. P., Oliveira, H., & Varandas, J. M. (2003). O contributo das tecnologias de informação e comunicação para o desenvolvimento do conhecimento e da identidade profissional. In D. Fiorentini (Ed.), *Formação de professores de Matemática: Explorando novos caminhos com outros olhares* (pp. 159–192). Campinas: Mercado de Letras.

Selwyn, N. (2011). *Schools and Schooling in the Digital Age*. Oxon: Routledge.

Selwyn, N., Potter, J., Cranmer, S. (2010). *Primary Schools and ICT. Learning from Pupil Perspectives*. London: Continuum.

Warschauer, M. (2003). *Technology and Social Inclusion. Rethinking the Digital Divide*. Cambridge: The MIT Press.

Enthusiastic, Hesitant and Resistant Teachers Toward the One-To-One Laptop Programme: A Multi-Sited Ethnographic Study in Catalonia[1]

Cristina Aliagas Marín[2] & Josep M. Castellà Lidon

Abstract

How do teachers make sense or struggle to make sense of the top-down process of classroom digitalization? This chapter tackles the fore concern by analysing the narratives of 12 teachers reflecting on the adoption and implementation of the one-to-one laptop initiative in the autonomous region of Catalonia (Spain), locally named *EduCAT1x1* programme. It examines the teacher's arguments and counterarguments towards that initiative considering their ideological and pedagogic positioning as techno-enthusiast, hesitant or resistant. It shows that teachers holding these three stances differ in the underlying assumptions regarding computers as tools for learning and in the educational benefits they think computers can bring about. Findings also indicate that all teachers, regardless the stance they take, have assumed the "discourse of inevitability" (Ferneding, 2003) that dominates viewpoints concerning technology and education. By looking at the teacher's narratives we claim that their experiences, opinions and feelings need to be placed in the centre of the debate on the digitalization of the learning/teaching process. This qualitative study is part of a wider multi-sited ethnography in 18 high schools, aimed at understanding how the educative actors (eg. headmasters, teachers, students, families) are dealing with this digital transformation in their everyday life in-and-out of school.

---

1 Data comes from the research project *IES2.0: Prácticas letradas digitales. Materiales, actividad de aula y recursos lingüísticos en línea* (EDU2011-28381; 2012-14), co-ordinated by Dr. Daniel Cassany and funded by the Spanish Government. More information about the project can be found here: https://sites.google.com/site/ies201x1/.

Moreover, the authors of this paper participate in the consolidated research project GR@EL, which has received a grant from the Catalan Government (AGAUR 2009 SGR 803, resolution 3-7-2009). We thank the high schools that have collaborated in this project for their generous co-operation, and especially the teachers being interviewed. Some members of our research team have participated in the process of gathering the data analysed here: Daniel Cassany, Sònia Oliver del Olmo and Glòria Sanz. Àngels Oliva has contributed a helpful linguistic revision of the final version of this chapter.

2 With the support of the Secretary for Universities and Research of the Ministry of Economy and Knowledge of the Government of Catalonia and the Co-fund programme of the Marie Curie Actions of the 7th R&D Framework Programme of the European Union (Beatriu de Pinós 2011-A).

Introduction

Inspired by the *One Laptop per Child* programme, in 2009 the Spanish Government launched the project *Escuela 2.0* (School 2.0), with the goal of introducing new technologies into classrooms. It was an ambitious and expensive educational reform, and 15 of the 17 autonomous regions plus the independent cities of Ceuta and Melilla decided to participate by co-financing part of the expenses. We could state that nowadays almost all the "traditional" classrooms have become "digital" or "2.0", as they have been equipped with a wireless internet connection, interactive whiteboards and low-cost netbooks.

The project of transforming the old pencil-and-paper classroom into a "2.0 classroom" is appealing, but what do the educative agents really think about this process of digitization of the classrooms? How do they make sense or struggle to make sense of this new educative reality? Is the Government investment having a real impact on the daily processes of teaching and learning in the so-called "wireless classroom"? This chapter reports on some fieldwork we are currently conducting in Catalonia to address these questions by investigating students', teachers' and families' perceptions of the use of portable computers in secondary schools. In the study, we qualitatively analyse teachers' for-and-against arguments to the one-to-one programme, based on the contribution of 12 secondary school teachers.

The digitization of the secondary classrooms

The debate on the digitization of education is part of a larger debate on the politics of education that takes a critical look at the role of technology in it, focusing on the social structures behind the use of technology in education rather than on its technical aspects. Ferneding (2003) argues that the narrative space of educational reform is feeding the cultural bias that equals technology with progress – an ideology for which technology-based policy remains unquestioned, sheltered by a discourse of "inevitability". Considering that technology is not a neutral or an apolitical tool, but an artefact tied up by global market economy forces, the technocentric discourse underlying the current educational reform policy could be seen as serving corporate market ideologies. Thus, one of the more astonishing educative implications is that behind this reform based on a technological determinism, the model of "student as a consumer" is consolidating. Ferneding's critical reflection on current American educational reform policy strongly resonates with the Spanish technology-driven reform.

The debate on the digitization of classrooms has been developed around four issues: a) digital natives, b) technology and learning outcomes, c) technology, teachers and classroom educative practices, and d) the barriers for integrating technology into instruction practices.

Digital natives

Most of the literature about this issue involves the work of Prensky (2010), one of the most popular supporters of the introduction of computers in the learning and teaching process. His distinction (2010) between the so-called "digital native" and "digital immigrant" has become trendy. In Spain, this dichotomy has become a commonly-accepted pillar of the digitization of education although, in fact, it has been wildly criticized for being inaccurate and deterministic.

From a critical stance, Thomas (ed. 2011) argues that the notion of "digital natives" cannot be empirically informed. An example of this is Brown and Czerniewicz's (2010) study, which demonstrated that the digital divide in South Africa University is not characterized by age, but by access and opportunity. Moreover, Bennett *et al.* (2008) make use of rigorous quantitative research to refute one important assumption underlying the notion of the "digital native": the idea that young people are imbued with sophisticated technical skills because they live immersed in technology. One of the counter-arguments regards multitasking, and how it can result in a loss of concentration (Bowman *et al.*, 2010). As for the implications for education, Bayne and Ross (2011) consider that Prenky's methaphor is a simplistic binary that constructs the teacher as lacking, as a digital immigrant doomed to have an illegitimate voice in the current digital age of education.

Technology and learning outcomes

The second main concern in the literature is the impact that technology has on the outcome of students' learning. Claims have been made both in favour of and against technology.

Researchers furthering the cause argue that substantial academic achievements have been reported in literacy skills, above all in writing and problem-solving tasks (Lowther *et al.*, 2003; Warschauer, 2006). Prensky (2010) argues that computers in the classrooms are the key to reducing the digital generation gap in the United States. This idea is consistent with the work of Warschauer (2006) who, after conducting a two-year laptop literacy study at 10 schools pointed out that having laptops in the classrooms helped to overcome the home-school divide. As laptops are devices that "travel" back and forth crossing these domains, they create a kind of "continuity" between these contexts socially associated with different values, practices and ways of using texts.

At the same time, the work of Cuban (2001) is driven by the goal of dispelling the assumption that more technology creates better learning and in fact, according to Hu (2007), some high schools have cancelled their one-to-one laptop programmes arguing lack of evidence of gains in achievement. Selwyn (2011) argues that the claim that technology improves learning is usually backed by personal beliefs, opinions and conjectures. Probably due to the lack of evidence to categorically state one or the other stance, other authors (Cassany, 2013) are beginning to dissociate themselves from this unanswered question, arguing that it is in fact too early to observe any solid relationship between laptops and academic benefits.

Technology, teachers and classroom educative practices

The third key issue in the literature is about the impact that one-to-one programmes may or may not have on everyday teaching practices. Are computers changing the ways teachers teach and the ways students learn? Nowadays there seems to be a tentative answer to these questions: so far, laptops have had a minor impact on classroom practices, and it seems that, apparently, whatever impact there is stems directly from the teacher's decisions, which, in turn, are closely influenced by many personal and institutional factors. Why do teachers struggle to include computers and ICT in their teaching practices? Let us consider two well-known explanations in that regard.

Prensky (2010) argues that the role of technology in teaching in the classroom consists of bringing about a change of teaching paradigm, of moving from the "old" pedagogy of teachers telling onto the "new" pedagogy of kids teaching themselves under the teachers' guidance. Prensky says that every teacher is at some point along the continuum between the old and the new paradigms. Teachers who are closer to the new paradigm (student-centred learning, problem-based learning and case-based learning) fit in the 2.0 classrooms, in which computers have become the instruments of such constructivist pedagogy. Prensky highlights that it makes sense that many teachers resist being taught to use technology because it is not they who should be using the technology to teach students, but rather their students who should be using it, as a tool to teach themselves. On that particular point, other advocates of the School 2.0 as Davies and Merchant (2009:7) argue that "teachers have a role to play in guiding their students' use of technology".

Digging a little bit more into this problematic, Cuban (2001) has been arguing for the past decades that computers in the US classrooms are underused both by teachers and by students despite the astronomical amount of government money invested in them. It is quite puzzling that nowadays teachers are more likely to use their home computers for personal, leisure and business issues than for classroom instruction. Cuban's point is that computers have been oversold by policymakers, constructing the image that ICT is the "panacea" to all the educative problems. Accordingly, computers were expected to motivate both struggling and good students, to help teachers to find better learning materials, to transform traditional instruction into active classroom learning and even to make education cheaper in terms of expenses in textbooks and paper. The problem is that policymakers driving the ICT educational reform expected the digitization of the classrooms to unleash a quick deep pedagogical revolution, which has not yet occurred. They naively assumed that, with the physical presence of laptops in the classrooms, student-centred education would naturally emerge, pushing teaching practices into autonomous learning, critical thinking and creativity.

The barriers for integrating technology into instruction practices

Research concerning the uses that teachers make of technology in their everyday teaching practices has been mainly tackled from a psychological stance, and through quantitative methodologies based on, for example, statistical analysis, cognition, beliefs or personality tests. The most salient issues concerning teachers and ICT in education have been a) the social and psychological factors that determine its uses, and b) the barriers that teachers should overcome to achieve the integration of ICT in their teaching practices.

The factors influencing teachers' decisions about technology have been largely identified in the literature. According to Liu (2011) some of these factors are: teacher professional development and training, administrative support, positive school environment, adequate technological resources, access to technology, technical assistance, adequate planning time, and sustained funding for technology. Instructional styles, attitudes toward learning, pedagogical beliefs, and personal characteristics have also been documented as being relevant influences. In relation to teachers' pedagogical beliefs, it seems that those who have strong constructivist pedagogical beliefs are more likely to use technology in the classroom than teachers who have more traditional pedagogical beliefs (Ertmer 1999).

Regarding the barriers, Kopcha (2012) lists some of the most frequently mentioned ones in the literature: access to technology, time, professional development and teachers' own beliefs about the integration of technology. Interestingly, Ertmer (1999) distinguishes between two types of barriers that influence teachers' usage of technology in the classroom. First-order barriers comprise those that are external to the teacher, including resources (both hardware and software), training, and support. Second-order barriers consist of those that are internal to the teacher:

teachers' confidence, beliefs about how students learn, teachers' perception of the value of technology within the teaching/learning process. Despite first-order barriers having been documented in the literature as being significant obstacles, it seems that second-order barriers are in fact the real challenge for achieving technology integration (Condie and Munro, 2007).

Concerning technology integration, Dwyer *et al.* (1986) identified the phases teachers go through during the process of introducing ICT into their classroom practices, starting at access and adoption onto a period of adaptation, appropriation and, finally, invention. On the grounds of this evolution, a key qualitative step is taken when moving out of a centralized control model in which teachers deliver information to a roomful of students and into a more entrepreneurial approach to learning.

The review of the literature regarding the digitization of schools is brief partly because computers are still relatively new as an educative tool. Much more research is needed to understand what the benefits and the drawbacks for students of handling a laptop every day all day long for academic purposes can be.

Our context: the one-to-one laptop programme in Catalonia

This study is based on an ongoing multi-sited ethnography in 18 high schools, which started in July 2012 in order to document the impact that the one-to-one initiative is having on Catalan secondary school classrooms (see previous studies by Cassany 2013). Our main goal is to describe the role that laptops have in the high school scenario, taking into account the insights of the different actors that are involved: headmaster, teachers, students and families. The data examined here is part of our corpus of 72 teacher interviews, although we focus the analysis on a sample of 12 teachers working in six different high schools (see Table 1 in the Appendix) which amounts to almost 10 hours. We classified the intensity of the teachers' points of view into three categories: techno-enthusiast, hesitant and resistant.

The context where this research is being carried out is Catalonia, one of the 17 autonomous regions in Spain, the second most densely populated one, with 7.5 million inhabitants. One of its most visible particularities is that two official languages (Catalan and Spanish) co-exist. The one-to-one programme arrived in Catalonia in 2009, when *La Generalitat de Catalunya* (The Government of Catalonia) accepted to co-finance the national project *Escuela 2.0*. In Catalonia, the programme was named as *EduCAT1x1 programme* (*Edu*=education; *Cat*= Catalunya/Catalonia; *1x1*= 1 student per 1 computer) and the Catalan Government encouraged the secondary schools to "voluntarily" join the project, arguing that it would imply a structural shift in secondary education by moving the learning and teaching practices from paper to screen. High schools could choose a total or partial involvement in the project.

All the high schools[3] that enrolled in the programme received funding for equipping their classrooms with *Wi-fi* and interactive whiteboards, and the Government bore the expenses associated with the Internet connection and the development of the educative digital platform (ATRIA). Families received a voucher to buy a small laptop at half-price; teachers were offered free-training courses on teaching with ICT; and publishing houses were forced to quickly digitize their textbooks. This investment clearly sought to create an environment of technological immersion.

According to news published on the official website of the Catalan Government[4], during the 2010–11 academic year, 539 out of 629 high schools (which means 95,624 students) had digitized their classrooms. In the following year, the economic recession deepened and coincided with a change of government from a left to a right-wing one, which decided to cut the funding of this scheme. Faced with this scenario, some of the high schools decided to go on with the technological programme even without financial help, convincing parents to assume a greaterpart of the expenses.

The six high schools involved in our study were public *Instituts* of secondary education (IES in their acronym in Catalan). The IES discussed are located in five different mid-size towns of the Barcelona area (except Montserrat, which actually was located in a wealthy neighbourhood in Barcelona). The next brief description shows that the IES had different ideological positions towards the digitization of education, backed by their institutional trajectories with ICT in education.

IES Vallès is in a middle class neighbourhood in Sabadell, a town 25 km from Barcelona. It was created in the mid-80s with the goal of experimenting with the Educative Reform, and therefore it is usually engaged in pedagogical innovations. IES Vallès carried out a pilot study with the platform DigitalText in two of their science subjects (biology and mathematics), becoming one of the first schools in Catalonia to launch multimedia learning materials. Then, the board decided to become fully involved in the first year of the *EduCAT1x1* programme, but were quickly disappointed with the materials for second cycle students, which they considered too childish to be suitable.

IES Torre del Palau is in a working class neighbourhood in Terrassa, a town 30 km from Barcelona. The immigrant population here is generally Latin and

3 Some of the teachers' and high schools' names are pseudonyms.

4 http://www10.gencat.cat/gencat/AppJava/cat/actualitat2/2010/00813programaeducat1x1.jsp.

Maghribian. In this context, this high school is an island that tends to attract families without financial problems. The centre is an ardent pioneer of ICT in education, considering that it has been participating in ICT programmes since 2002, much before the implementation of the *EduCAT1x1*.

Institut Giola is located in Llinars del Vallès, a small town 45 km from Barcelona. They became partially involved (sciences, technology, mathematics and English) in the *EduCAT1x1* project in its second edition. One of the promoters of the IES' participation in the project was the mathematics teacher who, after the experience, has completely changed his mind. In the fourth year, when the funding was cut, the school went back to the previous shared textbook scheme, a project that consisted of different generations of students sharing the same textbooks.

IES Passeig Muralla and IES Rambla Llibertat are high schools located in Girona, a city 100 km from Barcelona. On the one hand, **IES Passeig Muralla** was involved in the *EduCAT1x1* partially (the Departments of Catalan and Life Sciences). It has an attractive active webpage with news, book recommendations, some blogs and the centre's digital magazine, which is only published online. On the other hand, **IES Rambla Lliberat** has new technologies as one of the pillars of its educative project, and they were using Moodle[5] before the *EduCAT1x1*. They were partially involved in the *EduCAT1x1* programme in its second edition. When they had to decide about their involvement, 70% of the faculty voted yes. Some years after, 95% of the faculty voted in favour of quitting the programme. Both high schools now combine paper and digital textbooks.

IES Montserrat is the only high school in this sample that is located in Barcelona, in the area known as Sant Gervasi, one of the most affluent neighbourhoods. The building, surrounded by a beautiful historical garden, is equipped with ICT rooms, labs and a big lecture hall. Although they already had a good infrastructure to support the use of computers in the classrooms, they preferred to be prudent and wait for one year to hear about the experiences of other high schools. Initially, the IES faculty was a bit hesitant towards the initiative, but they received a formal request from the families and accordingly became fully involved. Now that funding has run out, the students' families have decided to stay in the project by assuming the expenses.

The following analysis seeks to present a detailed account of the teachers' points of view, focusing on their arguments and counter-arguments regarding the *EduCAT1x1* programme.

---

5 Moodle (https://moodle.org/) is an open source virtual learning environment that implements tools for online interaction.

Analysis of data

Techno-enthusiasts teachers

We defined techno-enthusiast teachers in our sample as ardent supporters of the one-to-one laptop programme and the use of digital tools in teaching/learning contexts, regardless of the degree of technological incorporation in their teaching practices.

a) Reasons to be in favour of 1x1 programmes

The most frequently repeated argument by the teachers who defended the use of laptops in secondary education was the recognition that we now live in a digital rather analogue world and hence education cannot turn its back on new technologies. Carme, a teacher of Catalan language, said "I can't imagine at this pointa classroom without technology." Montse, a science teacher, was convinced that by using ICT she was doing the proper thing an up-to-date teacher needs to do: "If I don't use the computer I'm not doing it right."

The idea that it is impossible to step down from the technology-driven world we live in was the key idea sustaining these teachers' point of view. In the case of IES Torre del Palau, one high school which had bet strongly on ICT before the beginning of the one-to-one programme, the teachers that we interviewed were quite outraged by the Catalan Government's decision to stop the funding. These teachers were fully convinced of the benefit of new technologies, and the headmaster of IES Torre de Palau even referred to the *EduCAT1x1* programme as the best educative reform ever brought in by the Government:

> The project EduCAT1x1 has been stopped, and now if we keep on working with 1x1 it is due to the good will of families and teachers. The question is: how do we carry on with a project (…) which I reckon is the strongest bet in recent years in the field of education in Catalonia, with such a revolutionary nature? The funding, the technical infrastructure is (…) debatable, but never has an educative centre had the technical infrastructure to make society and education act with one accord[6].
>
> (Evaristo, teacher of Spanish Language)

The teachers' conceptualisation of the world we inhabit as technology-driven was based on other very remarkable notions. Firstly, they were convinced that the fact of using laptops in their classrooms enhanced the following aspects of the teaching and learning process:

6 All quotations translated.

- The chance to use virtual learning environments such as Moodle, as it helped them make learning materials more accessible and organized.
- The improvement of student-teacher academic communication outside the classroom.
- The increase in readily-available impromptu feedback to students' doubts, which teachers regarded as helpful to promote significant learning.

When thinking of their particular disciplines, the teachers emphasized different aspects that laptops could strengthen. Carme stressed that laptops boosted the students' creativity in the writing tasks, thanks to linguistic projects such as running a radio broadcast. Evaristo was delighted with the fact that new technologies made oral competence more teachable, as students could analyse their speeches, having previously recorded them. The teacher of computer science, Enric-I, emphasized to what extent laptops offered the possibility to create contexts for awakening critical thinking and collaborative learning.

Secondly, these teachers felt enthusiastic about online open resources and teaching materials. For technology-enthusiastic teachers, these possibilities acted as a springboard from which to bounce away from paper and onto digital textbooks or even no textbooks at all (in Enric-I's case). They tended to prepare their own teaching materials using open resources, but just one of them (Enric-I) took advantage of online communities of teachers to share his educative, technological and pedagogical concerns.

Regarding the online resources that were more highly valued, language teachers stressed the usefulness of online dictionaries in writing activities, presentation software such as *PowerPoint* as a tool for structuring oral presentations, and they also highlighted the advantages of audio and video recording software. From the science field, Montse pointed out the potential of free online visual materials that made abstract knowledge more accessible to more students (e.g. simulators to represent everyday life situations and then doing physics calculations of motion and speed) as she explains below:

> There are a lot of tools which, if you don't use them, you are effectively clogging learning. For instance, simulators and the immensity of resources that you can find on the net, for free, and which help you understand important, complicated and sometimes abstract concepts of physics. I think that not using them (...) is a loss. You can't reach lots of students. There're students who struggle when you explain something abstract, but [*some of these*] students, if they see, if they perceive, it helps them a lot.
>
> (Montse, teacher of chemistry and physics)

Thirdly, another argument that emerged in the discourse of the interviewees was that computers and ICT made sessions more dynamic and contents more interesting.

Carme said that without computers her lessons were "more boring". Moreover, Enric-I, the ICT teacher, argued that laptops helped him centre his sessions on students' learning. For him, learning meant "doing" and "thinking", and that was why he had organized his sessions around tasks that the students —generally in pairs or in groups— had to solve using the information available on the Internet. In his classrooms, computers were used as tools for thinking, exploring and questioning. Intuitively driven by a constructivist theoretical orientation, he encouraged students to use the computer as a tool for active inquiry and problem solving. In order to illustrate his teaching philosophy he told us about a lesson in which students were asked to demonstrate the falseness of a webpage[7] which reported, scientifically and with scientific data and touched up videos, the existence of a tree octopus.

However,Enric-I was rather critical towards the reality of the 1x1 classroom, complaining about how the original idea underlying this programme, which was a methodological change in teaching, had not been achieved. He did not criticize the digital world, but the fact that the implementation had not been authentic enough, in the sense that the teaching methodology had not undergone deep qualitative changes. In the following quotation he compares traditional lessons with the typical situation in a 1x1 classroom. Underlying his comment there is a deep personal commitment to the digital world, rather than a critique.

> In a traditional lesson it's expected that the students sit, take notes, listen, remain in silence while the teacher explains. In a 1x1 class what is usually done is that the students sit, take notes, are quiet and the computer teaches a lot of things. Well, to do that it's better if they stay at home. For me, a 1x1 class is a class where you don't explain, the computer explains what students want to know, that is to say, they search for it. You prepare a problem, never say how to solve it, and it is they with these tools, the computer and the Internet who need to wise up to solve it. This way, they will learn how to solve that problem by themselves.
>
> (Enric-I, computer technician and teacher of ICT)

b) The toll to be paid

There was a general agreement that the two most difficult aspects of the programme were solving the technical difficulties and controlling students' access to the Internet, but each teacher indicated that the positive aspects of having laptops outweighed the negative ones. About the technical difficulties, Carme said that in the beginning it was unavoidable to use class time to solve problems and carefully explain how the tools work, but it was a good future investment. Regarding the

7 The link to this webpage is: http://zapatopi.net/treeoctopus/.

task of controlling the student internet access, she played it down arguing that the student who wants to get distracted, gets distracted with or without a laptop:

> It can happen that sometimes [*students*] can be playing some random game, but it is the same thing as if they were doodling with paper and pencil. I don't think that they are any more distracted. The one who wants to get distracted, will get distracted. And the one who doesn't want to, won't.
>
> (Carme, teacher of Catalan Language)

In connection with this last point, Enric-I thought that the chance of getting some students' attention stranded on the Internet was not enough to avoid the use of laptops in the classroom. In the following extract, he argues that the best strategy for tackling the hazards of using screens in the classroom was to control the risks:

> Do you forbid the use of computers in class because there is the chance that someone doesn't do the task, or do you control directly those who don't do it? This is a constant dilemma. There is a new tool that has some risks. What do you do? Do you prohibit it because it has risks or do you control these risks? Well, people who don´t know how to do it, and don't want to take care of the risks, what do they do? Off with the computers!
>
> (Enric-I, computer technician and ICT teacher)

Another trait of techno-enthusiastic teachers was that they felt comfortable with the reality that students are usually very experienced with new technologies. These teachers did not feel that this situation undermined their authority as experts in front of the pupils. They tended to think that in fact it is the students who are going to use the tools, so that it is no big deal if the student masters those tools more efficiently than the teacher. This idea has been suggested by Prensky (2010) when trying to convince teachers to use new technologies in their classrooms. Enric-I, who was rather critical of the preconception about young people's technological expertise, stated that teachers could contribute a lot of relevant issues to students' know-how, such as the personal elaboration of the information on the Internet and critical reading skills.

> I struggle seeing youth as digital natives! I believe that they are trained from childhood to do three or four tasks, and that´s all. When you try and go beyond that point…For instance, if you tell them "look up this information on the Internet", they will try any [*webpage*]. If you tell them "find out if this source is reliable", they answer "reli- what?". Wikipedia is God and that's all. They are trained to do a set of operations, and these they do very well, better than us, but not the others… they lack critical thinking skills when using these tools.
>
> (Enric-I, computer technician and ICT teacher)

Hesitant teachers

Hesitant teachers accepted the *EduCAT1x1* programme, but with some mistrust. They were moderate in their thoughts and opinions, in the sense that they were not extremists. They tended to have mixed feelings towards this initiative, and as a consequence their discourse was criss-crossed with confusing arguments. Moreover, they usually emphasized what they saw as unresolved concerns about the role of ICT in education. Hesitant teachers were initially quite enthusiastic with the one-to-one laptop initiative, but their enthusiasm wavered when they began to experience technical problems that affected their lessons.

a) Affinities and differences within techno-enthusiastic teachers

Hesitant teachers in this sample agreed with techno-enthusiasts on the idea that education cannot ignore the technological reality in which students are immersed. Although they did not hesitate to recognize the importance of introducing laptops in the educative context, hesitant teachers differed from the techno-enthusiasts in the degree of certainty of the potential academic benefits of computers. Hesitant teachers questioned the idea that teaching and learning with computers is perfectly positive, but they partially admitted to some of the benefits. Another particular trait of the group of hesitant teachers was that they were extremely aware of the difficulties that the process of socializing technology into the classrooms may unleash.

b) Reasons for staying on the edge

Although hesitant teachers were convinced that new technologies are the future, they had a lot of reasons to remain a little bit sceptical.

The first concern deals with the control over students when using the laptop in the classroom. Jordi argued that computers generated dispersion in the students, as they are not used to working with screens: "the first year it was terribly difficult because the habit of seeing the computer as a tool was missing: the computer was just a game". Pilar, the English teacher, claimed that it was essential to be able to monitor what students do in the classroom with their laptops, "so that you can see on the teacher's screen exactly what students are doing on theirs". She complained about feeling like a policewoman in the classroom ("no way if I have to be acting as a policewoman"). In her classrooms, students did not use their laptops, but she used the projector to show the digital textbook on the screen while the students used the paper version.

The second reason underpinning these teachers' sceptical position is purely technical. These teachers repeatedly complained about poor wiring, crashing servers, computers running too slowly and insufficient technical support. Pilar complained that she could not use Youtube videos in her English class because this site was blocked by default in her centre. They told us how they used to have a back-up plan when doing activities that involved Internet searches, PowerPoint presentations, or particular video and audio programmes, and even digital textbooks.

Some of the hesitant teachers constantly mentioned that digital textbooks were not as useful as they had expected. Enric-II said that the year when he used a digital textbook in his mathematics class, he experienced a lot of problems with electronic materials due to the Internet, the computer or the projector. Moreover, students also used to have problems with their computers or with the browser or they needed to install some programme. He felt demotivated and he went back to using photocopies. Another reason was that digital textbooks were slow and that students were unable to find the materials. Jordi was upset with the publishers he had chosen for three years because he missed some more interactivity in the digital textbooks, and he eventually reached the conclusion that there were not many differences between digital and paper textbooks, so finally he decided to go back to paper textbooks and use Moodle as a platform to organize all the learning materials. He did not want their students to merely be "spectators of screens".

The third key reason for staying on the edge was related to learning. Hesitant teachers accepted that laptops promoted some interesting learning benefits when combined with paper although, as Francesc states, they thought that it had not been definitely demonstrated that computers have a positive impact on learning: "I don't really know, in part because I'm not an expert, if the learning target improves substantially… what I can state is that methodologically it's beneficial". These teachers emphasized different specific benefits in their classrooms. Pilar cited listening activities, which she considered practical and excellent, how ICT made correction easier, and she valued the fact that online activities allowed students to check their understanding autonomously. Jordi said that ICT had improved their biology lessons by providing images and movement, as he now can use videos, simulators and also animations, that is to say, lab environments where experiments can be done virtually. Simultaneously, these teachers defended the traditionally handwritten processes: e.g. drawing in the biology class, and handwriting in the language classes to learn spelling and grammatical rules.

Regarding their usage of ICT in their lessons, it seems that these teachers tended to feel more comfortable using new technologies for teaching than as tools for the students to learn with autonomy. Hesitant teachers would use new technologies to show the knowledge of their disciplines in new ways. Francesc summed up this idea clearly: "I'm not interested in remaining as a language teacher with a book, a piece of chalk and a dictionary of the Royal Academy." Regarding learning, they asked students to use ICT as a complementary tool but hardly ever as the main tool. Enric-II argued that "the future will be hybrid". Starting from that idea, he claimed that computers should be integrated into formal learning because this is what teenagers will find in their lives, but "we don´t have to convert all things into digital".

Resistant teachers

Teachers who displayed resistant positioning in the interviews were sceptical about the benefits of computers in the classrooms. They did not see any advantages in using ICT in their sessions and consequently their discourse was characterized by a strong questioning of it.

a) Affinity with hesitant teachers

The resistant teachers we interviewed agreed with the hesitant teachers on some aspects, but they differed from them on the whole, in the sense that they made a negative global assessment of the experience with the *EduCAT1x1*. Resistant teachers agreed with the moderate ones on these points:

- They stressed the fact that they are not against the digital world and that they consider computers to be important future options on which education cannot turn its back.
- They had added some digital resources to their teaching practices: they used the digital blackboard and the Moodle virtual learning environment.
- These teachers believed that the optimal position in the technology conundrum is the combination of resources.

b) Reasons to be against the 1x1 project

One of the key arguments to be against the *EduCAT1x1* in resistant teachers' discourse was the evidence from the preceding experiences. Pere remembered that the pilot experiences had never demonstrated that this initiative was an improvement. Marga was very surprised when she knew that the programme was being implemented on a massive scale in Catalonia because she had heard that in Germany they had already decided that laptops should be used in combination with other non-digital resources, rather than a central educational tool. Almost all teachers were very critical of the exorbitant economic investment that went into the one-to-one programme, and some of them even described it as a "squandered public money project".

Moreover, these teachers suggested that the project had been implemented hastily:

> I don't know if the 1x1 originated in a pedagogical issue or in commercial pressure. It was a hurried decision, there were resources from Madrid and this was a necessary condition

> to profit from them (…) a more progressive implementation was needed, giving people time to digest things.
>
> (Pere, teacher of life sciences)

In relation to the hurried implementation of the 1x1 scheme, another argument was about the lack of training. The one-to-one laptop initiative caused uncertainty in teachers because they felt compelled to use a tool with resources that they had not had the chance to explore. Marga was very critical of this issue, arguing that there had not been any proper training for teachers.

For the resistant teachers, technical malfunctioning was another motive to be against the 1x1 programme, which continually emerged in the conversations with them. Some of the interviewed teachers said that they preferred to use their own computer because the one provided in the classroom was too slow or sometimes was uncomfortably located or did not have any desktop screen. Besides the infrastructure, their complaints were above all focused on the poor quality of the Internet connection. As Pere explains next, problems with connectivity made students become restless. He recognizes that this aspect has been improved in his high school.

> It was so distressing because every day you entered in the classroom and you didn´t know what you would find, whether [*the internet*] worked or not. It was a daily lottery… if a child would be able or not to enter the [*digital*] platform. Now connectivity has improved.
>
> (Pere, teacher of life sciences)

Another key complaint in their discourse was the fatigue of having to control students' activity when using laptops in the classroom. They were concerned about students being connected to social networks or playing computer games. Pere said that about 15 or 20% of his students used to be on Facebook. All resistant teachers were concerned that, unfortunately, students unwisely using the computer were the weakest ones.

> The issue is control: the big mistake is that children have a computer right there in the classroom. In overcrowded classrooms with more than thirty students it's not possible to control what they are really doing. The best students use the computer correctly, but those who would need the capabilities a computer can offer, those pupils don´t use it for studying, they do stuff that has nothing to do with studying.
>
> (Pere, teacher of life sciences)

Resistant teachers thought that the screen had an irresistible power of attraction, so they argued that using computers in the classroom was to put a candy in front of students, when they were not mature enough to understand that "they have to be in command of the tool and not let the tool control them" (Toni):

> When you're explaining something, and students have their screens switched on, it can be very difficult to get their attention. (...) They open Moodle, but at the same time they're on Facebook; if you put a candy in front of them, it's very difficult to keep them from eating it...
>
> (Jaume, teacher of music and informatics)

> It's very difficult to get students' attention when they have a computer right in front of them: even if they only get to see the desktop background, they will be staring at the desktop background, even when it's what they see every other day!
>
> (Marga, teacher of history and geography)

c) Reasons to be against digital tools

We found that these teachers' discourse against the *EduCAT1x1* project was impregnated with other underlying reasons to be against digital tools. These substantive grounds for refusal are related to the use of computer tools as a way to learn and not to the one-to-one project itself. Further research should be done on this issue. Here, we just summarize the most prominent motives underpinning these teachers' refusal, as they were revealed in the interviews:

- The computer resources promote mechanical work, on top of impulsive and impatient behaviour.
- The interactive materials dilute subject contents, as contents are presented schematically and in a rather unstructured way. (Toni: "Digital textbooks are more and more schematic, more insubstantial, shorter").
- The learning of reading and writing is better done on paper, and thus good students prefer it. (Marga: "The best students are more resistant to computers. Good students do a lot of handwriting").
- We don't believe in the supposed pedagogical shift brought about the one-to-one programme: students need pencil and face-to-face interaction to learn.
- Some cheekiness and cheating both on the part of students and teachers (e.g. copy-paste things from the Internet in the student's case, and self-assessed exercises that make teachers less aware of the students' learning).

Conclusions

In this first analysis of data of a multi-sited ethnographic study about the implementation of the one-to-one laptop programme in Catalonia, we have examined the arguments and counterarguments that enthusiastic, hesitant and resistant teachers use in order to justify their insights on that initiative. In the following, we provide a brief summary of each positioning.

- **Enthusiastic teachers** differ from the other two groups in their assumption that ICT can have a positive impact on students' learning, this being the main reason why they agree to take on the drawbacks. Their pedagogical philosophy is intuitively driven by socio-constructivist approaches to learning, and thus in their teaching they tend to stress task-based learning, creativity, learning through interaction and the collaborative construction of knowledge. They have integrated ICT within their curriculum and they recognize that, with the computers that the *EduCAT1x1* has brought to their classrooms, they can afford to teach things they could not have possibly taught before.
- **Hesitant teachers** think that computers might have an interesting impact on particular competences of the disciplines they teach, but they are all too aware of the fact that it is still not possible to demonstrate what the benefits or the damages are. Although they do not put up resistance to the one-to-one laptop initiative, they are especially aware of the disadvantages of using computers in the classroom in terms of setbacks in their teaching planning, and also because it increases the likelihood of students being inattentive. On account of this, hesitant teachers feel much more comfortable using ICT as a tool for teaching than as tool for the students to learn with autonomy. Their students keep learning on paper except for one-off activities where ICT is used because they are pedagogically relevant.
- **Resistant teachers** are sceptical about the use of ICT in the classroom. They have not found much sense in the integration of new technologies in their teaching practices, although they really believe that new technologies are a social reality that education cannot just ignore. These groups of teachers are critical to some particular aspects of the implementation of the one-to-one laptop program in Catalonia: previous experiences in European countries that demonstrate that digital tools should just be another tool and not the main one, weaknesses in teachers' training, technical blockage and the students' tendency to get distracted. Moreover, they have deeper underlying reasons to justify their dissenting stance, such as the fact that screens have the power of attraction that is hard to fight against.

All three groups of teachers agree on the fact that it is impossible to avoid the use of technology in the classroom. They have assumed the discourse of "inevitability" (Ferneding 2003), but they all differ in the educational benefits they think it can bring about. Regarding the *EduCAT1x1* initiative, they all refer to the same aspects (e.g. students' attitudes towards computers, the technical barriers) but they adopt different stances: for the most critical teachers, these facts are proof of the failure of the initiative, whereas for the enthusiasts these aspects are just a toll that has to be paid.

Therefore, this analysis suggests that there is a deeper stance that every teacher assumes regarding computers as tools for learning. Such views do not stem from classroom problems, but from teachers' will and motivation to overcome the barriers they might find. The potential of these new technologies to alter existing social practices of teaching and learning explains the ambivalent opinions that teachers have expressed about these powerful machines. Similar results were found in a study analysing primary school teacher's perspectives on digital technologies in the context of the Portuguese 'e.escolinha' one-to-one laptop programme (see the previous chapter by Pereira). Further research is needed in order to understand the influences that shape the teachers' viewpoints on ICT for learning, which could be tied in with the following aspects:

- the teachers' beliefs,
- their approach to teaching instruction and their insights on how learning is triggered,
- their particular personal relationship with new technologies,
- the subject they teach and the group attitudes of other teachers in their area, and
- the predominant social class in the school.

References

Bayne, S. and Ross, J. (2011). 'Digital native' and 'digital immigrant' discourses in R. Land and S. Bayne (eds.), *Digital Difference*. Rotterdam: Sense Publishers, p. 159–169.

Bennet, S., Maton, K., Kervin, L. (2008). The 'digital natives' debate: A critical review of the evidence. *British Journal of Educational Technology* 39(5): 775–786.

Bowman, L., Levine, L., Waite, B., Gendron, M. (2010). Can students really multitask? An experimental study of instant messaging while reading. *Computers&Education* 54(2010): 927–931.

Brown, C. and Czerniewicz, L. (2010). Debunking the 'digital native': beyond digital apartheid, towards digital democracy. *Journal of Computer Assisted Learning* 26: 357–369.

Cassany, D. (2013). 1:1 o cómo se lee y escribe en línea. *RELED* 1/1: 1–24. Available online: http://www.reading.org/Libraries/international/revista-electronica-leer-escribir-y-descubrir2.pdf.

Cuban, L. (2001). *Oversold and Underused*. London: Harvard University Press.

Davies, J. and Merchant, G. (2009). *Web 2.0 for Schools*. New York: Peter Lang.

Dwyer, D.C., Ringstaff, C., Haymore, J. (1986). *The Evolution of Teacher's Instructional Beliefs and Practices in High-Access-to-Technology Classrooms*. Report 8. ACOT. Available online: http://www.apple.com/nl/images/pdf/acotlibrary/rpt8.pdf.

Ertmer, P.A. (1999). Addressing first- and second- order barriers to change: strategies for technology integration. *Educational Technology Research and Development 47*(4: 47–61).

Ferneding, K.A. (2003). *Questioning technology*. New York: Peter Lang.

Hu, W. (2007). Seeing no progress, some schools drop laptops. *The New York Times*,4-5-2007. http://www.nytimes.com/2007/05/04/education/04laptop.html?pagewanted=all&_r=0.
Kopcha, T.J. (2012). Teacher's perceptions of the barriers to technology integration and practices with technology under situated professional development. *Computers&Education 59*: 1109–1121.
Liu, Sh. (2011). Factors related to pedagogical beliefs of teachers and technology integration. *Computers & Education 56*: 1012–1022.
Lowther, D.L., Ross, S.M., Morrison, G. (2003). When each one has one: The influences on teaching strategies and student achievement of using laptops in the classroom. *Educational Technology Research and Development 51*(3): 23–44.
Prensky, M. (2010). *Teaching Digital Natives.* Thousand Oaks: Corwin Press.
Selwyin, N. (2011). *Education and Technology*. London: Continuum.
Thomas, M. (ed.) (2011). *Deconstructing Digital Natives*. New York: Routledge.
Warshauer, M. (2006). *Laptops and Literacy*. New York: Teachers College Press.

Appendix

Table 1: Teacher sample analysed

Positioning	Teacher's name	Gender	Discipline	High school	Location	School's involvement in the EduCAT1x1
Techno-enthusiast	Carme	Female	Catalan	INS GIOLA	Llinars del Vallès	Partial
	Montse	Female	Physics Chemistry	INS GIOLA	Llinars del Vallès	Partial
	Enric-I	Male	ICT	IES Vallès	Sabadell	Total
	Evaristo	Male	Spanish	IES Torre de Palau	Terrassa	Total
Hesitant	Enric-II	Male	Mathematics	INS GIOLA	Llinars del Vallès	Partial
	Francesc	Male	Spanish	IES Vallès	Sabadell	Total
	Jordi	Male	Biology	INS GIOLA	Llinars del Vallès	Partial
	Pilar	Female	English	INS GIOLA	Llinars del Vallès	Partial
Resistant	Jaume	Male	Music Informatics	IES Montserrat	Barcelona	Total
	Marga	Female	History Geography	IES Vallès	Sabadell	Total
	Toni	Male	Spanish	IES Passeig Muralla	Girona	Partial
	Pere	Male	Life Sciences	IES Rambla Llibertat	Girona	Total

Animation: A New Method of Educational Communication in China

Vincenzo De Masi and Yan Han

Abstract

Animation has always been considered a minor art and it has been neglected by the media experts – although it has a very ancient history and is so successful on the world market. From 2006 to the present, the Chinese Government has considered animation a key sector for the birth of a new national identity and for cultural development in China. In 2004 China used to produce less than 30 titles with about 20,000 minutes of animation products for TV and cinema. Thanks to the Chinese Government's support, in few years China has become the world's leading producer of animation. All the animation products from the production to the distribution are under control of the State Administration of Radio Film and Television agency (SARFT). Animation is considered not only a business but also a new method of communication. The Chinese Government supports businesses but ask that the animation products made in their studios have to provide for an educational feature in order to teach and educate the next generation of young people in the context of soft power. In this paper, we try to outline the actual situation of animation in China, focusing on the new methods of production and distribution of animation in the country. We conduct the analysis from a comparative point of view, in order to better study and analyse the traditional way of creating animation and the new methods. The second part of the paper deals with the artists and the new methods of distribution used in China in the last 10 years. The aim of this paper is to give an overall view of the state of animation in China and above all to understand this new way of communication, such as animation, which can influence the new Chinese generation as well as foreigners.

The origin of the Chinese animation

In China the history of animation is closely linked to political events. The government is the largest producer and controller of each film and then allows for the creation of animations dedicated exclusively to education and propaganda. Although the animation industry has been dominated by American cartoons, China has been able to create its own art with traditional Chinese features and contents, known throughout the world as the "Chinese School" of animation[1]. The animation film from the beginning has been one of the most powerful means of communication for two reasons: 1) because it was used a lot in propaganda, both in the West and

1 He Huang (2007). *Journey to the East: the Re(Make) of Chinese animation*. Massachusetts Institute of Technology.

in the East, due to its simple way of communicating messages and ideas, and 2) because it spoke to a universal audience that included both children and adults. The animation pioneers were the Wan brothers (万氏兄弟, Wàn Shì Xiōngdì), who at the beginning, in the 30s were the only ones to experience and create animations for advertising, then propaganda, and they finally created animations with clear Chinese cultural characteristics (Quiquemelle, 1991). Chinese animation has a long history of education communication, which can be traced back to the Wan brothers' time. The Wan brothers once made a statement in a magazine stating that their works were not just for fun, but they spoke highly of and pursed the educational value. We can clearly see this point in those animation films produced in 1932, such as *The Hare and Tortoise* which came from the fairy tale and told the audience not be overconfident, *A New Wave* which expressed patriotic ideas, *Compatriots, Wake up* revealed the war's absurdity and abnormality and appealed to everyone to fight against the invading army.

The progressive animation cinema (1931–1936)

This historical period is marked by tensions between the Republic of China and the Japanese Empire, and in particular should be mentioned the so-called Manchurian accident (Mukden Incident of September 18th, 1931), which caused the destruction of the Japanese railway in Mukden in Manchuria, then under the sovereignty of the Japanese Empire. This attack, never proved, was the excuse used by the Japanese to accuse the Chinese terrorists, thus providing Japanese troops a pretext for the invasion of Manchuria and the annexation of this part to the Japanese Empire. In addition, this was one of the events that led later to the bloodiest clash between China and Japan: the Second Sino-Japanese War (Xiao-Bin, 1966).

At that time, Shanghai was still the city with the highest lifestyle, a city open to the West and with the highest percentage of artists throughout China. In 1930 there was the inauguration of the foundation of traditional Chinese Opera and of the second largest film studio in Shanghai, the Lianhua Film Company (联华影业公司, Liánhuá Yǐngyè Gōngsī).

Shanghai was the breeding ground for experimenting with new film styles and in this period there was the birth of the so-called *progressive cinema* (or *Left movement*). Even animation and the Wan brothers were influenced by this current cultural policy which had as its aim the production of films that focused on the social struggle and contents against the Japanese imperialist invasion.

Most of the films of this period were still silent, although some Chinese director-experimenters invented several devices that reproduced and synchronized the sound with the images. But the most important films of the '30s were still silent because they were linked to a narrative structure typical of the language of silent cinema. This period is also remembered as the first *Golden Age* of Chinese cinema, as it saw the establishment of actresses and famous actors who became then the stars and movie stars of the 30s (Zhang, 1995).

The influence of the policy was also important since the very beginning of film production: an example is the Lianhua Film Company in Shanghai, a studio supported by the political Left, which was the most productive in the 30s; in fact it produced films and animated films. In this very studio, the Wan brothers directed the first animated film that had as its basis the progressive propaganda, especially with anti-Japanese content.

This part of animation history has never aroused much interest, and therefore it has been neglected by scholars of animation movies. In fact, there are only a few papers that analyze this period in detail. Yet in some texts, sometimes, there is just a hint or a list of titles produced in this particular historical moment, and all that even happens in the research carried out by the same Chinese in the Chinese language.

In our opinion, it is exactly in this historical period and in this cultural background that the foundation of Chinese animation is laid, which is why it is considered important to carry out a thorough search of the content and techniques used by this kind of animation.

These films had the intent to educate the younger generation with political and anti-imperialist ideas, so they were not designed only for youngsters but also for the whole population: their aim was primarily to educate young people to be proud of being Chinese and to participate actively in the resistance.

Between 1931 and 1937, the Wan brothers shot many films with patriotic, anti-Japanese, anti-imperialist contents. The first film of this series was *Compatriots, wake up* (同胞速醒, Tóngbāo sù xǐng), of 1931, whose content is a clear patriotic appeal against the Japanese invasion and the new cultural progressive ideology. The story is very interesting and the narrative structure is simple to understand (Zhang Yuanmin, 1999) in order to facilitate the understanding of the content by a wide audience. The first images of the film are the sequences of peaceful landscapes, mountains, lakes and then of a huge lion asleep. But this peace is violated by the Japanese military artillery: the military aircrafts indiscriminately bomb all these places, causing huge lion to stir, who, with a roar, wakes up, pushes and encourages all the farmers and workers to resist the Japanese imperialist invasion (Lin 2002).

The film *Solidarity* (精诚团结, Jīngchéng tuánjié) of 1932 has the same style and narrative language: here the character is a bug (metaphor of the Japanese army) which is bad towards the humans who try to drive it away from their property. *Compatriots* and *Solidarity* are two movies in black and white whose exact length is unknown, because they are missing.

In 1932 one of the Wan brothers, Wan Dihuan, left the production of cartoons to start his own business, a photography studio based in Shanghai. Since then Wan Dihuan did not participate actively in the Wan brothers' film production anymore, but he made an important contribution to the most important productions of his brothers.

Very interesting are the two films *The detective dog* (狗侦探, Gǒu zhēntàn) and *Bloody Money* (血钱, Xuè qián) of 1933 and 1934. From the technical point of view, these two films use a very interesting technique, and in fact the characters in the film are real but they move in an animated world. The story of the *detective dog* is very unique because it tells the story of a student, played by Zhang Minyu, who, with her dog walks round the streets of Shanghai, and in one of these streets she runs into an opiumden. The girl is very disappointed by this discovery and encourages her dog to sniff everywhere searching for the source of the evil. The dog discovers that the evil comes from a military ship (it is unclear if the ship is of English or French origin) in which there is a load of opium. The student sets fire to the ship and destroys its cargo. The interpretation of this film is very complex, but essentially it wants to make clear that all products coming from abroad were dangerous to the Chinese economy and so had to be fought and burned (Lijun Sun 2011).

The film *Bloody Money* has the same ideological line, but it is much more explicit, and it tells the story of a student (Zhang Minyu) who, after finishing the lesson with his teacher, begins to fancy inventing a story whose character is a mysterious man. Thanks to a magical blood transfusion, this man is able to receive a briefcase with the words "Made in China" in which there is plenty of money to buy planes, tanks and guns to be distributed to the Chinese people in order to fight and destroy the Japanese products.

All these four films are typical examples of progressive animation and you can easily understand that they are definitely aimed at a young audience, as the stories are told in a metaphorical way, but far from the animated film for children, and moreover the topics covered convey a powerful message of patriotism (Wu Zhouguan, 1995), protection of products of the internal market against Japanese imperialism.

Other films of this genre were made by the Wan brothers, suchas *History of national pain* (民族痛史, Mínzú tòng shǐ) and *New Wave* (新潮, Xīncháo) produced in 1936 always in the Star Film Company studio based in Shanghai: the first contains anti-imperialist contents and part of the story tells about the Opium

War. Instead, the themes of the second film are especially the anti-feudalism and the movement of May 4th .

The special feature that unites all these films is their content imbued with a strong moral sense, and like the other progressive films, they use a narrative language which is very easy as it is dedicated to a very wide audience.

The year 1936 ends with this film, the progressive phase of animation is to be marked with the outbreak of the Second Sino-Japanese War.

Propaganda animation (1937–1941)

This cultural and historical phase of China goes from 1937, the year of the beginning of the so-called Second Sino-Japanese War, until 1941, when China joined forces with the Soviets and the Americans.

After the so-called *Marco Polo Bridge incident* (7th July 1937), Shanghai was one of the first cities to be occupied by the Japanese imperial army and this led to both the commercial decline of the city and the end of the first so-called *Golden Age* of Chinese cinema. The famous production studio Lianhua, where the Wan brothers and many other cinema artists worked, was forced to close as well as all the other large studios of Shanghai.

Before the Japanese invasion, most of the artists who worked in the Shanghai studio took refuge in other major cities, such as Hong Kong and Chongqing. But it was in Chongqing that there was the last hard resistance of the Chinese and where many artists joined the opposition party. The Wan brothers though moved to Wuhan, where they joined and worked for the China Film Studio (Chinese anti-Japanese National Film Association). Obviously, the war and the resistance represented the topics of all the animations created in this period, and the Wan brothers decided to take advantage of animation to communicate patriotism and the progressive ideologies, and especially to encourage everyone to stand up against Japanese imperialism (Needham 1962).

In 1938, influenced by the American and European productions, the Wan brothers experimented for the first time with animation in episodes and series. The first set of animations of this kind was *War slogans* (抗日歌辑, Kàngrì gē ji) made up of 6 episodes, and the second series called *Anti-Japanese war songs* (抗日歌辑, kàngrì gē ji) was made up of 7. The soundtracks of these series of animations were famous patriotic songs: memorable compositions of authors very famous at that time, such as Xian Xinghai (冼星海), Liu Xuean (刘雪庵), Sneah Kar Loon (Sheng Jialun) (盛家伦) and Lui (He) Luting (贺绿汀).

The technique of using musical videos in the form of animation was a great way to educate and inspire a good emotional impact on the audience, and it also managed to attract the attention of the entire population. Furthermore, using the music of famous composers turned out to be a good propaganda strategy for the ideas of resistance (De Masi, 2011).

With the end of the civil war in 1949 and the proclamation of the Republic of China by Mao, animation, even if controlled by the Communist Party, reached its maximum period of greatness, with production whose target was to educate following the examples of the traditional Chinese culture. Animation reached its second *Golden Age* during this period, and there was the opening of the Shanghai Animation Film Studio, the birthplace of the famous "Chinese school" animation (Bendazzi, 1998).

With the establishment of the new China, the Wan brothers worked for the government and passed on their idea of education communication, and they especially influenced the animation editors in Shanghai Studio. These animators of the Shanghai Studio followed Wan brothers' way stressing the education function in the animation films. There are many classic animation films that influenced Chinese children at that time, such as *Monkey King* (1961)[2], *Little Sisters On the Grassland* (1965), *Snow Kid* (1980)[3], etc. *Little Sisters On the Grassland* is based on a real report about two sisters in Inner Mongolia who get trapped in a big snowstorm. In order to protect the sheep, they set out to find the lost sheep in the storm. Unfortunately, the youngest sister has her foot amputated because of exposure to the freezing conditions for a long time, but not one sheep is lost. Lin Wenxiao, who took part in this animation film, said that protecting public property was a common value at that time, and the idea of the sisters' risking their lives to preserve the sheep is the core theme of this animation. In fact, this action affected a whole generation of Chinese who are in their 50s now, and they have a strong collective spirit and do not care about individual loss (Ye, 2012).

The cultural revolution and the re-education (1966–1976)

This period is a very dark one in the Chinese history of cinema and animation as there was the production of short animated propaganda films without any reference to the cultural past. The main characters of the film are always children who are forced to become "adults" to fight for high ideals, such as the class struggle or against the Americans. Obviously, the narrative formulas are very mature and

---

2 See: *The Monkey King: Uproar in Heaven – Full Version*, https://www.youtube.com/watch?v=dDrPx3RCqCE.

3 See: Snow Kids https://www.youtube.com/watch?v=OFF_UlghnAk.

closer to the thinking of adults, and in fact the animation loses its peculiarity to speak to a wide audience, especially a young one, favouring an ideal concept of revolution.

The Cultural Revolution began to reject all the traditional art and the so-called *Four olds* (old culture, old ideas, old habits and old behaviours), furthermore all places of worship were closed, looted, destroyed, occupied and turned into other purposes. One slogan was very famous at that time, which was also very direct and powerful, asserting that<<without destruction there is no reconstruction>>.

As already happened in Italy during Fascism and Nazism in Germany, even in China the cinema was forced to make revolutionary films leading to a re-education. The Shanghai Animation Film Studio was forced to close until 1972. Some artists succumbed and agreed to shoot the film imposed by the Party, because it was a matter of life or death for them. The Wan brothers and the great master Te Wei were forced to leave their families and sent to far-off areas of China where they had to learn humility and the revolutionary consciousness of the peasants (Sun 2010).

Even for this period, there is very little information and the official sources of the studio SAFS didn't report any animated film produced in those years. But actually, some films were produced, such as: *Shanghai arts and crafts* (上海工艺美术, Shànghǎi gōngyì měishù) but there isn't any certain information about it; *The village of the emerging Artists* (山村新苗, Shāncūn xīn miáo) , produced in 1966, whose music was of Wu Ying-Ju (吴应炬): the film tells the story of some children living in rural areas, who, with the help of the Party, founded a team and then becoming important members of the revolution; *The great affirmation* (伟大的声明, Wěidà de shēngmíng), there isn't any certain information about it; *Fruit* (果实, Guǒshí), of 1967, is dedicated to children but there is no information about the direction and the cast.

The years running from 1967 to 1972 were poor years because there was no production of any movies of any kind, and it is only in 1972 that there was the revival of artistic cinema. In fact, the artists of the studio SAFS were brought back to start the production again for the studio itself, but they could only make propaganda films after being subjected to a period of intense analysis of the Cultural Revolution ideas.

The first film after the reopening of the studio SAFS was *The Battle Hymn to achieve the hydraulic pressure machine* (万吨水压机战歌, Wàn dùn shuǐyājī zhàngē), whose direction was of Hu Jinqing and Wu Qiang who used the cut-paper technique.Very interesting are the contents of this animation because it tells the story of the era of the so-called Great Leap Forward, when there was an urgent need for plenty of water, necessary for the development of industry and agriculture. In Shanghai, the working class, despite not having useful technical information and the right equipment, based their ideas of design upon the principles of Chairman Mao's philosophy, successfully implementing a hydraulic pressure machine that was able to deliver the first million tons of water.

The animation film called *After school* (放学以后, Fàngxué yǐhòu), produced with the traditional technique by the director Yan Dingxian, tells the story of some young students, belonging to the so-called Small Red Guards, fighting against the bad songs learnt at school and taught by a soldier named Xiao Gang. But one of the boys, Li Guohua, is against all those songs and, with the help of the teacher Chen, discovers that the soldier is Huang Yilang, widely regarded as a notorious criminal.

The animation *Not bad, Half Penny* (不差半分毫, Bù chā bànfēn háo) also deals with the same ideas of the other animation films. The film was shot using the cut-paper technique by the directors Di (Li Andi) and Yanping Xiao and it was produced in the Xi'an Yaping Studio.

However, it is important to know that of these animations there are just propaganda cartoons based on the films, so it is impossible to have the chance to view the audio-video material of them.

Wang Shuchen and Yan Dingxian were back again with a propaganda film called *The trumpeter* (小号手, Xiǎo hào shǒu)[4] where there are all the features typical of the next propaganda films. In fact, the main character is taken up many times in the history of cinema. It is the story of a country boy who wants to help the army to defeat the enemies of the Nationalist Party. He learns to play the trumpet, he enlists in the army and goes directly to the battlefield where he is wounded and then forced to stay at home to recover. But he wants to find the enemies and punish them, so he adventures alone to the mountains. There he discovers the refuge of enemies and, thanks to the sound of his trumpet, he can call the Red Army. Unfortunately, he is discovered and later imprisoned, but the Red Army frees him and he, once again, wants revenge and chases the chief enemy, at night, who is running with his horse. The boy manages to hit the enemy on the run, who falls with his horse over a cliff. The film is characterized by both a good quality animation, much more mature than the others of the previous years, and a different narration whose language is more modern (Benecchi 2011).

We have to mention then the film called *The little coast guard* (东海小哨兵, Dōnghǎi xiǎo shàobīng)[5] which is very close to the story of the animation called

4 See: *The trumpeter* https://www.youtube.com/watch?v=hfnrEunowTY.

5 See: *The little coast guard* https://www.youtube.com/watch?v=AyijiSPeJJo.

The Red Scarf (1965), produced before the advent of the Cultural Revolution. But here the quality of the animation and the cut-paper technique is much improved, the characters are more real and the movement much more natural. In this period there is also the return of the puppet animation technique. A clear example of this is the film called *The small army of eighth road* (带响的弓箭, Dài xiǎng de gōngjiàn[6]) which covers the events of the Second Sino-Japanese War, and even here the character is a child hero who fights against the Japanese. Interesting are the aesthetic and somatic features of the characters, in fact, the child type character of this film, which seems to be the same in all other propaganda films: he has the same face, the same expression and the same adult attitude.

Te Wei also shot a film in 1976, whose title was *The golden geese* (金色的大雁, Jīnsè de dàyàn)[7]: it is the story of some Tibetan children, who led by the Communist Party, fight against their enemies. Te Wei tried to make a propaganda film different from the others, using a new style and features far from the ideals of the Cultural Revolution (Xiao, 2011).

With Mao's death in 1976, animation continued to promote revolutionary ideas and mourned the deceased. One of the most interesting recent propaganda films was *The Red rock* (火红的岩标, Huǒhóng de yán biāo)[8] because it tells the story of the people who mourn Mao's death, so they build a stone sculpture to celebrate their saviour who freed them from slavery. The Tibetan people decide to remain loyal to the Communist Party.

Until the late 70s, all the films continued to be of propaganda and in memory of the communist leader Mao.

The new animation dedicated to edu-entertainment

After the period of propaganda, the government has tried to help the animation industry with financial contributions and tax breaks, with the aim of creating an industrial virtuous chain, but all the films produced had to have as their main objective the education and the entertainment of the young generations.

One of the first animations that responds to the features of edu-entertainment is *Haier Brothers* (海尔兄, Hǎi'ěr xiōng, 1996)[9] which aimed at teaching children about the scientific and social knowledge of the nature world and in daily life. It

6 See: *The small army of eighth road* https://www.youtube.com/watch?v=UldyntGrg1w.
7 See: *The golden geese* http://www.tudou.com/programs/view/q9_9O4dpZjE/isRenhe=1.
8 See: *The Red rock* https://www.youtube.com/watch?v=FgJ59iv9Vx8.
9 See: *Haier Brothers* http://www.56.com/u77/v_OTYwNjAxNjI.html.

was broadcast in America as well and not only the American children liked it but also their parents who, in fact, spoke highly of it because they thought that it was quite different from the other animation films they had watched: there is no blood or pornography in it and it is full of useful knowledge (People, 2001).

Since 1999, in most of the Chinese television the series *3000 Whys of Blue Cat* (蓝猫淘气3000问, Lán māo táoqì 3000 wèn)[10] has been broadcast. This cartoon is in line with a new concept of animation called *'Knowledge animation'* (知识动画, Zhīshì dònghuà), focusing on informing and raising awareness in children about some topics such as ecology, cultural history, astronomy, biology, etc., so the intent was to create an animated children's encyclopaedia. Every day the Blue Cat is seen by 80 million viewers and broadcast by 700 different TV stations. In the context of the 'Knowledge animation', there are other animation products such as *The Boy Toad* (蟾童, Chán tóng, 2006) which, through the mythical characters of Chinese culture, aims at teaching children what to do in case of earthquakes, two years before the 2008 terrible Sichuan earthquake.

Many animations of this kind are made with an educational purpose, most are designed for the web like the Original Net Animation Series (ONAS) or for mobile devices, and they have different topics such as health, education, culture, etc.: most of them are funded by the regional governments, provincial or public institutions.

Many of these works do not have the qualitative features suitable to be broadcast by the Chinese televisions, although the ideas are sometimes very interesting and educational, as for example the animation series made by the Guangzhou Straw Animation Design (广州稻草动漫设计有限公司, Guǎngzhōu dàocǎo dòngmàn shèjì yǒuxiàn gōngsī) which created the cartoon titled *Emergency Superman* (急救超人, Jíjiù chāorén)[11], made in 3D, and talking about how to deal with the different emergencies in cases of necessity. The characters are: a man who is very similar to "Superman", a large tomato, a corn cob corn and Jimmy, who face various emergency situations. In general this cartoon does not meet the tastes of a television audience, because in some places it is very simple and obvious, but it might work well, with a few tweaks, on other platforms such as web or mobile devices (Variety, 2011).

Another very remarkable example is the animation made with educational features telling the history of the Chinese Communist Party entitled *Bugle* (号角, Hàojiǎo, 2013): it consists of 26 episodes available on the websites of CCTV (Chinese state television) and tells about the 90th anniversary of the Chinese

10 See: *3000 Whys of Blue Cat* https://www.youtube.com/watch?v=vmWnvm_JMJE.

11 See: *Emergency Superman* https://www.youtube.com/watch?v=hOUdyVJyksc.

Communist Party. Each episode has a slogan and the stories are very easy to understand, and they are set with a clear teaching method suitable for children. The various episodes deal with the initial creation of the Party, the Northern Expedition, the Agrarian Revolution, the war of liberation, the socialist revolution and the reform of openness, in the different historical periods (CNTV 2013).

In recent years there have been filmmakers who have also tried to talk about the social problems of the country using their animation. One of these is the famous director Pisan (the original name is Wang Bo). In his famous animated series *Kuang Kuang*, censored in China, he is highly critical of the social situation in China. The most interesting episode of this series is *Kuang Kuang Special edition year of the Rabbit* (Kuang Kuang 贺岁特别版兔年贺卡, Hèsuì tèbié bǎn tù nián hèkǎ)[12], where Pisan deals with the problem that struck China in 2008, which is the matter relating to the milk powder infused with melanin that caused not only the death of 6 children but also, according to reliable studies, the suffering of more than 300,000 children. In his animation, Pisan uses a metamorphosis to describe this serious piece of news: the common people are transformed into rabbits whose babies die soon after drinking milk. Therefore, the parents go to complain to the regulators, represented by tigers, who instead of helping them, beat up and kill them.

In 2005 Pisan opened his own studio in Beijing, named Hutoon Studio[13], where he created one of his most famous animation series: *Miss Puff*[14]. The original cartoon, aired on Youku, marks a turning point for his animation because it describes a modern China, where women have more power and are emancipated.

Since 2010 the Chinese Government has tried to promote the use of new technologies and therefore promulgated the National Outline of Mid-long Term Educational Reform (2010–2020) which emphasized the acceleration of the progress of education informatization[15] in all the schools, from primary to secondary ones, including the professional ones, to universities. The purpose of government is to get a "revolutionary impact on future generations that will create new ideas useful to shape the new social context."

In July of the same year, the National Education Plan states that as "information technology has a revolutionary impact on educational development, it must be highly valued". In fact, in 2011 the Notification on Several Key Jobs to Accelerate

---

12 See: *Kuang Kuang Special edition year of the Rabbit* http://www.youtube.com/watch?v=1B8SOuswczI.

13 Hutoon Studio: http://www.hutoon.com/.

14 Watch Miss Puff: https://www.youtube.com/watch?v=BHJSpMoOhUk.

15 http://www.edu.cn/li_lun_yj_1652/20130826/t20130826_1006648.shtml.

the Education Informatization was issued by 9 departments including the Ministry of Education. In the same year, the Ministry of Education started 682 national education informatization pilot[16] projects.

The Ministry of Education issued the Educational Informatization Plan for the next ten years in order to achieve this goal. In fact the Ministry is planning to launch the "China digital education 2020 action" programme in the near future, containing five major activities including the construction of a network for sharing high-quality data as a resource for learning in schools, the construction of a national system for interactive education, and the use of information technology in education in order to improve sustainable development[17].

Conclusion

We can see that the animation produced by Shanghai Studio from 1960s to 1980s played an important function in education communication, while it seems different nowadays. On the one hand, some animators think that we do not need animation films to educate anymore and entertainment is the only purpose; on the other hand, some other animators undervalue animation aimed to educate considering it as childish and shoddy and even causing bad effects on children. Just think about those dreadful stories about two boys (aged 5 and 8) burned by another boy (aged 9). They were playing together and mimicking the plot of burning the sheep, watched in the animation film *Pleasant Goat and Big Big Wolf* (喜羊羊与灰太狼, Xǐ Yáng Yáng yǔ Huī Tài Láng). Afterwards the parents of the two victims sued the producer of the animation for promoting violence (China Jiangsu Network, 2013)[18]. *Pleasant Goat and Big Big Wolf*[19] is the most popular animation, in fact about 17.3% of local audience viewers chose to see this TV series animation, hitting a ratings record. But at the same time, the scholars and critics think it is a poor work considering its artistic quality. That indeed is true. In the old animation *Snow Kid*, snow kid rushes into the firing house to rescue his friend little rabbit, but he himself melts into water. Many children were moved to tears and learnt that fire is dangerous rather than a funny game.

As the development of the animation industry progresses and its audience is expanding, entertainment is becoming the main purpose of some animation films.

---

16 http://www.edu.cn/li_lun_yj_1652/20130809/t20130809_999523.shtml.

17 http://edu.people.com.cn/GB/79457/17731942.html.

18 See: http://news.jwb.com.cn/art/2013/5/9/art_189_2866929.html.

19 Watch episode 10 of *Pleasant Goat and Big Big Wolf*: http://www.youtube.com/watch?v=xKG70_eP2hs.

But the animation companies and individual animators hope their works are suitable not only for children in the learning stage but also for adults. *One Hundred Thousand Bad Jokes* (*十万个冷笑话,* Shí wàn gè lěng xiàohuà) is an animation-series broadcast through the Internet. There are many classic characters in this animation. In one of the episodes, Fu Lu, wants to send their grandfather to the snake-shaped demon, which is the same as appeared in the old story of *Calabash Brothers* produced by Shanghai Studio in 1986. Beyond that, these two animation films are different in many aspects: the theme of the old one is the family love while the new one's is funny; the characters in the old one are smart while in the new one are stupid. All in all, the characters in the *One Hundred Thousand Bad Jokes* do not follow the former style. On the contrary, they become a funny element in the entertainment animation.

Animation in China is experiencing both an industrial and creative success. In fact, to date many animation films with an educational purpose have been produced but they have not been so successful with the public and the market, except for some we have previously analysed.

This is due to two main reasons: 1) young audiences do not like these products, and 2) the language of the narrative series is sometimes very obvious for a child audience and sometimes very complicated to understand even by adults. However, there are some positive aspects such as the development of the most interesting series regarding animation dedicated to education. For this reason, over the years, the studios have tried to make products closer to the tastes of younger audiences. But it is a real challenge not easy to achieve in a short time because it focuses on the educational value and entertainment.

References

Bendazzi G. (1998). *Cartoons, cento anni di cinema di animazione*, Venezia, Marsilio.

Benecchi E., Chen C. C., De Masi V. (2011), *Animated Canons. The Canons of Animation between the East and the West* in 'Il canone cinematografico the film canon', Grafiche Risma, Roveredo in Piano (PN) March, p. 307–312.

Blue Book animation (2011). Social Sciences Academic Press (2011), *Annual Report on Development of China's Animation Industry* (2011), Social Sciences Academic Press, Beijing.

China Jiangsu Network (2013). 烧伤儿童父母状告《喜羊羊与与灰太狼》制片方 (Burn the child's: parents sued the "Pleasant Goat and Big Big Wolf), Jike News, http://tgt.jike.com/news/industry/-4064760509254277124.html, Retrieved 22/05/2013.

CNTV (2013). 党史题材动漫片《号角》分集视频在线点播更多(Party themes animation film "horn" diversity online video-on-demand), http://donghua.cntv.cn/haojiao/, Retrieved 05/04/2013.

De Masi V., (2011). *Awards of animation*, in CMO Newsletter March issue, 2011, http://www.chinamediaobs.org/pag/newsletter.htm, access 02 October 2012.

Ji Xiao-Bin (1966). *Fact About China*, New England Public association.
Lent J. A. (2003). *Asian Cinema*, Asian Cinema Studies Society.
Li Xiao (2011). *Cartoon makers between rock and a hard place*, http://www.china.org.cn/arts/2011–11/30/content_24043193.htm, access 10 November 2012.
Lin Z. H. (2002). 20世纪中国动画艺术史 (20th Century History of Chinese Animation), 陕西人民美术出版社(Shaanxi People's Fine Arts Publishing).
Lijun Sun (2011). 中国动画史研究 (Research on the history of China's animation), (Zhongguo dong hua shi yan jiu) , Beijing : Shang wu yin shu guan. 20th Century History of Chinese Animation.
Needham J. (1962). *Science And Civilisation In China,* Volume 4-, Physics And Physical Technology, Cambridge: Cambridge University Press.
People (2001). 《海尔兄弟》将风行米老鼠的家乡 ("Haier Brothers" will be popular in the home of Mickey Mouse), People, http://www.people.com.cn/GB/wenyu/64/128/20010526/475180.html, Retrieved 05/04/2013.
Quiquemelle Marie-Claire (1991). "*The Wan Brothers and Sixty Years of Animated Film in China*," in Perspectives on Chinese Cinema (ed. Chris Berry), London: British Film Institute, 175–86.
Rosen S., Zhu Y. (2010). *Art, politics, and commerce in Chinese cinema,* Hong Kong: Hong Kong University Press.
Variety (2011). *China's toon biz is growing up, Recent hits avoid allegations of plagiarism.* http://www.variety.com/article/VR1118043656?refCatId=19, access 15 December 2011.
Wu Zhouguan(1995). 民国影坛风云录 (Story of the Republic of China's Movies), Kaifeng: Henan University Press .
Ye T., Zhu Y. (2012). Historical Dictionary of Chinese Cinema, Lanham: Scarecrow Press.
Zhang Y. (1999). 上海电影志/上海市专志系列丛刊 (Shanghai film collections), Shanghai: Shanghai Academy of Social Sciences Press.

Part Three – Subversions

Teaching the Unteachable: Networked Media, Simulation and Community Research/Activism

Judith Faifman and Brian Goldfarb

Abstract

This chapter considers opportunities that digital media culture presents for educators to engage pedagogical approaches and take on subject matter that within the current educational context has become increasingly "unteachable"; edged out of the curriculum by mandates that have taken hold during the transnational rise of the standards-based education reform movement. What we mean by this is twofold: first, unteachable in the sense of modes of knowledge that educational institutions have deemed illegitimate or unworthy of attention because they can't be measured; and second, discursive practices that fall afield of the authorized conception of schooling as a neutral space of learning rather than a site of intellectual debate and forum for discussion of public issues. These formulations of the "unteachable," have played a formative role in limiting the potential for participation in knowledge creation and democratic processes on local, regional and global scales. Our intention is to urge educators to consider how networked and digital technology/culture might be employed to activate dimensions of subjectivity truncated by this form of education. While there numerous fronts to take on this responsibility, here we zero in on digital practices that forward two particular goals: first, allowing active participation in the politics of knowledge through a broad conception of inquiry in contexts extending beyond the school and embedded in networks of life-impacting scientific research, and second, embracing the affective dimensions of communication that are crucial to how knowledge is negotiated in the spaces that connect intimate/personal and public experience.

Introduction

As educators working together from distant positions in the global north and south, and spanning distinct disciplinary arenas of the sciences, social sciences, arts and humanities, we are writing to synthesize our understandings of some specific educational impacts of the pervasive integration of computing and networked communication into spaces and practices of contemporary social life. What follows is a sketch of some of the ways that digital and networked media presents opportunities for, and in some instances, is, fostering challenges to standards-based approaches to learning. While we would caution that the same media forms can and are being developed in the service of normative modes of schooling that seeks to ensure that students learn prescribed knowledge and skills, our intention here is to highlight what we see as the potential of digital media for making learners and research more democratic in the sense that participants have greater input into the scope and goals of their inquiries. Our hope is that this discussion will direct educators to emphasize particular affordances of new media forms while resisting others. While there is a plurality of fronts to take on this responsibility, in this essay we are advocating the shaping of digital media practices with two particular goals: first, allowing active participation in the politics of knowledge through a broad conception of research as central to learning and knowledge creation in a global context, and second, embracing the affective dimensions of communication that are crucial to how knowledge is negotiated in the spaces that connect intimate/personal and public experience.

Research, as a capacity to make disciplined inquiries into those things we need to know, but do not know yet, is vital to the exercise of democratic citizenship. Intellectual inquiry, in this sense, is not something arcane or a practice reserved for an academic elite. It is something that threads through all dimensions of social participation and is crucial to the problem of teaching and learning at all levels. On these grounds, Arjun Appadurai has argued that research as a core aspect of self-determination should be framed as a "human right." (Appadurai, 2006) Certainly, people have always engaged in quotidian as well as formal inquiry in order to make those decisions presented to them in their personal and social lives. Digitally networked culture, however, has brought considerable transformation to the space, scope and form of research activity. The common use of search engines coupled with expanded access to modes of "publishing" (including blogs, home pages, etc) and distributing (email, listservs, newsgroups, craigslist, tweets, and other social media) have made the forms of inquiry associated with decisions at all levels of impact more visible and self-conscious. Mobile devices have visibly integrated the performance of research into the field of consumption. Cell phone conversations place the inquiry that subtends business and political negotiation into public and pedestrian spaces of restaurants and mass transit. Considerations of the use of digital media in learning should articulate to this shifting place of inquiry within contemporary culture.

Arguments for the centrality of research in education aren't new. Inquiry learning with its strengths, risks and limitations in one form or another has been part of the educational landscapes at least since the middle of the nineteenth century (Hodson, 2009, 1996; DeBoer, 2006 ; Rudolph, 2005). Notably, these developments can be tied to the growing economic importance of institutions and technologies of research. During the latter half of the nineteenth century the emergence of the science laboratory as a key component of science education was justified by the expressed goal of developing students' abilities to acquire knowledge independently freeing individuals from a dependence on the intellectual authority of others (DeBoer, 2006). Science and research more broadly were linked to the demands of democratic society[1]. In the early twentieth century, with enrollments in public secondary education expanding rapidly, John Dewey argued that education in a democratic society should aim to develop students' capacities to formulate significant and meaningful questions as well as their abilities for cooperative group inquiry to increase understanding of how reliable knowledge is generated. Dewey's Laboratory school pioneered at the same time theoretical perspectives and practices in the incorporation of inquiry to primary school, conceiving knowledge not as given but rather worked out in "communities of inquiry".

A significant thrust for the promotion of inquiry learning came in the early 1960s from the approach developed by Joseph Schwab who sought to shift the emphasis of schooling cultures away from learning as a rhetoric of conclusions towards an understanding of the process of inquiry. In the late 20th century, challenges to this pedagogical agenda gained increasing force in the name of standards-based reform. The 1983 Reagan administration report, *A Nation at Risk: The Imperative For Educational Reform*, sounded alarms about the decline of US education and triggered or at least announced the onset of standards-based education reform in the United States and globally. Throughout the 1990s state and national standards-based reforms began being implemented on a broad scale, at the same time the growth of World Wide Web, expanded Internet access and increasing centrality of computers to the workplace signaled an imperative to embrace digital media in education. At the same time that the Clinton Education Administration concretized the standards-based ideology forwarded under Reagan and G H W Bush in its reauthorization of the Elementary and Secondary Education Act (later renamed as "No Child Left Behind" under G W Bush), simultaneously deemed it necessary that every child would have a computer and access to the internet in order for US education to prepare them for a changing global economy. (US Dept of Education, 1996) While it is true that funding for school technology was largely directed at Title 1 schools (those serving low income families), this ideological nexus is important to understanding frictions and openings for resistance to standards based reform in the ways we reconceive the place of networked computing in schooling.

---

1 In 1894 the National Education Association in the U.S. produced the *Report of the Committee of Ten on Secondary School Studies* that articulated the need for inquiry teaching that enabled students' to develop their own ways of seeking knowledge. The report strongly urged teaching aimed at exercising students' independent intellectual powers crucial to living in a scientific age.

Situating the right to research: student/community inquiry into mining and water ecology in argentina

The recognition of the right to research as part of the "family" of human rights gains significance only in relation to the need for knowledge within situated contexts. For example, in the context of the multiplicity of social movements resisting new extractive methods of mining that require extensive use of water in the extraction of metals, shale oil or gas that has had broad environmental impact and directly undermines food sovereignty of poor and indigenous population around the world. The first and biggest open-pit mining project in Argentina, Minera Alumbrera gold mine, initiated in 1997, was authorized by the Catamarca government (among Argentina's poorest provinces) to extract 100 million liters per day of water from a natural reserve. In Argentina, a significant portion of the population lacks adequate access to safe drinking water. This is emblematic of a situation where an estimated that one in six people worldwide don't have access to safe water and 2.5 billion people, including almost one billion children live without basic sanitation (UNESCO, 2012). In this context, initiatives of vertical socialization of the scientific and technological discourse emerged in Argentina that leveraged universities and scientific public agencies to authorize these new mining extraction methods.

Arguably this state of affairs is made possible by an approach to education built upon what had been termed a deficit model of knowledge, envisaging the relation between scientific expertise and the public as asymmetrical assuming public deficiency but scientific sufficiency and adopting a one way, top down communication process in which knowledge flows from the source of science with all the required information to the scientifically illiterate general public (Gross, 1994). The status of public understanding of science in the deficit model is epistemologically diminished casting the public in a passive role while marginalizing the ethical and political implications of knowledge. Confronting pro-mining discourses buttressed by expert knowledges, neighbors in local communities attempted to build and strengthen a critical scientific discourse elaborating evidence on the damage and impact of these new ongoing extractive practices in the territories under exploitation. This is increasingly necessary in the context of strongly allied efforts of global corporations and government agencies that have poured great expense into elaborate popular educational media and venues. For example, Technopolis, an interactive world fair-like museum that comprises many technology bolstering and pro-industry exhibitions, features a "Yes to Mining" exhibition.

The struggle of local communities to confront mining initiatives is an example of informal educational processes that motivated what can be described as a dispersed learning network that has enabled effective community participation at various governmental levels. Between 2003 and 2008, as a result of multisectorial mobilizations and social networking articulating critical knowledges, seven provinces in Argentina enacted laws forbidding different aspects of these new extractive practices (Svampa and Antonelli, 2009). Public understanding of science became a cornerstone of political participation, but only as the joint product of scientific and local knowledges. Digital communication as a multidirectional flow has in notable cases begun to serve as a mechanism for integrating lay and expert knowledges and needs through deliberation and participation (Epstein, 1996). This emergent zone of interaction among academic and community-based expertise is key factor in the particular forms of inquiry-based education we advocated here.

These models of learning rely on an implicit model of public understanding of scientific knowledge embedded in the way digital technologies for learning are designed, developed and used. This demands critical attention to two key dimensions of digitalization of knowledge producing practices: First, the migration of mediating practices to multimodal networked environments involving new forms of sharing and making public as well as new dialogical practices (importantly, this involves the increasingly permeable boundaries among once distinct social and educational spheres and institutions); second, the design, implementation and use of new computationally enhanced, ways of manipulating, visualizing and analyzing information.

The kinds of performances and understandings possible shift when students' modes of inquiry are supported by multimodal networks and combined with use of models as both descriptive and generative tools. This can be better described through consideration of concrete examples of classrooms embracing the affordances of digital media for learning, specifically insofar as they are used to increase the agency of students and teachers in determination of a curriculum linked to their situated needs/interests. In the context of a Media Lab in a community school in the city of Buenos Aires, primary and secondary students and their teachers designed and developed research projects in different curricular areas aimed at developing interactive documentaries as a way to report their findings to part of the school community. What is distinctive about the curriculum design was that teacher encouraged students to formulate research questions in the classrooms that demanded active engagement with very diverse actors and archives in the community in order to find answers. Empirical evidence here, integrated the students' pursuit of scientific understanding with direct experiences of social and environmental impacts.

In one of these research projects, a group of secondary school students followed the steps of a lawsuit claiming health damage as well as environmental collective damage that reached the National Supreme Court. The suit at issue was initiated in 2004 by a group of residents of the Matanza-Riachuelo river basin, the most contaminated river basin in Argentina. At issue in the case was the identification and elimination/reduction of the multiple contributing processes that most contributed to this critical environmental situation; establishing responsibility; and determining effective interventions. Digital technologies allowed students to go beyond reading about the case as a past event through news stories and other historical accounts such as Silvestri's book *El color del río* (2003), and Raponi and Boselli' documentary *Riachuelo* (2006). They addressed the case as a living arena of contestation, recording and editing interviews with some of the residents that filled the legal claim, doctors in the local hospital, and lawyers involved in the case. Further, they were able to also to use computational models for sense making, and to maintain an online partnership with scientific researchers working in bioremediation, attempting to use plants among other organisms to contribute to the solution of environmental contamination problems.

The computational models designed by the students were informed by their observation of research at a bioremediation research lab as well as hands on experiments at school in bioremediation with plants based on advice of the lab researchers. These parallel activities enabled a dynamic online dialogue developed between students, their teachers and the researchers sharing their reflections on the topic as well as asking new questions. Throughout this process, the students' attitudes toward knowledge, their teachers and school assignments changed significantly. Notably, several secondary school students identified by their teachers as chronically disruptive to the learning environment, challenging of school rules, and with low academic achievement expressed surprised at their inclusion without exception in the small group visits to the research bioremediation laboratories. Teachers and researchers alike, who had been concerned about the inclusion of these students, enthusiastically commented a number of times that during the visits these students were particularly active in the lab practices and dialogue, formulating questions and pointing towards problematic issues. All the students involved in the project demonstrated an increasing facility in articulating their own arguments and presenting their unique perspectives in the analysis of environmental and scientific issues as well as listening and analyzing the approaches proposed by their peers, teachers and researchers. This evidently developed in the context of the ongoing practice of expressing their interests, outlining inquiry projects, posing goals, questions and knowledge problems where it was made clear that they were part of a meaningful inquiry with potential social impact. The creation of knowledge was presented to them as a work in progress in which they could participate.

The relations among school professionals and parents also changed significantly. Parents whose contact with school had been mainly to deal with problematic situations of their children found themselves supporting their children's research efforts, and attending presentations of the interactive documentaries reporting on the projects. A significant factor, in this regard, was that parents were familiar with the issues the students were researching and could observe the impacts of the pollution on members of nearby communities. As students have access to authoring positions that enable them to contribute to clarify and discuss issues of public relevance, the interest and recognition showed by parents goes far beyond the attitudes of formal monitoring of school achievement. Parents were given new possibilities for valuing students as productive citizens, not mainly as subjects to be regimented and disciplined.

Dimensions of digitally facilitated knowledge creation across global and local sites

This conception and execution of this curriculum rests on transformations of the last three decades that have seen the integration of computing and networking into academic research cultures has heralded diverse and intensive transformations in multiple fields. Every stage in the life cycle of a research project from how questions are constructed and posed, and how hypothesis are generated, through how data is obtained, contextualized, stored, organized and analyzed to how results are communicated have come to be mediated by information technologies in at least three ways. First, by the broader access they enable to both raw data and research products. Second, by new research approaches based on computer modeling, simulation and automated data analyses. Third, by the expansive communication and broad collaboration they make possible (Bartscherer and Coover, 2011; Foster, 2011; Dutton and Jeffreys, 2010; Olson, Zimmerman and Bos, 2008; Borgman, 2007).

Within the curriculum that followed the dispute over water management practices, students' use of digital networks to access diverse data and the findings of others facilitated forms of mobility (virtual and actual) and social/professional interaction that are key to active participation within the political economy of globalization. In this pedagogical approach students are encouraged to see inquiry, not simply as searching for verifiable sources of information, but as an iterative process of queries, investigations, analysis and interpretation in relation to impacts on vulnerable populations and those with other vested interests. Their online research is dynamically connected with facilitated opportunities for email and live interactions that are not only unplanned, but often unforeseen. The potential impacts of the students' research can be realistically considered as an integral component of the real world problematic. By helping students to understand how their research as embedded in the arena it seeks to understand, teachers also make them aware of ways that their work can feed back into the debate as another mediating party. This pedagogical approach builds on activist scientific practices such as those health-care advocacy groups addressing including AIDS and Breast Cancer, and articulates frameworks for understanding the situated nature of scientific knowledge best articulated in feminist science studies (Harding, 2008; Haraway, 1988).

The framing of inquiry as a situated practice within the Matanza Basin water management curriculum resonates in its pedagogical considerations of the use of new computationally based analysis tools such as modeling and simulations. The development of these tools in a rapidly expanding range of fieldsis not only connected with a continuous increase in the speed and capacity of calculation but is also closely associated with the capacity to process images, to handle sophisticated man-machine interfaces, and perhaps most importantly, expanded conceptions of the uses of visualizations (Küppers, Lenhard and Shinn, 2006). These emergent uses call attention to the nature of simulation as an observational instrument but one in which the concept "observation" assumes an entirely novel meaning. While classical observational instruments such as telescopes and microscopes render phenomena visible by affecting the scale of entities through optical processes of resolution, simulation renders visible the effects of parameters and forces such as time and dynamic interactions translating absolutely nonvisual events into a visual media often shifting the emphasis from opportunity to compare simulated images with real world objects or processes to the possibility to project the potential for initiating or impacting processes or events in ways that haven't yet been observed.

Ihde, a philosopher of science and technology, argues that technologies have played a deeper and stronger role in philosophy than is usually thought, playing major roles as metaphors, driving whole philosophical programs. Sometimes these metaphors produce what he calls an "epistemology engine", used to model the process of knowledge production. For example, the *camera obscura* played an explicit rolein early modern philosophy as a metaphor of how knowledge is structured through representation. In contrast with this epistemology centered in representations or what Ihde calls *isomorphic images*, that is, images that can be compared with the object imaged, computational imaging techniques are not depictions of a perceptible object. Imaging in the context of simulation and modeling is more analogous to a critical, interpretive practice that depicts composite features, than to isomorphic representations resulting from analogous transcription via optical lens systems or other more direct indexical methods. Nonetheless, the literature about the uses of models and simulations remains rife with representationalist language that is an artifact of this earlier observational approach. In this context, several issues arise with regards to the integration of models and simulations in schooling cultures that demand new nuanced approaches that articulate their limitations and affordances, given that what simulations depict are very complex composites constructed of multiple measurement instruments with their embedded assumptions, standards and conventions as well as their isomorphic vestiges (Ihde, 2006; 2004).

Students in the water basin curriculum learned important lessons about the nature of evidence created by models and simulations through comparisons with other forms of digitally enhanced observation that they engaged in. Video, with it's increased affordances for high-resolution observation and control over time (stop action filming and shifting frame rates in post production) allowed students to observe phenomena that were too fine-grained to be captured in their models. The broader and more insight that a situated critical approach to scientific learning can present is that knowledge is a force in the world rather than an objective reflection of it. With regard to laboratory models, we can teach how they may be used in different rhetorical ways, leading us to different understandings of how they relate to phenomena "in the wild." What we want to avoid is conceptual/interpretive practices that rule out as insignificant or anomalous, that which doesn't conform to abstract models (what are often termed outliers). Disability Studies, offers important theoretical insights into the virtual, stressing the differently embodied experiences of ideals vs norms: the former we know and conceive as unattainable goals, objectives or forms, the latter as that which seems achievable, but which lived experience doesn't match (Davis, 1995).

A critical pedagogy of simulation can draw on recent discussions that redirect emphasis from representation to mediative, productive and performative perspectives highlighting how models function as actors. Knuuttila frames this shift in thinking about scientific imaging by likening it to Peirce's focus in his later work on mediation and production of interpretants replacing his earlier focus on representation. (Knuuttila, 2006, 2010a, 2010b). The semi-independent functioning of models with respect to theory and data can be made palpable by considering how their design and the meanings they produce are directly tied to decision making processes that span contexts as diverse as economics, technological design, and architecture (Morrison and Morgan, 1999). Through this lens, simulation appears as a specific theoretical practice in which modelers construct idealized systems that selectively draw on a narrow set of properties that can be attributed to the targeted phenomena (Godfrey-Smith, 2006). Following this perspective the Matanza Basin water management project aims to teach students to employ models as multifunctional epistemic tools (Knuuttila, 2010b) whose value derives largely from our interaction with them by constructing and manipulating them as well as using them for various tasks.

What are the implications of the development of modeling and simulations in a rapidly expanding range of fields for educational practices? In traditional schooling cultures, where a heavy emphasis on coverage of content standards and high stakes summative assessments is prevalent, teachers often use models and simulations for demonstration purposes. Using models in this (re)presentational rather than a construction mode obfuscates students' understanding of the scope and limitations of models (Schwarz et al., 2009; Gilbert and Boulter, 1997). The distinction between lay and expert knowledge claims is articulated in the difference between this approach and that of academic researchers who create a model to help their own thinking and share their ideas with peers to discuss and debate whether they are convincing in the professional community. Schwarz et al. argue that involving learners in modeling practices can help them build not only subject matter expertise but also epistemological understanding of models as a valuable facet of expertise in the practices of generation and evaluation of knowledge. They suggest that it is crucial to involve learners in the construction of models, rather than primarily working with models provided by teachers or scientific authorities as they regard the pedagogical benefits of working with models rests critically on having students develop models to articulate their own understanding. Students' critical understanding of simulation rests on their experience of it as embedded in a politics of knowledge production and sharing. That is, we are advocating approaches that keep the problem of un-conceived or non-pursued alternatives within the field of vision (Stanford, 2006). This requires continually articulating the communities and forces that contribute to the designs we develop for simulation.

Schooling that embraces such an approach, necessarily requires fluid interaction with individuals, groups and institutions at a distance. In this regard digital networks are foundational to re-imagining and re-engineering the space and time of inquiry that is central to developing pedagogy for global participation. This is certainly apparent in the ways that students in the water management curriculum were guided to develop their modeling approaches in iterative ways that included accessing an expert team of scientists as well as engaging members of communities potentially affected by environmental impacts, legal scholars, governmental representatives, and economic entities linked to the toxic pollution of the Basin area. This highlights the third way in which the stages in the life cycle of research have come to be mediated by information technologies: the expansive reach of communication and broad collaboration they make possible literally stretch and compress the spatiality and temporality of knowledge producing practices.

In fields from habitat ecology to sociology digital media have enabled forms of disembodied fieldwork through handcrafted wireless sensor arrays and other networked surveillance techniques. With regard to these transformations in the technological landscape of research, Dutton (2010) poses significant questions concerning the reconfiguration of access to observation as one of the resources central to research: "Will researchers be more distant from their objects of study or closer to them? Will they have more direct or more mediated experiences in observing their subjects of study? Will researchers collect more data or be more dependent on data collected by others?" This provocative set of questions is of particular relevance for reflecting on the roles of digital technologies in education as open inquiry projects where students share agency and responsibility in formulating research questions and designing research approaches and strategies are replaced by open explorations of online simulations and modelizations or automated data collection practices.

To tackle the increasing amount of data and the consequent need for new data analysis methods in the context of these new forms of instrumentation one of the emergent issues involved is the development of an integrated framework for data management and digital libraries for data. In this regard Borgman, Wallis and Enyedi (2007) draw attention to the risks involved in standardization of processes and products as digital libraries of data can facilitate collaboration but can also be problematic by forcing abrupt standardization. Classifications and standards are themselves powerful technologies, highly political and ethically charged that become relatively invisible as they are embedded in working infrastructures. The social and political struggles and compromises that go into the constitution of standards emphasize the need to examine the ways in which standards reconfigure and shape knowledge producing practices. As Bowker and Star (2000) put it "Black boxes are necessary, and not necessarily evil. The moral questions arise when the categories of the powerful become the taken for granted; when policy decisions are layered into inaccessible technological structures." Lessons about standards, institutions and infrastructure are critical to a science curriculum that aims to carry out community informed research.

Teachers' mediating roles take on new significance in the context of students' interactions with digital tools that stimulate more in depth analysis, discussion and reflection on the implicit assumptions, underlying concepts and relationships. As students gain opportunities to express their own ideas, asking their own questions focusing on "how we know" rather than "what we know" teachers have greater need for skills for fostering and mediating shared discussion and debate rather that assessing comprehension of predetermined content and attainment of normative skill sets. Questions remain open with regards to the risks of marginalizing open-ended inquiry in the classroom in a context where certain lines of investigation are facilitated by software resources and online virtual learning environments.

A number of studies have drawn attention to significant changes in the organization of science, particularly the increase of collaborative work in academic research such as the increase in the number of multi-authored papers mostly in the physical and biological sciences but also in the social sciences and to a lesser extent in the humanities (Thagard, 1997). The transformation is markedly geopolitical: the increase in remote and transnational collaboration in the hard sciences has been exponential in recent years (Walsh and Maloney, 2002; Walsh and Bayma, 1996). Attempting to explain this change in the organization of inquiry, scholars make reference to a combination of key factors that play a role in prompting researchers to collaborate both within and outside their disciplines and institutions, including the increasing urgency, complexity, scale and scope of scientific problems, the need for access to new and expensive research instruments and technologies, and pressure from funding agencies as well as the dramatic affordances of networked technologies for collaboration at a distance (Olson, Zimmerman and Bos, 2008; Thagard, 1997; Walsh and Bayma, 1996). This trend toward the geographic distribution of knowledge production, like other dimensions of globalization, is heterogeneous and involves both new forms of inclusion as well as consolidation of control. Here it is worth emphasizing the role educators can play in engaging students in considering what forms of localized knowledge and expertise are included and excluded in the functioning of large-scale science, and how one can intervene in these asymmetries of the knowledge economy.

From scientific models to communication and cultural dimensions of the transformation of knowledge creation

Addressing expansive shifts in scientific practice at the level of primary and secondary schooling can seem daunting, however, parallel transformations in social and cultural realms that students are already implicated in, if not always critically reflecting on offer emergent opportunities for educators to actively engage students in responding to knowledge production across fields and disciplines. The terrain of young people's everyday lives as they engage with new media reconfigure the contexts for communication, friendship, play and self-expression and involve them in a plurality of modes of knowledge production and sharing. Social media, rather than simply enacting monolithic forms of youth identity, initiate collaborative practices that emerge in both mainstream uses of new media as well as in the context of more exceptional practices that represent emerging experimental modes of technological and media literacy.

Facebook is emblematic of a range of friendship-driven practices that for most youth integrate their online and offline encounters with peers in the age segregated contexts of schools and other local activity groups like cultural, religious and sports groups as their primary source of affiliation, friendship and romantic partners that involve them in a plurality of knowledge producing/sharing activities. Rather than simply mirroring or reinforcing existing real world social relationships and settings, today's hybrid online offline publics differ from traditional teen unmediated publics as they are characterized by their persistence, searchability, replicability and invisible audiences where personal networks and social connections are displayed to broader publics that have traditionally been available locally to teens (Ito et al., 2010a; Boyd, 2007). Significantly, students' participation in these publics involves homespun forms of inquiry that for better and worse mirror developments discussed above in relation to the transformative impact of digital communication, collaboration and surveillance on scientific inquiry.

We'd like to put some distance between our analysis and recent arguments that cast the current generation of students as "digital natives," in the sense that they already know/understand the technologies they live and breathe (Prensky, 2001), a characterization that has been critiqued widely in terms of its empirical accuracy as well as theoretical usefulness (Helsper and Eynon. 2010; Livingstone, 2011; Thomas 2011). Rather, young people on the whole are engaged across a spectrum of levels in heterogeneous activities of knowledge production. Online sites provide opportunities for youth to connect at a distance with interest-based groups that might not be represented in their local communities and constitute more intentional and chosen affiliations. This is an important mechanism for them to understand possibilities for countering the mechanisms that maintain distinctions among professional/expert and lay knowledge practices. YouTube and networked gaming sites, among other specialized communities, serve as virtual collaborative laboratories where young people engage with other creators or players to share expertise or mentor others, developing leadership and organizing experience. Amateur media production communities have become increasingly important sites of social, cultural, and technical innovation in today's networked media environment. The benefits from the activities of amateur cultural and knowledge production nowadays are difficult to ignore. Scholars like Mimi Ito, Yochai Benkler, Henry Jenkins, Lawrence Lessig, among others, have urged us to take in account a growing ecology of amateur cultural and knowledge production as forces to be reckoned. Ito draws attention to an emergent shift reordering the balance of power in research and theorizing between the arenas of professional and amateur cultural and knowledge production. In this regard she notes that successful amateur innovations get taken up and widely disseminated and appropriated by professionals just as the amateurs originally appropriated the professional's works (Ito 2010b, Varnelis, 2008).

Beyond their value for situating learning activities within communities of knowledge production, networked media presents significant affordances in the realm of affect and intimacy that, intentionally or not, recast classrooms as sites of engagement with personal knowledge and newly embodied aspects of difference (with respect to culture, gender, health/ability, class, etc). This is a crucial dimension of global citizenship and agency in a digital age that schools are beginning to respond to, mostly in a reactive rather than proactive manner. In this regard, we are observing new resistances to and negotiations of the cultural space of schooling that challenges the limits of standards-based schooling to establish fixed and predetermined requirements in terms of skills or knowledge. In the digital age, the classroom is newly porous in ways that are difficult to ignore. While educational theorists and governmental ministries celebrate and mandate students' use of networked media to access knowledge beyond the classroom walls, the processes of learning and the avenues of content delivery are increasingly entangled with those of personal interaction tethering research activities to issues and activities that schools have long battled to keep outside the curriculum. So, while the use of networked communication has been incorporated in curricula in ways explicitly embraced by proponents of standards-based reform (especially as a tool for preparing students to participate in a global economy), these same media embody a veritable Pandora's box that presents fundamental challenges to established goals of this movement to reign in and codify knowledge.

This contradiction has fueled an important agenda in school administrative policy and launched an industry whose main goal is to protect children from "dangerous content" and schools from liability for student exposure. Considerable amount of thought, technical innovation, and managerial effort has been sunk into the development and implementation of modes of computer use that restrict access to proscribed content and prevent students from sharing personal information or compromising their own or their peers privacy. These include technical solutions (ie, software for block particular URLs or search terms) as well as continually morphing policies for appropriate use of computers and smartphones. Yet by all accounts, this has hardly impeded what can be described as the virtual disintegration of the armored enclosure of learning institutions that were designed and proliferated globally throughout the twentieth century. This increased porosity of classroom walls that digital networks embody has far reaching implications in terms of struggles over the politics of knowledge and students self-determination of the direction and scope of inquiry.

In our discussion of natural sciences curricula mentioned above, we were concerned with active processes of using digital communication to foster understanding of the social political dimensions of research and experimentation. Here, we'd like to turn to some of the implications that arise with unintentional and unanticipated consequences of using the Internet and wireless networks to support inquiry in the social sciences, humanities and the arts. Because curricular concepts in these areas are already clearly linked to social contexts and the interpretive contingencies, the mandate to manage schools as neutral political sites has required administrators and teachers to draw careful lines around what are thought to be safe and appropriate issues and ideas for grade school classrooms.

Students' increased technology use has brought wide reaching transformation in their thinking about what constitutes public and intimate knowledge, and has spawned a spectrum of discourse modalities that lie between these poles. The volatile or unpredictable nature of incorporating networked research in schooling is conditioned by the rise in digital technology use in virtually all aspects of life beyond school walls. Today, personal boundaries are a site of continual contestation, modulation and maintenance. These lifestyle impacts have been rapid and have required teachers to think on their feet. Some of the fallout has been well documented and publicly reported such as high-profile cases of online bullying, 'sexting', stalking, etc. But the vulnerabilities that students are facing are more pervasive and nuanced. Outside the crosshairs of popular media there are a plethora of less hostile exchanges of intimate knowledge that inevitably dovetail with practices that harness the potentials of networked communication for classroom inquiry. Discussions with some of the expanding numbers of teachers who have begun to use new media practices (including students blogging, digital storytelling, student-produced media with recording devices in phones, and a plethora of new social networking platforms—many designed specifically for schools as safer sharing environments) yield rich accounts of the complex, unanticipated and often-unintended adjustments that they have had to confront. These can be openings for addressing key challenges to developing ethical dimensions of global citizenship, however, strategies for considering them as integral to classroom inquiry, rather than distractions, need to be developed and fostered.

Negotiating the intermingling of public and private knowledges: students collecting US veterans' life stories

The anecdotal experiences of teachers who have begun to embrace this challenge can allow us to critically consider possibilities for negotiating public intimacies, and develop strategies for dealing with vulnerabilities that accompany classroom inquiry. Marta, a Southern California teacher whose classroom we've worked with over the past 8 years, has participated with her students in Stories of Service, a US national project to develop an archive of audio-visual documents of the personal experience of US war veterans. Stories of Service was launched in California's

Silicon Valley in 1998 by the nonprofit Digital Clubhouse Network, created by NASA. It was one of the founding partners of the Veterans Oral History Project of the Library of Congress. While Stories of Service has involved K-12 schools throughout the country, individual teachers create their own curricula to address the general goals of creating a national archive of oral history of veterans. Marta's implementation of the stories of service project was integrated with the school's history curriculum, and it is a way of opening up critical discussion of a range of social issues and ethical concerns from conflicting views on war, global relations, and health care/disability (critical topics for veterans). But, as Marta points out, the modalities of contact with these subjects that are facilitated by digital media heightens the role of affect in the learning experiences, as students more directly come into contact with critical issues mediated through the voices and lived experiences of senior citizens who are family members and/or strangers. Taking up forms of interpersonal inquiry anchored in community and family, teachers are almost inevitably faced with unanticipated feelings and social dynamics that can reverberate through the classroom or initiate sensitive discussions at home.

In one instance, the Stories of Service Project excavated buried stories of a student's deceased grandfather that had never been revealed to her by her parents. The student had never known her grandfather who died before she was born. But eliciting accounts of his life from other family members divulged sensitive issues and reignited difficult feelings that her mother had never resolved. This impacted the scope and goals of the project in a variety of ways. When the student approached Marta about what was emerging from her interviews, she had many concerns. She was ambivalent about how much more she wanted to know—she felt that this was a really important opportunity to develop new connections and trust with her family, but was also overwhelmed. She was also faced with decisions about how much of the project she wanted to share with her peers and classmates. Part of what Marta has had to address in this instance and in other components of the Stories of Service Project is the students' development of skills and understandings of how to regulate different levels of privacy and publicness of knowledge. She had learned to coach them in making decisions about what to share and with whom. This means creating a classroom in which the rules and expectations for presenting work can be adjusted dynamically and involve collaborative determinations among the teacher and individual of groups of students.

The connection between inquiry and citizenship skills, then, is not simply about the situation of knowledge in relation to contexts of public and political deliberation, but also about how learning processes can more self-consciously acknowledge the emotional factors that shape ethical decisions. In this regard the recognition of the nuanced ways that knowledge production is situated within a learning community becomes key. It becomes more difficult to deny the radically distinct relationships that different members of a class have to curricular material. And this change comes about, not just in forms of inquiry such as oral history or digital story telling that put students in direct contact with live research subject, but also in processes of online research precisely because the internet has become a repository of such vast amounts of intimate information that resonates with students personal and family lives. Accessing the Internet's as a resource for developing the competencies in independent inquiry necessarily diminishes teachers' control over or ability to anticipate the forms of knowledge that students take up.

The collapsing of intimate/private experience and public discourse that has come with the rise of digital communication presents a formidable challenge to notions of schools as politically-neutral zones that proscribes discussion of the most intimate and politically charged issues students are exposed to. If the principle, "the personal is political", that was established by second wave feminists; the sea-change ushered in by networked and wireless media urges us to pay attention to this in new ways. As educators we do well to recognize moments when intimate knowledge spills out into our classrooms as an opportunity to deal more openly with the radical differences of life experience among our students.

Coda

In our itineraries exploring the roles of digital technologies in academic research and in young people's cultures and their implications for schooling cultures we drew attention to the opportunities, risks and challenges involved in the way these new tools are designed, developed and used. In our contemporary diverse societies, interpellated by advanced marginalization and degradation trends the risks involved in the use of digital technologies from vertical socialization perspectives demand a reconfiguration of our attentional economies in educational landscapes increasing the focus on "how we know" as new epistemic and communication tools and practices are integrated at any level to educational institutional scenarios around the world. In this context, increasing participation in processes of knowledge generation and legitimation as well as dialogic multimodal practices in interaction with a wide range of community actors seems to offer some tracks to confront the challenge of acknowledging the status and limits of available knowledge, identifying the benefits but also the risks of damage and negative externalities implied in knowledge based decision making.

We were inspired to pen this chapter in order to share thoughts on how digital media culture might allow teachers to engage what has within the current educational regime been "unteachable"; proscribed or edged out of the curriculum by mandates that have taken hold during the transnational rise of what has been termed the standards-based education reform movement. What we mean by this is twofold: first, unteachable in the sense of modes of knowledge that educational institutions have deemed illegitimate or unworthy of attention because they can't be measured; and second, unteachable in the sense of discursive practices that fall afield of the authorized conception of schooling as a neutral space of learning rather than a site of intellectual debate and forum for discussion of public issues. Both of these formulations of the "unteachable," have played a formative role in limiting the potential for participation in knowledge creation and democratic processes on local, regional and global scales. And both have been codified and reinforced through the movement for standards of learning that, paradoxically, with respect to our discussion, have dominated educational policy in tandem with the spread of digital communication practices. Some of the unteachables can be described as those forms of inquiry that are determined by localized and unanticipated activity/contexts. Others can be characterized as those discordant aspects of cultural and social life that educational officials have determined too politically charged to take up in classrooms. Our aim has been to push educators to consider how networked and digital technology/culture might be employed to activate dimensions of subjectivity truncated by this form of education.

References

Appadurai, Arjun (2006). The right to research. *Globalisation, Societies and Education* Vol. 4, N° 2, p. 167–177.

Bartscherer, Thomas and Roderick Coover eds. (2011). *Switching Codes: Thinking through digital technology in the Humanities and the Arts.* Chicago: University of Chicago Press.

Borgman, Christine L. (2007). *Scholarship in the Digital Age: Information, Infrastructure, and the Internet.* Cambridge: The MIT Press.

Borgman, Christine L., Jillian C. Wallis, and Noel Enyedi (2007). Little Science Confronts the Data Deluge: Habitat Ecology, Embedded Sensor Networks, and Digital Libraries. *International Journal on Digital Libraries* 7: 17–30.

Bowker, Geoffrey C. and Susan Leigh Star (2000). Invisible Mediators of Action: Classification and the Ubiquity of Standards. *Mind, Culture and Activity* 7: 147–163.

Boyd, Danah. (2007). Why Youth (Heart) Social Network Sites: The Role of Networked Publics in Teenage Social Life. *MacArthur Foundation Series on Digital Learning – Youth, Identity, and Digital Media Volume* (ed. David Buckingham). Cambridge, MA: MIT Press.

Davis, Leonard (1995). *Enforcing Normalcy: Disablity, Deafness, and the Body.* London: Verso.

DeBoer, George E. (2006). Historical Perspectives on Inquiry Teaching in Schools. In *Scientific Inquiry and Nature of Science: Implications for Teaching, Learning, and Teacher Education,* eds. Lawrence B. Flick and Norman G. Lederman. Dordrecht: Springer.

Durst, Anne (2010). *Women Educators in the Progressive Era: The Women behind Dewey's Laboratory School.* New York: Palgrave MacMillan.

Dutton, William H. and Paul W. Jeffreys eds. (2010). *World Wide Research: Reshaping the Sciences and Humanities.* Cambridge, MA: The MIT Press.

Dutton, William H. (2010). Reconfiguring access in Research: Information, Expertise, and Experience. In *World Wide Research: Reshaping the Sciences and Humanities,* eds. William H. Dutton and Paul W. Jeffreys. Cambridge, MA: The MIT Press.

Epstein, Steven. (1996). *Impure Science. Aids, Activism and the Politics of Knowledge*. Berkeley, CA: University of California Press.

Galison, Peter L. (1992). Introduction: The Many Faces of Big Science. In *Big Science: The Growth of Large-Scale Research,* eds. Peter L. Galison and Bruce Hevly. Stanford: Stanford University Press.

Gilbert, John K. and Carolyn Boulter (1997). Learning science through models and modeling. In *International Handbook of Science Education,* eds. Barry Fraser and Kenneth Tobin. Dordrecht: Kluwer.

Godfrey-Smith, Peter. (2006). The strategy of model-based science. *Biology and Philosophy* 21: 725–740.

Gross, Alan G. (1994). The roles of rhetoric in the public understanding of science. *Public Understanding of Science* 3: 3–23.

Harding, Sandra (2008). *Sciences from Below: Feminisms, Postcolonialities, and Modernities.* Durham, NC: Duke University Press

Haraway, Donna (1988). Situated Knowledges: The Science Question in Feminism and the Privilege of Partial Perspective. *Feminist Studies* 14: 575–599.

Helsper, Ellen Johanna and Rebecca Eynon (2010) Digital natives: where is the evidence?. *British Educational Research Journal* 36 (3): 503–520.

Hodson, Derek (2009). *Teaching and Learning about Science: Language, Theories, Methods, History, Traditions and Values.* Rotterdam: Sense Publishers.

Ihde, Don (2006). Models, Models Everywhere. In *Simulation: Pragmatic Construction of Reality,* eds. Johannes Lenhard, Günter Küppers, and Terry Shinn. Dordrecht: Springer.

Ihde, Don (2004). Has the Philosophy of Technology arrived? A State of the Art Review. *Philosophy of Science* 71: 117–131.

Ito, Mizuko et al. (2010a). *Hanging Out, Messing Around, and Geeking Out: Kids living and Learning with New Media.* Cambridge, MA: The MIT Press.

Ito, Mizuko (2010b). Amateur Media Production in a Networked Ecology. Closing Keynote at the 2010 ACM Conference on Computer Supported Cooperative Work, February 6–10, Savannah, Georgia, USA http://www.itofisher.com/mito/publications/amateur_media_p_1.html.

Knuuttila, Tarja (2010a). Some consequences of the pragmatist approach to representation: decoupling the model-target dyad and indirect reasoning. In *EPSA Epistemology and Methodology of Science: Launch of the European Philosophy of Science Association*, eds. Mauricio Suárez, Mauro Dorato and Miklós Rédei. Dordrecht: Springer.

Knuuttila, Tarja (2010b). Not just underlying structures: toward a semiotic approach to scientific representation and modeling. In *Ideas in Action: Proceedings of the Applying Peirce Conference, eds.* M. Bergman, S. Paavola, A. Pietarinen and H. Rydenfelt. Helsinki: Nordic Pragmatism Network.

Knuuttila, Tarja (2006). From representation to production: parsers and parking in language technology. In *Simulation: pragmatic construction of reality,* eds. Johannes Lenhard, Günter Küppers, and Terry Shinn. Dordrecht: Springer.

Küppers, Günter, Johannes Lenhard, and Terry Shinn (2006). Computer Simulation: Practice, Epistemology, and Social Dynamics. In *Simulation: Pragmatic Construction of Reality,* eds. Johannes Lenhard, Günter Küppers, and Terry Shinn. Dordrecht: Springer.

Livingstone, Sonia (2010). Digital learning and participation among youth: critical reflections on future research priorities. *International journal of learning and media,* 2 (2–3): 1–13.

Morrison, Margaret and Mary S. Morgan (1999). Models as mediating instruments. In *Models as Mediators. Perspectives on Natural and Social Science,* eds. Mary S. Morgan and Margaret Morrison. Cambridge: Cambridge University Press.

Olson, Gary M., Ann Zimmerman and Nathan Bos eds. (2008). *Scientific Collaboration on the Internet.* Cambridge, MA: The MIT Press.

Prensky, Mark (2001). Digital Natives, Digital Immigrants. On the Horizon, MCB University Press, Vol. 9, No. 5.

Raponi, Graciela & Boselli, Alberto (2006). *Riachuelo* (Video). Instituto de Arte Americano – Centro Audiovisual FADU – Universidad Buenos Aires.

Rudolph, John L. (2005). Epistemology for the Masses: The Origins of "The Scientific Method" in American Schools. *History of Education Quarterly* 45: 341–376.

Schwarz, Christina et al. (2009). Developing a learning progression for scientific modeling: making scientific modeling accessible and meaningful for learners. *Journal of Research in Science Teaching* 46: 632–654.

Silvestri, Graciela (2003). *El color del río. Historia cultural del paisaje del riachuelo.* Buenos Aires: Universidad de Quilmes-Prometeo.

Stanford, P. Kyle (2006). *Exceeding Our Grasp: Science, History and the Problem of Unconceived Alternatives.* New York: Oxford University Press.

Svampa, Maristella and Mirta A. Antonellieds. (2009). *Minería transnacional, narrativas del desarrollo y resistencias sociales.* Buenos Aires: Editorial Biblos.

Thagard, Paul (1997). Collaborative Knowledge. *Noûs* 31: 242–261.

Thomas, Michael, ed (2011). *Deconstructing Digital Natives: Young People, Technology, and the New Literacies.* New York: Routledge.

UNESCO (2012). The United Nations World Water Development Report (WWDR) http://www.unesco.org/new/en/natural-sciences/environment/water/wwap/wwdr/.

US Department of Education (1996). Getting America's Students Ready for the 21st Century: Meeting the Technology Literacy Challenge, Report to the Nation on Technology and Education. Washington, D.C.: GPO, http://www.ed.govJTechnology/PlanJNatTechPlan/.

Varnelis, Kazys (2008). *Networked Publics.* Cambridge, MA: The MIT Press.

Walsh, John P., and Todd Bayma (1996). Computer Networks and Scientific Work. *Social Studies of Science* 26: 661–703.

Walsh, John P., and Nancy G. Maloney (2002). Computer Network Use, Collaboration Structures, and Productivity. In *Distributed Work,* eds. Pamela Hinds and Sara Kiesler. Cambridge, MA: The MIT Press.

Beyond 'Beyond Schools': Young People's Unsanctioned Digital Media Use In and Around Schools and Classrooms

David Elliott & Scott Bulfin

Abstract

School classrooms employing digital media are often romanticised as places of revolutionary, technologically augmented learning, despite often replicating the traditional processes and power structures of more typical school environments. Indeed, in order to facilitate formal curriculum objectives, digital technologies are often subject to an expanded set of constraints, limitations, and restrictions, in comparison to more traditional classroom media. These constraints are often in response to a perceived need to protect students from harmful online content, the assumption being that all young people need protecting from online 'dangers'. In challenging this deficit framing of young people's 'digital literacies', we explore two case studies of the 'underlife' of digital learners, in which secondary school students participating in a games-based curriculum used digital media in transgressive ways in order to merge in-school and out-of-school literacy practices. Students engaged in a kind of self-directed digital 'learning', employing creative and collaborative strategies in overcoming the restrictions placed on school technology. These underlife strategies drew on a range of tech-based solutions and helped students share knowledge and extend their technological expertise. We argue that this underlife, in which students employ an informally-developed repertoire of techno-cultural skills to subvert school digital regulation, have a range of potentially desirable consequences for both teachers and students.

Introduction

This chapter presents two case studies of young people's unsanctioned digital media use in a public secondary school located in a low socioeconomic area in Melbourne, Australia. It uses these cases to argue for a more nuanced examination of school-based new literacies in general, and for an increased focus on 'digital underlife' (cf Bulfin 2008, 2009; Bulfin and North, 2007). Research into new literacies and informal learning has shown how many young people are engaged in rich learning beyond school (cf Carrington & Robertson, 2009; Knobel & Lankshear, 2007; Marsh 2012). While much of this new literacies research has documented valuable examples of new communication practices, especially those mediated by digital technologies, much of the research is limited in the contexts it investigates (cf Bulfin and Koutsogiannis, 2012; Prinsloo and Rowsell, 2012; Walton and Pallitt, 2012). The study reported in this chapter, from which the two cases are drawn, aims to redress some of these limitations, if only in a modest way, by expanding the range of contexts explored by new literacies research, in particular by examining the messy realities of digital media use by students in public secondary schools. In these schools, tightly stretched funding, limited staff expertise, low socio economic status (or SES) environments and limited available technologies, amongst other issues, represent challenges which mediate how new literacies are enacted in classrooms, and constrain the ability of teachers and researchers to engage in the kind of innovative work often envisioned by new literacies research (eg Alvermann, 2010; Gee, 2010; Ito et al., 2009; Lankshear and Knobel, 2011).

In addition to recognizing the usefulness of this sizeable body of research focusing on new literacies outside of schools, we argue that there is need for a more complex and nuanced engagement with new literacies in and around schools and classrooms. By using the phrase 'in and around schools and classrooms' we are signaling the way that researchers and education professionals can benefit from seeing schools as multi-sited and multi-faceted spaces mediated by more than official policies and teacher intentions. Rather than assume that not much is taking place with new technologies in schools and literacy classrooms, or that what is taking place is mundane and not worthy of critical attention, more serious attention needs to be paid to young people's use of new technologies in schools and the literacy and identity work performed through these uses. In particular, in this chapter we emphasise the importance of unauthorized or unsanctioned technological activity in understanding how young people are engaging with emergent digital media.

The chapter is in two main parts. First, we briefly sketch a theoretical framework for understanding young people's 'digital underlife' in schools. Second, we present the two case studies. The first case study, involves secondary school students playing the computer game, *Minecraft*. Here we argue that students' underlife practices highlight significant challenges associated with the use of digital media within the formal curriculum, highlighting the complex and fraught educational work involved in negotiating spaces for informal digital literacies within the secondary school literacy classroom. The second case study shows students' attempts to subvert, hijack, or remove restrictions imposed on their use of technology in school through a range of approaches, including LAN connections, proxies, and TOR browsers. We argue that these restrictions on the use of new technologies within schools often limit a range of learning opportunities, and are likely to negatively impact the skills students can develop in relation to digital media technologies. We conclude the chapter with some discussion of the cases, again highlighting complexities not often addressed in research focused on digital literacies and schooling.

Digital underlife in schools

This chapter draws on a framework developed by Bulfin and colleagues (Bulfin, 2008, 2009; Bulfin & Koutsogiannis, 2012; Bulfin and North, 2007;) and used to describe 'practices of negotiation' and tactical 'ways of making do' employed by some secondary school students when using digital technologies within educational settings to assert alternative forms of identity and underlife. While located across work in the new literacies studies (cf Gee, 2010) and work focused on the 'sociology of educational technology' (see for example De Vaney, 1998; Johnson, 2009; Monahan, 2005; Picciano & Spring, 2013; Robins & Webster, 1989; Selwyn and Facer, 2013), this research also has resonances with approaches to the sociology of education which emphasize the difficult mediating role schools play in the construction of young people's identities (cf Youdell, 2011).

The concept of 'underlife' as developed by Goffman (1962) in his work on asylums and other 'total institutions', can be understood as the activities (or 'information games') individuals use to indicate that their identities are different from and more complex than, the identities assigned to them by organisational roles within various institutions (cf Brooke, 1987). Goffman argues that all people employ underlife practices as part of their identity-making activities and everyday life-coping strategies. Schools, for instance, offer students particular schooled identities and require compliance with these before success is bestowed. But clearly schools are not places where people always willingly accept institutionally assigned identities. Goffman (1962) notes:

> Whenever we look at a social establishment … we find that participants decline in some way to accept the official view of what they should be putting into and getting out of the organization and, behind this, of what sort of self and world they are to accept for themselves. Where enthusiasm is expected, there will be apathy; where loyalty, there will be disaffection; where attendance, absenteeism; where robustness, some kind of illness; where deeds are to be done, varieties of inactivities. We find a multitude of homely little histories, each in its way a movement of liberty. Whenever worlds are laid on, underlives develop. (pp. 304–5)

Underlife practices allow for the take-up of critical, playful and irreverent stances towards expected roles and indicate (display or perform) this alternative position-taking to others. Importantly, Goffman observed two forms of underlife: disruptive and contained. Disruptive forms of underlife are those 'where the realistic intentions of the participants are to abandon the organization or radically alter its structure' (p. 199). Contained forms of underlife attempt to fit into or operate within 'existing institutional structures without introducing pressure for radical change' (p. 199). Goffman found that contained forms of underlife were more common in those sites he studied. Literacy studies researchers have also found that contained forms of underlife are common in schools (Finders, 1997; Gutierrez, Rymes and Larson, 1995; Larson and Gatto, 2004; Sterponi, 2007). These studies indicate how underlife practices in schools are employed by young people and adults in a range of subtle ways, not always in prototypical defiance to an oppressive power. The potential of underlife concepts in educational contexts becomes clearer when they are framed as orientations which young people might choose to employ during their time in schools and classrooms. Such orientations potentially allow young people to engage in practices of resistance, recontextualisation and solidarity (cf Dyson, 2003).

Work by Bulfin (2008, 2009) has developed the idea of 'digital underlife'. A study of 15–16 year olds across five secondary schools in Melbourne, Australia, indicated that young people employed digital underlife practices in schools for a variety of purposes. Three main underlife practices observed. First, students imported unsanctioned technologies, software and literacies into school. These imported practices and technologies represented challenges to school literacies by unsanctioned technologies and practices. Second, students devised tactical workarounds when confronted with school practices, hardware, software, rules, blocks and obstacles which restricted their engagement in unsanctioned practices, or which made it difficult to use technology in ways restricted by the school. These workarounds used knowledge and practices 'borrowed' from across different domains and from different sites, (re)introducing techniques from other contexts into the school. Third, students deliberately subverted school practices with sanctioned technologies available in the school. That is, they used technologies readily available in schools to engage in underlife behaviours which challenged traditional school practices and literacies. In effect, these students inverted school-authorised technologies and practices and used them against school ways of doing things.

In the case studies and discussion that follow, we explore this digital underlife framework with fresh data generated by Elliott in a study of secondary school aged young people using computer games in a literacy class in a low-SES school in Melbourne, Australia (see Elliott, 2012; 2013; forthcoming).

Study context and methodology

The two case studies discussed below are drawn from a larger ethnographic study conducted by Elliott during 2012 which explored the use of a computer game-based curriculum at a low-SES secondary school in Melbourne, Australia. The study was conducted in a literacy / language arts classroom over six months and involved a curriculum developed around *Minecraft*, a PC game currently popular with many middle school aged students. The study involved 17 participants between 13–14 years of age from one class who were completing their second year of secondary school ('Year 8'). The study school is located in the outlying northern suburbs of Melbourne (15km from the centre of the city), the second largest major city in Australia. It is bordered on one side by an extensive public housing zone, and by middle-class suburbs on the other. As a result the student population are drawn from a diverse range of SES and cultural backgrounds. This diversity has been the source of tension within the school community, with anxieties being raised about the impact of low-SES students on the academic performance of those from more affluent families. A majority of student participants were active users of new technologies regardless of economic background, with most owning an internet-enabled smartphone.

The computer game-based curriculum was developed in conjunction with the classroom teacher, Cynthia, who provided background on students, suggested strategies for shaping curriculum towards the needs of individual students, and acted as a liaison and broker between the school administration and Elliott. Multiple forms of data were generated. Initially, students were asked to complete a questionnaire dealing with both their in and out-of-school technology use. Weekly focus group interviews were held where students were encouraged to discuss their experiences with the game-based curriculum, with technology in the school, and with their own use of digital media outside of school. Detailed one-on-one interviews were also conducted with selected participants. In depth interviews were also conducted with selected teaching and support staff, and the school principal, with topics ranging from the challenges and complexities of using digital technologies in the school, to the challenges of departmental school funding models. All interviews were audio recorded. Artifacts retrieved from the study site included print and digital objects, ranging from written documents to photographs taken from inside *Minecraft*, to copies of actual digital content generated in the game by students.

Minecraft as an alternative literacy curriculum

Minecraft is an independently produced PC game which has received attention by teachers and researchers (Goetz, 2012; Lastowka, 2012; Moore, 2011; Short, 2012). The open-ended and relatively unstructured nature of the gameplay has proven very popular with young people, many of whom use it as a tool of collaboration and creativity. A growing number of informal accounts of *Minecraft*'s pedagogical potential have already been recorded, with teachers from a range of disciplinary backgrounds reporting that the game has been useful in strengthening some formal learning outcomes, and providing digital alternatives to legacy-based teaching approaches. While these informal accounts tend to be overly positive, for students, even those only partially engaged in digital cultures and gaming, *Minecraft* seems to offer a bridge of sorts between the digital literacies used beyond school and the formal learning outcomes being pursued by formal and mandated curriculum. The study reported in this chapter used *Minecraft* in a literacy / language arts classroom as a way of heightening engagement with school-based activities, and providing a digital alternative to a legacy media-based curriculum. Rather than building curriculum around the more commonly used print texts such as novels, newspapers, poetry, plays and short stories, this game-based curriculum allowed student digital literacies to be mobilised as part of a formal classroom curriculum through new media texts, including video games. The study generated data regarding the 'underlife' of study participants, as they demonstrated a complex array of practices and skills through their formal and informal uses of the game.

The computer game-based curriculum employed a combination of designed and free-play pedagogical approaches, in which the strengths and affordances of *Minecraft* as a new media text were combined with the necessarily designed nature of secondary school curriculum. This approach did, however, necessitate a careful and sensitive integration of *Minecraft* into the unit, with a view to ensuring that the game's structure was not adversely affected by the surrounding curriculum, and to support the game's out-of-school cultural profile. The curriculum was non-linear, and was designed around the prediction of activities that students *may* engage with while participating in the *Minecraft* unit, with assessments and links to policy embedded in the curriculum design. Using this non-linear, 'activity matrix' approach, students were given autonomy, and were able to participate in a curriculum that was largely 'negotiated' (cf Boomer, Lester, Onore & Cook 1992). The formal aspects of secondary curriculum design – assessment, feedback, scaffolding, and the positioning of staff expertise in terms of student needs – were able to comfortably co-exist alongside a text that is emergent, participatory, and duologic. Class activities ranged from creative design, with students working together to build houses, farms, factories, towers, and town centres, to 'farming' and the generation of a sustainable ecosystem in which students' characters could live in the game, to questions of economics and law, as students designed their *Minecraft* community's rules of engagement, punishments for transgressions, and a tradeable currency based on the scarcity of in-game elements.

The game-based curriculum adopted elements of a multiliteracies stance (cf Mills, 2011; Pahl and Rowsell, 2012) during the planning and design phases. Rather than look to text-based responses, such as essays and short response questions, as metrics for evaluation and assessment, multimodal content was acceptable as assessable material. *Minecraft* levels, photographs and images, written text presented via blogs, audio and video content, and objects created using *Minecraft's* in-game tools were all used to evaluate the effectiveness of the study curriculum in terms of student learning, and allowed a deeper understanding of how the game-based curriculum contributed to meeting formal objectives mandated by the school and State curriculum objectives.

There were, however, complex questions regarding the nature of 'free' play of the game during classes, and how we as researchers might come to understand the presence of 'underlife' practices in the case studies presented below. From a student perspective, the curriculum offered the opportunity for some forms of 'free play', in that students were not instructed or required to complete a set list of linear, scaffolded and assessable tasks, beyond a self-directed group project, and a self-directed formative assessment task. Student activities in-game were both peer-led with interference from both the participant teacher and the researcher minimised.

This kind of in-class 'freedom', however, was still bound by various restrictions imposed by the school. Student laptops remained the property of the school for instance, and were subject to numerous layers of filtration, a kind of technological mediation that was often perceived as overly invasive by students, and student behaviour in both the 'real' and virtual spaces was expected to retain the school's core values of respect, tolerance, and inclusivity. The play of *Minecraft* could be described as 'free', in the sense that students were permitted to participate in self-directed ways which fell within the confines of *Minecraft's* ludology – students were not permitted to hack the game, exploit or cheat, or manipulate *Minecraft's* code, and the restrictions imposed on the laptops as a result of school policy was intended to police this. Similarly, students were expected to follow the broader behavioural policies of the school, and would be disciplined if they destroyed the work of others, attacked other students, abused or ridiculed one another, or used *Minecraft* to disrupt their class, or the classes conducted in the surrounding rooms.

These conditions of use and play indicate some of the complexities in how the study conceptualised 'sanctioned' and 'unsanctioned' activities. While useful, this binary is not representative of the nuanced and complex policy environment of the study school. Certainly, it may be interpreted that *Minecraft* became a 'sanctioned' text the moment it was introduced into the classroom, even as a part of an 'alternative' or trial curriculum with the participating class, but we argue that this is a position which rejects the complexity of school policy, Government policy regarding technology, and of the highly unstable and unpredictable nature of teacher ideology. In this sense, *Minecraft* was a sanctioned study text as it was attached to a piece of formal curriculum, but at the same time, it presented a kind of unsanctioned text as the highly restrictive nature of this school's internet filtration, and the broader regulation of the school laptops, required a deliberate *breaking* of mandated policy in order to allow the game to function at all. In order to become a 'sanctioned' study text, it was necessary for it to simultaneously become an 'unsanctioned' study text in order for the technology to function at all. This kind of activity was seen by many staff members as subversive, and potentially dangerous, cultivating a transgressive environment which made some within the school community uncomfortable.

As *Minecraft's* status as a 'sanctioned' text became increasingly contested by the technological restrictions of the school, questions regarding the sanctioned and unsanctioned nature of student participation were raised, and were often equally ambiguous. Students were not compelled to engage in specific tasks during the games-based curriculum, but they were expected to be bound by the behavioural standards set by the school for offline behaviour. They were also expected to respect the technological limitations imposed on their laptops, and to ensure that they do not exploit the relative freedom afforded to them by the alternative curriculum by using it for 'inappropriate' behaviour.

Below, we present the two case studies and explore some of the nuances and complexities of how digital underlife manifests in each example and what the cases might mean for thinking about digital literacies in schools. We position digital underlife as the product of the messy business of formal schooling, and as multiple practices which manifest across a range of policy/curriculum architectures in different ways. In pursuing these nuances we explore the thinking invoked by language which is oppositional—sanctioned/unsanctioned, free/restricted—and suggest that digital underlife can be observed in a variety of shapes and contexts, and often stems from seemingly contradictory, ambiguous environments. All participant names in the following case studies have been anonymised.

Case study 1: Collaboration and invasion

Setting up a game-based curriculum at the study school proved far more challenging than originally anticipated. From the beginning, the logistics of fairly straightforward tasks such as co-ordinating student logins were complicated by the highly regulated school internet. Provided by the state education department, the restrictive internet connection made it very difficult to deploy *Minecraft* on the school laptops. *Minecraft* uses a network of authentication layers, each one needing to be unblocked at both the school and education department level—a task requiring extensive planning and negotiation with school and department personnel. The particular incident described here occurred a fortnight into school-based data generation. Students were able to run local versions of the *Minecraft* client on their laptops but could not connect to servers beyond the school, and were thus incapable of authenticating their client, an essential part of completing the installation of the game. Fortunately, *Minecraft* features a LAN (local area network) function, enabling computers to connect to each other via wi-fi, bypassing the need for an internet connection. One machine operates as a simple server, and others can connect to it provided they are connected to the same network. In planning the game-based curriculum this option had not been considered, but on this particular afternoon a student, Paul, showed both Elliott and the classroom teacher, Cynthia, his laptop screen, revealing that he had created a *Minecraft* LAN server, and ten boys from the class had already connected to it.

During the game-based curriculum unit, the more or less settled social dynamics of the class changed, as students formed new groups based on their objectives in-game, with students who had rarely communicated in the past now working in collaboration. Paul had already built a large structure on the server—a wooden house set into the side of a mountain beneath a waterfall, and a group of other boys were adding to it, building stairs, windows, cutting into the mountainside to divert water. When asked by Elliott if they could build something from scratch in order to display their collaboration process, they immediately established a rally point in the game, began to delegate tasks, and set to work. As the group worked to develop a new structure, discussion about gameplay focused on analysing the group's strategic and design decisions. Their digital avatars swarmed around their in-game construction (in this case, a warehouse) as they requested materials from each other, delegated roles as needed, and engaged in peer-led evaluation of their colleagues' performance. Students demonstrated project management skills, discussed the question of 'ownership' and virtual objects, collaborated on designs, negotiated both function and form of their collaborative creations, and worked with both their hardware and software to maintain the *Minecraft* LAN server's performance. This was a sophisticated and layered set of largely self-generated and self-sustained activities, which incorporated intensive skill development for some students (not all Paul's collaborators in this instance were similarly skilled at the game). Many of these skills are much in demand in the typical mandated curriculum that students would normally be working with, but these skills were much more clearly on display in this instance. Such a display, it is worth bearing in mind, was facilitated partly through a piece of software, a game, which, required a temporary suspension of regular school policy in order to be used as a part of the alternative game-based curriculum.

During this same classroom session, a group of users, not recognised by the group, and not operating within the classroom appeared on their server. The *Minecraft* server which the group had set up and which was running on a LAN network, could be joined by anyone within physical proximity of the host machine. The group interrogated these 'invaders' via text chat, demanding to know who they were. Without responding the 'invaders' proceeded to collect the resources necessary to create both 'flint' and a set of 'fire-burning torches' (both virtual objects that can be made or crafted in the game). They then set the group's constructions alight. Paul's original structures, as well as the new buildings that had been the results of collaborative effort between the group, were ablaze. It was clear that these anonymous attackers were not in the classroom, but the boys had suspicions as to who the invaders may have been. Cynthia, the classroom teacher, responded to this instance with a mixture of amusement and horror, as the classwork completed by the boys, in the form of their *Minecraft* structures, was virtually burning to the ground. After the group explained how such an invasion was possible, Cynthia investigated adjacent classrooms in an attempt to track down the source of the incursion. The group, however, self-organised and began a kind of emergency response operation—re-routing water from nearby mountains to douse the flames, delegating roles for the speedy reconstruction of damaged buildings, and debating the best course of action for removing the invaders from the LAN server.

Despite the levity and unpredictability of the situation, the instance above illustrates a potential site of skill and knowledge development typically prized by formal curriculums. Students demonstrated an eagerness for engaging in high level digital and spatial literacies, requiring them to: think and act collaboratively, to manage resources, to delegate tasks and to negotiate responsibilities in the service of a group agenda, to think geometrically and mathematically. In effect, they were required to imagine their participation in an emergent and real time in-game narrative (cf Gee, 2007). The 'invasion' required the group to re-assess their task distribution to quickly respond to the invading students and, while beginning to rebuild, reimagine their designs as a means of repairing the damage done by the attack.

The instance highlights issues related to 'contained' forms of digital underlife (cf Goffman, 1962): those which attempt to fit into or operate within 'existing institutional structures without introducing pressure for radical change' (p. 199). Students in Cynthia's classroom were using a game that had effectively been recontextualised within her classroom for the purposes of the alternative game-based curriculum. The game was an unsanctioned artefact that had been temporarily designated a space within Cynthia's classroom. Within the classroom, students were using the game to practice and perform the kinds of skills and understandings valued as part of 'digital age' practice. Without *Minecraft* being given temporary sanctioned status, these digital age practices are effectively be banned from the classroom, or at least from being exercised through an artefact such as *Minecraft*. Beyond this particular classroom, the game of course continued to have other meanings for other students (the invaders, for instance). Hacking into someone else's *Minecraft* server when you're not at school, has a certain cultural capital associated with it. Contained forms of underlife are therefore highly contextualised, shaped by the situations and institutions in which they are enacted and performed. Practices designated sanctioned in one room, can be non-sactioned in the adjacent room. The *digital* complication in this instance is that students in both rooms can be operating in the same gameworld simultaneously, but have their actions make meaningful in different ways.

Case study 2: TOR and school internet filtration

Internet filtration is an ongoing and contentious issue in schools (cf Deibert, Palfrey, Rohozinski & Zittrain, 2008; Hope, 2008, 2012; Rosenberg, 2001; Wells & Lewis, 2006). In Australian public schools, internet use is regulated across multiple levels of policy. Due to the complex methods of filtration currently employed it is often difficult to accurately pinpoint the parameters of acceptable internet use. State and regional education department variations, along with regulation at an individual school level, has led to a confusing and unpredictable system of filtration and blocking for both students and staff. Such systems can often have unintended effects on the use of new technologies in classrooms. Many new media texts, such as video games, wikis, and social media platforms, are subject to regulation and can often be blocked and banned from school computers even when they contain educationally useful material and activities.

Students at the study school had created a range of 'workaround' solutions to the problem of internet filtration, and had used available hardware and software to ameliorate what they generally saw as unfair censorship of the internet. These workarounds included:

- using the HTTPS prefix, an SSL prefix, in place of a traditional HTTP address
- using external internet proxies
- installing VPN software, such as Hotspot Shield
- using Google Apps to run a proxy server from their home PC.

A smaller group of students were using a particularly potent technique for subverting internet regulation via the Tor browser (The Onion Router), an encryption service originally sponsored by the US Naval Research Laboratory, before being financed by the Electronic Frontier Foundation. Through Tor, user anonymity is protected, and internet activity is shielded from external monitoring. Tor is often used for the transmission of digital content by activists and dissident movements in oppressive regimes, by journalists and whistleblowers and also by law enforcement professionals. Because of the software's ability to anonymize online activity is has also been co-opted as a tool for sharing child abuse material, and for the illegal trading of drugs and firearms.

The presence of Tor in the study school was troubling because of the notoriety some Tor user communities have for operating in dangerous and lawless environments. The discovery that some students were using Tor within the school was an ethical conundrum for Elliott, requiring serious reflection on the nature of internet regulation, and to questions about the limits of student underlife when engaging with genuinely dangerous software.

Sophie and John

Sophie was a student who had demonstrated an aptitude for design when participating in the games-based curriculum. After being asked to demonstrate some of her *Minecraft* creations, Elliott noticed the Tor browser installed on her laptop. When asked what the software was, she immediately took her laptop away in alarm. She insisted that it was 'nothing', and that she 'didn't know what it was'. Below is a follow up exchange where Sophie gives a part-explanation of why she uses Tor:

Sophie:	It lets us use the internet properly
Elliott:	Where did you get it from?
Sophie:	John gave it to us
Elliott:	Did he?
Sophie:	Promise that you won't say anything to our teacher. She'll take it away.

The exchange highlights the difference Sophie sees between the 'proper' internet and the 'school' internet. Here, Sophie defines 'using the internet properly' as having access to an 'unregulated' connection. This awareness of the limitations of the official, regulated school internet is crucial in understanding how students perceive the integrity of the online environment, and value the kinds of unregulated access which they often experience outside of school. As noted above the incident raised important ethical responsibilities for Elliott as a teacher-researcher, which while needing to be observed challenged many of Elliott's assumptions regarding unregulated student access to the internet. Leaving students with unmonitored access to the Tor network could place them in a potentially harmful situation, with the possibility of a student unwittingly accessing child abuse material, or material dealing with the trade of drugs or firearms. Cynthia was unaware of Tor, and suggested that the majority of the school staff would be similarly unfamiliar with the software. Later, the school's ICT co-ordinator confirmed that she had no knowledge of Tor.

John, the student who had initially distributed the Tor software to fellow students, was taken into Cynthia's office for a meeting, where he was asked to explain his understanding of Tor. He became immediately distraught, insisting that he didn't mean to do anything 'wrong', and that, similar to Sophie's claims, he believed that Tor was simply a web browser that allowed him to use the internet 'properly'. He explained that a lot of his fellow students were angry and frustrated about the restrictions of the school internet, and that Tor was able to restore the internet to an acceptable level of functionality. John became increasingly upset as the potential dangers of Tor were explained to him. John was counselled and asked to not pass the software on to any other students. After school, Cynthia rang John's mother to let her know about the situation.

This example presents a challenge to educators and researchers working in the media and technology space. While Elliott had considered himself an opponent of censorship, and had concerns about experiences of internet filtration expressed by staff and students, during the study he had been placed in a situation which prompted him to immediately act as a censor in shutting down Sophie and John's digital underlife activity. This seemed to run contrary to his original intention as a teacher-researcher—to invite informal digital literacies into the classroom space and allow them to be mobilised as productive classroom identities and activities. Students' use of the Tor browser, despite the fact that no illegal activity was seen, complicated Elliott's teacher-researcher intentions by generating a response that conflicted with his original, and possibly evangelical, positioning of digital media as a useful school literacy resource.

As Bulfin (2008, 2009) argues, digital underlife activities in schools can often be defined as engaging at least three primary practices: the importing of unsanctioned software and literacies into school, the use of tactical workarounds to combat efforts made to regulate technology use in school, and the use of sanctioned technologies in order to subvert school practices. Sophie's description of the Tor-enabled internet as 'proper' internet can be similarly viewed through this analytical frame. She used underlife practices to 'restore' what she perceived to be a modified, inauthentic school internet, by using a combination of sanctioned (laptops, the school's internet connection) and unsanctioned (Tor) technologies.

In using Tor to engage in underlife activity, however, students weren't simply challenging reductive school policies, or having benign 'fun'. Without their knowledge, their use of the technology had placed them in a space that was potentially dangerous, and represented a digital environment which arguably is not appropriate for school-aged young people. Elliott's challenge, then, was to reconcile this tension, and to unpack the potential incompatibility between his own anti-censorship stance, and a necessary intervention given his status as an invited guest, researcher, and teacher with a clear duty-of-care to students. At the core of this tension are questions of legality versus taste. While it could be argued that he *was* acting as a kind of censor, the source of that censorship was not based in aesthetics, or in taste, in social or political framings of online content, or as a response to the perceived threat of digital media in a legacy classroom.

For teachers and researchers working in the media and technology space, several complex questions might be asked: what are the limits of digital underlife in school contexts? How might researchers and educators begin to navigate the complexities inherent in offering students relatively unregulated access to digital spaces? In answering these questions, Elliott first found it necessary to be aware of the legal implications of the media being accessed by students. The 'undesirable' content which he felt it necessary to regulate was content which could result in legal problems for the students, teachers, and the school itself. This was not a question of perspective, and just as *any* illegal materials are not permitted on school grounds, the same restrictions must apply to digital objects of an illegal nature. The tensions between the intentions of the study and Elliott's response to the presence of Tor, then, do not only raise questions regarding censorship, but raise questions regarding consistency in how educators and researchers conceptualise illegal materials. Just as students are not permitted to bring weapons or drugs into schools, Tor gave students potential access to the trade in these materials via a digital space, and as such were subject to the same necessary restrictions placed on illegal objects in physical spaces.

This case serves to highlight some limits and complexities of digital underlife in schools, and presents an example of a key element of research on digital literacies: educators and researchers need be aware of the potential uses of new technologies, and need to be able to navigate the complex philosophical space in which material is assessed and help their students do the same (cf Buckingham 2007).

Discussion and conclusion

The two cases presented above point to some of the complexities related to young people's use of digital technologies in and around schools, and in particular, those which tend to be less frequently discussed in the research on new and digital literacies. In both cases, students' understanding of and interaction with the internet is mediated through a complex network of social and technical regulation so that student experience of the internet is confined to a domesticated and schooled space; in the students' terms a 'pretend' or 'fake' experience of the internet. The forms of digital underlife visible in the cases question the parameters and reach of school-based technology regulation, and challenge assumptions about the ways that formal education contexts typically frame student access to the internet (eg Hope 2012). Both cases can be seen as student attempts to replicate the less restricted nature of internet access which they enjoy during their out-of-school lives. In the first case, the kinds of activities which students often engage in informally beyond school—construction and design, collaboration, and conflict with other groups—are introduced into the classroom through both contained and partially disruptive forms of digital underlife, demonstrated by the study participants, and the invading students. In the second case, students attempt to reclaim the 'proper' internet by working around blocks and restrictions of online material.

In addition to challenging these particular school practices, students' digital underlife points to some broader tensions and issues relating to young people's use of digital technologies in school. We discuss two points briefly here: (1) the complex situated nature of digital underlife; and (2) the useful distinction between technologies, text and practices.

In Cynthia's classroom, *Minecraft* as a game was a provisionally sanctioned text (or set of texts), in the sense that it had been given a kind of temporary 'visa' to travel in this particular classroom space for a time. The kind of gameplay characteristic of *Minecraft* was also sanctioned. The game (and some aspects of its gameplay) were, however, simultaneously an unsanctioned' text, as both school and departmental policy have not authorized the use of the game in other classes and areas of the school; indeed the formal technological architecture of the school is configured to prohibit the use of such games. In order to 'make' *Minecraft* a sanctioned text, certain technological and social/relational conditions had to be negotiated. First, internet filters blocking unauthorized online content must be temporarily disrupted and school laptops configured to ensure that filter disruption can be maintained. Second, students and staff must be vigilant in reporting the multiple possibilities for the reblocking of content, such as the censoring of authentication layers, and the revoking of access to Windows system files which allow the game to be modified. In addition to these technical negotiations, which are of course social in nature too, a set of negotiations and provisional understandings needed to be established with teachers and other staff, students and parents. Teachers and the school principal, for example, gave tentative in-principle support for the game-based curriculum despite reservations about how a 'games' curriculum might be seen by parents to be less rigorous and serious than regular curriculum and classroom work. This in-principle support was always provisional and was based on the smooth and trouble free progress of the game-based curriculum with the class. The 'invasion' incident, with the multiple shaping contexts of its two different groups of users suggests that the sanctioned (and the unsanctioned) nature of *Minecraft* was heavily situated and context dependent. The place of the text was often contested by other students and staff, who seemed puzzled by the less regulated space that had been established inside the school for the game and the alternative game-based curriculum.

In the second case, understanding student use of Tor as digital underlife activity is also context dependent, and illustrates the useful difference between object and utility (or for example 'game' and 'gameplay' as above). Tor is, in itself, not a dangerous piece of technology. It is a browser with expanded anonymising functionality, allowing users to bypass many kinds of online filtration and regulation. In a secondary school context, however, potential problems are raised by the presence of Tor—questions of safety, of the responsibility of staff to provide a harm-free and supportive environment in schools, and of the internet's position as a potential threat to student welfare. In this particular context, with these kinds of issues being raised by the presence of the software, Tor becomes conceptually weaponised, and regardless of the ways in which students are *actually* using the client, it is constructed by teachers and administrators as the kind of potential threat which necessitates the filtration which drove students to it in the first place. Sophie's use of Tor, however, is in the context of a 'broken internet'—one which is so different to the internet she has experienced outside of school—and the browser is not an attempt to disrupt, but is instead an attempt to negate an existing disruption in the form of her school's filtration attempts. Attempting to tease out the technologies, the text/s and the practices, is one way of attending more closely to the significance of use, rather than to make a fetish of devices. There is, of course, a duty of care issue at work in the second case, and while Tor certainly *can* be used for illegal activity, just as knives are not in and of themselves dangerous, their application in specific scenarios certainly can be. If we are to accept that the digital and 'real' worlds should be bound by the same freedoms, the same opportunities for choice, and the same abilities for self-direction and consumption, perhaps they should also be bound by similar attempts to ensure that environments are as safe and inclusive as possible. The challenging question is about how this safety and inclusion might be democratically produced.

Cases such as those above encourage researchers to engage with more complex understandings of the social, cultural and political dimensions of digital literacies in and around classrooms and schools. Engaging with this complexity means moving beyond the common narrative in which informal and out of school digital literacies are seen as rich, engaging and colourful, in opposition with the sterile, lifeless, archaic literacies of traditional secondary school education (cf Bulfin and Koutsogiannis 2012). The notion of a student digital underlife in and around classrooms and schools worth paying attention to (to say nothing of a teacher digital underlife) is an encouragement to move beyond the 'beyond schools' argument: that researchers should look beyond schools for clues as to the real future of education. These two 'underlife' cases illustrate the limitations of digital technologies as they are often manifest in schools, but the cases also suggest that resolving these issues is not as simple as looking elsewhere (or in eliminating all online regulation from schools). A more complex and nuanced approach is needed, in which a sensitive and granular understanding of the relationships between young people and digital technology is brought together with a realistic sense of the responsibilities of educators and the often limited opportunities which exist for the kinds of 'transformative' digital pedagogies espoused by techno-evangelists.

References

Alvermann, Donna (Ed.). (2010). *Adolescents' online literacies: Connecting classrooms, digital media, and popular culture*. New York: Peter Lang.

Boomer, Garth, Lester, Nancy, Onore, Cynthia, & Cook, Jon (Eds.). (1992). *Negotiating the curriculum: Educating for the 21st century*. London: Falmer.

Brooke, Robert. (1987). Underlife and writing instruction. *College Composition and Communication, 38*(2), 141–153.

Buckingham, David. (2007). *Beyond technology: Children's learning in the age of digital culture*. Cambridge, UK: Polity.

Bulfin, Scott. (2008). Renegotiating digital literacies in and around the curriculum (pp. 1–18). Paper presented at the AATE/ALEA Conference, 6–9 July 2008 Adelaide Convention Centre, Adelaide.

Bulfin, Scott. (2009). *Literacies, new technologies and young people: Negotiating the interface in secondary school.* (PhD), Faculty of Education, Monash University.

Bulfin, Scott, & Koutsogiannis, Dimitris. (2012). New literacies as multiply placed practices: Expanding perspectives on young people's literacies across home and school. *Language and Education, 26*(4), 331–346. doi: 10.1080/09500782.2012.691515.

Bulfin, Scott, & North, Sue. (2007). Negotiating digital literacy practices across school and home: Case studies of young people in Australia. *Language and Education, 21*(3), 247–263. doi: 10.2167/le750.0.

Carrington, Victoria, & Robinson, Muriel. (2009). *Digital literacies: Social learning and classroom practices*. London: Sage.

de Certeau, Michel. (1984). *The practice of everyday life*. Berkeley: University of California Press.

De Vaney, Ann. (1998). Can and need educational technology become a postmodern enterprise? *Theory into Practice, 37*(1), 72–80.

Deibert, Ronald, Palfrey, John, Rohozinski, Rafal, & Zittrain, Jonathan (Eds.). (2008). *Access denied: The practice and policy of global internet filtering*. Cambridge, MA: MIT Press.
Dyson, Anne Haas. (2003). *The brothers and sisters learn to write: Popular literacies in childhood and school cultures*. New York: Teachers College Press.
Elliott, David. (forthcoming) *Rebooting the system: A study of computer games in a secondary literacy classroom*. PhD, Faculty of Education, Monash University.
Elliott, David. (2013). *The playing field*. Paper presented at the conference of the Australian Association for the Teaching of English (AATE), Brisbane, Australia, 4–7 July.
Elliott, David. (2012). Together alone: Computer games as curriculum. *IDIOM, 48*(3), 16–18.
Finders, Margaret. (1997). *Just girls: Hidden literacies and life in junior high*. New York: Teachers College Press.
Gee, James Paul. (2010). *New digital media and learning as an emerging area and 'worked examples' as one way forward*. Cambridge, MA: MIT Press.
Goetz, Christopher. (2012). Tether and accretions: Fantasy as form in videogames. *Games and Culture, 7*(6): 419–440. doi: 10.1177/1555412012466288.
Goffman, Erving. (1962). *Asylums: Essays on the social situation of mental patients and other inmates*. Chicago: Aldine.
Gutierrez, Kris, Rymes, Betsy, & Larson, Joanne. (1995). Script, counterscript, and underlife in the classroom: James Brown versus *Brown v. Board of Education. Harvard Educational Review, 65*(3), 445–471.
Hope, Andrew. (2008). Internet pollution discourses, exclusionary practices and the 'culture of over-blocking' within UK schools. *Technology, Pedagogy and Education, 17*(2), 103–113.
Hope, Andrew. (2012). The shackled school internet: Zemiological solutions to the problem of over-blocking. *Learning, Media and Technology, 38*(3), 270–283. doi: 10.1080/17439884.2012.670646.
Ito, Mizuko, Baumer, Sonja, Bittanti, Matteo, Boyd, Danah, Cody, Rachel, Herr, Becky, Tripp, Lisa. (2009). *Hanging out, messing around, geeking out: Living and learning with new media*. Cambridge, MA: MIT Press.
Johnson, Nicola F. (2009). *The multiplicities of internet addiction: The misrecognition of leisure and learning*. Surrey, UK: Ashgate.
Knobel, Michelle, & Lankshear, Colin (Eds.). (2007). *A new literacies sampler*. New York: Peter Lang.
Lankshear, Colin, & Knobel, Michelle. (2011). *New literacies: Everyday practices and social learning* (3rd ed.). Maidenhead, UK: Open University Press.
Larson, Joanne, & Gatto, Lynn Astarita. (2004). Tactical underlife: Understanding students' perceptions. *Journal of Early Childhood Literacy, 4*(1), 11–41.
Marsh, Jackie. (2012). Purposes for literacy in children's use of the online virtual world 'Club Penguin'. *Journal of Research in Reading*, 1–17. doi: 10.1111/j.1467-9817.2012.01530.x.
Mills, Kathy Ann. (2011). *The multiliteracies classroom*. Bristol, UK: Multilingual Matters.
Monahan, Torin. (2005). *Globalization, technological change and public education*. New York: Routledge.
Moore, Christopher. (2011). The magic circle and the mobility of play. *Convergence17*(4), 373–387.
Pahl, Kate, & Rowsell, Jennifer. (2012). *Literacy and education: Understanding the New Literacy Studies in the classroom* (2nd ed.). London: Sage.
Picciano, Anthony, & Spring, Joel. (2013). *The great American educational-industrial complex: Ideology, technology and profit*. New York: Routledge.

Prinsloo, Mastin, & Rowsell, Jennifer. (2012). Digital literacies as placed resources in the globalised periphery. *Language and Education, 26*(4), 271–277.
Robins, Kevin, & Webster, Frank. (1989). *The technical fix: Education, computers and industry.* Basingstoke: Macmillan.
Rosenberg, R. S. (2001). Controlling access to the internet: The role of filtering. *Ethics and Information Technology, 3*(1), 35–54.
Selwyn, Neil, & Facer, Keri (Eds.). (2013). *The politics of education and technology: Conflicts, controversies, and connections.* New York: Palgrave Macmillan.
Short, Daniel. (2012). Teaching scientific concepts using a virtual world—Minecraft. *Teaching Science, 58*(3), 55–58.
Sterponi, Laura. (2007). Clandestine interactional reading: Intertextuality and double-voicing under the desk. *Linguistics and Education, 18*(1), 1–23.
Walton, Marion, & Pallitt, Nicola. (2012). 'Grand Theft South Africa': Games, literacy and inequality in consumer childhoods. *Language and Education, 26*(4), 347–361.
Wells, John, & Lewis, Laurie. (2006). Internet access in U.S. public schools and classrooms: 1994–2005 (NCES 2007–020). Washington, DC: National Center for Education Statistics, U.S. Department of Education.
Youdell, Deborah. (2011). *School trouble: Identity, power and politics in education* Milton Park, Abingdon: Routledge.

Digital Introductions as Critical Practice

Julie Faulkner

Abstract

The possibilities for new kinds of writing afforded by digital technologies and social media now permeate digital worlds. Conceptualisations of literacy in relation to how we learn and practise multimodal forms of communication have undergone significant evolution over the past few decades. In education, research suggests that while young people are deeply engaged with a proliferating range of digital technologies, many classrooms continue with print-based textual approaches. Multiliterate understandings engage complex relationships among visuals, space and text as well as interpreting a range of symbols in critically and culturally appropriate ways. I explore in this chapter the reshaping of semiotic form and disruption of author (and reader) expectations, expanding to wider debates around technology, representation and communication. In this project, I created a digital introduction task to replace a traditional written student introduction which began a 12 month class in an English teaching method. The task required students to construct aspects of themselves digitally, present this representation and then critically reflect on the practices and technologies involved. The task was structured as an open-ended 'problem', grounded in a literacy concept. The framework we chose as the best fit for the task was Bill Green's (1988) 3D literacy model, which describes three interrelated dimensions of literacy: operational, cultural and critical. Operationally, students had to understand and use digital technologies, employing a repertoire of (multi)literate practices strategically and appropriately for their audience (the cultural dimension). Introducing themselves to a new cohort of peers called upon social and deliberate meaning-making. To participate in the critical dimension, students explored the self reflexive, or constructed nature of identity and representation. One aim of the interaction was to push students into a less comfortable space. This space was created through their need to learn new media skills, and critically reflect on the capacity of technology to shape their purposes, as well as the choices they needed to make to characterise themselves for a particular audience. These 'pedagogies of discomfort' (Boler, 1999) were, in turn, constructed by me as generative learning conditions in which students might be forced out of habituated practices. The study, while small in scope, has resonances which can extend to other intercultural settings. These environments are ones where digital technologies, used creatively, can serve as provocations for new forms of critical thinking.

Introduction

Bill Green (2001), speculating on the implications for subject English in the 21st century, points to 'the proliferating phenomenon of techno-textuality'(p. 249). The possibilities for new kinds of writing afforded by digital technologies and social media now permeate digital worlds. Conceptualisations of literacy in relation to how we learn and practise multimodal forms of communication have undergone significant evolution over the past few decades. This has precipitated, according to Peel et al. (2000), the 'biggest seismic shift' in curriculum history.

Can such a claim can be substantiated and, if so, how do we identify and describe such a shift? In education, research suggests that while young people are deeply engaged with a proliferating range of digital technologies, many classrooms continue with print-based textual approaches (Papert, 1992; Lankshear & Knobel, 2006; Morris, 2010).

A dimension of this techno-textuality, however, has been the opening up in terms of what can now be authored, not only of new kinds of content, but also of form (Green, 2001). Multiliterate understandings engage complex relationships among visuals, space and text as well as interpreting a range of symbols in critically and culturally appropriate ways. I explore in this chapter the reshaping of semiotic form and disruption of author (and reader) expectation, expanding to wider debates around technology, representation and communication. I then link these concepts to Green's (1988) critical dimension of literacy, asking how the introductions mobilise mode and content as 'constructed and contingent experiences' (Duffelmeyer, 2001: 359).

In this project, I created a digital introduction task to replace a traditional written student introduction which began a 12 month class in an English preservice teaching method. The task required students to construct a version of themselves digitally, present this representation and then critically reflect on the practices and technologies involved. The task was structured as an open-ended 'problem', grounded in a literacy concept. The framework I chose as the best fit for the task was Bill Green's (1988) 3D literacy model, which describes three interrelated dimensions of literacy: operational, cultural and critical. Operationally, students had to understand and use digital technologies, employing a repertoire of (multi)literate practices strategically and appropriately for their audience (the cultural dimension). Introducing themselves to a new cohort of peers called upon social and deliberate meaning-making. To participate in Green's critical dimension, students explored the self reflexive, or constructed nature of identity and representation.

One aim of the interaction was to push students into a less comfortable space. This space was created through their need to learn new media skills, and critically reflect on the capacity of technology to shape their purposes, as well as the choices they needed to make to characterise themselves for a particular audience. These 'pedagogies of discomfort' (Boler, 1999) were, in turn, positioned by me as generative learning conditions in which students might be forced to reconsider habituated practices associated with learning and teaching.

Background

Universities and schools are increasingly populated with learners who are shaped by their relationships with information and communication technologies (ICT) in ways unimaginable to many current educators (Green and Bigum, 1993). These students actively develop their literacy skills in online environments – they are adept at multitasking, collaboration, sophisticated in their uses of electronic technologies, and used to a trial and error approach to solving problems. This stands in stark contrast to a more logical, rule-based approach by previous generations (Oblinger, 2003; Oblinger, Martin and Baer, 2004). New Literacy Studies (Street, 1984; 2003) argues that formal learning practices which decontextualise ways of knowing increasingly lead to student disconnection with school learning. One commentator notes:

> [It is] no surprise that when we incarcerate teenagers of today in traditional classroom settings, they react with predictable disinterest […] They are skilled in making sense not only of a body of content, but of contexts that are continually changing. (Economist.com)

Differences within ways that in-school and out-of-school literacies are organised have been usefully analysed by Bernstein (1999). While schooling values vertical, segmentally-structured discourses of knowledge, popular (and digital) ways of knowing to which everyone has potential or actual access can be described as 'horizontal'. They are 'likely to be oral, local, context-dependent and specific, tacit, multi-layered and contradictory across … contexts' (p. 8). Young people take up valued knowledge by word of mouth and there is a rapid turnover of what is required to be a participant within and across a number of cultural contexts. Students as readers and producers of Green's techno-textuality thus need to dis-embed themselves from familiar, and increasingly multiliterate ways of thinking, in order to immerse themselves successfully in formally-constructed knowledge, knowledge which continues to privilege print forms of language. Moreover, while pre-school learners naturally discover the world in multimodal ways, the *balkanization* of school curriculum serves to fracture and isolate approaches to learning (Kalantzis and Cope, 2012).

Under the new knowledge economies however, not only has the conceptualisation of literacy undergone significant evolution, but also how we learn and practise multimodal forms of communication. Multiliteracies call for understandings of complex relationships among visuals, space time and text and interpretations of a range of symbols in critical and culturally appropriate ways. Arguing that we are now experiencing a 'visual turn', Kress (1995) examines the cognitive shift from print to illustrative text. Syntactic demands on print language have lessened as visual material becomes more complex and abstract. While the move away from print has been resisted by traditionalists, Kress sees the increasingly sophisticated emphasis on visual material as creating a rich rescripting of what we mean by 'literacies'.

Given these disparate discursive formations of learning, how is education negotiating the new capacities, forms of knowledge and skills demonstrated by our contemporary learners? The debates around schooling in the digital age are sometimes 'overpowered' in relation to technology's promise, and founded on narrow research questions, argues Selwyn (2011). This has often produced, he maintains, a kind of techno-evangelism which ignores the complexities of social, economic, political and cultural contexts. Notwithstanding the transformative hype, however, the patterns of educational life have been changed by actual and potential uses of ICT.

> Many people would argue that education has proved to be a particularly significant site for the reconfigurative properties of the digital. In particular, many people see the primary concerns of education as resonating especially closely with those of digital technology – ie. the production and dissemination of information and knowledge through communication and interaction with others. (Selwyn, 2011, p. 8)

The theory of multiliteracies (The New London Group, 1996; Cope and Kalantzis, 2000) takes reconceptions about literacies in a technologized, globalised environment and maps them on to more established notions of situated practice. Through building a social-semiotic theory of multimodality, Kress develops the notion of affordances. Crucial to choices individuals make when designing multimodal artefacts are the potential resources available for socially and culturally-shaped uses of different modes. The rules and norms of cyberspace create a different, and distinctive sense of spatial awareness, involving a 'fracturing of space' (Lankshear and Bigum 1999). We can now shift back and forth between different modes of meaning, creating new design patterns. Space is no longer closed and purpose-specific, but 'open, continuous and fluid' (Knobel and Lankshear, 2007: 11).

Kress (2003) calls the ways that we can purposefully mobilize these resources *synaesthesia,* or the remaking of semiotic resources *within* modes (transformation) and *across* modes (transduction). Within each mode exist different systems, or organizing logics which affect the ways that the semiotic elements are integrated, or 'braided' (Mitchell, 1994). While multimodality is not new, through rapidly-changing technologies, we can, and increasingly do, deploy innovative ways to overlay image, word, gesture, image, sound and space. Three dimensional space opens prospects for cognitive reshaping of texts, which have become, Kress (1997) argues, affordances. In this sense, the producer's relationship with the text has become something more generative and creative. The processes which drive this shifting meaning-making create qualitatively new forms from those that have previously existed, pre-internet. Users of formerly static systems have become remakers, or transformers, of representational resources. Potter (2012) argues that the term 'curation' can be appropriated to describe these forms of digital self-representation, capturing not only the idea of writing and creating but adding the acts of collecting, distributing, assembling and disassembling in a digital space.

I sought to understand how pedagogical design could encourage authors – tertiary students in this case – to use digital technologies to represent themselves in new ways. If synaesthesia, or shifting back and forth between modes were evident, how might students conjure and recombine elements from available resources? While students who engage in social media may be experienced 'curators' (Potter, 2012) of their own digital lives, I wanted to bring their practices into the formal learning environment. In this sense, the task was designed as a form of personal rhetorical persuasion aimed at producing a particular set of peer responses and interpretations. Author consciousness through reflection would then link multimodal practices to critical frameworks.

A critical multimodal approach

In exploring whether and to what extent my participants exploited the potential of digital technologies to create innovative, synthesised forms of authorship, related questions emerged. Awareness of communication and representation on the part of the creators is integral to confident literate practice. As a way of heightening media awareness, the written reflections would, I hoped, detail the combinative approaches the authors used, simultaneously developing appreciation of the creative processes involved.

Multimodal texts offer high levels of playfulness and creativity for young people, who are generally expert readers of their complex semiotic worlds (Kress and van Leeuwen, 2001; Johnson-Eilola, 1997). However, while young people make discriminations about and within their chosen texts, they do not always consciously evaluate or articulate the criteria they use (Buckingham, 1994; Doecke and McCleneghan, 1998). Articulating tacit knowledge examines one's own meaning-making processes, and thus self-reflexivity, or a critical knowledge of the constructedness of students' own texts, became integral to the process of writing the technologies. I wanted to investigate how far students' reflections suggested understanding of Green's (1988) critical dimension of literacy. The critical reflections and student use of metalanguage, along with the introductions themselves, contributed to observations I made from the responses.

The digital introductions

This study explored changing forms of textual practice using new technologies and asked how far participation invited a critical awareness of (self)representation. In asking students to create a digital innovation, I also wanted to discover pedagogical resonances, or the 'disruptive' possibilities for re-imagining routinised teaching practices. The small-scale observation was, then, heavily loaded as an exploration of how students used the technologies for rhetorical purposes and the pedagogical potential of the task for more critically reflective professional practice.

Twenty-four education students completed the introductions as part of their English preservice teaching method course. The introductions were prepared as students' first task in the first semester of a year-long course. Students arrived from an undergraduate degree to complete their Diploma of Education unfamiliar with the university, me or their peers.

They developed and presented a 5 minute digital introduction to me, as course lecturer, and their fellow postgraduate teaching method students. The purpose of the elements of the task was to introduce students to a new cohort, extend their current digital knowledge from where it currently stood (Green's 1988 notion of 'operational' literacy) and consider the potential of software choices for their purpose and audience ('cultural' dimensions of literacy). More critically, students were asked to link their self-representation processes to literacy theory from their readings and then to think reflexively on what they had learned (the critical dimension) and the implications that the learning held for their teaching practice.

I sought preservice teachers' permission to use their introductions and reflections for investigation of my research questions. I also invited written responses to a series of questions asked. Extended survey responses were followed up in further directed discussion with nine of the original twenty-four participants, as I sought clarification and elaboration.

From this, I highlighted, grouped and regrouped different patterns of response, complicating and refining themes and categories. Exploring contradictions and assumptions in the writing, I investigated prevailing discourses underpinning contributions, and linked these to ideas emerging from the literature in relation to multimodality and disruption.

Discussion

The preservice teachers' interview data, their reflections and the digital introductions themselves provided a number of valued insights into the research questions.

The introductions ranged in from limited, in terms of exploitation of form, to rich and boundary-pushing. At the limited end, the presentations used the task as a kind of digital scrapbook, posting photos of friends, family and pets, following a chronology from baby to university student, occasionally supported by a favourite music track. The visual and audio resources in these cases mimicked print resources of self-representation; they tended to be linear in structure, relied more strongly on written text and drew upon known conventions such as photo albums.

However, other students consciously wrestled with the 'messiness' of ICT (Bigum, 1995), producing conceptually and visually spectacular introductions. Working at the edge of personal digital expertise, their range of programs included iMovie, Prezi, Xtranormal, Movie Maker, PowerPoint, Google Earth, Animoto, websites and blogs. A number of reflections detailed hours spent on learning new software, time willingly expended in pursuit of a program that would achieve self-representation ends. Music, for example, was often problematic to add to images. Yet, reflections suggest that students read guides, searched Youtube instructions and sought advice in their efforts to have their chosen digital platform achieve the effects they wanted for their intended audience.

In some cases, authors 'bent' genre conventions as they played with identity constructions. This was done from a distanced perspective and, often using knowing humour. Amy, for instance, filmed people talking about her and talking 'as' her – at no point did she ever either appear or reveal anything substantive about herself. Employing documentary and vox pop techniques, Tom edited clips of his family and friends discussing him posthumously, with one brother struggling to remember he had even existed. Another introduction engaged an animation program with computer generated, HAL-type voices, to parody his decision to become a teacher education student. He chose a Napoleonic war scenario to request safe passage to the outer suburb where he would commence his teacher education diploma (http://www.xtranormal.com/watch/12353479/rmit-english-digital-intro-2011).

In terms of 'braiding' elements to create new spaces, a number of students experimented successfully with technological possibilities. Koh from Singapore constructed an on screen digital jigsaw puzzle with his name written in the centre piece. Other digital pieces contained hyperlinked identity features (a Google map link to his street, satay recipes, a trailer to a favourite television series). Clicking and dragging the irregular pieces to the centre piece completed his jigsaw, which formed a map of his home country.

Liam filmed himself in profile, intermittently speaking. He then stood opposite his interactive screen profile and conducted a conversation with himself – a playful, decentred expression of authorial voice.

Google Earth provided a platform for Matt to offer an annotated tour of the history of his relationship and work with a Japanese tent theatre company. He uploaded to Google Earth photographs and notes of events that took place in Tokyo and Melbourne linked to his ongoing collaboration, 'flying' us to Tokyo and pasting theatre photos on relevant points of the map. The blending of literal and figurative modes extended his understanding of communication and representation. No two dimensional form could replicate the geographical space Matt wanted to overlay as an architectural layer to his photographic images.

The level of 'orchestration' (Kress, 2003) in these examples was high, as students borrowed and experimented with combinations. This was not, however, an effortless process, as evidenced by Gert:

> I felt a bit scared as I know my ICT smartness is not exactly fed every day by trying out and using new technologies (but I think it should be, if only to keep up with what some students might know about or like to use.) Also, a sense of playfulness kicked in pretty quickly, connected to the challenge to organize one's life into a 5 minute digital show.

Caroline discussed the semiotic shift to the visual, linking image to authorial voice:

> A very real challenge for me was to 'let the images do the talking'. I observed some of my peers make extensive use of the spoken and written word, which did make me consider how easy it might be to fall into the trap of providing the students with too much of a teacher's voice and not allowing them to develop their own.

Some written reflections alluded directly to the shifting between modes – Kress's 'synaesthesia'. David understood this as a 21st century teaching tool:

> The digitally-based problem solving that the introduction exercise provided was extremely important, as it provided the impetus to think creatively with new media, and to use it as an instrument of alternative pedagogy … Some people see the digital medium as a way of reframing what is … Others seem far more willing to manipulate space, image, sound, and notions of interactivity and clusters of disparate media – and they seem to handle it with far greater success.

What could be seen as surface play is linked by Matt to increased potential for depth of exploration:

> The point is that these technologies are only special in as much as they allow us to see pictures, hear sounds and read text close to instantaneously, and from places that might usually have taken a week to order through libraries. It is this fluency of information flow that allows questions to be researched more deeply.

As well as mixing and blurring genres, students integrated voice, gesture, image, film and animation to engage audience attention. To different degrees, they controlled the 'version' of themselves they revealed through both content choice and the mediation of that content.

Did the presentations and reflections enable awareness of communication and representation processes? Caroline writes 'I had the benefit of watching others' introductions and processing ideas about what I had seen while still structuring my own. I began to reflect even before presenting.'

Linking his introduction to more complex understandings, Matt reflected on the potential of the task to develop critical perspectives:

> The creation of a digital introduction was an interesting process because it forced me to examine perceptions of my own identity. It required that I construct a version of myself and my story for a particular context and audience. Beyond instances of fact, considerations of 'truth' are relatively constructed. Upon reflection I understand, to a greater extent than I did before, the role of my ideological viewpoint in constructing a discourse that is not universally shared. I think this is important for a prospective teacher to understand.

Matt's appreciation of knowledge as contingent is taken further by David, as he articulates the significance of the introductions for reconceptualising pedagogy. David claims:

> The digital introductions were an immediate challenge [digital media being largely dismissed as lacking in academic rigour or pedagogical value]. The digital introductions immediately legitimised digital spaces as valuable and dynamic sites of classroom activity. With the structural and aesthetic possibilities presented by the task, it was remarkable to see the potential of a multiliteracy approach manifesting through my classroom experiments with digital media.

Lankshear and Knobel's 'ethos stuff' (2006) entails a Web 2.0 mindset that is oriented to collaboration and folksonomic, or building knowledge from the ground up. While the notion of 'Web 2.0' itself has been contested (see, for instance, Allen 2012), features of this disposition are alluded to by Kirk:

> Teens today appear to learn far more intuitively and laterally by using forms of ICT, than if they were expected to learn exclusively through methods of rote learning, engagement with paper-based (static) texts, or through physical face-to-face socialisation. As I see it, digital technology actively encourages contemporary learners to explore new ways of visual, auditory, kinaesthetic and metacognitive representation. Learners are provided with a new channel through which to socialise, interact and collaborate, and it constantly changes and regulates itself in response to the collective needs of those who use it. Digital technology invites content creation from its users in such a way that a hierarchical, top-down, unitary or "classical" model of teaching and learning has become increasingly invalid or inapplicable to teenagers' lives.

Not all students reflected in such depth and detail, nor exploited the multimodal affordances of the technology. Some introductions made few connections beyond self-evident statements. It could be argued that the range of artefacts and responses from the students (aged between 22 and 37) complicate any simple notion of 'digital natives' whose learning objects transcended prosaic traditional pedagogies. Moreover, David Buckingham (in Thomas, 2011) asserts that 'most of young people's use of digital technology is mundane rather than spectacular: it is characterised not by dramatic manifestations of innovation and creativity, but by relatively routine forms of communication and information retrieval' (p. x). To encourage new combinations and expression of students' local knowledge, then, the role of the teacher becomes significant.

Conclusion

The creativity of Kress's synaesthetic affordances is thus not inevitably implicated in digital technologies. The inventive play with time and space by students described in this study could have been mediated through other technologies. In this sense, technology works as a language through which pedagogies are explicated. Selwyn (2011: 18) points to Guile's argument that enhanced learning often occurs because teachers have designed innovative contexts and scaffolding to encourage new practices. In this task, there was, a central focus on semiotic communication and representational interrelationships. Moreover, the task design emerged from a belief that critical understanding, rather than encouraged as a theoretical concept, is 'better achieved when students have some grasp of how media texts are actually produced' (Durrant, 2011: 76).

Authors indicated that personal learning in relation to attempting something new and motivated included strategies such as trial and error, collaboration, just-in-time and point-of-need instruction. Some students considered how frequently they had seen such 'bootstrapping' practices (Gee, 1994) in classroom contexts and the implications of such approaches for their own digital pedagogies. Animating new challenges enabled reflexivity in relation to personal framing (Green, 2001) and thus provided agency to think from new positions about 'doing school'. David describes the activity in terms of his own background as a digitally-connected person, and the implications for his own teaching:

> For me, it was a validation of the kind of pedagogy that I wanted to embrace and promote during my career. Technology, gaming, and the Internet have always been passions of mine in everyday life, and throughout my own education I had little – if any – opportunity

to use them as tools of learning. As a preservice teacher, I was expecting to be placed in a relatively powerless situation in which I would be confined to the same forms of print media that I had been given as a student.

The digital introductions were designed to explore identity boundaries through potentially innovative technological spaces. The mode in this case potentially 're-formulated' and expanded communicative possibilities. However, prevailing discourses in schools around generational and technological determinism continue to be interrogated in the literature, as contextual influences influence and limit educational change. It is therefore still in the classroom, perhaps, where the teacher can play with what is possible.

References

Allen, M. (2012). Gaining a past, losing a future : Web 2.0 and internet historicity, *Media international Australia* (143) pp. 99–109.

Bernstein, B. (1999). Vertical and horizontal discourse: An essay *British Journal of Sociology of Education 20*(2), pp. 157–73.

Bigum, C. (1995). Schools and the internet. Reinventing the 1980s? Incorporated Association of Registered Teachers of Victoria (IARTV) Seminar Series, no. 47.

Boler, M. (1999). *Feeling Power: Emotions and Education* New York: Routledge.

Buckingham, D. (2003). *Media Education: Literacy, learning and Contemporary* Culture Cambridge: Polity Press.

Buckingham, D. (1993). *Children Talking Television: The Making of Television Literacy* London: Falmer Press.

Cope, B., and Kalantzis, M. (2000). Multiliteracies: The Beginnings of an Idea. In B. Cope and M. Kalantzis (Eds.), *Multiliteracies: Literacy Learning and the Design of Social Futures.* London: Routledge.

Doecke, B. and McCleneghan, D. (1998). Reconceptualising experience: Growth pedagogy and youth culture. In W. Sawyer, K. Watson and E. Gold (eds) *Re-viewing English* Sydney: Clair Press pp. 46–57.

Durrant, C. (2011). The 3D model and media education in B. Green and C. Beavis (eds) *Literacy in 3D: An integrated perspective in theory and practice* Melbourne: ACER pp. 76–95.

Economist.com 'From literacy to digiracy: Will reading and writing remain important?' http://www.economist.com/science/PrinterFriendly.cfm?story_id=11392128 Retrieved 18th April, 2013.

Gee, J. P. (1994). First language acquisition as a guide for theories of learning and pedagogy, *Linguistics and Education 6* pp. 331–354.

Green, B. (2001). English teaching, 'Literacy' and the Post-Age In C. Durrant and C. Beavis (eds) *P(ICT)ures of English: Teachers, learners and technology* South Australia: AATE.

Green, B. and Bigum, C. (1993). *Aliens in the classroom* in Australian Journal of Education 37(2) pp. 119–134.

Green, B. (1988). Subject-specific literacy and school learning: a focus on writing in *Australian Journal of Education 32*(2) pp. 156–179.

Johnson-Eilola, J. (1997). Living on the surface: Learning in the age of global communication networks. I. Snyder (Ed) *Page to screen: Taking literacy into the electronic era* Sydney: Allen and Unwin (pp. 185–210).

Kalantzis, M. and Cope, B. (2012). *Literacies.* Port Melbourne: Cambridge.

Knobel, M. and Lankshear, C. (2007). *A New Literacies Sampler* http://everydayliteracies.net/files/NewLiteraciesSampler_2007.pdf Retrieved February 16th, 2013.

Kress, G. (2010). *Multimodality: A social-semiotic approach to contemporary communication.* London and New York: Routledge

Kress, G. (2003). *Literacy in the New Media* Age. London: Routledge.

Kress, G. and van Leeuwen, T. (2001). *Multimodal discourse*. London: Edward Arnold.

Kress, G. (1997). Visual and verbal modes of representation on electronically mediated communication: the potentials of new forms of text in I. Snyder (ed) *Page to Screen: Taking literacy into the electronic era* St Leonards Sydney: Allen and Unwin.

Kress, G. (1995). *Literacy or literacies: Thoughts on an agenda for the day after tomorrow* Unpublished paper.

Lankshear, C. (1997). *Changing Literacies.* Buckingham, UK: Open University Press.

Lankshear, C. and Bigum, C. (1999). Literacies and new technologies in school settings. *Pedagogy, Culture and Society* 7(3) pp. 445–465.

Lankshear, C. and Knobel, M. (2006). *New Literacies: Everyday practices in classroom learning*. Berkshire, England: OUP.

Mitchell, W. (1994) *Picture Theory*. Chicago: University of Chicago Press.

Morris, D. (2010). Are teachers technophobes? Investigating professional competency in the use of ICT to support teaching and learning Procedia – *Social and Behavioural Sciences 2*(2), pp. 4010–4015.

Oblinger, D. (2003). *Boomers, gen-Xers and millenials: Understanding the new students* EDUCAUSE Review, 38 (4), 37–47.

Oblinger, D., Martin, R., and Baer L. (2004). *Unlocking the potential of gaming* technology National Learning Infastructure Initiative Annual Meeting, 26th of January 2004. San Diego: CA.

Papert, S. (1992). *The children's machine: Rethinking school in the age of the computer*. NY: Basic Books.

Peel, R., Patterson, A. and Gerlac, J. (2000). *Questions of English: Ethics, aesthetics, rhetoric and the formation of the subject in England, Australia and the United States*. London: Routledge.

Potter, J. (2012). *Digital media and learner identity: the new curatorship*. New York: Palgrave McMillan.

Selwyn, N. (2011). *Schools and schooling in the digital age: A critical analysis*. London and New York: Routledge.

Street, B. (1984). *Literacy in theory and practice*. Cambridge: CUP.

Street, B. (2003). What's 'new' in New Literacy Studies" Critical approaches to literacy in theory and practice *Current Issues in Comparative Ecucation 5*(2) pp. 77–91.

The New London Group (1996) A pedagogy of multiliteracies: Designing social futures *Harvard Education Review 66*, pp. 60–93.

Thomas, M. (Ed.) (2011). *Deconstructing digital natives: Young people, technology and the New Literacies*. NT: Routledge.

Redefining Students' Reflections: Opportunities and Challenges of Video-Enhanced Blogging

Dennis N. York and Ronald D. Owston

Abstract

In the age of Web 2.0 dominance universities are under increasing pressure to investigate the educational applications of user-created content within the traditional culture of knowledge. There is a growing realization in the literature that the incorporation of user-created web video into the curriculum provides a number of pedagogical opportunities for active forms of learning and student-centred teaching practices. Predicated on the precepts of constructivism, this paper aims to explore the pedagogical application of the critical appropriation of user-created web video in a university classroom. Operating in a mixed-method paradigm, the authors analyzed data collected from a non-randomized convenience sample of 17 master's students in education at a regional university in the United States. Evidence suggests that the critical appropriation of web video allowed students to relate new concepts and ideas acquired from the assigned readings to self-selected user-created web video. This study led the authors to conclude that the proposed learning architecture was critical to student's success by creating conditions for them to properly balance user-created web video with scholarly knowledge and to become active participants who are accountable for their learning.

Introduction

In the educational literature examining the adoption of web video, researchers have made a variety of claims regarding the benefits of web video use and production for university education, including the potential for web video to facilitate an understanding of complex concepts (Bonk, 2008; Ghasemi, Hashemi, & Bardine, 2011; Kay, 2012; Trier, 2007), to enable advancement of analysis and reflection (Kong, Shroff, & Hung, 2009; Lazarus & Olivero, 2009; Saljo, 2009), and promote the cultivation of originality and creative multimodal composition (Bishop, 2009; Burke & Snyder, 2008; Godwin-Jones, 2012). Despite these claims, leaders in the field of educational technology continue to call for better management of the application of Web-based technology and its integration into curricula; they also urge educators to revisit their pedagogies and personal philosophies as to the nature of knowledge and the way it is produced and distributed (Bates & Sangra, 2011; Dede, 2008; Jenkins, Clinton, Purushotma, Robinson, & Weigel, 2006).

Contemporary researchers have inquired into the educational benefits of viewing either video lectures or digital video as supplementary learning resources. In most of these studies, researchers have primarily focused on videos produced in proprietary formats, such as lecture capture recorded by or with the help of instructors or enterprise educational videos produced by established media companies (Bassili, 2008; Bracher, Collier, Ottewill, & Shephard, 2005; Copley, 2007; McGarr, 2009; Scutter, Stupans, Sawyer, & King, 2010). Although these video programs demonstrate a high regard for credibility and video quality and are mostly trusted by instructors, their content is often contingent on the knowledge and experience of particular individuals. Similarly, enterprise video programs (which are produced, owned, and controlled by media companies, professional groups, or educational institutions) tend to expose students to video material that represents "filtered" information – sometimes an outdated account of the subject matter studied – and favours one side of the issue (Bracher et al., 2005). Consequently, we would argue that these video formats may isolate students from continually emergent knowledge, provide little or no opportunity for interaction with authentic experiences, and hold them back from taking intellectual risks while constructing knowledge and searching for new meanings. Furthermore, the process of proprietary video production and publishing is expensive and strictly regulated by peer review guidelines, and students' access to the content of such videos is controlled under strict copyright licensing. Much of this research is of somewhat limited use and does not meet the current educational needs of students who are faced with the rapid growth of user-created content (Burgess & Green, 2009) and require a new set of skills to process this information (Jenkins et al., 2006).

Thus, for university instructors and instructional designers, the question is one of how user-created web video, best epitomized by YouTube video, can be integrated into formal curricula so that the value of academic knowledge presented in scholarly publications would not be overshadowed or diminished in university academic culture. Mezirow (1997) suggested that meaningful learning "requires new information to be incorporated by the learner into an already well developed symbolic frame of reference, an active process involving thought, feelings, and disposition" (p. 10). Furthermore, the importance of studying course material in combination with video has been discussed for quite a long time. Sherwood, Kinzer, Hasselbring, and Bransford (1987) suggested that the use of video (in the form of videodiscs) tends to benefit student learning as it provides rich context for their learning, increased comprehension, and maximizes student attention to the topic.

In this paper, we aim to examine the pedagogical application of critical appropriation of existing web video in the form of video-enhanced blogging. Because little research has examined the incorporation of user-created web video as an integral part of academic curricula, it was of particular interest to explore the influences of user-created web video from an empirical basis and thus to provide some evidence to fill the gap in the research literature on web-enhanced learning.

Theoretical framework

The theoretical framework for this research is conceptualized as a confluence of two constructivist theoretical approaches – the theory of situated cognition (Barab & Duffy, 2000; Brown, Collins, & Duguid, 1989; Herrington, Oliver, & Reeves, 2003; Lombardi, 2007) and the theory of distributed cognition (Cole & Engestrom, 1993; Pea, 1997; Salomon, 1994) – which provides clues on how potentially rich learning opportunities of using web video might best be harnessed to foster student-driven meaningful learning and facilitate transformations of learning practice in the context of traditional university instruction.

The situated perspective assumes that information cannot be consumed and converted into knowledge in isolation. The situatedness in rich contexts of authentic practice is required. When learning is embedded in rich situations and social contexts where meanings can be constructed, students pick up both implicit and explicit knowledge (Barab & Duffy, 2000; Brown et al., 1989). Under this framework, the concept of situatedness is fostered by critical appropriation of existing user-created web videos that allows students to observe authentic experiences from multiple perspectives. Video provides much richer specific contexts than general, text-based narratives or verbally mediated ones (Sherwood et al., 1987). There is no need for learners to come out of their putatively "artificial" learning context in order to engage in authentic practice. Video sharing websites and networks are well supplied with "just-in-time" content that can be personalized and delivered to the student immediately.

Furthermore, the idea of appropriation (Francis, 2010) is embedded in the instructional design of the critical appropriation of web video to help students establish synergetic relationships between text- and video-mediated cultures (Sherwood et al., 1987), authoritative and participatory cultures (Jenkins et al., 2006; Mitra, Lewin-Jones, Barrett, & Williamson, 2010), and authentic and formalistic learning (Barab & Roth, 2006; Brown et al., 1989; Herrington et al., 2003). In other words, the learning process is predicated on the coordination of three sources of knowledge: (a) scholarly knowledge (i.e., represented by the instructor's lectures and prescribed course readings); (b) contextual or situated knowledge (i.e., represented by the user-created web video content selected by students on their own); and (c) students' prior knowledge and learning experience. It is our assumption that the critical appropriation of user-created web video content and its combination with other knowledge sources can help students examine the topic presented in the assigned readings and in class lecture, modify their existing knowledge about the topic, and perhaps construct new knowledge and develop new understandings about the topic being studied within the course.

The theory of distributed cognition views the knowledge-building process as an interaction between students and knowledge artefacts. In this study, we view a user-created web video as a designed artefact that carries the intelligence of the author(s) or producer(s) and has the capacity of facilitating deep and reflective understanding. The research project was intended to engage students into active, participatory, and meaningful learning mediated with web video, as well as to provide them with opportunities to situate the course content and to test for their comprehension validity in real-world contextual circumstances with the help of constructive web-enabled peer commentary and classroom discussions in small groups.

Methods

This research was conducted in a graduate-level educational technology course at a public university located in a rural community in the United States. This course was a mandatory degree requirement for the master's programs in teacher education that was intended to give students the foundational skills for integrating educational technology into classroom settings and to help them achieve a greater understanding of the process of technology integration in K-12 educational settings. The research project utilized a case study approach to gain a better understanding of what was happening when students were introduced to video-enhanced blogging. In this mode of inquiry, we combined a quantitative approach with a "less-dominant" qualitative approach (Creswell, 1994; Greene, Caracelli, & Graham, 1989) in order to explore the affordances and challenges of video-enhanced blogging, as well as its impact on perceived learning within the authentic context of an ongoing university course.

During a six week period, 17 participants were engaged in the critical appropriation of web video in the form of video-enhanced blogging. As part of a video-enhanced reflection assignment, students were asked to find an existing web video clip (on video sharing networks, such as YouTube) that was both relevant to the weekly readings and meaningful to them, and to bring the self-selected clip into the reflective discussion of the assigned readings[1]. The intent of video-enhanced reflection was to help students make connections between what they have read and acquired during the lecture, their reflection on the relevant web video they have selected, and their prior knowledge of the subject matter. An example of student's

1 The project curriculum also included an assignment of the creative production of student's own web video in order to enable them to document their thinking in a rich media format that was further streamlined and shared over the Internet. In this paper, the authors sought to address the issue of appropriation of existing user-created video.

video-enhanced blog is given in Appendix A. In addition to blogging, students were asked to provide constructive commentaries to their peers' blogs and engaged in classroom small-group discussions (see Figure 1).

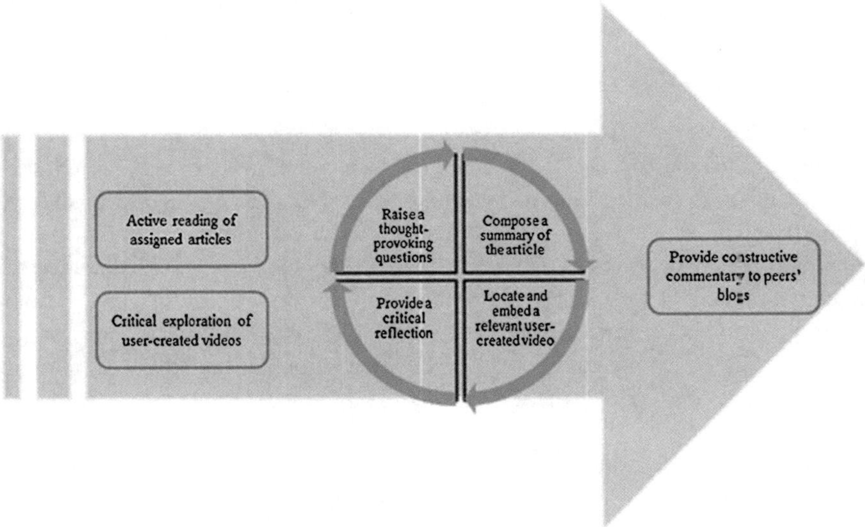

Fig. 1: Learning events of video-enhanced blogging assignment

Multiple sources of evidence were collected: repeated surveys and in-depth interviews. Repeated surveys were administered before, in the middle, and after the implementation of research treatment to measure the effects of video-enhanced blogging on participants' perceptions of user-created web video, its affordances, constraints, and learning value. In-depth interviewing was used to describe and understand events and actions of individual participants. Analysis of data included descriptive and inferential statistical analysis that was complemented with the findings derived from qualitative analysis (such as frequent occurrences of thematic fragments in participants' responses) and illustrative examples of qualitative data).

Results

Demographics

The sample of the case study included 17 participants; seven (41.2%) were male and 10 (58.8%) were female. Half of the sample (52.9%) was under 30 years old; about one third of the participants belonged to a 30 to 45 year-old group; three participants (17.6%) were over 45. The gender and age proportions within the sample concur with the demographic characteristics of a typical class of master's students in education at the participating university. The pretest survey responses showed that the overwhelming majority of the participants were rarely or never engaged in Web 2.0 mediated learning activities as part of formal course curricula.

Perceived affordances of web video for learning

The purpose of the "affordances" section of the survey was to explore the functional significance and distinct attributes of web video for learning, and to measure participants' perceptions of the benefits of web video integration, such as opportunities for content contextualization, opportunities for student-driven learning, and impact on student achievement. The survey results indicated that students perceived web video and blogging as an indispensable Web 2.0 technology combination for learning. A repeated-measures MANOVA revealed the significant effect of the study on students' perceptions of the learning value afforded by the combination of web video and blogging, $V = .49$, $F(2, 13) = 6.01$, $p = .014$.

The rate at which participants reported their positive perceptions of web video attributes was quite high during both pre- and posttest administrations. At the pretest, web video's multimodality (i.e., a capability of digital capturing and sharing, including embedding) was highly valued by the participants (76.5%), followed by its entertainment value (70.6%), and the varying degrees of oversight of content production (52.9%). By the end of the study, these qualities received an overwhelmingly positive feedback from the participants, ranging from 76% to 100%. The results of repeated-measures ANOVA showed that 3 of the 5 "web video attributes" variables were significantly affected by the research treatment. In particular, the Project had significant effects on participants' perceptions of the "entertainment" web video attribute, $F(1, 16) = 8.73$, $MSE = 4.24$, $p = .009$, $\eta = .35$; the "multiple perspectives" attribute, $F(1, 16) = 9.26$, $MSE = 2.38$, $p = .008$, $\eta = .37$; and the "multimodality" attribute, $F(1, 16) = 5.89$, $MSE = 5.89$, $p = .027$, $\eta = .27$.

The results of statistical analysis were supported by students' comments in their personal statements, which emphasized their appreciation for the ways in which web video use could break up the monotony of lectures and capture the attention of both visual and non-visual learners. The statements also reflected positively on students' experience of embedding videos in their blogs to illustrate their thinking. Qualitative data analysis gave evidence of additional valuable attributes of web video for students, such as instant gratification and easy searchability. Furthermore, when comparing web video to earlier video technologies, such as television, DVD, films and the like, participants in interviews identified four attributes differentiating web video from those technologies (see Figure 2). The distinct quality of web video that students noted most frequently was its accessibility (33.3%), meaning that video sharing websites provided easy and immediate access to the required video content. The next unique quality of web video, from students' perspective, was related to customization (25.9%), meaning that video sharing websites allow students to search for web video according to their own individual learning needs. The third most noted quality of web video could be described as content diversity (18.5%), including internal diversity (in terms of content) and the diversity of the form of available videos (i.e., multiple media formats). Finally, the last web video quality most worthy of mention could be defined as multimodality (7.4%), referring to the numerous capabilities for embedding, re-mixing, and managing, and storing video content on the Web.

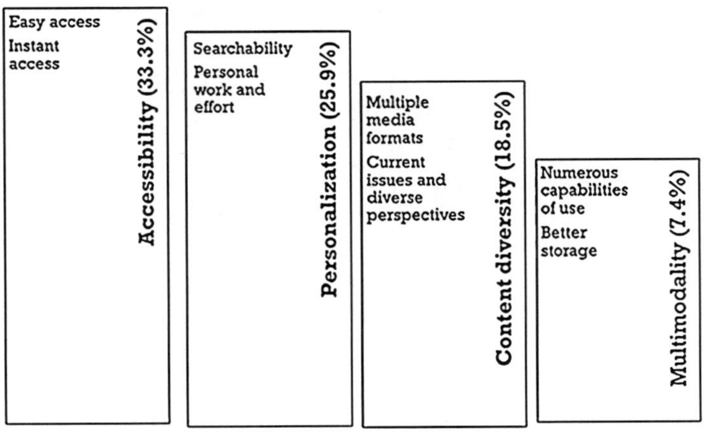

Fig. 2: Percentage of thematic units representing participants' perceptions of distinctive attributes of user-created web video

Perceived constraints of web video for learning

The purpose of the "constraints" survey section was to explore students' anticipated and actual perceptions of web video constraints for learning. A commonly perceived barrier to learning was associated with web video technology constraints. An overwhelming majority of respondents reported concerns about the compatibility of video sharing websites with various types of web browsing software (76.4%), as well as concerns about the bandwidth and internet speed needed to support streaming video experiences (64.7%). Repeated-measures ANOVA on the outcome measures revealed only one significant treatment effect on the perceived lack of ability to download a video clip, $F(1, 16) = 4.81$, $MSE = 4.97$, $p = .043$, $\eta = .23$. These results of statistical analysis were confirmed by qualitative data analysis of participants' written responses, suggesting that technology and website constraints were two of the most frequently cited problems (featured in 30% of thematic units) during the project. Most of the issues were related to incompatibility with web browsers and the time-consuming process of loading web videos to view.

The next group of constraints – the lack of web video searching skills – relates to the difficulties and frustrations perceived by students when navigating video sharing websites in their quest for relevant video clips, as well as the obstacles they encountered when storing and organizing web video content. Nearly 47% of participants anticipated that the lack of web searching strategies could hinder them from managing web videos efficiently. Upon completion of the Project, most students appeared to have developed the navigation and searching skills needed to participate successfully in the project.The results of repeated-measures ANOVA revealed two significant treatment effects on the perceived lack of ability to find a relevant web video, $F(1, 16) = 12.75$, $MSE = 5.77$, $p = .003$, $\eta = .44$, and the perceived lack of ability to store and organize web video efficiently, $F(1, 16) = 5.88$, $MSE = 4.97$, $p = .028$, $\eta = .27$. Qualitative data analysis revealed that students rarely mentioned any frustrations caused by a lack of web video searching skills (featured in 10% of thematic units) during the study. Most of their frustrations came from encountering in their search results a high number of web videos with unnecessary information which required extensive sorting. However, at the post-test, there were no reports of a perceived lack of skills required for effective web video searching.

Another group of constraints is associated with the lack of conceptual understanding of user-created web video and the way it is produced and delivered. Nearly 60% of participants reported difficulty grasping the concept of user-created web video. They communicated their anxieties about the credibility of web video producers or video uploaders (41.2%), and about the accuracy and reliability of web video content (47.1%). The results of repeated-measures ANOVA showed that participants' perceived lack of conceptual understanding of web video was not significantly affected by the project. Qualitative data analysis indicated students' lack of understanding of web video, and demonstrated that most of them were concerned by the quality of web video content since it was produced with minimum content oversight. Furthermore, in their responses participants suggested that skills for assessing the accuracy of web video content should be made mandatory components of university instruction.

Perceived impact of video-enhanced blogging

During the research project, nearly 60% of participants reported that they accessed video sharing websites for browsing and viewing web videos regularly. Almost 30% of the participants searched video sharing websites on a daily basis. Only a few participants (11.76%) visited video sharing websites infrequently. Most of the students (84.6%) self-reported that they predominantly used YouTube for the project, while other video sharing platforms (such as EduTube, MetaCafe, TeacherTube, and Vimeo) were reported only by two most dedicated participants.

The perceived impact of embedding a borrowed web video into a blog was assessed through two survey questions pertaining to: (a) participants' motivations for selecting a web video germane to the discussion of the assigned reading, and (b) their perceptions of the learning benefits of video-enhanced blogging activity. The participants appeared to have a positive response to all of the decisive factors contributing to their web video appropriation task, which entailed locating a user-created web video relevant to the weeks' assigned readings. The results of rank order analysis indicated that most participants (76%) selected an appropriate web video clip that conveyed a sense of real-life situations, had substantial relevance to the week's topic, and spoke to the assigned readings. Qualitative data analysis of interviews gave further support to evidence produced by the posttest survey, which revealed students' selection of web video to be predicated on the video's practical relation to the issues raised in the week's readings.

In the posttest survey, participants were asked whether they agreed or disagreed with a series of statements about the impact of borrowing existing web video on their learning and the development of their understanding of subject matter. The results indicated that over 80% of the participants were quite positive about the value of adding borrowed web video to facilitate their comprehension of the assigned scholarly readings. Among the benefits of the video-enhanced blogging activity, the top three functions of web video appropriation in facilitating learning were revealed: (a) an opportunity to consider issues uncovered in the readings more deeply, (b) an opportunity to make new connections to the assigned readings, and (c) an opportunity to engage in active and thoughtful reading. Data analysis from interviews and personal statements identified three ways in which web video appropriation may have helped students increase their understanding of the underlying complexity of issues or concepts presented in the assigned articles: (a) by stimulating connection-making between textual and visual information; (b) by relating abstract concepts from class readings to practical real-life situations, thereby rendering them concrete, specific, and applicable; and (c) by allowing for the negotiation of multiple perspectives pertaining to the article. Some of the participants' reactions are worth noting in order to illustrate these implications of web video appropriation.

Discussion

The results indicated that students felt comfortable with the idea of documenting their thinking in a rich media format and then broadcasting it in the form of video-enhanced blog postings. In particular, the participants noted that video-enhanced blogging gave them opportunity to relate new concepts and ideas acquired from the assigned readings to self-selected user-created web video, and that they were able to do so in ways that built upon their existing knowledge structures and previous learning experiences. For instance, over 80% of the participants were quite positive about the learning value of adding borrowed web video to facilitate their comprehension of the assigned scholarly readings. The participants identified the following three factors as the most important learning benefits of the video-enhanced blogging activity: (a) an opportunity to consider issues uncovered in the readings on a deeper level; (b) an opportunity to make new connections to the assigned readings; and (c) an opportunity to engage in active and thoughtful reading. In analyzing participants' perceptions about web video affordances for learning, the analysis indicated that the project came very close to meeting the essential characteristics for authentic learning, as described by Herrington et al. (2003). It possessed such qualities as real-world relevance, ill-defined challenges, sustained investigation, the use of multiple sources, multiple perspectives, integrated self-assessment, and confronting the complexities and ambiguities of real-world professional practice.

A major challenge for many students appeared to be the ability to connect knowledge previously acquired from the assigned articles with relevant, self-selected user-created web video in a critical reflection. Failure to locate relevant web video may have been influenced by technology incompatibility, constraints of video sharing websites, and the lack of web video searching skills. The ability to locate and retrieve relevant web video appeared to be affected by the level of video searching skills and the ways in which those skills were acquired in the first place. In other words, students should apply their knowledge and skills to practice in the context, otherwise they will not be able to transfer that knowledge and skills to a new situation or context. When confronting the tasks of appropriating existing web videos and producing one's own web video, students experienced problems related to the technical processes of web video use (e.g., embedding web video into a blog), and to the cognitive processes (e.g., making connections, drawing meaningful conclusions, getting their message across through blogging). In these tasks, students were required not just to complete the assignment on a technical level, but, more importantly, to demonstrate critical reasoning by providing connections to the readings and determining the relevancy of appropriated web video to what was discussed in the readings.

This study reinforces the argument by Sherwood et al. (1987) and Lee (2010), who examined the use of video to facilitate students' comprehension. Sherwood et al. (1987) have concluded that videos provide much richer context and demonstrate particularities better than solely verbal communication, and Lee (2010) argued that pedagogy needs to reduce reliance on textual readings and verbal lectures in order to satisfy a diversity of learning preferences and styles. The study was designed to engage students in the sophisticated integration of web video and blogging technology with more traditional authority-driven textual discourses of knowledge making (in the form of articles); it was also intended to create room for students to direct their own learning. In effect, evidence suggests that the embedding of web video into blogging appears to serve students not just as an illustration of practical examples of how concepts can be applied to real life, but it also gives them additional cognitive opportunity to integrate new knowledge into existing knowledge structures, to place the abstract issues they read about into practical context, and to explore new concepts through applying them in authentic situations as represented in web video fragments. These findings thus suggest that participation in video-enhanced blogging activity enables students not only to contextualize theoretical concepts, but also to apply them convincingly by capitalizing on the "borrowed" web video complementing the scholarly knowledge.

In conclusion, findings from this research are presented as a first step towards understanding the impact that user-created web video has on students' learning when mobilized as an integral part of university curricula. Data analysis confirmed that students felt comfortable and gained knowledge of and skills in applying web video for their learning. Furthermore, students appeared to be enthusiastic about fitting web video into their learning strategies, and were capable of diagnosing the affordances as well as the constraints of integrating web video into their learning while experiencing it firsthand. Although a number of concerns were voiced about the accuracy and reliability of web video content and its appropriation for learning, it is possible to conclude that students eventually may have found benefits of learning with web video, benefits attributable to its distinct properties such as immediate accessibility, customized searchability, multimodal functionality, diversity of perspectives, and instant gratification among others. Despite the challenges and barriers, the opportunities for web video integration are also very clear. In particular, this investigation has provided evidence that web video is largely supported by students and perceived as a catalyst for facilitating learning by enabling students to engage in authentic activities, explore alternative aspects of the subject matter, and exercise critical evaluation of different knowledge sources and multiple opinions.

References

Barab, S. A., & Duffy, T. M. (2000). From practice fields to communities of practice. In D. H. Jonassen & S. M. Land (Eds.), *Theoretical foundations of learning environments* (pp. 25–56). Mahwah, NJ: Lawrence Erlbaum.

Barab, S. A., & Roth, W.-M. (2006). Curriculum-based ecosystems: Supporting knowing from an ecological perspective. *Educational Researcher, 35*(5), 3–13. doi:10.3102/0013189X035005003.

Bassili, J. N. (2008). Media richness and social norms in the choice to attend lectures or to watch them online. *Journal of Educational Multimedia and Hypermedia, 17*(4), 453–475. Retrieved from http://www.editlib.org/p/25218.

Bates, A. W., & Sangra, A. (2011). *Managing technology in higher education: Strategies for transforming teaching and learning*. San Francisco, CA: John Wiley & Sons.

Bishop, J. (2009). Pre-service teacher discourses: Authoring selves through multimodal compositions. *Digital Culture & Education, 1*(1), 31–50.

Bonk, C. J. (2008, March). *YouTube anchors and enders: The use of shared online video content as a macrocontext for learning.* Paper presented at the American Educational Research Association 2008 Annual Meeting, New York, NY. Retrieved from http://www.publicationshare.com/SFX7EED.pdf.

Bracher, M., Collier, R., Ottewill, R., & Shephard, K. (2005). Accessing and engaging with video streams for educational purposes: Experiences, issues and concerns. *ALT-J, Research in Learning Technology, 13*(2), 139–150. doi:10.1080/0968776050010416l.

Brown, J. S., Collins, A., & Duguid, P. (1989). Situated cognition and the culture of learning. *Educational Researcher, 18*(1), 32–42.

Burgess, J., & Green, J. (2009). *YouTube: Online video and participatory culture.* Malden, MA: Polity.

Burke, S. C., & Snyder, S. L. (2008). YouTube: An innovative learning resource for college health education courses. *International Electronic Journal of Health Education, 11*, 39–46.

Cole, M., & Engestrom, Y. (1993). A cultural-historical approach to distributed cognition. In G. Salomon (Ed.), *Distributed cognitions: Psychological and educational considerations* (pp. 1–46). Cambridge, England: Cambridge University.

Copley, J. (2007). Audio and video podcasts of lectures for campus-based students: Production and evaluation of student use. *Innovations in Education and Teaching International, 44*(4), 387–399. doi:10.1080/14703290701602805.

Creswell, J. W. (1994). *Research design: Qualitative & quantitative approaches.* Thousand Oaks, CA: Sage.

Dede, C. (2008, May/June). A seismic shift in epistemology. *Educause Review*, 80–81. Retrieved from http://net.educause.edu/ir/library/pdf/ERM0837.pdf.

Francis, R. (2010). *The decentring of the traditional university: The future of (self) education in virtually figured worlds.* London, England: Routledge.

Ghasemi, B., Hashemi, M., & Bardine, S. H. (2011). UTube and language learning. *Procedia – Social and Behavioral Sciences, 28*, 63–67. doi:10.1016/j.sbspro.2011.11.013.

Godwin-Jones, R. (2012). Digital video revisited: Storytelling, conferencing, remixing. *Language Learning & Technology, 16*(1), 1–9. Retrieved from http://llt.msu.edu/issues/february2012/emerging.pdf.

Greene, J. C., Caracelli, V. J., & Graham, W. F. (1989). Toward a conceptual framework for mixed-method evaluation designs. *Educational Evaluation and Policy Analysis, 11*(3), 255–274. doi:10.3102/01623737011003255.

Herrington, J., Oliver, R., & Reeves, T. C. (2003). Patterns of engagement in authentic online learning environments. *Australian Journal of Educational Technology, 19*(1) 59–71. Retrieved from http://www.ascilite.org.au/ajet/ajet19/herrington.html.

Jenkins, H., with Clinton, K., Purushotma, R., Robinson, A. J., & Weigel, M. (2006, October 19). *Confronting the challenges of participatory culture: Media education for the 21st century* (White paper).Cambridge, MA: MIT. Retrieved from http://www.macfound.org/press/publications/white-paper-confronting-the-challenges-of-participatory-culture-media-education-for-the-21st-century-by-henry-jenkins/.

Kay, R. H. (2012). Exploring the use of video podcasts in education: A comprehensive review of the literature. *Computers in Human Behavior, 28*(3), 820–831. doi:10.1016/j.chb.2012.01.011.

Kong, S. C., Shroff, R. H., & Hung, H. K. (2009). A web enabled video system for self-reflection by student teachers using a guiding framework. *Australasian Journal of Educational Technology, 25*(4), 544–558. Retrieved from http://ascilite.org.au/ajet/ajet25/kong.html.

Lazarus, E., & Olivero, F. (2009). Videopapers as a tool for reflection on practice in initial teacher education. *Technology, Pedagogy and Education, 18*(3), 255–267. doi:10.1080/14759390903255528.

Lee, G. (2010). *SecondLife as an educational platform for collaborative learning by the millennial generation at a laptop university* (Doctoral dissertation). Retrieved from ProQuest Dissertations and Theses (UMI No. 3426227).

Lombardi, M. M. (2007). *Approaches that work: How authentic learning is transforming higher education (ELI Paper No. 5)*. Retrieved from Educause Learning Initiative website: http://net.educause.edu/ir/library/pdf/ELI3013.pdf.

McGarr, O. (2009). A review of podcasting in higher education: Its influence on the traditional lecture. *Australasian Journal of Educational Technology, 25*(3), 309–321. Retrieved from http://www.ascilite.org.au/ajet/ajet25/mcgarr.html.

Mezirow, J. (1997). Transformative learning: Theory to practice. *New Directions for Adult and Continuing Education 74*, 5–12. doi:10.1002/ace.7401.

Mitra, B., Lewin-Jones, J., Barrett, H., & Williamson, S. (2010). The use of video to enable deep learning. *Research in Post-Compulsory Education, 15*(4), 405–414. doi:10.1080/13596748.2010.526802.

Pea, R. D. (1997). Practices of distributed intelligence and designs for education. In G. Salomon (Ed.), *Distributed cognitions: Psychological and educational considerations* (pp. 47–87). Cambridge, England: Cambridge University.

Saljo, R. (2009) Videopapers and the emergence of analytical perspectives on teaching practices. *Technology, Pedagogy and Education, 18*(3), 315–323. doi:10.1080/14759390903255593.

Salomon, G. (1994). No distribution without individuals' cognition: A dynamic interactional view. In *Distributed cognitions: Psychological and educational considerations* (pp. 111–138). Cambridge, England: Cambridge University.

Scutter, S., Stupans, I., Sawyer, T., & King, S. (2010). How do students use podcasts to support learning? *Australasian Journal of Educational Technology, 26*(2), 180–191. Retrieved from http://ascilite.org.au/ajet/ajet26/scutter.html.

Sherwood, R. D., Kinzer, C. K., Hasselbring, T. S., & Bransford, J. D. (1987). Macro-contexts for learning: Initial findings and issues. *Applied Cognitive Psychology, 1*(2), 93–108. doi:10.1002/acp.2350010203.

Trier, J. (2007). Cool engagements with YouTube. *Journal of Adolescent & Adult Literacy, 50*(5), 408–412. doi:10.1598/JAAL.50.5.7.

Appendix A: Screenshot of Participant's Video-Enhanced Blog Posting

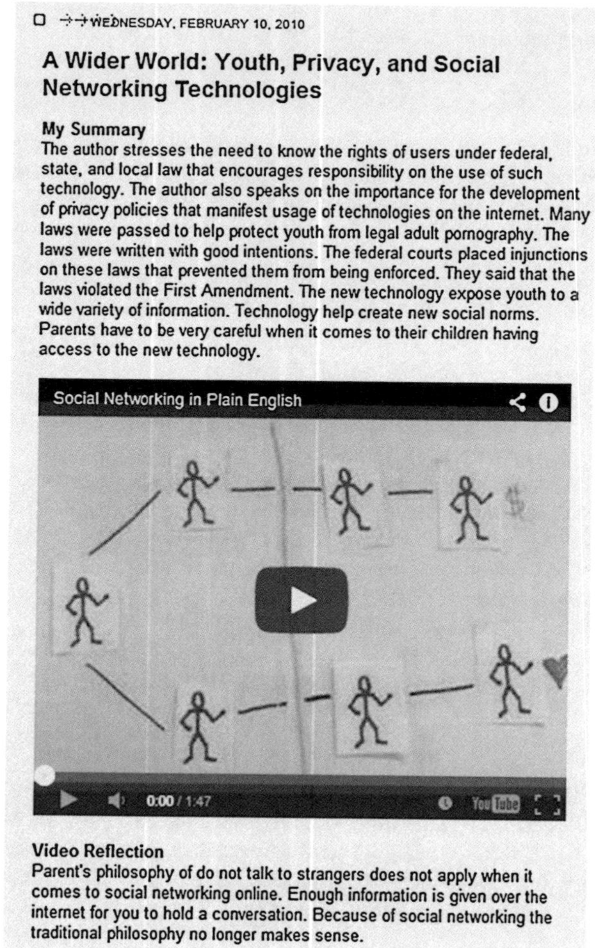

WEDNESDAY, FEBRUARY 10, 2010

A Wider World: Youth, Privacy, and Social Networking Technologies

My Summary

The author stresses the need to know the rights of users under federal, state, and local law that encourages responsibility on the use of such technology. The author also speaks on the importance for the development of privacy policies that manifest usage of technologies on the internet. Many laws were passed to help protect youth from legal adult pornography. The laws were written with good intentions. The federal courts placed injunctions on these laws that prevented them from being enforced. They said that the laws violated the First Amendment. The new technology expose youth to a wide variety of information. Technology help create new social norms. Parents have to be very careful when it comes to their children having access to the new technology.

Video Reflection

Parent's philosophy of do not talk to strangers does not apply when it comes to social networking online. Enough information is given over the internet for you to hold a conversation. Because of social networking the traditional philosophy no longer makes sense.

Emancipative Technology in Formal Education: The Case for "Free and Open Source Software (FOSS)"

Gloria Gómez-Diago

Abstract

In a world where the widespread use of the Internet offers to many citizens the technological opportunity to actively participate in the creation of Cyber culture, downloading and using applications and software for different purposes, the use of privative software in formal education has no sense because it imposes unnecessary barriers and constraints on learning practices and the freedom of students. Based on the results of a pilot study, in this chapter I argue for the importance of Free and Open-Source Software (FOSS) as a suitable alternative model to foster innovative learning, democratic education and ultimately an emancipative pedagogy.

Introduction

Discussing research in education technology, Selwyn and Facer (2013) argue for the need of a critical perspective capable of going beyond the mere description of "best practices" or the documentation of lived digital cultures as cultural studies offer. Going further is possible by evaluating and analyzing, instead of just describing or reciting.

In this chapter, and in an effort to take this suggestion seriously, I discuss the main problems associated with the use of privative software in formal education from a communicative perspective. In my approach, the unit of analysis is not the single user but the context of interaction and the outcomes resulting from it (Gómez-Diago, 2013a). As Lievrouw observes (2011), a 'contextual' approach is very needed not just in technology and education research but also in media research. In this way, people's engagement with media can be conceptualized in terms of expression, organization, relations, and interaction rather than reception and consumption, as is usually the case. My main argument is that, in formal education, Free and Open-Source Software (FOSS) must replace commercial software, which I refer to here as 'privative' software because its use deprives users the right to see and to modify its source code, the right to install it in various devices or the right to distribute it. If users cannot control their programs, then it is the program and its manufacturer that control its users – which is the case when using privative software. The chapter describes the main advantages of the former and the disadvantages of the latter as experienced in educational practices in formal education. This study provides a framework for further research which can be oriented, for example, on identifying and evaluating Free and Open-Source Software (FOSS) to achieve different purposes in formal education.

My concern about the detrimental effects of the use of privative software in formal education began in 2011, when I was asked to teach the use of a privative software for vector graphic design to third-year students of Advertising and Public Relations at the University of Vigo in Spain. Since the price of this software was more than EUR 400 and well beyond the budget of most our students, I suggested teaching an open-source software for graphic vectorial design capable of performing the same operations as the privative software. The suggestion was rejected despite the fact that the professor responsible for the course agreed with me on the benefits of the alternative I suggested. Therefore I had to teach students to use the privative software. Unfortunately, however, because the price of this software is pretty high, the university did not have a legal version of this software for teachers, and students could not install it on their personal computers in order to familiarize themselves with its use in their spare time. This fact alone, the confinement of the learning experience, within the temporal and spatial boundaries of formal education, made the learning curve quite steep and difficult to tackle, and consequently the use of this software became a source of anxiety.

The difficulties and complications I encountered in teaching the software to the students inspired a pilot study (Gómez-Diago, 2013) based on an action research framework. The goal of the study was to identify the problems associated with the use of privative software in formal education and to help pupils address them. Action research in the classroom seemed a suitable approach because it allows the teacher to detect the problems connected with a given pedagogical model, to test the effect of alternative models on class dynamics, and to introduce and experiment with new didactical tools, etc. Teachers who conduct "action research" in the classroom have to critically evaluate their didactical methods and their perspectives in an effort to gain a deeper access to students, their experiences, their views and assessment of learning. As Sagor pointed out (2009: 10), by engaging in 'action research,' teachers subscribe to a professional ethic that 'requires the professional educator to continuously ask, "How can my work be modified to produce better results"? Persisting with practices that do not succeed is the antithesis of professionalism.

For three months, I collected impressions in the classroom through direct observation and interaction with 41students who were divided into two groups which received 12 hours of instruction in privative software. To give stronger grounds to my first impressions of the nature and roots of the problems we encountered in the training programme, I designed an open and anonymous questionnaire to facilitate reflection and creative thinking (O 'Cathain & J. Thomas, 2004). Fourteen students answered the questions about their relation with the software, and the type of knowledge they had acquired after the instruction.

My pilot study confirmed my concerns. The use of privative software in formal education limits students' knowledge of computers, limits the learning environment to the classroom, and limits the types of skills gained by the students. A more detailed discussion of that study is available (Gómez-Diago, 2013a) Below I present a commentary on the opportunities for learning and innovation associated with the use of open-source software in education.

The privative software model: dependency, piracy and professional ignorance

The dependency of students on privative software they have been trained to use in the years of their education continues during their professional life, sometimes even when they are unable or unwilling to pay for it. According to Software Alliance, the software piracy rate in the world is 42%. On their website, this organization encourages users to denounce enterprises which use pirate software so they can punish them with economic sanctions. Those most directly concerned by the commercial damage of these 'pirates' however, have good reasons to be more flexible.

By enforcing the learning of privative software, educational institutions contribute to the "tolerance piracy strategy" (Heger, 2009), a strategy that Bill Gates admittedly used in his company in order to avoid pushing the users towards free software (Chopra, 2011). This 'strategy' effectively construes illegality as a better alternative to 'choice'. In this strategy, for example, the widespread use of pirate software among small business is preferable to the enforcement of actions that may increase the popularity, diffusion and ultimately the competitiveness of alternative software.

The research conducted by Llyas (2008) about the Maldives suggests that the facility of access to pirated software there prevents people from using free software. In 2008, this country had no copyright law and this encouraged many software vendors to sell pirated versions of famous commercial software and many government offices to use pirated software. The use of Linux was very rare and pirate software so easily accessible that the emergence of a local community of software developers or locally customized software was effectively inhibited.

Chopra and Dexter (2011: 175–176) point out that exorbitant prices of much proprietary software do not necessarily restrict access to the software because copyright infringement of software is common and tolerated. From the perspective of an information justice, what is most troubling is the users' dependency on the vendor proprietary software promoted by licensing terms. These authors describe what happened to the Philadelphia public school system in 2011 when Microsoft threatened legal action against the practice of installing Microsoft products on more computers than the licensing terms allowed. Under a Free and or Open Source Licence, the Philadelphia school system could have acquired the software freely and made unconstrained decisions about its use, installation and customization but also about whether it would support this software by purchasing service and support from competing outside vendors or by hiring and training IT staff to service and improve the software for the entire system.

The use of technology must be seen as a deeply social and political matter (Selwyn, 1998), because technology is far more complex than being "simply a tool" and it does not exist as a neutral or value-free assumption – "a wrong idea typically associated with commonsensical perceptions of technology" (Ferneding 2007: 1332). Students, professors and teachers are becoming 'workers' for privative software companies while at the same they are being expropriated of the results of their 'work'. In fact, when they use any such products, they are unavoidably involved in the process of testing by using and commenting on it, hence contributing to the search for solutions to its problems and to the development of the software itself (Soler 2008: 15).

If to witness the adaptation of curricula to the learning of privative software may be upsetting, even worse is to see instances of social research which justifies its scientific character based on the use of privative software that in many cases has unaffordable prices and is accessible to just a few. In these instances, when research institutions are linking research and the use of privative software, the message they are sending is more about marketing than about knowledge, and more about exclusion than inclusion: scientific research can be done just by the few who can afford the purchase of that software. Instead of citing privative software as a way of giving authority to their research, researchers, departments and universities in general should be more interested in designing software, tools, devices and procedures which allow citizens to do things that would be more difficult to do without them.

Rushkoff (2010: 130–133) argues that America is falling behind most developed and many developing nations in computer education because most public schools do not teach programming. Kids learn how to use popular spreadsheet, word processing, and browsing software so that they can operate effectively in the high-tech workplace. But these basic skills will not help them adapt to the technologies of tomorrow. By contrast, kids in other countries – from China to Iran – are not wasting their time learning how to use off-the shelf commercial software packages; they are finding out how computers work. According to Rushkoff, programming is the sweet spot, the high leverage point in a digital society. If we do not learn to program, we risk being programmed ourselves.

Computer techniques have profound effects on all aspects of the disciplines they are applied to (Berry, 2011: 8). We can think, for example, about visual artistic creation, visualization of data or even literary creation, with the emergence of new literary forms based on hypertext possibilities.

All disciplines are being modified by the use of technology, and this is because their practitioners, that is the persons who construct disciplines, have access to technological devices, tools, and platforms that allow them to achieve actions which before were not possible or, at least, were too difficult to achieve. The Internet has carried the most important changes in how disciplines and formal education are built. Thanks to the possibility of being in touch with people who are geographically distanced, collaborative creation can be achieved with ease.

In an emancipative perspective, and in a way compatible with democratic ideology, formal education must be understood as a context of freedom where students are motivated to create and to access knowledge. If we constrain the abilities of students to using privative software, we are in fact prioritizing the promotion of that software over the development of the students' skills. It is fundamental to be educated in a context where we can understand the software as an environment whereby we can achieve a diversity of goals by being aware of the multitude of software available, and of the differences between them. All educational activities – at school and elsewhere – influence the future of society through what they teach. So schools should teach exclusively free software, to transmit democratic values and the habit of helping other people – not to mention a future generation of programmers to master the craft! To ground education on privative software means to foster the dependence of the educated on the owner of this software, a practice that contradicts the democratic mission of public education (Lee, 2013). Introducing students to the use of free and open-source software will make them understand how culture and technology are linked, and how they can contribute to the development of both. As Lévy pointed out (2000: 5), the relationship between a technology (part of the cause) and a culture (which would undergo its effects) is not a direct one. Between the two there is a multitude of human agents who variously invent, produce, use and interpret technologies. When colleges and universities move to a Linux standard for academic computing, they become full participants in a growing movement to use open-source software as a means of achieving social justice worldwide. They become engines of open-source software development – and the results could make a genuine difference in helping to formulate effective remedies for the international inequalities in access to information technology (Pfaffenberger, 2000).

The use of privative software in formal education generates serious problems that, in turn, greatly affect the contexts of interaction in the classroom and beyond. Firstly, privative software is expensive and usually it can only be installed on one computer because what we buy is not the software but a licence. This licence, 'furthermore is a 'closed' one: it does not allow the user to access the source code of the software itself. The developer of privative software hides the functionality of the software by distributing digital objects whose underlying design is opaque to their users (Lessing 2006: 54).

When the code cannot be accessed, transformed, or updated, etc., users have a relation of dependency with the manufactures. Until the manufacturer releases updates of the software, users cannot utilize it in ways other than the ones for which it was created. If the discussion about the importance of creativity and innovation in education is taken seriously, how can anyone believe that both those skills can be effectively developed if students (and teachers!) have to comply with software limitations dictated not by the affordances of technology itself but by the commercial interests of the company that manufactures the software?

As Rushkoft notes (2010), digital technology is a form of technology that depends on programming and on programming skills. In a digital age, emancipative learning requires learning how to *make* – rather than merely *use* – the software. The risk, otherwise, is that of *becoming* the software. It is not too difficult or too late to learn the code behind the things we use – or at least to understand that there is a code behind their interfaces. Otherwise, we are at the mercy of those who do the programming, the people paying them, or even the technology itself.

In this perspective, the popularity of privative software is unmotivated and its influence on curricula detrimental. If the goals of education are interpreted within an emancipative pedagogy, it is not reasonable to constraint the work, the progress and the knowledge of students through the use and dependency of privative software. The core of this type of software is fundamentally at odds with the values on which scientific practices and excellence are supposed to be based.

These programs are designed according to what Raymond (1998) defines as the 'cathedral-builder view' of programming. In this methodology, bugs and development problems are tricky, insidious and deep phenomena. It takes months of scrutiny by a dedicated few to develop confidence that you have winkled them all out. This leads to long release intervals and the inevitable disappointment when long-awaited releases are not perfect. By contrast, open-source software is created through the collective effort of different people and all the improvements, changes and corrections are done quickly because the source code is available and public.

Raymond (1998) defines this style as 'bazaar view' and explains that this working methodology assumes that bugs are generally shallow phenomena – or, at least, that they turn shallow pretty quickly when exposed to the expert attention of a thousand eager co-developers, pounding on every single new release. Through this method, new releases are issued often in order to get more corrections, and as a beneficial side effect one has less to lose if an occasional botch gets out the door.

Cyberspace, cyberculture and the challenge of innovation

According to Internet Usage Statistics, by June, 30, 2012, there were 1,405,518,376 Internet users in a world which has a population of 7,017,846,922 – or an equivalent of 34.3%. The growth in the number of Internet users from 2000 to 2012 was 566.4%.

The communicative possibilities of the Internet affects the interactivity of new media, which as Schulzt notes (2004: 10), turns recipients into communicators, allowing them to establish and to maintain networks for different purposes. Taking into account that clear socio-economic differences exist in individuals' predilection to produce rather than consume online content (Lewthwaite, 2011), and agreeing with Selwyn (2012) when he points out that it is idealistic to imagine social media as providing a level playing field for all, it is evident that thanks to the widespread use of the Internet throughout the world, the creative production made by individuals is more visible and has more possibilities to be recognized and incorporated into the industry.

New media technology is evolving rapidly, new media applications are proliferating and creative possibilities are multiplying. In the digital age, users' network-building capacity supports the social capital that Putnam (2000) described in terms of connections among individuals, social networks and norms of reciprocity and trustworthiness (see the chapter by Melissa Harness &Sultana A. Shabazz in this volume). Hughes (2000: 294) cites a definition of learning coined by Wenger (1998) in which learning is understood as mutual engagement with others and participation in communities of practice which have a common enterprise or purpose and negotiate their own meanings and repertories. He argues that taking part in a learning community of practice involves identity transformation when members move from peripheral to full membership of the community. He illustrates that idea by explaining that a student does not learn physics (except perhaps by rote) but learns to think and to act like a physicist by engaging with a community of physicists: experts (through their texts), teachers and other physics students.

Innovation must be an objective not just for the enterprises but also for universities. The International Principles on the Application of Human Rights to Communications Surveillance (July 2013) acknowledge the role of formal education in innovation. Universities, in particular, are called upon to shape digital models of scholarly discourse for the newly emergent public spheres of the present era to model excellence and innovation in these domains, and to facilitate the formation of networks of knowledge production, exchange, and dissemination that are at once global and local. But innovation requires a space where active learning is possible and where students are not treated as passive receptors of information: not as mere users or 'consumers' of software but as agents who work in environments which are open to be used, modified, adapted and improved.

Free software movement exemplifies a form of organization of production and distribution within a knowledge economy based on common property, on innovation through open collaboration with the creators and on the private appropriation and commercial use of applications and products resulting from software development connected to this form. The point is not to abolish private property, but the privileges that block innovation and the distribution of wealth across mankind (Castells, 2005).

Non-privative software models and innovation

The approach to software development that generates free and open-source software is based on a non-privative model. The acronym FLOSS (Free Libre and Open Source) embraces both types of software and it is used to designate the outcome of motivated teamwork: the results of specialist work by many individuals, sharing an interest in a common project, for a variety of motivations, but without any single person or entity having the possibility to assert any right to exclude others from the outcome of the project or parts of it (Benkler, 2006: 6).

The social experience and practice of open source software projects teach us that users can create, produce, diffuse, provide user field support, update, and use complex products by and for themselves in the context of user innovation communities (Hippel, 2005). For authors such as O' Reilly, it is useful to see open source as an expression of three deep, long-term trends: the commoditization of software, network-enabled collaboration, and software customizability (software as a service). Free software is responsible for some of the most basic and widely used innovations and utilities on the Internet today (Benkler, 2006: 438).

By publishing software along with its source code, open-source developers establish a mutually encouraging network to correct each other's mistakes, and improve each other's work. Rather than competing they collaborate, and they do not hide the way their programs work. As a result, everyone is invited to change the underlying code and the software can evolve with the benefit of a multiplicity of points of view (Rushkoff 2003: 56).

eProperty in open source is configured fundamentally around the right to distribute, not the right to exclude (Weber 2004: 1–3). The practice of granting extensive rights to users through licensing dates back to the free-software movement that Richard Stallman launched in the early 1980s called Free Software Foundation to counter the trend toward proprietary development of software packages and the release of software without source code. Then, in 1998, several prominent computer hackers, including Bruce Perens and Eric Raymond, launched the Open Source Initiative. The social anthropologist of technology, Bryan Pfaffenberger (2000: 114) distinguishes the Open Source Movement from Free Software Foundation primarily on philosophical grounds. According to Pfaffenberger, the participants of the Open Source Initiative prefer to emphasize the practical benefits of its licensing practices, while the members of the Free Software Movement are more inclined to emphasize the moral importance of granting users the freedoms offered by both free and open-source software.

The main difference between the Open Source Initiative and Free Source Foundation resides in the type of conditions they impose for regulating the use of the software. Free Software advocates the unrestricted attribution of rights to the users. Its licences are designed to rule out the possibility that one software licensed as free software can be studied and used to develop privative software. The point of this is to make sure that anyone using the work of the community also contributes to developing improvements and additions that reach back to the community (Rajani, 2003: 25–26). By contrast, in the Open Source model, licences may allow users to study and use the code of given software to develop privative software.

Both models, however, clearly state the importance of making the source code available for study and use. Stallman explains that 'free' refers to the possibilities or to the actions which are available to users with this software: 1 the freedom to run the program for any purpose; 2. the freedom to study how the program works, and change it to do what you wish; 3.the freedom to redistribute copies to help your neighbour, and 4. the freedom to distribute copies of your modified versions to others. As Suber states (2012), while the notion of 'gratis' is used to mean the removal of price barriers alone, the notion of 'libre' designates both the removal of price barriers and of permission barriers.

The current open-source development model is rooted in the academic computer science of a decade or more ago. What makes open source dramatically more successful today, however, is the growth in the volumes and speed of circulating information made possible by the Internet. Open source has been born into a digital renaissance made possible by the Internet, just as modern service was made possible during the Renaissance by the invention of the printing press (Dibona, 1999). The Internet amplifies the possibilities for communicating, for creating and for sharing knowledge. Contrary to how the mass media work, the Internet is the first modern communication medium that expands its reach by decentralizing the capital structure of information, culture and knowledge (Benkler 2004: 30).

Depending on the objective, it could be useful having students working with social media. The knowledge tools that encourage and create social networks are fostered by professors of communication who encourage students to manage them and also to maintain their profile. Accordingly to Lanier (2010), however, sites such as Facebook originate standardized presences and anonymized fragments of creativity as products that might have fallen from the sky or been dug up from the ground, obscuring the true sources. To address this limitation and the important problem connected to it, teachers could familiarize their students with open source social media such as idiaspora, n-1, friendica, thimbl, identi.ca or kune. By inviting students to study and more extensively engage with these open tools, teachers will help them to understand their design more critically, and to see how, for example, the interface design of social media has an influence on the type of discourse generated by the users.

Users or used? Software and emancipation

Despite all the advantages that Internet brings to their users, sentences such as "The Internet as we know it today is dominated not by business but by users whose free communication prevails in cyberspace" (Feenberg, 2012: 12) are not close to reality.

In 2013, for the first time, Internet surveillance has become a major concern for citizens around the world. The Snowden documents show that the NSA (National Security Agency) runs surveillance programs through partnerships with major US telecom and Internet companies. Some of these relationships go back decades, others are more recent, established notably in the wake of the attacks of 9/11.The division inside the NSA that deals with collection programs that focus on private companies is Special Source Operations. According to the Guardian, the biggest single contributor to NSA's intelligence reports is PRISM, a "downstream" program – which means the agency collects the data from Google, Facebook, Apple, Yahoo and other US Internet corporate giants. While the Guardian claims that NSA has direct access to their servers, the companies involved have hotly disputed this claim, arguing instead that they only comply with lawful requests for user data.

Media educator and activist Dan Guillmor (2013) expresses his concern about the fact we have become so accustomed, even addicted, to the easy-to-use convenience of Google and its peers that not enough of us will opt for genuine safety. He wishes that the marketplace would come up with more products and services that are easy to use, robust in function and designed for security from the ground. Media scholar Rushkoff (2010: 137) explains what is behind the easy-to-use convenience of most of the software and applications. The user-friendly interfaces hide an effort to make people dependent on the features provided by the software and to increase the distance between programmers and users. He compares the interactivity exercised by users who build a profile on a social networking site with the interactivity exercised by a person who sends a text message to a TV talent show, telling them which of their ten contestants she thinks sings the best. In both cases the ways in which we are allowed to interact have been programmed for us in advance.

Free and open-source software is not always user friendly and it is not always secure. However when it is developed in the 'open', with open bug trackers, open mailing lists, open governing structures, and open-source code, it is much more difficult for these projects to have a policy of betraying their users like Microsoft has (Lee, 2013). Berry (2011: 6) discusses the importance of the code for digital humanities arguing that its understanding is fundamental to approach the cultural production more deeply because computation is the key issue underlying the changes across media industries and economies. Considering that technologies and networks have the potential to reshape our economy, our ecology, and our society more profoundly and intentionally than ever before in our collective history (Rushkoff, 2010: 143), it seems wiser to get involved in this development.

The more people become involved in the design of commonly used software, the more these tools will end up being people-inspired.

Conclusion

There is no reason to continue using privative software in the academic context. Utilizing this software in formal learning generates contexts of interaction where users become slaves of the programs, firstly in the classroom, then in the workplace, and globally in our private context, where we innocently use tools that are actually using us.

In communication studies the existence of courses aimed to encourage students to create profiles on popular social networks are common. Opening a profile on social networks requires no instruction because the interfaces are designed so that there is no room for doubt. What is needed is to train students to carry the design of new devices and tools intended to satisfy different necessities, among them, the need to protect ourselves from the surveillance exercised by those using the 'back doors' and/or windows included in proprietary software.

The ideal of a society based on innovation requires schools and universities to teach innovation. But this cannot be done if the learning environment and the educational context are those shaped by the influence of privative software. Formal education should not become the place for the promotion of the closed tools created by companies which ask for a lot of money in exchange for licences full of prohibitions. An innovation-prone educational context must enable students to acquire knowledge and interest in designing their own tools and maintaining their security. If formal education is not used to motivate students to manage the source code of software, the companies who program will control all that we do, designing our contexts of interaction and having access to our privacy.

It is not by chance that Linux has no viruses. By contrast, when using other operating systems we must rely on powerful antiviruses which slow down our computer. For that reason it is not surprising that The United Space Alliance has switched from the Windows XP computers aboard the International Space Station to Linux, arguing reasons based on the need of having an operating system that was stable and reliable.

It is time that educational institutions switch to open-source and free software. This change must be made at all the levels of the institutions and especially in the classrooms and in the curricula because the students will build and contribute to the development of the Internet environment where we spend more and more of our time. This global system of networks can be used to progress, to be freer and for being more united and safer. But to be part of it without constraints, code must be accessible in educational contexts.

References

Baab, P. (2013). Video: Orwell's '1984' has nothing on the current surveillance state. November 5, 2013. Infoworld. Technology video worth watching. Retrieved 23 December 2013 from http://www.infoworld.com/t/internet-privacy/video-orwells-1984-has-nothing-the-current-surveillance-state-230259.

Benkler, Y. (2006). *The Wealth of Networks . How Social Production Transforms Markets and Freedom*. New Haven and London: Yale University Press. Retrieved 23 December 2013 from http://www.benkler.org/Benkler_Wealth_Of_Networks.pdf.

Castells, M. (2005). Software Libre. *La Vanguardia.* 30/01/2005. Retrieved 23 December 2013 from http://www.rebelion.org/noticias/2005/1/10741.pdf.

Century, M. (2000). Open Code and Creativity in the Digital Age. Retrieved 23 December 2013 from http://www.nextcentury.ca/Papers/Code.html.

Chopra and Dexter (2011). Free software and the economics of information justice. In *Ethics and Information Technology*.13, pp. 173–184, DOI 10.1007/s10676-010-9226-6.

Coll, H. & Bri, D, García, M, Lloret, J. (2008). Free software and open source applications in higher education. 5th wseas / iasme international conference on engineering education (ee'08), heraklion, greece, july 22–24, 2008. Retrieved 23 December 2013 from http://www.wseas.us/e-library/conferences/2008/crete/education/education51.pdf.

Cusumano, M. (2007). The Changing Software Business: From products to Services and Other New Business Models. Retrieved 23 December 2013 from http://ebusiness.mit.edu/research/papers/2008.01_Cusumano_The%20Changing%20Software%20Business_236.pdf.

Dibona, C. et al. (1999). Prologue in Open Source. In *Voices of the Open Source Revolution*. Sebastopol: O' Reilly Media.

Dourado, E. (2013). Let's Build a More Secure Internet. *The New York Times*. Opinion Pages. October 8, 2013. Retrieved 23 December 2013 from http://www.nytimes.com/2013/10/09/opinion/lets-build-a-more-secure-internet.html?_r=0.

Feenberg, A. (2012). Introduction in *(Re) Inventing the Internet*. Feenberg & Fiesen (Eds.) Rotterdam:Sense Publisher.

Ferneding, K. (2007). Understanding the message of the medium: Media technologies as an aesthetic. *International Handbook of Research in Arts Education Springer International Handbook of Research in Arts Education*, Volume 16, pp. 1331–1354.

Gómez-Diago, G. (2013a). Identificación de consecuencias negativas de incluir la enseñanza y/o aprendizaje de software privativo en el aula universitaria. Estudio piloto. *Razón y Palabra,* 82. Retrieved 23 December 2013 from http://www.razonypalabra.org.mx/N/N82/V82/28a_Gomez_V82.pdf.

Gómez-Diago, G. (2013b). Aplicando el concepto de diseño de la comunicación para realizar investigación aplicada. Dos posibles vías: Diseñando herramientas de comunicación y metodologías de diseño. Brainflowing. II Congreso Nacional de Metodología de la Investigación en Comunicación. Asociación Española de Investigación de la Comunicación.Segovia, Mayo, 2–3. 2013. Retrieved 23 December 2013 from http://uvadoc.uva.es/bitstream/10324/3071/1/Aplicando%20el%20concepto%20de%20dise%C3%B1o.pdf.

Gómez-Diago, G. (2012). Cyberspace and Cyberculture. In M. Kosut (Ed.), Encyclopedia of gender in media. (pp. 58–60). Thousand Oaks, CA: SAGE Publications, Inc. doi: 10.4135/9781452218540.n24. ISBN: 9781412990790. Retrieved 23 December 2013 from http://knowledge.sagepub.com/view/genderinmedia/n24.xml.

Grundy, S. (1982). *Three Modes Of Action Research.* In Kemmis,S. and McTaggert, R. (eds) (1988). *The Action Research Reader* (3ed). Geelong: Deakin University Press.

Grundy, S. (1987). *Curriculum: Product or Praxis* London: The Falmer Press.

Guillmor, Dan (2013). Google, Yahoo et al. have the power (and money) to fight back against the NSA. The Guardian. 1 november, 2013. Retrieved 23 December 2013 from http://www.theguardian.com/commentisfree/2013/nov/01/google-yahoo-nsa-surveillance-reform.

Heger, A (2009). Software piracy and producers developer's strategies. 3rd FLOSS International Workshop on Free/Libre Open Source Software. Department of Economics. University of Padua. July, 2–3. Retrieved 23 December 2013 from http://www.decon.unipd.it/personale/curri/manenti/floss/heger.pdf.

Hippel, Von (2005). *Democratizing Information.* Massachusetts London, England: The MIT Press Cambridge. Retrieved 23 December 2013 from http://web.mit.edu/evhippel/www/democ1.htm.

Holmstrom, H. & Jacobson, M. (2002). Using models in virtual world design. Proceedings of the 34th Annual Hawaii International Conference on System Sciences. Hawaii, IEEE.

Hughes, G. (2000). Social software: new opportunities for challenging social inequalities in learning? *Learning, Media and Technology*. Vol. 34, No. 4, December 2009, 291–305.

International Principles on the Application of Human Rights to Communications Surveillance. Retrieved 23 December 2013 from https://en.necessaryandproportionate.org/text.

Internet Usage Statistics. Retrieved 23 December 2013 from http://www.internetworldstats.com/stats.htm.

Lanier, J. (2000). *You are not a gadget. A manifesto.* Alfred A. Knopf. New York 2010. Retrieved 23 December 2013 from http://r-u-ins.org/resource/pdfs/YouAreNotAGadget-A_Manifesto.pdf.

Lee, M. (2013). Encryption Works. How to Protect Your Privacy in the Age of NSA Surveillance. Freedom of the Press Foundation. Retrieved 23 December 2013 from https://pressfreedom foundation.org/encryption-works#trust.

Lessing, L. (2006). *Code Version 2.0*. Basic Books. Retrieved 23 December 2013 from http://codev2.cc/.

Lévy, P. (2001). *Cyberculture*. Minneapolis: University of Minnesota Press.

Lievrouw, A. L. (2011). Preface in (Re) *Inventing the Internet*. Feenberg & Fiesen (Eds.) Rotterdam: Sense Publisher.

Llyas, S. (2008). FLOSS and the Computer Culture of the Maldivas (pp. 270–278), in Mansoux, A & De Valk, M. (Eds). GOTO10 & Open Mute. Retrieved 23 December 2013 from http://flossart.randomlab.net/pdf/FLOSS%2BArt.pdf.

Mitchell, J. (2013). With-Open-Platform-Stanford seeks to reclaim MOOC Brand. The Chronicle of Higher Education. Retrieved 23 December 2013 from http://chronicle.com/article/With-Open-Platform-Stanford/142783/?cid=wb&utm_source=wb&utm_medium=en.

O' Cathain, A., & J. Thomas, K (2004). Any other comments? Open questions on questionnaires, a bane or a bonus to research? BMC *Medical Research Methodology,* 4:25 doi:10.1186/1471-2288-4-25. Retrieved 23 December 2013 from http://www.biomedcentral.com/1471-2288/4/25.

O'Reilly, T. Paradigm Shift. Retrieved 23 December 2013 from http://tim.oreilly.com/articles/paradigmshift_0504.html.

Pfaffenberger, B. (2000). Linux in Higher Education: Open Source, Open Minds, Social Justice. Retrieved 23 December 2013 from http://www.linuxjournal.com/article/5071?page=0,2

Putnam, R. (2000). *Bowling Alone: The Collapse and Revival of the American Community*. New York: Simon & Schuster.

Rajani, N. (2003). Free as Education. Significance of the Free/Libre and Open Source Software for developing countries. Helsinki, Finland: One World Finland and KEPA. Retrieved 23 December 2013 from http://www.itu.int/wsis/docs/background/themes/access/free_as_in_edu cation_niranjan.pdf.

Raymond, S. E. (1998). The Cathedral and the Bazaar. First Monday, Vol. 3, No. 3. Retrieved 23 December 2013 from http://www.firstmonday.org/issues/issue3_3/raymond/.

Rushkoff, D. (2010). *Program or be Programmed. Ten commands for a digital age.* New York: OR Books.

Rushkoff, D. (2003). *Open Source Democracy. How online communication is changing offline politics*. Demos. Retrieved 23 December 2013 from http://www.demos.co.uk/files/Open SourceDemocracy.pdf.

Sagor, R. (2009). Collaborative Action Research and School Improvement: We Can't Have One Without the Other, *Journal of Curriculum and Instruction* (JoCI), January 2009, Volume 3, pp. 7–14.

Schnapp, J. and Presner, P. (2009). Digital Humanities Manifesto 2.0. Retrieved 23 December 2013 from http://www.humanitiesblast.com/manifesto/Manifesto_V2.pdf.

Sebastian, A. (2013). International Space Station switches from Windows to Linux, for improved reliability. May 9, 2013. Extreme Tech. Retrieved 23 December 2013 from http://www.extremetech.com/extreme/155392-international-space-station-switches-from-windows-to-linux-for-improved-reliability?utm_source=rss&utm_medium=rss&utm_campaign=international-space-station-switches-from-windows-to-linux-for-improved-reliability.

Selwyn & N. (2013). *The Need for a Politics of Educational Technology,* in Selwyn & Facer (Eds) New York: Palgrave Macmillan. Retrieved 23 December 2013 from http://www.academia.edu/4692005/The_need_for_a_politics_of_education_and_technology.

Selwyn, N. (2012). Social Media in Higher Education. Retrieved 23 December 2013 from http://www.educationarena.com/pdf/sample/sample-essay-selwyn.pdf.

Selwyn, N. (1998). *Education and Technology. Key issues and debates.* New York, London: Continuum International Publishing Group.

Soler, P. (2008). *Artists and Free Software. An Introduction* (14–17) in FLOSS + Art. Poitiers. France: GOTO10 & Open Mute. Retrieved 23 December 2013 from http://flossart.randomlab.net/pdf/FLOSS%2BArt.pdf.

Stallman, R. (2013). Why Free Software Is More Important Now Than Ever Before (09.28.13). *Wired.* Retrieved 23 December 2013 from http://www.wired.com/opinion/2013/09/why-free-software-is-more-important-now-than-ever-before/.

Stallman, R. (2002). *Free Software, Free Society*: Selected Essays of Richard M. Stallman. Edited by Gay. Free Software Foundation 59 Temple Place.

Suber, P. (2012). SPARC Open Access Newsletter, issue #164 Retrieved 23 December 2013 from http://legacy.earlham.edu/~peters/fos/newsletter/06-02-12.htm.

The Digital Humanities Manifesto 2. Retrieved 23 December 2013 from http://www.humanitiesblast.com/manifesto/Manifesto_V2.pdf.

The Guardian. NSA Files. Retrieved 23 December 2013 from http://www.theguardian.com/world/interactive/2013/nov/01/snowden-nsa-files-surveillance-revelations-decoded#section/1.

Thu Hien, T.T. (2009). VNU *Journal of Science, Foreign Languages* 25 (2009) 97–106 . Retrieved 23 December 2013 from http://tapchi.vnu.edu.vn/nn_2_09/b4.pdf.

Vardi, V. M. The End of The American Network Can the Internet be liberated from government meddling? Communications of the ACM, Vol. 56 No. 11, Page 5. Retrieved 23 December 2013 from http://cacm.acm.org/magazines/2013/11/169021-the-end-of-the-american-network/fulltext.

Weber, S. (2004).*The Success of Open Source*. Cambridge, Massachusetts, and London, England: Harvard University Press. Retrieved 23 December 2013 from http://www.cui-zy.cn/Course/Courses2011/LRR/StevenWeberSuccess_of_Open_Source.pdf.

Directories of Free and Open Source software

List of free and open-source software packages. Retrieved 23 December 2013 from http://en.wikipedia.org/wiki/List_of_free_and_open-source_software_packages.

The Free software directory. Retrieved 23 December 2013 from http://directory.fsf.org/wiki/Main_Page.

Open Source Initiative. Retrieved 23 December 2013 from http://opensource.org/.
Open Source Living. Retrieved 23 December 2013 from http://osliving.com/.
Floss Foundations Directories. Retrieved 23 December 2013 from http://flossfoundations.org/foundation-directory.

Free and Open Source Software

Graphic Design

Blender. 3D creation for everyone, free to use for any purpose. Retrieved 23 December 2013 from http://www.blender.org/.
Font forge. Outline font editor. Retrieved 23 December 2013 from http://fontforge.org/.
Gimp. Bitmap image editor/creator. Retrieved 23 December 2013 from http://www.gimp.org/.
Gimpshop. Image editing software. Retrieved 23 December 2013 from http://www.gimpshop.com/.
Inkscape. Vector image editor/creator. Retrieved 23 December 2013 from http://inkscape.org/index.php?lang=es.
Irfanview. Photo manager with some editing and plugin ability. Retrieved 23 December 2013 from http://www.irfanview.com/.
Minepaint. Graphics application for digital painters. Retrieved 23 December 2013 from http://mypaint.intilinux.com/.
OpenSCAD. Software for creating solid 3D CAD models.Retrieved 23 December 2013 from http://www.openscad.org/about.html.
Pencil. Animation/drawing software to create traditional hand-drawn animation (cartoon) using both bitmap and vector graphics. http://www.pencil-animation.org/.
Scribus. Desktop Publishing. Retrieved 23 December 2013 from http://www.scribus.net/canvas/Scribus.
Synfig Studio. 2D animation software. Retrieved 23 December 2013 from http://www.synfig.org/cms/.

Audio, Video and Web editors

Amaya.Web editor. Retrieved 23 December 2013 from http://www.w3.org/Amaya/.
Audacity. Audio editor and recorded. Retrieved 23 December 2013 from http://audacity.sourceforge.net/.
Avidemus. Video editor. Retrieved 23 December 2013 from http://avidemux.sourceforge.net/
Kdenlive. Video editor. Retrieved 23 December 2013 from http://kdenlive.org/features

Miscellaneous

Arkos. A project to help users self-host their websites, email, files and more. Retrieved 23 December 2013 fromhttps://arkos.io/.
Cytoescape. Network Data Integration, Analysis, and Visualization in a Box. Retrieved 23 December 2013 from http://www.cytoscape.org/.
Jap. Anonymous proxy. Retrieved 23 December 2013 from http://anon.inf.tu-dresden.de/index_en.html.
MediaPortal.Listen music & radio, watch video's and DVD's, view, schedule and record live TV. Retrieved 23 December 2013 from http://www.team-mediaportal.com.

Pure Data. Visual programming language. Retrieved 23 December 2013 from http://puredata.info/.
VirtualBox. Cross-platform virtualization application. Retrieved 23 December 2013 from https://www.virtualbox.org/.

Free and Open Software Social Media

diaspora. Retrieved 23 December 2013 from https://joindiaspora.com/.
friendica. Retrieved 23 December 2013 from http://friendica.com.
identi.ca. Retrieved 23 December 2013 from https://identi.ca/.
kune. Retrieved 23 December 2013http://kune.ourproject.org/.
n-1. Retrieved 23 December 2013 from https://n-1.cc/.
thimbl. Retrieved 23 December 2013 from http://www.thimbl.net/.

Index